Teaching to Learn, Learning to Teach

A Handbook for Secondary School Teachers

Teaching to Learn, Learning to Teach

A Handbook for Secondary School Teachers

Alan J. Singer
with
**Maureen Murphy, S. Maxwell Hines,
and the Hofstra New Teachers Network**

2003

LAWRENCE ERLBAUM ASSOCIATES, PUBLISHERS
Mahwah, New Jersey   London

Lawrence Erlbaum Associates, Inc., Publishers
10 Industrial Avenue
Mahwah, New Jersey 07430

Cover design by Kathryn Houghtaling Lacey

Library of Congress Cataloging-in-Publication Data

Singer, Alan J.
Teaching to learn, learning to teach : a handbook for secondary school
    teachers / Alan J. Singer with Maureen Murray, S. Maxwell Hines and
    the Hofstra New Teachers Network.
        p. cm.
        Includes bibliographical references and index.
ISBN 0-8058-4215-2 (pbk : alk. paper)
1. High school teaching—Handbooks, manuals, etc. I. Title.
LB1737.A3S56   2003
373.1102—dc21   2003044360
                                                                          CIP

Books published by Lawrence Erlbaum Associates are printed on acid-
free paper, and their bindings are chosen for strength and durability.

Printed in the United States of America
10   9   8   7   6   5   4   3   2   1

This book is dedicated to the members of the Hofstra New Teachers Network

Students, Friends, Colleagues and Partners in the struggle to build better schools and create a more just society.

Venceremos—We will triumph!

CONTENTS

PREFACE:
OUR APPROACH TO TEACHING

This book is based on the following ideas:

1. Classroom practice should be based on goals and an understanding of students as complex and diverse human beings.
2. Preservice and beginning teachers will benefit from learning about the experiences of other preservice teachers, new classroom teachers, and veterans.
3. There are principles of effective teaching in secondary schools that span the subject disciplines and it is important that new teachers make connections with the work of their colleagues in other content areas.
4. Although content expertise and the mastery of pedagogical skills are essential for teachers, empathy with students and a sense of personal mission are the keys to successful teaching.
5. Learning takes place all of the time—but students are not necessarily learning what teachers intend them to learn.
6. Everything that takes place in the school and classroom is part of the curriculum.
7. Learning is social—teachers should build on it, not fight it.
8. Effective teaching in inclusive middle school (6–8) and high school (9–12) classrooms with diverse student populations can involve the same student-centered pedagogical practice with differences in degree or emphasis based on student needs rather than differences in kind of instruction—everyone can be treated like an honors student.
9. Developing classroom community and student leadership is the most effective way to promote student learning—the only people teachers can control are themselves.
10. An overall goal in secondary education is to promote greater freedom for students as they assume increased individual and collective responsibility for their own learning.
11. People can learn to be student-centered, constructivist, critical teachers.
12. Although it takes extended experience (3 to 5 years) and hard work to master the skills needed to be an effective teacher, these skills are neither magical nor inexplicable, and can be developed by beginning teachers.

13. Every teacher must make a decision: Will you rock the boat—"fight the power"—or become "another brick in the wall" of an educational system that rewards some students, tracks many into limited options, and leaves others behind?

ABOUT THE AUTHORS

Drs. Alan Singer (social studies), Maureen Murphy (English), and S. Maxwell Hines (science) teach introductory secondary school methods classes, subject methods classes, supervise secondary school student teachers, and lead classroom analysis seminars in which student teachers reflect on their pedagogical practice, reconsider their teaching philosophies and goals, and examine ways that teachers can develop personal connections and build classroom communities with students from diverse racial, ethnic, and class backgrounds. They are also the faculty advisors and facilitators for the Hofstra New Teachers Network, which provides support for new teachers working in urban and suburban minority school districts.

The text was primarily written by Alan Singer (author of *Social Studies for Secondary Schools: Teaching to Learn/Learning to Teach*, LEA, 1997). Maureen Murphy and S. Maxwell Hines participated in its conceptualization and development, contributed specific sections, edited the entire manuscript, and helped members of the New Teachers Network frame and write their contributions.

RATIONALE AND DESCRIPTION

In secondary school general methods classes and classroom analysis seminars that accompany student teaching, preservice teachers are frequently obsessed with two problems: classroom control and figuring out exactly what is the role of the teacher. These problems are exacerbated by methods books that compartmentalize different aspects of teaching (practical, theoretical, critical). This book is designed to bridge these divisions and integrate the practical, theoretical, and critical considerations in secondary school teaching. It draws on the theoretical work of Michael Apple (1979), George Counts (1969), Lisa Delpit (1995), John Dewey (1916, 1927/1954), Paulo Freire (1970, 1995), Howard Gardner (1993), Maxine Greene (1993), Martin Haberman (1995), Herbert Kohl (1994), Gloria Ladson-Billings (1994), and Nel Noddings (1992), and it offers different ways of looking at the dynamics of classroom interaction for understanding social, cultural, and developmental influences on student behavior; for organizing lessons, units, and curricula; and for defining and establishing the diverse roles of teachers.

The book is designed as a handbook for preservice and beginning teachers. We anticipate that some readers will examine the entire package in the order that material is presented, whereas others will sample topics selectively based on their interests and needs. We hope the book works both ways. We apologize in advance for any repetition between chapters, but felt it was necessary so that each chapter could stand on its own.

The book opens and closes with challenges to preservice and beginning teachers to reflect on what they liked and did not like about their own school experiences and to consider their goals as teachers. It argues that many problems students perceive of as individual are really a result of the way that schools and classrooms are organized.

In the book, we address broad topics in secondary school teaching rather than the needs of specific subject areas. Although examples are included from different subject disciplines, the focus of the book is on the relationships between disciplines (concepts, skills, practices) rather than distinctions. While discussing different approaches to secondary school teaching (middle school, 6–8, and high school, 9–12), the book offers a model student-centered approach based on a series of PRO/CLASS Practices. It includes sample "Nuts and Bolts" teaching techniques that can be used in different types of classrooms and by teachers employing different pedagogical approaches (lesson and unit design, activities, questions, projects, team learning, community building). Although the broad principles of PRO/CLASS Practice are presented as part of an integrated approach to teaching, preservice and beginning teachers are encouraged to reinterpret the principles and continually redefine them as they develop their own reflective practice. Conversations with preservice teachers, interviews and conversations with teachers, essays about classroom issues and reflections on teaching goals and process, and the "Nuts and Bolts" of classroom practice are integrated throughout the text.

REFERENCES AND SUGGESTIONS FOR FURTHER READING

Apple, M. (1979). *Ideology and curriculum*. New York: Routledge.

Counts, G. (1969). *Dare the school build a new social order?* New York: Arno Press.

Delpit, L. (1995). *Other people's children*. New York: The New Press.

Dewey, J. (1916). *Democracy and education*. New York: Macmillan.

Dewey, J. (1954). *Experience and education*. New York: Collier/Macmillan. (Original work published 1927)

Freire, P. (1970). *Pedagogy of the oppressed*. New York: Seabury.

Freire, P. (1995). *Pedagogy of hope*. New York: Continuum.

Gardner, H. (1993). *Multiple intelligences: The theory in practice*. New York: Basic Books.

Greene, M. (1993). Diversity and inclusion: Towards a curriculum for human beings. *Teachers College Record, 95*(2), 211–221.

Haberman, M. (1995). *Star teachers of children in poverty*. West Lafayette, IN: Kappa Delta Pi.

Kohl, H. (1994). *I won't learn from you and other thoughts on creative maladjustment*. New York: The New Press.

Ladson-Billings, G. (1994). *The dreamkeepers: Successful teachers of African American children*. San Francisco: Jossey-Bass.

Noddings, N. (1992). *The challenge to care in schools*. New York: Teachers College Press.

CONTRIBUTORS

Contributors (with their school districts) include the following members of the Hofstra New Teachers Network: Christina Agosti-Dircks (Half Hollow Hills, NY); Anna Ardito (Long Beach, NY); Dean Bacigalupo (Island Park); Melisa Baker, Goldie Baldwin (Brooklyn, NY); Jennifer Bambino (Carle Place, NY); Jackie Benjamin (Freeport, NY); Kiesha Boatley (Uniondale, NY); Steve Bologna; Dawn Brigante (Levittown, NY); Vonda-Kay Campbell (Valley Stream, NY); Chris Caponi; Jennie Chacko (Amityville, NY); Severin Cornelius (Bronx, NY); Lynda Costello-Herrara (Uniondale, NY); Stacey Cotten (Hempstead, NY); Jennifer Debler (Baldwin, NY); Kelly Delia (Hicksville, NY); Richard DeLucia (New York, NY); Ken Dwyer (Oceanside, NY); Robin Edwards (Levittown, NY); Mahmoud Elder (Brooklyn, NY); Chris Erickson (Westbury, NY); Gena Ferrara (Wheatly, NY); Michael Ferraresse (Brooklyn, NY); Donna Hill Fielding (Plainview, NY); Joslyn Fiorello (Northport, NY); Lawrence Frohman; Howard Fuchs (Long Beach, NY); Hillary Licht Fuhrman (Hempstead, NY); Charlie Gifford; Clinton Grant (Uniondale, NY); Joseph Hartig (Hicksville, NY); Stephanie Hunte (Uniondale, NY); Patti Kafi (Lawrence, NY); Ken Kaufman (Brooklyn, NY); David Kettner (Brooklyn, NY); Laurence Klein (Queens, NY); Robert Kurtz (Oyster Bay, NY); Jessica Lopez (Queens, NY); Steven Love (Wantagh, NY); Darren Luskoff (Mineola, NY); Jewella Lynch (Syosset, NY); Michael Maiglow

(Brooklyn, NY); Michelle Manisclco (Syosset, NY); Tammy Manor (Queens, NY); Seth Margolin (Deer Park, NY); William McDonough (Baldwin, NY); Daniel McKeon; Donniella McLoughlin (Sewanhaka, NY); Gayle Meinkes-Lumia (Brentwood, NY); George Milliken (Hempstead, NY); Deon Gordon Mitchell (Brooklyn, NY); Dennis Mooney (Great Neck, NY); Maria Tartaro Musacchia (East Meadow, NY); Jayne O'Neill (Paterson, NJ); Jennifer Palacio (Long Beach, NY); Laura Pearson (Syosset, NY); Maritza Perez; Jennifer Pesato (Massapequa, NY); Laura Peterson (East Rockaway, NY); Michael Pezone (Queens, NY); Susan Sotiriades Poulos (Glen Cove, NY); Giovanni Reynoso-Perez (Brentwood, NY); Lauren Rosenburg (Brooklyn, NY); Stacey Saltzer; Michael Sangiardi (Brooklyn, NY); Rachel Santiago (New York, NY); Robert Schimenz (Queens, NY); Pedro Sierra (Brooklyn, NY); Katherine Simons Smith (Portland, ME); Stuart Stein (Bellmore, NY); Richard Stern (Rockville Centre, NY); John Syffrard; Richard Tauber (Uniondale, NY); Adeola Tella (Uniondale, NY); Nicole Theo (Islip, NY); Rachel Gaglione Thompson (Queens, NY); Louis Tolentino (Hewlett, NY); Robyn Tornabene (Long Beach, NY); Bill Van Nostrand (Connectquot, NY); Alice Van Tassell (Floral Park, NY); Nichole Williams (Westbury, NY).

Contributors include the following public school teachers and administrators: Rhonda Eisenberg (Oceanside, NY); Cecelia Goodman (Brooklyn, NY); Frederick Heckendorn (Bellmore-Merrick, NY); Evelyn Kalibala (Brooklyn, NY); Rozella Kirchgaessner (Queens, NY); Riza Laudin (Herricks, NY); John McNamara (Princeton, NJ); David Morris (Brooklyn, NY); Cheryl Smith (Hicksville, NY); Thomas Troisi (Valley Stream, NY).

Contributors include the following university-based teachers: Gary Benenson (City College of New York-CUNY); Judith Kaufman (Hofstra University); Sally Smith (Hofstra University); Judith Y. Singer (Long Island University-Brooklyn Campus); Sandra Stacki (Hofstra University).

The following Hofstra University teacher education students commented on versions of the manuscript: Lisa Accardi, Guiseppi Accardo, Danielle Albers, Stacey Albert, Claire Bowler, Charles Cronin, Richie Diaz, Anthony Disanti, Dina Disanto, Sarah Dmuchowski, Carlos Fernandez, Julie Fortier, Peter Franzese, Christine Giberti, Daniel Gross, Megan Hamm, Cherilyn Holmes, Jaimee Kahn, Megan Kennedy, Amy Keyishian, Jay Kreutzberger, Christine Kutzman, Joshua Levin, David Levy, Sharon Maltbie, Thomas McCann, Brian Messinger, Rachel Montagno, Dara Pakor, Catherine Pisicano, Rosa Posillico, Jayme Riekers, Jeannette Rosello, Holly Ryder, Nicholas Santora, Michelle Sarro, Maureen Serp, Alexis Stansky, Christopher Stevens, Ken Tapfar, Patrick Turk, Andrew Tutora, Scott Valentine, Laura Vosswinkel, Mariam Wahahzada, LeShawnda Williams, Thomas Zervas.

In addition, the following Hofstra University adjuncts, faculty, administrators, and staff members made important contributions: Jeannette Balantic, Frank Bowe, Mary Carter, Karleen Edwards, Sherri Fass, Doris Fromberg, Monalisa Fuller, Jane Goldman, Mary Hodnett, James Johnson, Janice Koch, Andrea Libresco, Maureen Miletta, Regina Follo Morris, Rose Marie Paternastro, Linda Rabino, Leo Silverstone, Ann Tarantino, Bruce Torff, Debra Veny, and Sharon Whitton.

We wish to thank Dennis Banks (SUNY Oneonta), Terrie Epstein (Hunter College), Yoan K. Pak (University of Illinois at Urbana-Champaign), and E. Wayne Ross (Louisville University) for critical readings and suggestions; Margaret MacCurtain (University College, Dublin) for her support; and Naomi Silverman and the staff at Lawrence Erlbaum Associates.

I

GOALS AND RESPONSIBILITIES FOR TEACHERS

A LETTER TO FUTURE TEACHERS

Dear Future Teachers,

According to a 1997 report issued by an organization called Public Agenda, education professors are "out of sync" with public school teachers and parents on fundamental issues such as what and how teachers should teach. A survey found that classroom teachers and the general public want discipline and basic reading, writing, and math skills to be the top priorities in public schools. However, university-based teacher educators insist that schools prepare children "to be active learners," and that teachers help students develop their "curiosity" and "a love of learning."

Deborah Wadsworth, executive director of Public Agenda, concluded that professors of education are not "arming graduates of their programs for the real world they face." She was supported by Sandra Feldman, president of the American Federation of Teachers, who said the survey confirmed what her union's membership already knew. "College education hasn't prepared them for the realities of the classroom."

As you prepare to become a teacher, you need to consider whether schools of education and out-of-sync professors are really responsible for poor student performance on standardized tests, our country's failure to achieve international standards, violence in and around urban schools, poverty, drug abuse, alienation, teenage pregnancy, inadequate school funding, overcrowded classrooms, and deteriorating buildings.

We live in a society that pays considerably more to educate the children of the affluent—children who already have numerous advantages—than the children of the working class and poor. In the New York City metropolitan area where I live and work, private schools charge as much as $20,000 a year for tuition. Some wealthy suburban districts spend almost the same amount of money per student. At the same time, during the late 1990s, New York City spent slightly more than $6,000 a year to educate students in mainstream regular education classes.

The kind of student-centered inquiry-based examination of our world proposed by education professors is expensive, and in our society it is only made available to the few. Does that mean that classroom teachers in less affluent communities who value this kind of teaching are doomed to fail and foolish to try?

I believe the answer is a resounding "NO!" The beginning and experienced teachers who worked with me to write this book are committed to the idea that the way we teach can make a significant difference in the learning and lives of our students. We refuse to give up on public education and our students.

As a social studies teacher in New York City public high schools for 14 years, I learned that there are no simple solutions to changing education and no magic formulas for teaching young people. Teaching is hard work and involves constant learning by educators. Successful teaching requires an understanding of children, a vision for their future, and a strategy for connecting students with that vision.

As teacher educators, my colleagues and I use our own experience as teachers; our understanding of the theories of thinkers like John Dewey, Paulo Friere, and Maxine Greene; and insights gained from educational research to help the next generation of teachers become ready for the classroom. New teachers always worry whether they will know enough to teach and whether they will be able to control students. They often do not agree with what we think is important. But we try to share with them some of the things that we have learned and value.

- We know that when lessons relate to student interests, involve them in activities, and are appropriate to their academic performance level, they will stimulate student curiosity and engage them as active learners.
- We know that students who feel that their teachers care about them as human beings and are willing to respond to their needs and concerns do better in class.
- We know that learning is social. Students do better academically as they develop a sense of relationship with each other and their teachers, and as they take responsibility for what happens in their classroom.
- We know that change never happens instantaneously. Why should children behave any differently from other people? Being an effective teacher means engaging in a long-term struggle to convince students that your goals for the class make sense and are worth examining.
- We know that as a teacher you cannot change everything in the world, in your school or even in your class. But we also know that as you become a better teacher you will be able to make an impact on more people.
- "Fingerpointing" does not help. Universities blame high schools. High school teachers blame middle school teachers. Middle school teachers blame elementary school teachers. Elementary school teachers blame preschools and parents. Parents blame schools and teachers. Instead of focusing on blaming each other for what has not worked, we need to discover and implement ideas and practices that will make a difference.

My primary goal as a high school teacher and as a university professor is that every student in my classes should become a thinking, caring, literate human being and an active citizen who helps shape our community, society, and world. If this is unrealistic and undermines what is really important in education, I gladly plead guilty.

At the May 2000 annual conference of the Hofstra New Teachers Network, Jennifer Palacio, a third-year teacher, told the group, "When I first started teaching, I tried to do all the things the exact way I learned them in methods classes and nothing worked. I thought I was a failure. When I began to discover my own ways to do these same things, I started to become a teacher. You cannot be someone else. You have to be you."

This book does not offer a recipe for becoming a successful teacher. How could we? Alan Singer, the principal author of the book, and Maureen Murphy and S. Maxwell Hines, who worked with him, do not always agree on where to place priorities. Of the three, Maureen places a higher emphasis on content expertise, "Max" on teaching approaches, and Alan on framing and achieving goals. Instead of a recipe, this book offers an approach to teaching and some suggestions on how to do it. But each of you will have to experiment with your own way of teaching as you teach to learn and learn to teach. We want you to JOIN THE CONVERSATION. We do not know any other way to become a teacher.

Are your university education professors lost in an ivy-covered tower? As you take this class, participate in field placements, and prepare to become a teacher, you need to answer this question yourself. What is the job of the teacher? As you come up with answers, please keep in touch. My e-mail address is CATAJS@Hofstra.edu.

Sincerely,
Alan Singer

1

GOALS: WHY DO YOU WANT TO BE A TEACHER?

Traditionally union organizers have used songs to encourage coworkers to join their ranks. Woody Guthrie, perhaps America's best known labor minstrel, rewrote a religious hymn, "Jesus Walked This Lonesome Valley" as "You Gotta Go Down and Join the Union." The point of Guthrie's song is that no one can make the decision to join a union for you. You have to make that decision for yourself. That advise holds true for teaching as well. Other people's ideas and experiences will only take you so far. You need to practice teaching, think about teaching, and talk about teaching for yourself. The idea that teachers have to continually evaluate what they are doing in their classrooms is called reflective practice. To help you develop the habit of reflective practice, sections in this book generally end with an activity that invites you to JOIN THE CONVERSATION and present your own ideas. Share your ideas with classmates in education classes and with other teachers. You will discover that you have much to offer your colleagues and it will make the process of becoming a teacher much more exciting.

JOIN THE CONVERSATION—SOME THINGS TO THINK ABOUT

Budget cuts. Strikes. Public debates. Curriculum revisions. "Five and a homeroom." High-minded theories and the daily grind. Working with TEENAGERS.

Why do you want to be a secondary school teacher?

Why would anybody want to be a secondary school teacher?

How do secondary schools work? Do they work? Can they work?

What did you like and dislike about your own school experiences?

Thirty years until retirement: Do I want to get involved in this? If I decide to give it a shot, what do I have to do to survive? To be good at it? To make a difference?

Question to Consider:

Why do I want to be a teacher?

SECTION A: THE CHALLENGE

A number of people helped to write this book, but the primary voice is mine—Alan Singer. When a piece is written by another author, it bears his or her name. Otherwise, although other people contributed ideas to help shape mine (or perhaps to confuse me), I take full responsibility for these ideas. In Yiddish, the language of my Eastern European Jewish ancestors, there is a word that I love—*Ungapochka*. It means just the way it sounds; something is all "mushed" up together. If you find this book a little too *Ungapochka* for your tastes, you only have me to blame.

I became a teacher and I am writing this book, because I sincerely believe that if you like teaching it can be the greatest job in the world. I also know that if you dislike it, it is 30 years of purgatory until retirement. Let me warn you now—do not be surprised when you hear teachers who enjoy their profession advise preservice teachers and beginners to steer clear of the faculty lounge.

The participants who put this book together are secondary school classroom teachers and university-based teacher educators. We want to begin by issuing you a challenge. Some of you may remember the movie *The Faculty* (1998), in which a group of space invaders took over the bodies of high school teachers and tried to use this as a base of operation for conquering the world. One of the songs in the sound track was Pink Floyd's "Another Brick in the Wall (Part II)," which accuses teachers of trying to brainwash children so they fit in and support the status quo. During the song a group of elementary school age children chant that they don't need no education, at least not the kind traditionally offered in schools.

Another movie, Spike Lee's *Do the Right Thing* (1989), opens with Rosie Perez dancing to a song by Public Enemy, "Fight the Power." In this song, the hip-hop group says they have no choice but to fight back against unjust authority that is intruding into their community.

This book is based on the premise that every teacher must make a decision: Will you "fight the power" or become "another brick in the wall" of an educational system that rewards some students, tracks many into limited options, and leaves others behind? In 1996, the Children's Defense Fund organized a march in Washington, D.C., and invited Americans to "Stand for Children" by working against inequality and injustice and by working for programs such as quality education for all children. Teachers cannot make all the difference in the world, but we can make a difference. In this book we are challenging you to become a teacher who stands up for children.

Chapter 1 introduces educational philosophies we feel you should consider as you define your own teaching philosophy and presents the thoughts of "new" teachers whom we believe "Stand for Children." It concludes with excerpts from reflective journals written by two preservice teachers who were taking their first education class and a summary of my own "pedagogical creed (beliefs about teaching)."

JOIN THE CONVERSATION—MAGIC WORDS

As student teachers prepare for job interviews they try to anticipate the questions they will be asked. I always recommend they think about the big issues that are being discussed in the field. The "magic words" change periodically, sometimes because the substance of the discussion has shifted and sometimes because educators, parents, and politicians are using a new vocabulary. These are the eight terms teachers are expected to understand and be able to discuss at the time of this writing—but maybe not tomorrow or when you read this book. I have listed them alphabetically. I do not think anyone would agree on an order of importance. As you prepare to become a teacher, these are the big issues you should think about (in case you are worried, we will return to discussion of how to find a teaching job a number of times in the book).

Assessment	**Content Knowledge**
Differentiated Instruction	**Diversity** (a.k.a. Multiculturalism)
Inclusion	**Literacy**
Standards	**Technology**

Questions to Consider:

1. How do you define these terms?
2. What other terms would you add to the list? Why?
3. Which terms, if any, would you drop from the list? Why?
4. Select three terms that you believe are important for teachers to think about and explain your views on why they are important.

SECTION B: HOW DO YOUR BELIEFS ABOUT THE WORLD SHAPE YOUR TEACHING?

Have you taken a philosophy course in college? Most of us usually think of philosophers as people who think deep thoughts about big ideas. The stereotype is that they are so preoccupied with their ideas that they are disconnected from the world around them and look and act a little weird.

Of course, there are other ways to think about philosophers and philosophy. In the movie, *The Wizard of Oz* (1939), the Scarecrow wanted a brain. In answer to his request, the Wizard gave him a degree in philosophy. I always find the scene funny, but there is a deeper message. In a sense, we are all philosophers. Everyone has a philosophy that gives direction to her or his beliefs and actions. The key is whether we think about it so that it becomes a conscious and considered aspect of our lives. You may not think about your philosophy; you may not even be aware of it, but you have one. Maybe it is something as simple (or as complicated) as the Judeo-Christian Golden Rule, "Do unto others as you would have them do unto you," or Frank Sinatra's "I did it my way."

Just as every individual has a philosophy of life, every teacher has a philosophy of education that shapes the way she or he looks at teaching. It includes their beliefs about life and the importance of learning, their goals, and their understanding of how to achieve them. Their philosophy includes views about "big ideas" such as democracy, equality, social justice, merit, a hierarchy of rewards, and the need for social structure and control, ideas that shape both our understanding of society in general and of education. In some areas, our beliefs are open to examination by ourselves and by others. At other times, they can be deeply hidden and we may not be conscious of them. But whether we are aware of them or not, we have beliefs that shape the way we think and act. This essay discusses the ideas of philosophers who were also educators. Their ideas may help you to clarify your own beliefs about the world and about teaching.

JOIN THE CONVERSATION—ARE YOU A PHILOSOPHER?

Questions to Consider:

1. Do you think of yourself as a philosopher? Explain.
2. Do believe that teachers should be philosophers? Explain.
3. Read about John Dewey, Paulo Friere, and Septima Clark. Make a list of the major ideas of each philosopher. Are any of their beliefs about the world and about education like yours? Explain.
4. Write an essay titled "My Pedagogic Creed" that explains your ideas about people, society and the world and how these ideas influence your philosophy of education.

John Dewey's Philosophy of Education

John Dewey, one of the most important thinkers about education in U.S. history, made a list of his basic beliefs back in the 1890s. He called it his "pedagogic creed." Dewey's progressive educational philosophy was concerned with the need to educate people for life in a democratic society. Key concepts for Dewey were experience, freedom, community, and "habits of mind." He believed that there was an "organic connection between education and experience," that effective teachers are able to connect the subject matter to the existing experience of students, and that they can expand and enrich students' lives with new experiences (Dewey, 1927/1954, p. 25).

According to Dewey, students learn from the full range of their experiences in school, not just the specific thing they are studying in class. They learn from what they are studying, how they are studying, who they are studying with, and how they are treated. In racially segregated or academically tracked classes, students learn that some people are better than others. In teacher-centered classrooms, they learn that some people possess knowledge and others passively receive it. When teachers have total control over classrooms, even when they are benevolent or entertaining, students learn to accept authoritarianism. During his career, Dewey continually reflected on the experiences educators need to create for students so they would become active participants in preserving and expanding government of, by, and for the people.

For Dewey, the exercise of freedom in democratic societies depends on education. He identifies freedom with "power to frame purposes" or achieve individual and social goals. This kind of freedom requires a probing, critical, disciplined habit of mind. It includes intelligence, judgment, and self-control—qualities students may never acquire in classrooms where they are subject to external controls and are forced to remain silent. In progressive schools that use a Deweyan approach, students engage in long-term thematic group projects where they learn to collectively solve problems; classrooms become democratic communities where "things gain meaning by being used in a shared experience or joint action" (Dewey, 1927/1954, p. 67; 1916, p. 263).

Dewey believed that democratic movements for human liberation were necessary to achieve a fair distribution of political power and an "equitable system of human liberties." However, criticisms have been raised about limitations in Deweyan approaches to education, especially the way they are practiced in many elite private schools. Frequently, these schools are racially, ethnically, and economically segregated, so efforts to develop classroom community ignore the spectrum of human difference and the continuing impact of society's attitudes about race, class, ethnicity, gender, social conflict, and inequality on teachers as well as students. In addition, because of pressure on students to achieve high academic scores, teachers maintain an undemocratic level of control when they arrange the classroom experiences of their students. Both of these issues are addressed by Paulo Freire, who calls on educators to aggressively challenge both injustice and unequal power arrangements in the classroom and society.

FIG. 1.1 Excerpts from John Dewey's pedagogic creed.

1. "The only true education comes through the stimulation of the child's powers by the demands of the social situations in which he finds himself."
2. "Education being a social process, the school is simply that form of community life . . . that will be most effective in bringing the child to share in the inherited resources of the (human) race, and to use his own powers for social ends."
3. "Education is a process of living and not a preparation for future living."
4. "The social life of the child is the basis of . . . all his training or growth."
5. "The true center of correlation on school subjects is not science, nor literature, nor history, nor geography, but the child's own social activities."
6. "The only way to make the child conscious of his social heritage is to enable him to perform those fundamental types of activity which make civilization what it is."
7. "The active side precedes the passive."
8. "Education is the fundamental method of social progress and reform."
9. "Education is . . . the process of coming to share in the social consciousness."

JOIN THE CONVERSATION—DEWEY'S PEDAGOGIC CREED

Questions to Consider:
1. Rewrite these statements by Dewey in your own words.
2. Which of these ideas do you agree with? Which ones do you disagree with? Why?

Paulo Freire's Philosophy of Education

Paulo Freire was born in Recife in northeastern Brazil where his ideas about education developed in response to military dictatorship, enormous social inequality, and widespread adult illiteracy. As a result, his primary pedagogical goal is to provide the world's poor and oppressed with educational experiences that make it possible for them to take control over their own lives. Freire shares Dewey's desire to stimulate students to become "agents of curiosity" in a "quest for . . . the 'why' of things," and his belief that education provides possibility and hope for the future of society. But he believes that these can only be achieved when students explicitly critique social injustice and actively organize to challenge oppression (Freire, 1995, pp. 105, 144; 1970, p. 28).

For Freire, education is a process of continuous group discussion that enables people to acquire collective knowledge they can use to change society. The role of the teacher includes asking questions that help students identify problems facing their community, working with students to discover ideas or create symbols that explain their life experiences, and encouraging analysis of prior experiences and of society as the basis for new academic understanding and social action.

In a Deweyan classroom, the teacher is an expert who is responsible for organizing experiences so that students learn content, social and academic skills, and an appreciation for democratic living. Freire is concerned that this arrangement reproduces the unequal power relationships that exist in society. In a Freirean classroom, everyone has a recognized area of expertise that includes, but is not limited to, understanding and explaining their own lives, and sharing this expertise becomes an essential element in the classroom curriculum. In these classrooms, teachers have their areas of expertise, but they are only one part of the community. The responsibility for organizing experiences and struggling for social change belongs to the entire community; as groups exercise this responsibility, they are empowered to take control over their lives. Freire believes that there is a dynamic interactive relationship between increasing academic literacy and the desire to understand and change the world around us (Freire, 1995, p. 105; Kohl, 1995, p. 6).

FIG. 1.2 Defining a Freirean curriculum.

Paulo Freire was a Brazil educator and political activist. Identify the main idea about education in each quotation that follows. Use these "main ideas" to write a paragraph presenting Freire's philosophy of education.

1. "In order for the oppressed to be able to wage the struggle for their liberation, they must perceive the reality of oppression not as a closed world from which there is no exit, but as a limiting situation which they can transform." Source: *Pedagogy of the Oppressed*, p. 34.

2. "In the banking concept of education, knowledge is a gift bestowed by those who consider themselves knowledgeable upon those whom they consider to know nothing. Projecting an absolute ignorance onto others . . . negates education and knowledge as processes of inquiry. The teacher presents himself to his students as their necessary opposite; by considering their ignorance absolute, he justifies his own existence. . . . The teacher teaches and the students are taught; the teacher knows everything and the students know nothing." Source: *Pedagogy of the Oppressed*, p. 58.

3. "Those truly committed to liberation must reject the banking notion . . . adopting instead a concept of men as conscious beings. . . . They must abandon the goal of deposit-making and replace it with the posing of the problems of men in their relations with the world." Source: *Pedagogy of the Oppressed*, p. 66.

4. "Without a minimum of hope, we cannot so much as start the struggle. But without the struggle, hope . . . dissipates, loses its bearings, and turns into hopelessness. . . . Hence the need for an education in hope." Source: *Pedagogy of Hope*, p. 9.

JOIN THE CONVERSATION—FREIREAN CURRICULUM

Questions to Consider:

1. A key idea in Freire's work is defining the curriculum by thinking about problems. Examine a newspaper for current events articles about education in the United States. Make a list of your questions about the issues raised in the articles.

2. Should students participate in defining the curriculum? Why or why not? To what extent?

3. In your opinion, do all people have an area of expertise that can be integrated into the curriculum? Explain your answer.

Septima Clark's Philosophy of Education

Septima Clark probably never would have described herself as a philosopher. She was a teacher and a civil rights worker in the U.S. south during the 1950s and 1960s. In her autobiography, *Ready from Within* (1986), she explained how she became an activist while working as a teacher in South Carolina. She sent a letter to Black colleagues asking them to protest a state policy that barred city or state employees from belonging to the National Association for the Advancement of Colored People (NAACP). Her thinking was that "if whites could belong to the Ku Klux Klan, then surely blacks could belong to the NAACP." Even though she wrote more than 700 letters, only 26 teachers answered her. Clark later wrote that "I considered that one of the failures of my life because I think that I tried to push them into something that they weren't ready for.... You always have to get the people with you. You can't just force them into things" (p. 37).

This experience played a crucial role in shaping Clark's approach to teaching, which was based on the idea that people had to be "ready from within." She wrote: "I never once felt afraid, not on any of those marches. Bullets could have gotten me, but somehow or other they didn't. I felt very good about going, about talking to people. I knew that people had gotten to the place where they saw the type of meanness that was being shown throughout their little towns. They hadn't noticed it before, but now they were ready from within to do something about it" (p. 71).

One of the more powerful stories in her autobiography is her account of teaching reading and writing to adults so they could qualify to vote. "To teach reading I wrote their stories on the dry cleaner's (paper) bags, stories of their country right around them, where they walked to come to school, the things that grew around them, what they could see in the skies. They told them to me, and I wrote them on dry cleaner's bags and tacked them on the wall. From the fourth grade through the sixth grade they all did that same reading. But they needed that because it wasn't any use to do graded reading when they had not had any basic words at all" (p. 106).

Clark had no problem admitting that everything did not work. But she felt that her mistakes were key to her learning to be a successful teacher. "Many times there were failures. But we had to mull over those failures and work until we could get them ironed out. The only reason why I thought the Citizenship School Program was right was because when people went down to register and vote, they were able to register and vote. They received their registration certificate. Then I knew that what I did must have been right. But I didn't know it before. It was an experiment that I was trying . . . I couldn't be sure that the experiment was going to work. I don't think anybody can be sure. You just try and see if it's coming" (p. 126).

JOIN THE CONVERSATION—SEPTIMA CLARK'S PHILOSOPHY

Questions to Consider:

1. Is Septima Clark a philosopher? Explain.
2. Are you a philosopher? Explain.
3. In your opinion, do you have to "buy" a philosopher's entire package, or should you feel free to pick and choose what makes sense to you? Explain.

Other Educational Thinkers You Should Know

In this book, Maureen Murphy, S. Maxwell Hines, and I want to offer education students, student teachers, and beginning teachers a research- and theory-based approach to teaching that will make it possible to have a positive impact on the lives of students and on schools. Most preservice and beginning teachers are preoccupied with the mechanics of teaching practice (the "how to") and tend to shy away from the "why." In a focus group set up to discuss this chapter, a teacher education student lamented that "every major theorist we look at has someone else who argues the exact opposite point." A beginning teacher added that "these theorists live in a utopian world that is not the world where I teach. They are not eval-uated on how well their students do on standardized tests." Or as Melisa Baker, a student teacher said, "I just don't do the Dewey."

Whatever your initial reservations about educational theory may be, I think you will gradu-ally discover that the "why" of things, the reasons we do them, plays a significant role in shap-ing the things we decide to do as teachers. By the end of our discussion, Melisa conceded that maybe the reason she did not "do the Dewey" was because she is a "closet Freire."

At this point I would like to briefly introduce other educational thinkers and research-ers who have influenced my work as a teacher. During the course of your teacher educa-tion program and your career as a teacher, I hope you get to read some of the things they have written.

In 1932, during the midst of the Great Depression in the United States, George Counts (1969, pp. 3–4) of Teachers College at Columbia University issued a challenge to teachers and all of America: "Dare the School Build a New Social Order?" Counts believed that schools were "in the grip of conservative forces," but that they could play a transformative role and help create a more just society. The key was whether educators would "pay the costs of leadership: to ac-cept responsibility, to suffer calumny, to surrender security, to risk both reputation and fu-ture" in order to build the new social order. Maxine Greene (1993), another social activist, calls on teachers to unleash the "creative imagination" of their students. As a product of the turbu-lent "sixties," I was eager to join Counts and Greene in this struggle.

But how do you change an institution that appears as monolithic and imposing as THE SCHOOL? Michael Apple (1979) offered a clue in his work exposing the "hidden curriculum." Apple built on Dewey's idea that students learn from the full range of their experiences in school, but he gave it his own twist. He argued that children did not simply learn the skills and information presented by teachers, but that they actually absorbed the values, prac-tices, and injustices of society from the way schools and classrooms were organized and people were treated.

Whereas Apple helped me understand the nature of schools, people such as Howard Gardner (1993), Christine Sleeter (1996), Martin Haberman (1995), and Herbert Kohl (1994) gave me a better idea of what to do in the classroom. Gardner presented a theory of "mulitple intelligences" that called on teachers to recognize and develop the full range of hu-man potential. Sleeter offered an approach to multiculturalism that honored diversity and promoted social justice. Haberman systematically analyzed successful teaching. Kohl showed how to navigate the system and survive by utilizing "creative maladjustment."

The problem still remained of connecting to students. Here, Nel Noddings (1992), Lisa Delpit (1995), and Gloria Ladson-Billings (1994) were the greatest help. Noddings champi-oned a feminist pedagogy based on caring and relationships. Delpit called on teachers to re-spect "other people's children" instead of blaming them for problems in the classroom. Ladson-Billings argued for a "culturally relevant pedagogy" that linked instruction with the "context" of students' lives.

At any rate, these are the people and ideas that were helpful to me. As you become a teacher, you have to decide which ones are useful to you. Maybe you will turn out to be a "closet Freire" as well.

REFERENCES AND SUGGESTIONS FOR FURTHER READING

Teachers who want to learn more about the ideas of John Dewey should read *Experience and Education* (New York: Collier/Macmillian, 1927/1954) and *Democracy and Education* (New York: Macmillian, 1916). Highly recommended books by Paulo Friere are *Pedagogy* of the Oppressed (New York: Seabury, 1970) and *Pedagogy of Hope* (New York: Continuum, 1995). I also learned much about Freire from Herbert Kohl, "Nurturing One's Dream," in *Rethinking Schools*, 10(1), Fall, 1995; Ira Shor and Paulo Freire, *A Pedagogy for Liberation: Dialogues on Transforming Education* (South Hadley, MA: Bergin and Garvey, 1987); and Ira Shor, ed., *Freire for the Classroom* (Portsmouth, NH: Heinemann, 1987). Septima Clark's story is told in Cynthia Brown, ed., *Ready from Within: Septima Clark and the Civil Rights Movement* (Lawrenceville, NJ: Africa World Press, 1986).

I think the following books will also be useful to you as you define your own philosophy of education and translate it into classroom practice. George Counts's *Dare the School Build a New Social Order?* (New York: Arno Press, 1969) is difficult to find, but excerpts appear in a number of collections. Maxine Greene has written many books. I especially recommend an article, "Diversity and Inclusion: Towards a Curriculum for Human Beings," in *Teachers College Record*, 95(2), 211–221, 1993. Michael Apple is the author of *Ideology and Curriculum* (New York: Routledge, 1979). Howard Gardner presents his ideas in *Multiple Intelligences: The Theory in Practice* (New York: Basic Books, 1993). Christine Sleeter has also written a number of books and articles. I find *Multicultural Education as Social Activism* (Albany, NY: SUNY Press, 1996) is particularly accessible to readers. Martin Haberman's *Star Teachers of Children in Poverty* (West Lafayette, IN: Kappa Delta Pi, 1995) is a short book with many challenging ideas.

Herbert Kohl explains his approach to teaching in *I Won't Learn from You and Other Thoughts on Creative Maladjustment* (New York: The New Press, 1994). George Wood and Debbie Meier write about schools using similar approaches in Wood, *Schools that Work* (New York: Dutton, 1992) and Meier, *The Power of Their Ideas: Lessons for America from a Small School in Harlem* (Boston: Beacon, 1995).

Among Nel Noddings's many writings is *The Challenge to Care in Schools* (New York: Teachers College Press, 1992). Lisa Delpit is best know for *Other People's Children* (New York: The New Press, 1995). Gloria Ladson-Billings is the author of *The Dreamkeepers: Successful Teachers of African American Children* (San Francisco: Jossey-Bass, 1994).

The newspaper, *Rethinking Schools*, and the essays from the newspaper that have been collected in book form, are especially valuable. They can be ordered from their Web site, www.rethinkingschools.org.

As you proceed in your career as a teacher you also may become interested in the research that lies behind educational ideas and practices. The American Educational Research Association is the principal organization in the United States concerned with promoting and disseminating research on teaching, learning, school organization, and assessment. It publishes a magazine, *Educational Researcher* (published nine times a year), four quarterly journals, and the annual periodical *Review of Research in Education*. In recent years, essays in the *Review of Research in Education* have examined topics such as "The New Narrative Research in Education" (Casey, 1995–1996: 211–253); "Professional, Personal, and Political Dimensions of Action Research" (Noffke, 1997: 305–343); and "Preparing Teachers for Diverse Student Populations: A Critical Race Theory Perspective" (Ladson-Billings, 1999: 211–248).

SECTION C: HOW IDEAS SHAPE OUR TEACHING

One thing that I learned, and I suspect that you are starting to learn, is that simple questions can have very complicated answers. I prepared this handout as part of a discussion over whether the dialectic spoken in inner-city Black communities should be considered slang, proper English, a different form of English, or as an entirely different language. The question you need to consider is which one of the passages below is "English"?

Which One Is English?

Beowulf, 8th-Century England

Heald pu nu, hruse, nu haeled0 ne mostan, eorla æhte! Hwæt, hyt ær on 0e gode begeaton. Gup-dea0 fornam, feorh-bealo frecne fyra gehwylcne leoda minra, para 0e pis lif ofgeaf, gesawon sele-dreamas.

The Canterbury Tales by Geoffrey Chaucer, England, 1386

Whan that Aprill with his shoures soote
The droghte of March hath perced
   to the roote,
And bathed every veyne in swich licour,
Of which vertu engendred is the flour;
Whan Zephirus eek with his sweete breeth
Inspired hath in every holt and heeth
The tendre croppes, and the yonge sonne
Hath in the Ram his halve cours yronne,
And smale fowles maken melodye
That sleepen al the night with open ye—

Hamlet by William Shakespeare, England, circa 1600

Alas, poor Yorick! I knew him, Horatio: a fellow of infinite jest, of most excellent fancy: he hath borne me on his back a thousand times; and now, how abhorred in my imagination it is! my gorge rises at it. Here hung those lips that I have kissed I know not how oft. Where be your gibes now? your gambols? your songs? your flashes of merriment, that were wont to set the table on a roar?

The Adventures of Huckleberry Finn by Mark Twain, Anglo-American, Rural Midwest, 1850s

You don't know about me, without you have read a book by the name of "The Adventures of Tom Sawyer," but that ain't no matter. That book was made by Mr. Mark Twain, and he told the truth, mainly. There was things which he stretched, but mainly he told the truth. That is nothing. I never seen anybody but lied, one time or another.

Gettysburg Address by Abraham Lincoln, United States, 1863

Four score and seven years ago our fathers brought forth upon this continent a new nation, conceived in liberty, and dedicated to the proposition that all men are created equal. Now we are engaged in a great civil war, testing whether that nation, or any nation so conceived and so dedicated, can long endure.

The Gilded Six-Bits by Zora Neale Hurston, African American, Rural Deep South, 1920s

"Humph! Ah'm way behind time t'day! Joe gointer be head 'fore Ah git mah clothes on if Ah don't make haste. . . ."

"Who dat chunkin' money in mah do'way? . . . Nobody ain't gointer be chuckin' money at me and Ah not do 'em nothin'. . . ."

"Ah ain't, Joe, not lessen you gwine gimme whateve' it is good you got in yo' pocket. Turn it go, Joe, do Ah'll tear yo' clothes. . . ."

"Unhhunh! Ah got it. It 'tis so candy kisses. Ah knowed you had somethin for me in yo' clothes."

Now Ah got to see whut's in every pocket you got."

Aunty Roachy Seb by Louise Bennett, Jamaica, West Indies, Contemporary

"So fi-we Jamaica Language is not no English Language corruption at all, a oh! An we no haffi shame a it, like one gal did go a Englan go represent we Jamaican folk-song 'One shif me got' as 'De sole underwear garment I possess,' and go sing 'Mumma, Muma, dem ketch Puppa' as 'Mother, Mother, they apprehended Farther'!"

FIG. 1.3   Which one is English?

Most people think of languages as static, unchanging, like a photograph. But languages are probably more like movies with images that continually change. New words are constantly being invented or borrowed from other languages. Even grammar evolves. Part of the debate over whether something is slang, a dialect, or a new language arises because some additions eventually become permanent whereas others are temporary and disappear. Another issue is over who gets to decide what is proper or standard usage.

Haitian Creole is a good example of how language evolves. It originated out of a blend of French and different African languages among Africans who were enslaved in Haiti. At first, most of the non-French words were considered slang. However, after independence and emancipation, Creole became established as the home dialect of the common people with its own distinct grammar and spelling. In the second half of the 20th century, Creole was accepted as an official language in Haiti. It is now taught in school and used in the workplace and government administration.

Significantly, although books and newspapers are now printed in Creole, Haitians who want to pursue higher education or to work in professions outside of Haiti must be multilingual. They are literate in their home language, Creole, and standard French, English, or both of these languages.

In 1974, the National Council of Teachers of English approved the following resolution that supported diversity while students work to master "standard" English: "We affirm the student's right to their own patterns and varieties of language . . . Dialects of their nurture or whatever dialects in which they find their own identity and style. Language scholars long ago denied that the myth of a standard American dialect has any validity. The claim that any one dialect is unacceptable amounts to an attempt of one social group to exert its dominance over another."

I believe it should be possible to respect a student's home dialect or language, while still preparing them to read, write, and think in the "standard" dialect. Their home dialect adds poetic richness to our language and helps it evolve, while mastery of the standard dialect is necessary for advanced study, professional training, and participation in a broader exchange of ideas.

JOIN THE CONVERSATION—WHICH ONE IS ENGLISH?

Questions to Consider:

1. In your opinion, which one of these passages should be considered English? Explain.
2. How does your response to this question shape the way you look at your students? Explain.
3. In your opinion, what should be a teacher's attitude toward a student who speaks "Black English" or any other home dialect in class? Explain.

REFERENCES AND SUGGESTIONS FOR FURTHER READING

Beowulf (c. 750). (Reprinted in *The Norton anthology of English literature*, 6th ed., vol. 1, p. 26, by M. Abrams, Ed., 1993, New York: Norton).

Chaucer, G. (1386). *The Canterbury tales*. (Reprinted in *The Norton anthology of English literature*, 6th ed., vol. 1, p. 81, by M. Abrams, Ed., 1993, New York: Norton).

Hurston, Z. (1933). The gilded six-bits. (Reprinted in *Black writers of America: A comprehensive anthology*, p. 613, by R. Barksdale and K. Kinnamon, Eds., 1972, New York: Macmillan).

Morris, M. (Ed). (1993). *Aunty Roachy Seb by Louise Bennett*, p. 3. Kingston, Jamaica: Sangster's.

Shakespeare, W. (1600–1601). *Hamlet, prince of Denmark*. (Reprinted in *The Works of William Shakespeare*, p. 1164, 1937, Roslyn, NY: Black's Readers Service).

Stern P. (Ed). (1940). *The life and writings of Abraham Lincoln*, p. 788. New York: Modern Library.

Twain, M. (1876). *The adventures of Huckleberry Finn*. (Reprinted in *Anthology of American literature*, 5th ed., vol. II, p. 145, by G. McMichael, Ed., 1989, New York: Macmillan).

SECTION D: BECOMING A TEACHER 1: NEW TEACHERS DISCUSS THEIR IDEAS

According to a report by the National Commission on Teaching & America's Future (September 1996), "New teachers are typically given the most challenging teaching assignments and left to sink or swim with little or no support. They are often placed in the most disadvantaged schools and assigned the most difficult-to-teach students.... Alone in their classrooms, without access to colleagues for problem solving or role modeling, discouragement can easily set in (p. 39)." As a result of conditions like these, one urban district estimates that one sixth of its new teachers leave the school system after 1 year and about a third leave within 3 years (Schwartz, 1996). Many quit teaching altogether, whereas others leave for higher paying positions in surrounding suburban communities.

To help prepare new teachers for these difficult first years, the Hofstra University School of Education organized a New Teachers Network. Alan Singer, Maureen Murphy, and S. Maxwell Hines, who worked on this book, are its principal advisors. At this writing (Spring 2002), the network is 6 years old. It has evolved to include bimonthly meetings, semiannual conferences, formal and informal collaborations with schools, an e-mail network, peer mentoring, mentoring of teacher education students by network participants, university faculty visits to schools, and visits by new teachers to education classes. Members of the network also participated in preparing this book, telling their stories as new teachers, and reviewing the other material that is included.

Most of the beginners in our programs worry about content knowledge—will they know enough—and teaching skills—how do you lead a certain activity. Some of the younger students worry whether they are mature enough to become teachers and take responsibility for students and for a full-time job. I know I had all of those worries when I was 21. But from this vantage point in my career as a teacher, I think we are too concerned with information and mechanics. They will come with experience and a commitment to learn.

Based on my work with new teachers in the Hofstra New Teachers Network, I believe that the two most important qualities for becoming a successful teacher are the ability to empathize with your students and to have a personal sense of mission of broader social goals that you hope to achieve during your career. In the stories that follow, members of the network discuss their own philosophies of education and the sense of personal mission that helps them to be successful in the classroom. In a second group of essays in chapter 2 ("Responsibilities"), another group of teachers explain how they draw on their personal experience as students in order to help them empathize with the young people they work with. Additional personal stories by beginning teachers are scattered throughout the text in sections labeled "Becoming a Teacher." You will find that as a group they are very diverse. What they share are their commitments to their students and to becoming excellent teachers. The first set of stories are by teachers who work in predominately "minority" schools. Experiences in different school settings are discussed in other chapters.

I have tried to tell you something about each teacher in a brief introduction (written in italics). As you read these stories by teachers in the New Teachers Network, consider your own ideas about teaching—your own philosophy of education. Ask yourself, how can your beliefs about students, teaching, schools, and society help you become a successful teacher?

REFERENCES

NCT&AF (September 1996). *What matters most: Teaching for America's future.* New York: National Commission on Teaching & America's Future.

Schwartz, F. (1996). Why many new teachers are unprepared to teach in most New York City schools. *Phi Delta Kappan*, 78(1), 82–84.

JOIN THE CONVERSATION—ARE ANY OF THESE PEOPLE LIKE ME?

1. As you read the stories of these new teachers, ask yourself, are any of these people like me? Which ones? How are their ideas like mine? How are they different?
2. What does it take to become a successful new teacher, especially if your initial assignment is working with students in urban and minority schools? What qualities do these teachers bring with them? What type of support do you think they need to sustain them in their work?

Questions to Consider:

1. Make a list of your beliefs about education.
2. Use your list to write an essay, "My Beliefs About Education and Society."

My Dreams and Hope
By Christina Agosti-Dircks

Christina Agosti-Dircks grew up in an affluent suburban community and attended an Ivy League college as an undergraduate. Her parents are Italian immigrants, and the family is Roman Catholic and deeply religious. In her early 20s, after a year in the secondary education program, Christina spent 2 weeks as an intern in an urban high school. Based on this experience, she accepted a position as a special education teacher working with students who were labeled emotionally disturbed. Her family, friends, and several of her classmates tried to discourage her with "horror stories of young, naive women facing dangerous situations." However, Christina not only decided to work in "the city," she moved into an apartment not far from the school.—Alan Singer

My sense of duty has its origins in my religious beliefs. My uncle worked as a missionary in the shantytowns of Nairobi, Kenya. He opened my eyes to social inequality and injustice and showed me the power of hard work, love, and a positive outlook. As a college student, I decided that I needed to act based on my beliefs. I became a literacy volunteer tutoring migrant school children having difficulty with English, a Big Buddy to a truant teen who needed someone to care, a soup kitchen volunteer delivering food and conversation, and a volunteer at the local Red Cross Emergency Shelter for the homeless. As part of a college-based religious community, I participated in a week-long social outreach project in the Appalachian region of Kentucky. These experiences exposed me to diversity in human circumstances and made me personally aware of material and spiritual poverty for the first time in my life.

During my sojourn in Kentucky, I had a religious and social epiphany when I spotted the face of a small child longingly peering out of the grimy, cracked window of his dilapidated house. This image stayed with me and stirred in me the desire to change the life chances of children who feel trapped and resigned to their lives. I want to use my life to "help them find the light within themselves," as Paulo Freire writes. Through use of my time, energy, and talents, I hoped to help them reach their full potential.

After college, I worked as a youth placement counselor in a rural, economically depressed area. I tutored low-income youth and created a mentoring program that paired teens at risk of dropping out of school with other members of their community. During this job, I realized the awesome potential and great responsibility teachers have to influence their students' lives. This was my calling—to take action, to be a good teacher, to have a classroom of my own where I could promote social change.

At that point, the only missing piece was the confidence of knowing whether as a White, suburban-born female, I could handle the challenge and be effective as a teacher of urban, minority students. To help me make this decision, I enrolled in a course with a teacher who gave me the opportunity to spend 2 weeks in his high school in Brooklyn. Attending classes, interacting with students, and getting a general sense of the atmosphere and organization of school life in the city dispelled my qualms and stirred a deep emotional chord within me. I headed out for the summer break content and confident. I decided that I wanted the chance to teach my own sets of beautiful, happy, young faces, and have been honored with that opportunity ever since.

Paulo Freire says that "dreams are the movers of history" and "there is no dream without hope." These words by Paulo Freire capture my feelings as a teacher. Dreams and hope have motivated, challenged, sustained, and rewarded me.

* * *

Race and U.S. Politics and Education
By Howard Fuchs

Howard Fuchs grew up in a religious Jewish family in a White, upper middle-class suburban community. Until eighth grade, he went to a private Jewish day school. After graduating from high school, he attended a small private liberal arts college. When he completed college, his parents expected him to become a lawyer. Instead, he decided to teach high school.—Alan Singer

As a child I was sheltered from what life is like in urban America. I was taught that if the Jews could come to this country after all the hardships they have experienced throughout their history and live the American dream, anyone could. I believed that those who were poor or claimed discrimination were people who did not want to work hard. These were people who were just trying to take the easy road.

While at college, my experience and opinions began to change. I was a politics major and would sit in classes about race and U.S. politics. These were the most uncomfortable classes I have ever taken. Here we were, a group of mostly White students, one Black student, and a White teacher talking about racism in America. It would frustrate me to watch the White students in the class picking their words carefully when answering questions and looking at the

Black student to make sure they did not say the wrong thing. It puzzled me to watch the professor acting worse than the students. I became fairly good friends with the Black student and we used to talk about how the class would react to his presence. He was very conscious of the situation. The funny part was that he was from a rich neighborhood in Ohio. It turns out that he had less experience with urban minorities than most of the kids in the class. He confided in me that this class was the first time that he felt like a Black man. This was the first time that he had been treated differently because of the color of his skin.

I began to take a long hard look at the school. It bothered me that the college, which prided itself on being fairly left wing, did not actively recruit in urban minority schools, and that the tuition prohibited most lower income students from attending.

After college, I entered law school where I spent the better part of a year miserable, trying to figure out how I would tell my parents that law school was not for me. I also discovered what I wanted to do with my life. The law school sent us to speak to high school students about the criminal justice system. I visited a school in one of the poorest neighborhoods in Brooklyn, New York. My experience at this school made me realize how lucky I was to receive the education that I did and that the students in urban minority schools do not have the same opportunity that I had. It really bothers me that a child's socioeconomic situation dictates the quality of education they receive. The children who need the extra resources are not getting them. This experience inspired me to want to teach and I enrolled in a secondary education program.

In one of my education classes, we were assigned to read the book *Savage Inequalities* by Jonathan Kozol. It discusses the horrendous conditions that exist in some of the poor urban schools. The class was appalled at this situation, but few people were willing to take any action. Most wanted to teach in suburban schools with students like themselves. But I decided I wanted to work with minority students where I thought I could make a difference.

I believed I knew how to teach before I went to graduate school. I learned over a very difficult year that I did not have a clue about what to do. I came in with desire, but I needed to learn the tools to be a teacher. During my student-teaching experience I had one of the best cooperating teachers. She taught me all about classroom organization, that you do not have to yell at kids, that you can be caring to people, and that there are ways of getting a class to cooperate with you. It is not all about walking into a class and slamming the door and screaming at kids. It is about understanding and appreciating them.

When I started, I expected my students to be instantly motivated to want to learn. But I soon realized that my job was to motivate students to want to learn and to help them connect to what we were studying. In my experience, a lot of teachers underestimate the importance of motivation.

I always let my students know who I am—that I am a Jew. There is often a lot of tension between Blacks and Jews. The kids see too much on television and they begin to think that all Jews are one way and that Black people and Jews are supposed to have an antagonistic relationship. It is important for them to understand that there are people teaching in their school whom they like and who care about them, and they are Jews.

* * *

I Want to Give Back to the Community
By Pedro Sierra

Pedro Sierra is a social studies teacher and the dean of students in a troubled inner-city high school. His parents were originally from Puerto Rico. He grew up in the neighborhood near the school, but earned his high school diploma from an alternative educational program. Pedro at-

tended a suburban college where he earned his teacher education credentials and was exposed to a level of affluence and comfort he had never imagined. Even though he worked hard to get out of the ghetto, Pedro decided to return to this community to teach, live, and raise a family. He feels he "spent years tearing down my community. Now I dedicate the rest of my life to making it a better place. It is my calling. This is why I am here."—Alan Singer

I decided to become a teacher because teachers taught me to imagine a brighter future. Life was hard for me growing up. My mother was a drug addict and an alcoholic who became infected with HIV. My younger brother and I were on our own since I was 14. For a while we lived in a furnished room that was not much more than a rat hole. We survived by selling drugs, numbers, and guns or robbing homes. I was living on the edge. My whole mentality was that I never would live to reach 21 anyway. I finally ended up at an outreach center where teachers gave me the "tough love" I needed, not only to graduate from high school, but to go to college and do something better with myself.

The two teachers who had the greatest influence on me were social studies teachers. One was an African American male who was able to reach me because he had been the way I was when he was younger. This connection was our starting point. It is also the starting point I use with my own students. A Jewish woman won me over because she respected us. We were on a first-name basis. These teachers worked hard to earn our respect and we responded to them. They motivated us by making connections with our lives. I spent 6 years in high school but because of these teachers I finally graduated.

One of the seeds they planted in my head was to give back to my community. I spent years tearing it down. Now I dedicate the rest of my life to making it a better place. It is my calling. This is why I am here. This community is where I feel comfortable. This is where I grew up. If I leave here to go somewhere else, I can make more money or have a nicer house, but it will not help the people I leave behind. In the outreach program, teachers compared our lives to rockets. We could use our lives for destruction or to carry people to a higher place. I want to carry people to that higher place.

In college, I read two books that had a profound impact on me. *The Autobiography of Malcolm X* and *Down These Mean Streets* by Piri Thomas. Both were written by men who spent time in prison but made something out of their lives. Piri Thomas says that even though he was locked up in jail, he was not really incarcerated because he learned to read and it freed his mind and his life. I feel the same way about my life. Because of my education, I have become free.

I tell students, "You are street smart. You can take off those baggy pants and turn them into slacks and turn those Timberland boots into shoes. You can take off your hood and put on a shirt and tie and learn to talk standard English instead of talking slang. You can use your survival skills in the workplace. There are a lot of people who have privileges growing up, so they never learn what you know. You have to decide what you want out of life. You can make a better life for yourself and others if you work hard to achieve your goals."

To be a successful teacher, I had to learn many things. I had to become a good listener and hear what my students were saying. In my education classes, I was taught to "think outside the box" in order to come up with creative solutions to problems. Now I had to learn to "listen outside the box," so I was not blinded by my assumptions about a student.

Many students do not have someone there for them as they grow up, so I try to be that someone in their lives—their spiritual mother and father. When one of my students gets in trouble, I say, "I love you to death like you are my little brother. I will help you. I will go all out for you. But if you do something that is wrong, I will have to burn you." Students want adults to set limits. This is one of my basic beliefs.

A good teacher must be compassionate and have passion. When I come into this building I never say to myself, "Oh my God, I have to go to work." I love coming into this building. I love being a teacher. Hopefully, I will not leave here until the day that I retire.

* * *

A Moral Obligation to Care About Others
By Gayle Meinkes-Lumia

Gayle Meinkes-Lumia grew up in a middle-class, predominately White neighborhood of New York City, but attended a public high school where the students were overwhelmingly Latino, African American, and Caribbean American. Among the students in her high school, she was one of a tiny fraction who were Jews. Gayle was a student in my high school class. We met again when she began her teacher education program. She teaches English in a suburban middle school with students who are primarily Latino. She is convinced that "the transformation of society must begin in our schools. Teachers have to motivate, encourage, coddle, and connect. Our own lives were touched by people who cared; it is our obligation to care about others."—Alan Singer

My decision to teach in a predominately minority school stems from my experience attending an underprivileged high school. It helps me empathize with the urban/inner-city plight. At this school, I was influenced by having friends from families with lower socioeconomic status and by teachers who inspired me. I was also lucky to have parents who instilled confidence in me.

Minority students in urban environments are victimized. They are subject to a system that discriminates against them and caters to the affluent. As a result, their self-esteem and confidence disappears and their school performance suffers. As educators, it is essential to motivate minority students and provide them with some sense of direction in their lives. They must be able to visualize alternatives.

As a graduate student in the School of Education, I was impressed by the writing of Paulo Freire and Maxine Greene and I try to incorporate their ideas in my educational philosophy. I especially admire Freire's work with illiterate farmers and Greene's idea that democracy cannot exist without freedom fighters. I love literature and introduce students to authors like Frederick Douglass, Alice Walker, Henry James, and Maxine Hong Kingston, so they can understand that freedom is something that must be struggled for.

Although the middle school I teach in is physically located in the suburbs, it reminds me of urban schools because students are mainly from low-income/single-parent households. Many of my students have a parent who works two or three jobs simply to meet the family's basic needs. My work with these students is a continuous challenge. It is extremely difficult to accomplish educational goals when a student's concerns are elsewhere.

I find that my students need to be motivated and empowered in different ways than their wealthier, white, counterparts. My eighth-grade "low-reading-level" class is reading *Fahrenheit 451*. The characters' minds have turned into mush because books are banned and burned. In discussions in class we centered on the consequences of eliminating choices and alternatives, and my students wrote beautiful essays dealing with aspects of their own lives that are censored or suppressed.

I am proud of the emotional support I gave one student after he attempted suicide. The boy wrote a wonderful journal entry that expressed his desire to communicate with people. We sat for hours and discussed everything, from goals to gardening. At the end, I felt rejuvenated. I believe that teachers receive as much as they give.

You have to go into teaching with a notion that you want to motivate the kids. I went into teaching because #1, I love English literature, I have always been an avid reader, and I wanted to inspire students to learn and to love literature. I had some horrible and some great teachers in high school. Once we were reading Oscar Wilde, and I loved him, so I asked if we could read another one of his books. The teacher just said, "No. No one tells me what to teach in my class." I just stepped back and thought, "I am never speaking to this woman again." I still remember ignoring her and just passing notes the rest of the term. The next year I had a great teacher. And that changed my notions about English literature and teaching completely. Now I wanted to become a teacher so I could inspire students to learn.

I want to make a difference. A teacher cannot just be there for the paycheck. I run two extracurricular clubs, a book club, and a newspaper club, because I want to do it. One of my colleagues said to me, 2 years ago, "Why do you do all of this? For tenure?" My answer is that I love being there. I love the kids. I chaperone, volunteer for all events. The students have so much energy and enthusiasm. If you work with them, you will have it too.

* * *

Teaching as an Act of Resistance
By Michael Pezone

Michael Pezone has taught in a junior high school and a high school in New York City. He is a White male, from a working-class Italian American family, who grew up in a suburban community with people from similar backgrounds. He attended an Ivy League college, worked in the corporate world, and, in his mid-30s, decided to start a second career as a secondary school teacher. A political radical and an intellectual, he was dissatisfied with the academic level and ideological limitations of most of the students and professors in the teacher education program he attended. Because of his political beliefs, he chose to student teach in a predominately minority suburban school district. After a series of unsuccessful job interviews, he opted for a teaching position in "the city."—Alan Singer

The ideal teacher is a political prisoner who resists bondage by continuing to educate himself, and to educate others. He teaches for one reason only: to create a world of equality and freedom. My role model as a teacher is Prometheus as described in classical Greek mythology. Prometheus was the teacher of all arts and the giver of all good to mortal men, who, as a result of his transgression, was severely and eternally punished by Zeus. When Zeus offered him freedom in exchange for betraying mankind, Prometheus responded, "There is no torment or contrivance in the power of Zeus to wring this utterance from me; . . . none of these things shall extort from me the knowledge that may ward off his overthrow." I believe teaching can be an act of resistance to an oppressive social order.

I live in the suburbs and tried to find a job there. I knew I would have to downplay and disguise my peculiarly political ideal of education. At 35 years of age, my overriding concern was to get a job and begin my second career. My first interview was quite brief. The personnel administrator, who did the initial screening for her district, looked over my resume with a quizzical expression. She commented on my Ivy League background, then asked why I was sitting there with her. She listened suspiciously as I stated my desire to work with young people. She suggested that I look for a job teaching in college and showed little real interest during the remainder of the interview.

At one interview, I was asked to discuss my attitude toward "revisionist history." At the second, I was asked to describe my feelings toward "multiculturalism." A third interviewer asked me to discuss "political correctness." The three interviewers each made clear, by tone and gesture, their disdain for the topics. I was being asked to distance myself from so-called revisionism, PC, and multiculturalism.

The new term was less than 3 weeks away and I was growing more and more desperate. I answered cautiously, with circumspection. But no matter how cautious and circumspect, I was unable and unwilling to respond in a conservative manner. As I spun out my answers, I could see, quite literally, their spirits harden and my job prospects dissipate.

A few days before the school year began, the (union) chapter leader of a city school whom I had met in a graduate course set up a last-minute interview at his junior high school. The interview was informal. The chapter leader's endorsement, and my assurance that I had no problem with discipline and control, were enough for the principal. I was hired on the spot.

I have spent the last 6 years devoting myself to a never-ending battle to free my classroom from all vestiges of authoritarianism and other relationships of domination. I have helped students conduct free speech fights, one over the flag salute and another over an underground newspaper. My classes regularly produce a magazine written and edited by students. Happily, I have discovered some like-minded colleagues with whom I can share ideas and find support. At the same time, I am alienated from a significant percentage of my colleagues. To some, I am an object of hostility and ridicule. Others have comforted themselves by defining me as an oddity, a deviant with an unhinged mind.

I am proud to say that my students have responded to me in a positive way. They particularly appreciate the self-expression they enjoy in my classroom. One result of my practice is that I have very few problems with student behavior. This has made it easy for the administration to believe that, despite my heterodoxy, I am a good teacher. Despite the school system's logic of control, I have been able to create a space for freedom inside its walls, or so I like to think. I also like to hope that inside these prison spaces children may laugh and learn, and may choose to keep the divine fire burning for the benefit of mankind.

* * *

Faith in God Gives Me Faith in Myself
By Deon Gordon Mitchell

Deon Gordon Mitchell was born in a rural community on the island of Jamaica in the Caribbean. She was raised by her grandparents until she joined her mother in New York City when she was 14 years old. Deon is a high school teacher and deeply committed to her Pentacostal Church. She works with the church youth group and writes articles for its newsletter discussing the importance of education. Deon believes that with God by her side "my life is filled with hope and love." She teaches young people in school and in church "to fill their lives with hope and love."–Alan Singer

Attending high school in New York City was scary for me. In Jamaica, teachers were very strict. Students had to wear uniforms, sit up straight, and use proper language. When I got here it was the extreme opposite. Classrooms were chaotic. I was considered a very good student and got grades in the 90s, but it baffled me why. Was it because I was quiet and obedient or because I really excelled? I graduated from high school in the top 20 in my class and was accepted at a prestigious branch of the state university.

When I got to college I was quite confident—until I started classes. I had problems writing and comprehending reading material and was placed on academic probation. I was on the verge of getting thrown out of school and was terribly embarrassed. I pushed myself harder and harder, staying up nights to study and going to tutoring. My skin broke out from stress, I grew terribly thin, and at one point I fainted because of dehydration. In my family, we were taught that with God you can do anything. Having faith in God gave me faith in myself. I continually prayed to God to grant me the strength to succeed and eventually I got my grade point average up.

College was really my first experience with White people and my first experience with racism. One year the college banned Black students from donating blood because it was afraid we would spread AIDS. We took over the school's administration building in protest. I had teachers who denounced the Black Student Union in their classes because we invited a controversial figure to speak on campus. In my senior year, the college started a diversity requirement and White students protested against it.

When I finished college I did not have a good impression of White people; however, I decided to attend a graduate program where most of the students were White. I believe that in this country, if you want the best education, you have to go to a school where White people go. I forced myself to complete remedial classes in order to qualify.

As a student teacher, I realized that some of my ideas about race were naive. I assumed that because I was Black and my students were Black, they would listen to me. During my first lesson, one of the students said, "That's a stupid question." I panicked as I remembered what students did to teachers at my high school and I just lost it. Once again I turned to God for the strength to continue. I told myself and God that "I can do this. I am going to do this."

I decided to become a teacher for many reasons. They include the strength of my religious beliefs and the knowledge that young people need my love and hope. Students need a teacher who cares about them and can show them a path out of a very rough environment. Christ came for the people who were most needy. I walk in God's footsteps when I choose to teach the students who need me the most.

I believe I have a responsibility to contribute to society so another generation does not receive the inadequate education I received in high school. It is my duty. Even though it is hard, if I can change one person's view of themselves from negative to positive, I feel I have fulfilled my responsibility.

* * *

SECTION E: WHY DO YOU WANT TO BE A TEACHER?

In the Hofstra University secondary education program we continually ask students, "Why do you want to be a teacher?" and we help them to rethink their answers as they define their own philosophies of education. Here are excerpts from answers by students in one introductory methods class for undergraduates.

- Danielle Albers: "I have wanted to be a teacher since high school. I love English, especially American Literature, and I hope to help my students learn to love (or at least understand and appreciate) it."
- Claire Bowler: "I have wanted to be a teacher for as long as I can remember. I had great elementary school teachers who helped me academically and also taught me how to 'break out of my shell' and gain self confidence. My goal is to make history fun, exciting and meaningful. Many people see social studies as a discipline involving a lot of memorization. I think of it more like putting together a giant puzzle or trying to solve mysteries."
- Sarah Dmuchowski: "My goals as a teacher are to encourage kids to read and help them to love to read. I want to introduce them to different genres and styles of literature so that they might find something that they really like and that they find moving."

- Carlos Fernandez: "I am becoming a teacher because I was greatly affected by many of my teachers and I feel that it is my duty to do the same for other young people. Most of the time I did not like high school, but I certainly liked hanging out with my friends. I want to make a difference."
- Cherilyn Holmes: "When I was in high school I tutored a student in Spanish and his grades began to improve. I took a student who was failing Spanish and helped him become an 'A' student. I feel that teaching is the most rewarding career because as teachers we have the ability to positively impact another person's life."
- Amy Keyishian: "I want to become a teacher because I believe the greatest weapon we as human beings have to fight ignorance and the 'evils' of the world, is education. I want to become a teacher because I love literature and there is so much in literature that we can benefit from by applying its truths to ourselves. I am someone who likes to volunteer in my spare time, and I see teaching as a way of helping others."
- Rachel Montagno: "I wanted to drop out of school and this teacher would not allow me to. She helped me find my place and encouraged me to go on to college. To this day, that teacher remains my friend as well as my mentor. That is why I want to be a teacher."
- LeShawnda Williams: "I want to become a teacher to teach the history that was never taught to me when I was in school—the history of Africa and African people in America. I went to a predominantly white high school, and it was a struggle just to make it through each school day. I want to make it different for students—all students."

JOIN THE CONVERSATION—WHY YOU WANT TO BE A TEACHER

Questions to Consider:
1. Whose ideas come closest to your own? Explain.
2. What or who inspired you to become a teacher? Why?
3. Write a brief statement explaining why you want to be a teacher.

SECTION F: FIRST-SEMESTER EDUCATION STUDENTS REFLECT ON THEIR EXPERIENCE

Alice Van Tassell and Maritza Perez were students in the same graduate secondary education methods class for preservice teachers. It was their first class in the Hofstra University teacher education program. In reflective practice journals they wrote during the semester, Alice and Maritza discussed their feelings and ideas as they tried to decide if they really wanted to be teachers. As you read about their experiences, think about your own ideas, concerns, and hopes as you prepare to become a teacher.—Alan Singer

My Secondary Education General Methods Reflective Practice Journal
By Alice Van Tassell

Excerpt A: A humbling experience.

Tonight we discussed our personal experience in high school, how it still shapes the way we see ourselves, and how it influences our ideas about teaching. I was surprised at how many people described negative experiences and talked about the way they learned to see themselves as failures. Two women, Maritza and Irene, said they felt stupid in high school and they continued to feel that way for a long time after they graduated. Alan (our teacher) asked us to think about whether the failure people described was because of their inadequacies or failure by teachers and schools.

My own high school experience was primarily positive, very different from the ones described by Maritza and Irene. I am starting to realize that this was largely due to the excellent teachers with whom I was fortunate enough to come into contact. I remember many different types of teachers, but the ones that made the most lasting impression on me were less concerned with the subject matter than they were with helping us learn to think and develop life skills. My advanced placement Calculus teacher always broke up the classroom with jokes and told stories of his previous job with NASA where he learned to apply Calculus. His down-to-earth manner and constant interaction with us made Calculus accessible to me. I was someone who had begged and pleaded to be taken out of advanced math only a few years earlier.

Tonight's class was a humbling experience for me. In the past, I always believed that my academic success was due solely to my intelligence and effort. Now, I see that things could have been very different if I had gone to an average school with average teachers, or even worse, a school where teachers didn't care. No matter how intelligent I may (or may not) be, I owe a lot of credit to teachers who always tried to teach us in creative ways.

Excerpt B: Mike's total rejection of 'the system' is very disconcerting to me.

Tonight's class was very heated. Our class argued about topics that are politically relevant to education and the country as a whole. Mike, a New York City teacher, visited our class, and he was very angry. He said that the American educational system institutionalizes racism, oppression and failure and he expressed disgust with mainstream America. Hector, a philosophy major, presented a diametrically opposed viewpoint. He believes that poverty and oppression are no excuse for educational failure. He feels people will be successful if they have strong family and academic values.

I think Mike and Hector are both wrong. Hector should realize that the phrase "family values" is a political slogan. Some conservatives want to impose their ideas on other people and many feel this is oppressive. As an English major, I read August Wilson's play *Fences* and Robert Pirsig's novel *Lila*. Hector should read these books. They would help him re-evaluate his opinion.

On the other hand, Mike's total rejection of 'the system' is very disconcerting to me. While I do see a need for change, I believe that such an absolutist position is counterproductive to his goals. In my opinion, change will have to come from within, especially with an issue which is as politically charged as education.

Personally, I feel family values are very important and I want to instill them in my children. But I recognize that there is something wrong with blaming the problems of education on the values of students. I don't know yet how I will handle this issue as a teacher. The only thing that I do know is that there is more than one side to this question.

Excerpt C: What struck me . . . was Alan's use of humor.

Tonight we spent about half of the class with Alan demonstrating mini-lessons in four different subject areas: Physics, Math, English and Music. It was very interesting for me because I got to see different ways to help students think about the main goal of the lesson. In each case the specific content area came second to the goal of getting us involved in the discussion.

What also struck me as very interesting was Alan's use of humor. I don't remember classes in high school being so much fun. I also don't remember being taught concepts like "duality" in science or "equality" in math. Important concepts like these were usually reserved for English classes—which may be part of the reason I chose to be an English major. I find lessons that engage students in discussion of the big issues by presenting smaller examples for examination are the most interesting. I suspect other people do too.

The props Alan used in class (like passing melting ice around the class to illustrate the duality of being) were very creative. "Is water a solid, a liquid or a gas?" The liveliness that the props added to the lesson helped keep me interested in what was going on and helped me better understand the concepts being introduced. Later when we evaluated the mini-lessons, we compared the props to the metaphors in a poem.

Excerpt D: I thought I was prepared before I got up.

Tonight we started doing our own mini-lessons with the class. One of the math students went first and he did very well. I was actually interested in what he was teaching. After his lesson we discussed ways to connect math to the lives of students so it is not taught in a vacuum. We also spoke about the idea of multiple intelligences. Different students can look at the same problem and think about it in different ways.

Then it was my turn. I thought I was prepared before I got up, but in retrospect, I don't feel I was. I had a good idea, but I didn't get it across clearly at all. I also found myself standing behind the desk too much and not connecting with the "students." Part of the problem was that I was very nervous, much more than I had expected to be.

After the mini-lesson, the entire class discussed how it went. At first, I was upset with the criticism, but very quickly I realized that I need it in order to improve. We discussed ways to make the lesson better, and then I got a chance to do the same lesson again. I was happy that Alan and the class didn't feel my ego was too fragile for them to openly raise their questions and that I got to do my lesson a second time in front of the class. Next time, I will work on laying out my plan better and will try to have everything clearer in my head.

Excerpt E: I was getting rebellious . . . pretending to be her student.

Tonight we worked on writing lesson plans. They are our strategies for teaching. We started looking at a two-week long unit, broke it down into daily lessons, and then broke the lessons down into shorter activities and questions. The idea of starting with a broad picture and then finding smaller building blocks we can use to convey understanding to students seems very logical and should help me to plan my lessons. I feel that better organization is one thing that will make a big difference in my next presentation to a class.

I want to comment on some of the mini-lessons people did in class tonight. Donnie was great. She spoke slowly and clearly and I never once had that uneasy feeling I get when I'm not sure where a lesson is going. However, the next mini-lesson made me feel like I was in sixth grade again. The teacher spoke clearly and made her points, but I would have been afraid of her as a student. During the fifteen minute mini-lesson, I was getting rebellious sitting in my chair pretending to be her student. I used to think I wanted to be the kind of teacher students respected with an ounce of fear. But I am starting to see that this isn't necessarily the most effective way to teach.

Excerpt F: The saying that you learn as you teach was very true for all of us.

We started class by examining a research project done with students at a California state university. Evidently, Asian students were consistently getting higher grades in freshman Calculus than students from other ethnic groups. After observing students during the semester, researchers concluded that the reason for this disparity in performance was not the intelligence of particular students or the amount of time they studied, but because the Asian students were more likely to work outside of class in unofficial study teams. Other studies have found that group work can facilitate learning at all age and academic levels.

This does not mean that if teachers put children into groups they will automatically become better students. We discussed ways that teachers can design groups to make them work more effectively. All team members should have clearly defined responsibilities. Teachers should be active participants in each group, advising, stimulating and monitoring the performance of students where necessary.

The class worked through a cooperative learning activity using an old high school algebra final exam. Each team had people who were comfortable with math, people who were just okay, and people who were terrorized by math problems. Our goal was to prepare a student who has "math phobia" to teach a problem to the rest of the class. The key to the activity was that we had to help the person who did not understand math, not only to understand, but also to explain the problem to the class. The saying that you learn as you teach was very true for all of us.

At first, I thought this kind of group activity wouldn't work very well. When I was put in a group in high school, I found the "smart person," and I just floated along. But the ideas of clearly defined responsibilities and of teacher-as-active-participant have potential and I can see myself getting enthusiastic about cooperative learning.

I also like the idea of having teams work on a term project. This type of long term activity teaches students how to work together, how to plan their time, and how to organize their thoughts. Group term projects will allow students with different talents to contribute them and make everyone's work better.

Excerpt G: I need to strike a balance.

As an opening exercise, we worked in groups writing questions to ask students about a reading passage. I hadn't realized how hard it would be to come up with good questions. After each group presented their questions to the class, we examined our questions using a system called Bloom's Taxonomy. Bloom organizes questions into a hierarchy ranging from simple, recall questions, to questions requiring comparisons, conclusions, and complex thinking. Personally, I like the structure Bloom provided for thinking about questioning, but some people were concerned that teachers who applied his formula could become rigid and only ask "higher order" questions. We also had difficulty deciding the differences between some of his categories. It might be more useful to locate questions on a continuum instead of placing them in distinct categories. Certain questions will have the tendency to draw thoughtful responses, even though they don't initially seem that sophisticated. Alan says his most important question is "Why?"

My second mini-lesson went much better than the first one. I prepared more questions and was more relaxed with the topic. Because my first mini-lesson was somewhat dull, I tried to make this one more exciting and the class got a little rowdy. I see that I need to strike a balance between the two and keep the discussion a little more civilized. I was also speaking too fast and cutting people off before they could finish presenting an idea. These are both nervous habits that I have to address before student teaching. Anyway, I worked hard and people felt that I improved.

Excerpt H: Many students feel that your grade defines you.

Tonight we discussed grading students in high school and also how we would be graded for this class. People raised good points and things came up that I hadn't considered before. I feel that grading is a negative part of our educational environment, but it is so intricately woven into the "system" that I have trouble envisioning schools without grades. Someone in class said that grading helps a teacher see who is doing well and who needs help to improve. I said I think it is unfair to label students as doing "better" or "worse." It seems like stereotyping people and tracking them in another way.

Alan introduced the idea of mastery learning. Instead of having students compete against each other for grades, students have to demonstrate that they have achieved a mastery level of material and skills. Success is measured by competence. This is an interesting idea because it leaves open the possibility that everyone will do well and get a high grade. It also fits in well with the ideas of cooperative learning. Students will have a cooperative classroom environment because they are not competing for grades.

We also discussed another option for grading called portfolio assessment. In this system, students present their work to a panel. I think this offers students a chance to really show what they know. Marking is done by a panel so there will be greater objectivity. However, I confess that the idea of going before a panel is very intimidating to me. I wonder what kind of an effect it would have on certain students. Someone who is outspoken will feel comfortable and may even be able to disagree with the panel. But a student who has been brought up to "toe-the-line" and respect and fear authority may not be able to breathe until later.

One thing that bothered me was Alan's statement when we were talking about grades for this class. He said, "A grade is just a grade. It measures performance on a task but it does not say anything about your qualities as a human being." Many of us, including myself, feel that your grade defines who you are. For Alan's statement to be correct, it needs to be incorporated into the philosophy of the school. It cannot just be rhetoric to make students feel better at report card time.

* * *

My Secondary Education General Methods
Reflective Practice Journal
By Maritza Perez

Excerpt A: My first day of class in ten years.

Today was my first day of class in ten years and I am doubting myself. I don't know if I made the right decision in going back to school. I don't know if I really want to be a teacher or if I would be a good one. I work in an art program for second to fifth grade children. An experience I had there explains why I am here now.

My second graders were designing patterns so they could make bracelets. As I was speaking to the class, I noticed one little boy was not doing the project. I went to help him, but the teacher said I should not waste my time because he never listens and is not smart. She felt he should be put back into the first grade.

I got the class started on the project and I went to talk with him anyway. I asked him why he wasn't working, and another boy told me that he didn't understand English, "He is Spanish." I bent down and in Spanish I asked him if we could do the project together. While I explained things to him in Spanish, the other children were whispering to each other, "She speaks Spanish." When Carlos completed his bracelet, it was one of the best in the class and he was very proud. I knew that for at least one class I had helped a child feel important and confident. That is why I am in the teacher education program.

Our teacher asked if any of us did not like high school and I raised my hand. I told the class my story of being the only Spanish-speaking student. I did not think I was smart enough to do the work, so I went into the vocational program and became a beautician. Alan said something interesting to me. He asked, "Why are you still blaming that fifteen year old girl for all the problems she had in high school?" I never really thought about it before. Maybe if some teachers had taken an interest in me, things would have turned out differently. Maybe, someday, I will be that teacher and I can make a difference in life for a teenager that is lost.

Excerpt B: I'm going home.

We were asked to read this paper and write a paragraph about what it means. I began to read the article but I didn't understand it. There was a lot of noise in the classroom and I couldn't focus. I sat in my seat not knowing what to do because I was so upset. I complained to myself and then I came to a conclusion—I don't have what it takes to get my Masters and I'm going home. I decided to talk with Alan after class and tell him why I couldn't do the assignment. Just then, Alan asked who didn't understand the reading. I raised my hand. I told him it was too hard, and I just was not as smart as the rest of the class. After I spoke, others began to open up. To my surprise, only two people in the class understood the article. The conversation started to change now. This is how students feel in school when the teacher tells them to read something that they don't understand. I have felt and struggled with this feeling all my school life. I was running away from this feeling when I became a beautician. When we looked at the article together as a class, I discovered two things. If you feel you have support from other people, you can confront the unknown and work it out. There are also different ways of teaching the same subject matter. It can be boring and oppressive, or it can be interesting and even fun. A teacher needs to remember the students and use appropriate lessons to teach them. Don't go over their heads.

Excerpt C: It really doesn't look right when the teacher chews gum.

Today, five students did mini-lessons. For many of the students in our class it was the first time they were in front of a group teaching, and some had a hard time. They lost the class in the middle of the lesson and could not figure out how to follow through and bring their mini-lesson to a conclusion. I learned some important points from what they did. 1. I have to keep focused. 2. Don't sit and point at the board. 3. Things go better when you are organized. 4. Be direct and ask lots of questions. 5. You have to understand what you are teaching. 6. Try to look confident. 7. It really doesn't look right when the teacher chews gum.

Excerpt D: You have to be in charge.

The people who did mini-lessons today clearly learned from the first group, and they did much better. Today I learned: 1. If you are nervous, it shows. Try to keep calm. 2. Don't be so rigid. Go with what works. 3. Participation from students is essential. It lets you know if they understand the lesson. 4. When students participate they get motivated to learn more. 5. Use different materials to make the lesson more interesting. 6. Do not assume students know what you are talking about. You have to explain things to them. 7. Try to limit the number of things that are not related to the subject. 8. Body language is important. Watch out for the signals you are giving the students. 9. If you are the teacher, you have to be in charge.

Excerpt E: I understood the concept.

The first half of the class we were doing some sample math problems. I hadn't done anything like this for several years and I didn't remember how to do them. When we finished—or gave up—Alan divided the class into groups. We would review the problems, and then someone who had trouble with the math would teach the problem to the entire class. In my group it was going to be me.

The people in my group tried real hard to help me but I still wasn't getting it and I panicked. Alan came over to see what was happening. He sat down and took off his shoe. It was silly, but we started to all compare our shoes and now I understood the concept. When I went up to the front, I explained to the class about congruent shoes and congruent triangles. When Alan took off his shoe he caught my attention, it got me to relax, and I was able to learn and teach the math. In the second half of the class we watched and discussed a video with a math teacher who found all sorts of ways to get her class into the lesson. She allows them to build, cut, play games, and she sings and dances, whatever it takes to motivate students and explain the concepts. Sometimes the more ridiculous you are, the more interested students become. I think I am starting to understand just a little bit of what math is all about.

* * *

JOIN THE CONVERSATION—REFLECTING ON YOUR EXPERIENCE

Questions to Consider:
1. Which of the experiences described in this section comes closest to your own as a student? Explain.
2. Alice and many of the students in this class were very concerned about being graded and assigning grades to their own students. How do you feel about being graded? Why?
3. Maritza lists things she learned from watching student-taught mini-lessons in class. What did you learn from your first mini-lesson?
4. What did you learn from Alice and Maritza?
5. Write a letter to either Alice or Maritza comparing your experiences as students and in teacher education classes with theirs.

SECTION G: ALAN'S PEDAGOGICAL CREED—
WHAT I KNOW ABOUT TEACHING AND LEARNING
(WITH APOLOGIES TO JOHN DEWEY)

Earlier in this chapter, I discussed John Dewey's "pedagogic creed," in which he listed his basic beliefs about education. In bringing this chapter to a close, I would like to list some of my basic beliefs. Most of Dewey's writing was heavily philosophical. However, in his pedagogic creed, he was much more concrete and practical. The ideas I present here are also intended to be concrete and practical, but as with Dewey, they are grounded in my broader philosophy of education and society, my experience working with students, and my goals as a teacher.

I am not calling the list a pedagogic creed because I think my ideas are on par with Dewey's. I am simply borrowing his approach and using it as a way to honor him for his seminal contributions to education.

This does not work:

Drill Kills: This approach to teaching (drilling basic skills) is based on the assumption that students either did not understand something because they were not paying attention or because they are too stupid to think. If we make them do it over and over again, they will learn through repetition or to avoid punishment. The approach seems to work for certain physical skills (shooting baskets, marching, or hitting tennis balls) and practice does make people more proficient as musicians and artists (but probably not if they experience it as punishment), but there is no evidence that drilling helps people understand complex ideas. On the other hand, constant drilling destroys enthusiasm and interest in learning. Drill kills.

Bore Snore: Boring teaching is a form of social control, not a necessary evil in conveying information. Its goal is to beat students into submission so they "behave." Boring instruction is a pretense at education so schools can say "we taught it but they didn't learn it"—therefore, "the problem must be them."

Repeat Defeat: Extended school day. Summer school. Remedial classes—Drill 'em, kill 'em. Bore 'em, snore 'em. If at first it didn't succeed, do it the same way again. Can you imagine a general or a football coach who employed this strategy? They wouldn't last very long. This is a form of punishment, not an approach to teaching.

Fact Attack: If you say it fast—fact attack—the words almost rhyme. The myth behind "fact attack" is that somehow, if we present students with mountains of detail, cram it all in and threaten them with a test, it will all be absorbed. In chemistry, when a suspension is supersaturated, particles precipitate out at the same rate they are absorbed. The liquid just can't hold anymore. In classrooms, most kids just give up. The others memorize data for the test and then trash it as quickly as possible.

Control Patrol: Hall patrols. In-house detention. Bathroom passes. Five points off. Threatening calls home. Pile on the work. Give them another quiz. Test, test, test. Post the rules, recite, copy, and memorize them. Sign the rules. Your mother signs the rules. Rules, rules, rules, and more rules. And if you break the rules—WHAM!

This works:

Engaged Learning: Imagine a world, or just a classroom, where people love to learn. A world where learning is exciting, where students are constantly exploring and trying to figure things out. Look at a baby and see how it engages its world, sorting things out, searching for patterns, seeing what goes together, and learning what to avoid. If one word could summarize the way young children learn, it would be curiosity. Instead of destroying it, teachers need to nurture *curiosity* and direct it so that students become engaged learners.

Standards Are Goals: "Because I said so" or "It is on the test," are the last phrases of desperation used by parents and teachers when all else fails and they want their directives followed—IMMEDIATELY. Why can't standards be flexible, targets to achieve, but not at a precise time or in a specified fashion? Maybe classrooms can have enough room so that students can make choices about how they will learn something.

Constructing Metaphors: Everybody does not understand the same thing in the exact same way. One size does not fit all. Teaching means helping students discover or create their own meaning or metaphors. All human understanding is a product of making connections between old ideas and new ones—constructing personal metaphors.

Reading and Writing Are Like Talking: Children learn to talk because they are surrounded by language. They discover that words have an agreed-on meaning and they can interact with others if they use the right ones. Of course we get better with practice, but we learn language by listening and talking. Children learn to read and write the same way, by being immersed in an environment where people use the written word to communicate. In learning environments where they are surrounded by printed material, where adults and older children model how to do it, and where children have a chance to practice, they learn to read and write. In fact, all meaningful learning takes place this way.

Classroom Community: A place where everyone learns and students care about and take responsibility for each other. Rules are designed to help the community function more effectively and achieve its goals, so community members help to establish the rules and remind each other why they are important.

My Motto: You do not have to know this for the test. You need to know this for life.

JOIN THE CONVERSATION—YOUR PEDAGOGICAL CREED

Questions to Consider:

1. Which of these statements do you agree with? Which do you disagree with? Why?
2. Compose your own list of your basic beliefs about education based on your experience in school, your ideas, and your goals.

2

RESPONSIBILITIES: WHAT IS A TEACHER?

During my first 3 years of teaching, my lessons were largely hit or miss. Sometimes it seemed like I had the entire class in the palm of my hand and I could do no wrong. On other days, the students acted like I was not even present. But the worst part was that I could not predict when lessons would work or why. I read a book called *The Last Unicorn* by Peter S. Beagle (1968) and I found it captured the way I felt about my teaching. It is the story of a hapless young magician who is trying to save unicorns from extinction. Sometimes he finds that he has great magical powers, but then, inexplicably, the magic is gone. The magician eventually realizes that humans cannot control magic. It only comes when there is a great need. During those years, I frequently felt that I was that hapless magician. I was always hoping for the magical lesson, but I never knew when it would appear.

As I learned how to teach, I realized that experience brought increased skill, better judgment, and greater knowledge. There was no magic formula, only practice and hard work. I now believe that it takes between 3 and 5 years of classroom teaching experience before you learn how to teach—and that does not include teacher education courses or student teaching. When you finish these programs, you are a certified beginner, but that is all.

As you might suspect, I am not a big fan of rapid preparation programs like *Teach for America* (but of course if they want to use this book they can). Unless the people who run those programs have discovered a magic potion that eluded me, or the students they turn into teachers are just much more talented than I was, the programs will not have a major impact on schools and teaching. In fact, because it only requires a 2-year commitment from participants, most of the people recruited by *Teach for America* are little more than "accidental tourists" who leave the profession just when they are really learning how to be effective teachers (Darling-Hammond, 1994, 2000).

This chapter examines the "job of the teacher" from different perspectives. In a section titled "My Best Teachers," I introduce a friend who helped me figure out how to become a teacher by modeling his own idiosyncratic approach. The "Becoming a Teacher" section focuses on childhood experiences of new teachers that have helped them define the "job of the teacher" for themselves. The chapter concludes with autobiographical sketches by two veteran teachers who explain how they learned to teach and an essay about teachers with a sense of mission who define their job very broadly.

In addition, in response to my much delayed understanding about what it requires to be a teacher, chapters include "Nuts and Bolts of Teaching" activities designed to demystify the mechanics of teaching. Remember, you only get better if you work at it. Think of teaching as lifting weights. If you start by pressing 100 pounds and work at it diligently, you will build muscle mass while increasing the number of your "reps" and the weight you can comfortably lift.

SECTION A: MY BEST TEACHERS 1: DIRECTED EXPERIENCE, SCAFFOLDING, AND CREATIVE MALADJUSTMENT

Some of my best teachers did not consider themselves teachers at all. I did not meet them in schools and I was already an adult when our paths crossed. My experience with these teachers reinforces the idea that teaching and learning go on all the time and in all places—but also, that certain conditions make teaching more effective.

According to John Dewey the key to effective teaching is directing classroom experience so that students are able to achieve educational goals. When learners use their understanding of these experiences to build on what they already know, they are able to construct new meaning or knowledge. Lev Vygotzky called this process scaffolding.

The experiences I am going to describe in this section and in "My Best Teachers 2" took place in a summer sleep-away camp located in the Catskill Mountains of New York State. Camp Hurley was sponsored by the United Community Centers, a community center in Brooklyn, New York. I worked at Camp Hurley during the summer between the ages of 19 and 24. It is here, as a result of my directed experience and scaffolding, that I learned how to be a teacher.

My best teacher at Camp Hurley was a man named Jerry Harris. When we first met in 1969, Jerry was in his early 50s, a World War II veteran who had spent most of his working life as a machinist making tools and parts out of metal. I was a college student, a novice and unskilled community volunteer who joined Jerry and other women and men on work weekends as we prepared the camp for the summer.

Jerry was kind of gruff and irascible. While he was not interested in being buddy-buddy with the younger volunteers, he definitely enjoyed working with us. What Jerry did best was demystify tools and help us become problem solvers by creating directed experiences and building on our prior knowledge.

Lesson #1. Keep your cool. Analyze the problem. Find a solution. The younger volunteers, especially college students caught up in the political activism of the "60s," had a tendency to glorify work and place skilled workers like Jerry on a pedestal. We considered their skills as nearly magical, rather than things that could be learned. Jerry let us watch him as he worked as long as we did not disturb him. If we were especially attentive, he let us try our hand at the task and work with him. He also supervised us in our initial efforts to use a tool before he sent us off to work on a cabin somewhere out in the woods. Once, one of the drivers lost the keys to our school bus. Most of us were on the verge of panicking. Jerry, with my minimal assistance but avid attention, proceeded to rewire it, bypassing the ignition switch so we could drive it home.

Lesson #2. If you work hard, you can learn to do the job. Jerry taught us that tools were for performing tasks, not totems to be worshipped; they were to be respected but not feared, and they could be used safely and skillfully if we cared to learn. Under his tutelage, I learned to use a chain saw to cut up a fallen tree, to use hydraulic jacks to lift a cabin so we could replace rotten foundation supports, and to locate a plumbing problem, dismantle the system, and reconnect and solder joints.

Lesson #3. Don't be afraid to bend the tools or the rules. Jerry believed that technical solutions had to be within the limitations of tools, the environment, our skills, and money available for materials. He valued what he could do, and he understood what he could not.

He continually reminded us that we were repairing cabins and plumbing, not creating art. Once the director of the camp discovered a bent screw driver, and he wanted to know who had broken it. A bunch of us started to laugh, and we told him to look at the screw driver again. It had been bent at a right angle and fashioned into a new tool, used to work in narrow places. The only member of the crew capable of such precision work and resourceful enough to do it was Jerry.

Lesson #4. Explanations cannot substitute for hands-on experience. Jerry stressed that we were not learning skills for the sake of mastering a skill, but to help us solve problems in the real world of work. Camp Hurley stretched for more than 120 very hilly acres. Jerry could not be everywhere and he could not give us detailed instructions to fit every situation in advance. Generally, he stayed at our centrally located toolshed where we could come and discuss a project with him and get needed tools, materials, and advice. But we had to come to him with a plan, a strategy for solving our problem. We had to know what our tools could do, we had to understand the materials, and we had to figure out what was broken and how to fix it. Although he would discuss it with us, he insisted that he had already taught us how to work through repeated modeling, so we should be able to solve the problem. Hard work, skill, and understanding, not magic, were required.

Lesson #5. Don't be afraid to do something you believe is right. In later years, I was continually reminded of Jerry when I read books about teaching. For example, in one passage in his book *The Pedagogy of Hope* (1995), Paulo Freire, a Brazilian educator, described the detailed, but frequently unappreciated, knowledge of skilled Chilean agricultural workers. Freire reported on a conversation where the workers insisted on deferring to his expertise because they felt that they had nothing to offer a man of his learning. Freire challenged them to a contest where he and they would take turns asking each other questions aimed at stumping their opponent. After a few rounds it became clear to all of the participants that the knowledge of the agricultural workers was different from, but not inferior to, the knowledge of the college professor. Jerry had similar knowledge to these workers, knowledge based on careful consideration of years of experience. It was knowledge vital for understanding the world and solving problems.

One reason that Jerry and I tended to get along was that we were both usually impatient with authority. In fact, I think Jerry independently discovered the concept "creative maladjustment" that Herbert Kohl describes in his book, *I Won't Learn From You and Other Thoughts on Creative Maladjustment* (1994). Kohl argues that effective teachers, especially teachers working with inner-city disenfranchised youth, have to learn how to break arbitrary or oppressive rules and get away with it. They need to find ways to manipulate "the system" in order to protect their students from injustice, create safe places for learning, and design lessons that connect with student lives and motivate them to learn.

My best example of Jerry's "creative maladjustment" to what he perceived of as irrational rules happened when we needed a six foot length of 1 in. by 2 in. (1 × 2) pine board to fix a window screen. I rummaged around the woodshed but could only find a large enough piece of 1 × 2 oak, intended for flooring, which was considerably more expensive per foot than pine board. Jerry told me to use the oak to repair the window, but I hesitated, concerned that the camp's director would not be happy when he discovered what I had done. Jerry looked at me as if I were from another planet. He said our time was worth more than a piece of wood and that it would cost more to go to town to buy pine than either the pine or oak was worth. He proceeded to cover the oak board with a coat of white paint. Then he handed me the camouflaged board, still dripping with paint, and sent me to go fix the window screen. Covered with paint, it made no difference whether it was a pine or oak board and no one could tell.

The lessons I learned from Jerry about work and his approach to solving problems have helped me in every project I have undertaken as a student, worker, and teacher.

1. Learning skills make sense when you are doing real projects. You learn best when you have a reason to learn.
2. Whether it is a hammer, an idea, or an approach to teaching, you have to know how to use your tools.
3. Experience, particularly directed experience, is the best teacher.
4. Reflect on and value your experiences, they are the basis for knowing.
5. Do not depend on memorized formulas.
6. Step back from a problem. Think about what you are doing. Figure out how to solve it.
7. Do not be afraid to do what you know is right.
8. Remember, the solution is there, if you learn how to see it.

Because of what I learned from Jerry and my other "best teachers," this is a "why to" rather than a "how to" book. I believe that teachers, and most people, will figure out much of the "how" as they think about and try to apply the "why."

JOIN THE CONVERSATION—CREATIVE MALADJUSTMENT

Mahmoud Elder, a New York City high school teacher, was a student in both the undergradute and graduate social studies education programs at Hofstra University, so he clearly found something of value in the experience. However, Mahmoud was disturbed by this essay because he felt it encourages teachers to break rules and challenge authority. He is concerned that if teachers break rules, students will feel justified in breaking them also and the result will be chaotic.

Questions to Consider:

1. What is your attitude toward obeying and breaking the rules? Explain.
2. How do you view Jerry's approach to teaching? Why?

SECTION B: NUTS AND BOLTS OF TEACHING 1

To help us examine the mechanics of teaching, I want to introduce you to a guide developed by the U.S. Army Air Corps during World War II. At the start of the war, the United States not only had a severe shortage of mechanics, but it had an even greater shortage of people who could teach other people how to be mechanics. The Air Corps Technical Schools developed a guide for vocational teaching (*Air Corps Technical Schools, Vocational Teaching (Temporary)*, M-26, Department of Mechanics, April 9, 1942) that is clear, easy to follow, hands-on, student centered, and, I think, still useful today. I want to thank Eric Simons, a former student, who discovered it among his family's artifacts. Many of the "Nuts and Bolts of Teaching" activity sections will discuss ideas from the Air Corps manual.

Although many of its ideas remain fresh, there is language in the document that is antiquated, especially when it refers to gender. The manual clearly would be different if it were designed for use by the contemporary United States military. In the passage that follows, while the manual originally said that "he must know," I substitute "teachers must know."

FIG. 2.1 Selections from the Air Corps teachers' manual. (Adapted from *Air Corps Technical Schools Teachers' Manual*, April 9, 1942)

DEFINING TEACHING

"Essentially, teaching is the process of assisting other people to learn the things you already know. A simple definition of teaching follows: Teaching is helping learners to acquire new knowledge or skills. Teaching consists, mainly, of *telling, showing, guiding the learner in performance tasks* and then *measuring the results*. Whenever you have shown someone how to do something; such as kicking a football, or pitching a curve, or fixing a flat, you have been teaching. The success of the Air Corps in fulfilling its mission, like your success, depends upon the success of the graduates from your classes."

RESPONSIBILITIES OF THE TEACHER

1. Teachers must know thoroughly the subject they are to teach. Teachers must be able to separate the nonessential content from the whole subject.

2. Teachers must look at the course from the learner's point of view. They must put themselves in the other fellow's place and ask whether the instruction is getting across. A teacher must show students the "how" and the "why" of each operation, tell them what to look for, or what to do at each step. This means analyzing step by step what the teacher does so easily and then explaining each step to the students. Teachers must also see that students continue in the correct way until they have mastered the operation.

3. Teachers must know what results to expect as standard performance of the job.

4. Teachers should develop to the utmost their skill as instructors. Teachers must present work clearly, set high standards and have students meet them, at the same time maintaining a cheerful, sympathetic attitude toward the class and arousing in them an interest in the job and real enthusiasm for it. "Without enthusiasm," said Emerson, "nothing great was ever accomplished." An interested, enthusiastic instructor who knows the subject will generally have students who are interested and engaged in purposeful activity.

PROFESSIONAL TRAITS OF THE TEACHER

1. Mastery of your subject is necessary. You can teach others only what you know yourself. You must do more than know your subject, however. You must so vitalize it by tying it up with the experiences, the needs, and the problems of your students that its importance will be clear to them. The successful instructor's knowledge of the subject must be far broader than any text being used. A teacher reads widely and continues studying to keep abreast of the latest developments in the subject and allied fields. In a word, a teacher is both thorough and up-to-date in his or her knowledge of the subject. A teacher maintains a professional attitude toward the work.

2. Executive ability is required to manage the affairs of the class in a businesslike fashion. This involves detailed planning of the course, the securing and distribution of supplies and equipment, the keeping of records, the reduction of waste, the adjustments of the program to the needs of students, the making of reports, and the examination and rating of students.

3. Most important of all is skill in teaching. The instructor must develop the knack of "getting a lesson across to a class," to give students new knowledge, understanding, and skills, new insight into what was unclear before, new power to use such knowledge and abilities as they already have to do the old jobs better or the new jobs well. This is a task calling for the utmost in personal industry and resourcefulness, but it is a task that brings profound satisfaction. A knowledge of the principles and facts underlying the science of teaching is not enough. One must have, also, the ability or the art to apply this knowledge in teaching a subject to a class.

JOIN THE CONVERSATION—DEFINING GOOD TEACHING

Questions to Consider:

1. How do you define teaching? Explain your definition.
2. The Air Corps manual lists four responsibilities for teachers: content knowledge, ability to place yourself in the position of the learner, an understanding of standards or expected performance outcomes, and skill as an instructor. Do you agree with this list? How might you alter the list or the explanations? Explain.
3. How would you rate these responsibilities in order of importance? Why?
4. According to the manual, teachers have three key "professional traits": subject mastery, executive ability, and skill in teaching. Do you agree with this list? How might you alter the list or the explanations? Explain.
5. How would you rate these traits in order of importance? Why?
6. Select a teacher (from the past or present) whom you really respect. What makes him or her a good teacher? What "professional traits" does he or she exhibit? How?

Some of the preservice teachers and teachers who helped with this book had vocational training in high school, in the military, or in industry. Many felt that vocational training, when done well, prepared them for later learning and for becoming teachers. After reading the Air Corps manual, two of them asked to share their experiences with new teachers.

I Was Not a Great Student
By Christian Caponi

I was not a great student in high school or later in my college career. Teachers mostly lectured and it was difficult for me to learn that way. In my mid-20s, I went to work for the telephone company as a technician after I earned my bachelor's degree. The initial 3-week training was run pretty much the same way as high school: lecture and read. We read books and watched videos about how dial tones worked. We received very little "hands-on" training and when we did, we used state-of-the-art equipment under "ideal" conditions.

During my training I was led to believe that working for the telephone company would be easy and enjoyable. I would get to work outdoors with my hands and sometimes even be able to flex my brain muscles. When I was sent into the field to work on actual telephones, I was in complete "shell shock." The new equipment we had practiced on in training did not exist in the field and conditions were never as "neat" as they had taught us. It quickly became apparent that my training was inappropriate and did not prepare me for the real job.

The company's management and the union that represents employees decided on a joint venture to retrain all of the technicians. They called our new training "cable college." It was 5 days of intensive "hands-on" training led by 25-year veterans. In cable college we used realistic equipment that prepared us to face scenarios that might actually occur on the job. In those 5 days I learned far more than I had from "hands-on" training in the original 3 weeks of videos and manuals.

When I started my teacher education program, I fell back into my old pattern of being a passive student waiting for instructors to lecture on what to do. This approach to learning did not work for me again. When I went out to student teach I did not really know what I was doing and had almost disastrous results. Fortunately, my field supervisor and cooperating teachers were veteran teachers who worked with me as I realized how to teach. Student teaching became my "cable college" and I finally realized what teaching and learning are all about. I learn best when I do something, not when I am told about it, as do most of the students in my classes. The funny thing is that I coach lacrosse, and coaching is hands-on teaching. It took me a while to understand that coaching and learning how to install phone lines by actually doing it is really what good teaching is all about.

* * *

"By the Book" Versus "the Real World"
By Steve Bologna

During my junior year of high school, I was placed in a vocational training program for aircraft mechanics. They taught us to do everything "by the book." We were supposed to follow directions and work step by step according to the manual. The best part of the program was that it taught me how to handle tools and how to work with others. I had a big surprise when I began working as an aircraft mechanic. The old-timers quickly initiated us into the real world. They put the manual aside and took shortcuts as they worked. In the beginning, I questioned their methods, but as time passed I realized they understood the job. Being a mechanic was about solving problems, not simply following instructions. This is the most significant thing I learned from my vocational training and I think it will help me wherever I go, whatever I do. People learn best by doing and the most important learning is figuring out how to solve problems.

* * *

JOIN THE CONVERSATION—THE VALUE OF VOCATIONAL TRAINING

Question to Consider:

Do you believe vocational training can be a model for effective academic instruction? Explain.

SECTION C: BECOMING A TEACHER 2: NEW TEACHERS DISCUSS THEIR PERSONAL EXPERIENCES AS STUDENTS

Did you like middle school and high school? Why or why not? What did you like? What did you dislike? Do you think everyone in your classes felt the same way you did? Were some individuals or groups favored? Stereotyped? Victimized? Alienated? Who was responsible? Could anything have been done to change their experiences?

Not everyone has the same experience in school, even when they attend the same one. I have a colleague who went to the same high school as I did, though a couple of years earlier. She remembers our high school as a place where there was excitement about learning and where teachers were connected to their students. I remember it as a place of alienation and oppression, where my relationship was with a small group of friends who felt little connection with the school or the teachers. The same school, similar people, different experiences, and very different memories. Can we both be right?

If you have ever seen the Japanese movie *Rashomon* (1951) or the American movie *When Harry Met Sally* (1989), read the novel *Chronicle of a Death Foretold* (1993) by Gabriel Garcia Marquez, or heard different "eyewitnesses" describe an accident, you understand how people can experience and describe the same high school in such different ways. Part of the reason for different memories is that people filter what they see through all of the other things that are going on their lives; part of the reason is because our experiences and our perspectives are just not the same. Memories are so complex because our lives are different and complicated.

Many people decide they want to become teachers because they liked school, a teacher, or a particular subject and really would like to return. Often they are unaware that not everyone shared their experiences and that, at least at the beginning of their careers, they will probably be teaching students who are not doing well and do not want to be there. When I interview prospective applicants to the secondary education program at Hofstra I often ask them, "What subject in high school did you like the least? How could you have reached 'you' in that class?" That is because most of their students will feel about the applicant's favorite subject the way they felt in the class where they did not understand what was going on, and they were sure that the teacher did not care if they learned or even attended.

As you read these stories about teachers in the New Teachers Network, consider your own background—your own story. Ask yourself: How can your experience help you become a successful teacher?

JOIN THE CONVERSATION—LISTENING TO THE DIVERSE VOICES OF URBAN AND SUBURBAN MINORITY SCHOOL DISTRICT EDUCATORS

Maureen Murphy, Judith Singer, and I wrote a research study (*Educators for Urban Minorities, 1*(1) Fall, 1999, pp. 9–17) based on discussions with teachers working in urban and suburban minority schools. We found that among successful teachers, a consistent theme was their ability to draw on personal experiences that made it possible for them to empathize with people whose lives were often very different from their own. Sometimes their memories were very personal. They acknowledged having them, but were not comfortable discussing them with others. Significantly, they all had important personal memories.

Question to Consider:

Explain what has happened in your life that enhances your ability to empathize with others.

A Student Who Did Just Enough to Get By
By Stacey Cotten

Stacey Cotten is an African American young woman who earned her teaching certification as an undergraduate and later returned to Hofstra University for her master's degree. She was born and raised in a working-class, largely minority, suburb of New York City. When she was interviewed for this chapter at the end of her first year as a teacher, Stacey said she believed her decision to become a teacher was a good decision, but she still had reservations.—Alan Singer

My mother is a housekeeper who works at a local hotel. I do not know my father. In the schools I attended as a child, the students were mostly Black like me. Some of the kids were Caribbean. Some were Latino.

In high school, I was the kind of student who did just enough to get by. It may seem funny, but that helps me now as a teacher. Most of the kids I work with are just like I was. They do just enough to get by, getting 75 or 80. They know how to work the system. They do not do every homework assignment but maybe every other assignment. They talk with their friends in class, but they do not talk too much, so they stay out of trouble. Every now and then they raise their hand—just enough to keep the teacher off of their case.

I usually can pick out when one of my students is going through the motions. I go over and talk to him or her and say, "You need to do more. A 75 is a good grade, but it is unacceptable because you know you can do more." I try to encourage them to pump out a 110% effort.

The Black kids in my classes like to see a Black teacher, especially someone like me who is young. They cling to me. A lot of the Black kids hang out in my room when they have lunch or a free period. I make sure that my room is open to everybody and other kids come too, though not as regularly.

I like teaching, but I just wish I knew the content the way the experienced teachers do. Things just roll off the top of their heads. Nothing rolls off the top of my head. I have to sit and organize myself and put it together. And then I have to teach it. Sometimes I feel like there is so much that I do not know. Even when I know something, I cannot always figure out, why it is important to teach about it. I worry: If I do not understand, how will my students? It gets so weird that sometimes I feel I should not be teaching. There are battles going on inside me, and I go back and forth. But then one of my students comes up to me and I figure out what is bothering him or her when nobody else can, and I know these kids need me to be their teacher.

For me, the key to successful teaching is making a personal connection with every student. If my classes are too large, I cannot make it around the room to help everybody during the period. Instead of talking to my students, I become intimidated by the size and I just lose control. I end up trying to keep them quiet by giving them a lot of work, but they do not really understand it or learn it. They need a more intimate setting so we can make connections. That is the kind of teacher I needed as a teenager and the kind of teacher I want to be with my students.

* * *

I Was Once in Their Shoes
By Susan Soitiriades

Susan Soitiriades is a Greek American whose family speaks Greek at home. She grew up and attended public school in an ethnically diverse section of New York City. As a teacher, Susan continually thinks about her own experiences as an adolescent and a student. She earned her teacher certification as an undergraduate.—Alan Singer

Since kindergarten, there was one factor in my neighborhood that could never be overlooked: We were all very different from one another. We did not look the same, we did not speak the same, and we did not dress alike. Growing up in the city is a difficult task for adolescents who are trying to figure out who they are and where they belong. Ethnic gangs were formed and in order to be accepted you had to belong to one. In high school, I dated a Puerto Rican boy and chose to be part of his Hispanic circle. I hid my Greek heritage and took on a new identity. Reflecting on my personal experience later convinced me that I wanted to become a teacher and help kids such as myself.

As a high school student, I was an activist torn between two worlds. I was a favorite of teachers and met with the school's principal, but I also had friends who dealt drugs, carried weapons to school, or had babies. I know how easy it is for teachers to ignore the world of their students and pretend that there are no problems. My experience as a teenager strad-dling both worlds helps me see things that other teachers do not see. I am always suspicious when students walk into school with designer clothing that I know they cannot afford. I get concerned when a bright student misses school because her mother cannot take care of her baby.

Every day I battle to figure out how I will help my students succeed. I ask myself, "What must I do to get through to them and make them understand that education is so very im-portant in today's world?" I have my students write personal essays about themselves and their backgrounds. From these essays, I have learned many wonderful things and some not so wonderful things about my students. I write back to them sharing my life story. At first, they were all curious to know my age because I was very young to be a high school teacher. I told them I was 21 and I finished college in 3 years, because I was determined to make a change in this world.

I always remember that I was once in their shoes. I contemplated dropping out of high school many times, but luckily I had teachers who went beyond their call of duty. I hope to do the same for all students. We must listen to what they are saying, not how they are saying it, if we want to help them succeed personally and academically.

* * *

I Hated Teachers Who Were Controlling
By Jennifer Bambino

Jennifer Bambino is a White, Italian American, young woman who earned her teaching certifica-tion as an undergraduate. She grew up and attended public school in an overwhelmingly White, middle-income, suburban community. In high school, Jennifer hung out with a rough working-class crowd. She hated teachers because they were controlling. She believes that if she had a teacher like herself when she was in high school, it would have saved her from some of the pain she went through as a teenager. Jennifer student taught in the predominately African American suburban school district where she is now a middle school social studies teacher. To her surprise, she dis-covered that the adolescent turmoil and alienation from school that some of her students experi-enced was amazingly like her own when she was their age.—Alan Singer

I chose to teach minority students because I can relate to where some of them are. I still re-member an eighth-grade girl I spoke with briefly while waiting in a principal's office to be in-terviewed for my first job. The girl was crying. She was accused of threatening another girl and was suspected of carrying a razor blade in her mouth. The young girl had problems at home. Her parents were both dead and she was living with her grandmother. She sounded as if she had no one at home she could talk to and just needed some attention. She reminded me of how I felt sometimes when I was 13. My friends and family think I took that job because I wanted to save kids. Honestly, on my first day, I thought I would save all 180 of them. On my second day, I hoped I would be able to get through to at least 1.

The most important job of a teacher is to understand and relate to the kids. You have to be able to reach them first so they can really learn what you expect them to. You cannot or-der them to learn, but you can motivate them to seek success. Kids want to be in my room. Students who rebel against other teachers behave with me. Some of my students need nur-turing and I provide an environment to help them feel they matter. I set high expectations for my students, and may seem demanding at times, but I am also very caring. One of the most rewarding benefits of my job are the wonderful things that they share with me through their work and through class discussions.

Sometimes my educational philosophy brings me into conflict with other teachers. A teacher barged into my classroom with a student from my homeroom class. She was trying to embarrass him by yelling at him in front of my class. She had thrown him off a field trip and asked the kids in my class if anyone wanted to buy his ticket for the trip. When she left, I took him outside and asked what happened. He told me that he fooled around in her class because he could not understand the work. She did not explain it very well to the class. They just copied notes off of the board while she yelled and screamed. Field trips are fundamental to learning, especially for the students that I had in my classes. I believed his story and decided to fight to get him back on the trip. I was sick of this teacher verbally abusing kids.

When I evaluate my work as a teacher, I always ask myself, "Am I bored?" If I am, chances are that my students are bored as well. To keep my middle school classes interesting, my students are assigned many individual and group projects, and I am always amazed by what they create. I am also using portfolio assessment with some of my classes to keep the kids motivated. It is important for students to reflect on their progress throughout the year.

* * *

I Was Called "Spic"
By Lynda Costello-Herrera

Lynda Costello-Herrera grew up in an affluent, White suburb. She was raised and identifies as an Italian American, although her biological father was Puerto Rican. After student teaching as part of a masters degree program, she was hired by a suburban junior high school that is more than 90% African American and Caribbean. She is glad she was given the opportunity to teach in the school where she teaches and is quick to challenge people who she feels are demeaning her students because of their racial and ethnic backgrounds.—Alan Singer

I made the decision to work with minority students because I felt that minority students were at a disadvantage. Many Americans are racist on some level and view people from minority groups as inferior. I want to help minority students realize that they can accomplish anything that they set their minds to achieve.

My experience as a child definitely shapes my goals as a teacher. I grew up having students calling me "spic." The worst part about these incidents was that teachers overheard what was said but never reprimanded the students or pointed out why it was wrong. I want to protect students so they never feel the way that I did growing up.

I believe that the most important element in my teaching is not ideology or method but being who I am. I am successful as a teacher because I respect my students, and, in turn they respect me. My behavior toward them is key. They are just children. That is how I look at them, not as people who are members of this or that category.

That does not mean I ignore the racial and ethnic backgrounds of my students. I do not put any students down, but I do try to bring them back into reality. They sometimes forget how society might perceive them. I help them understand they must rise above and challenge these stereotypes.

When I say I teach in this district, people always ask, "How is it teaching there?" This reaction is extremely disturbing to me because it means that the person is insulting my students. I always respond by asking them, "Is that a racist statement?" This sends the person into a stammering panic and they try to explain themselves with excuses like, "It is just, you know, so poor there, is all I meant." I tell them that it is not a poor area and that I teach children from all economic backgrounds. I have students whose parents are doctors, lawyers, and nurses. I have students from single-parent families, extended families, and welfare families. This usually quiets them.

I believe that I can make a difference where I am and I think that is the main goal of teaching. My students are children in a world that they did not create. I am here to teach what it means to be a person, a human being, in a world where there is racism, sexism, and violence.

* * *

I Was the New Kid and I Was Scared
By Stephanie Hunte

Stephanie Hunte is a young African American woman of Caribbean ancestry. Both of her parents are immigrants from Barbados. Stephanie was born in New York City and grew up and started school in a largely West Indian community. She earned her teacher certification as a graduate student.—Alan Singer

Families are complicated. I do not know what my father does. I have not seen him in many years. I have an older sister. I also had an older brother, but he died from Sudden Infant Death Syndrome. I did not even know about him until I was in high school. One day my mother said, "Oh, did you know your brother is buried in this cemetery?" I think I responded, "Really, what brother?"

When my mother first came to this country, she was a maid; then she was a secretary at the hospital where I was born. Today, she is a college graduate with a masters degree and is a registered nurse. School was always very important in my house. I remember when my mother was becoming a nurse, she dissected a cat in the house. All of her nursing buddies were sitting down with this black cat. I was only about 8 years old, but I remember this so clearly. My mother is still going to school; now she is learning about computers.

I attended elementary school in New York City before my family moved to the suburbs. I still remember my first day of kindergarten. I was crying. I started school a month later than the other children because I had to wait for my fifth birthday. By that time everybody else knew each other. I was the new kid and I was scared. When I was in second grade, I had the lowest reading scores in my class and the teacher considered putting me into a slower class or even holding me back a grade. That year is still fresh in my memory. The boy who sat in front of me had been hit in the back of the head, and he had horrible scars there. I was scared to sit behind him, so I did not want to go to school. I am not sure if there is a connection between my fear and my performance, but I did not do well in second grade.

As a student, I had a major breakthrough in fifth grade. Suddenly, I started to read. By the time I was in sixth grade, I had the highest reading scores in my school. Once I learned how to read, I loved it, and I read a lot. Now I realize that when I understand how to do something it becomes fun for me, not just a task. My mother and the teachers who cared about me deserve credit for the way I was finally able to perform in school.

I decided to become a teacher because I never wanted to leave school. I want to help children who are frightened of school learn to love it. I tell my students that every effort is a good effort. But they have to do more and more so they will get better. My mother taught me that as I get better, things will be less frightening.

I remember a lot about school and growing up and how I felt about things. This will help me be a good teacher. Some of my students feel that everyone else knows how to do something except them. They get easily embarrassed. One boy in my class did not want to say that his favorite music was Spanish music. He thought he had to like rap or the other students would make fun of him. I want to teach my students that they can be different from everybody else. They can be who they are.

* * *

I Could Not Speak English
By Jayne O'Neill

To look at her today, Jayne O'Neill is a typical young, harried, White, suburban mother, working hard to both raise her family and continue her teaching career. What keeps her going is her memories of being a poor child of immigrant parents who was shunted aside in school because she could not speak English.—Alan Singer

My parents came to this country from Czechoslovakia (now the Czech Republic) in 1969 without money and unable to speak English. My mother was already pregnant with me when they arrived. My childhood in our new country was very difficult. My parents separated, and my mother was forced to go on public assistance. There were days when she did not eat in order to put food on my plate. Because I could not speak English, I was a lonely child and school was very hard. I went to a Catholic school, but no one there spoke Czech, and there was no ESL program.

In response to my loneliness and my uncertainty with English, I became very introverted and stressful situations threw me into a tailspin. Whenever I had to take an exam I would feel sick to my stomach. I was never invited to birthday parties because none of the other children in my class could communicate with me. Once my mother came on a class trip with me. It was awkward, but at least I had someone to talk with.

Memory is a funny thing. Looking back, it is as if I woke up one day and decided to change my entire life. I imagine I was 13 years old at the time I underwent this metamorphosis. I became more outgoing, less crippled by my family situation, and able to make friends. I still was not a good student and even after college I was not sure what I wanted to do with my life. My mother had remarried and had two more children, much younger than myself. I found I enjoyed being around them and decided to try teaching.

At my first teaching job, the principal was very demanding and I had a very difficult time. He gave me a poor initial evaluation and I started to feel I had made the wrong decision by becoming a teacher. Worse, I found myself slipping backward personally, once again becoming that lonely introverted girl unable to speak English and unable to stand up for herself. I could not accept this. Finally, I marshaled all of my inner strength and went to speak to him. Basically I said, "What do I have to do to become a good teacher?" From that day on his attitude toward me changed. But more important, my attitude toward myself changed and I began to improve.

My experiences growing up with immigrant parents, living in poverty, and unable to speak English made me strong and are the keys to my teaching. Currently, I work in a vocational program where most of my students are from families that recently immigrated from Spanish-speaking countries. Sometimes I wonder what my students see when they look at me. I know that when I look at them I remember that I was once in their position. I know how hard the road is. With my help, I know they can succeed.

JOIN THE CONVERSATION—REMEMBERING OUR OWN EXPERIENCES

Stacey Cotten "was the kind of student who did just enough to get by." Susan Soitiriades was "once in their shoes." Jennifer Bambino "hated teachers because they were controlling." Lynda Costello-Herrera remembers being called "spic." Stephanie Hunte remembers when "I was the new kid and I was scared." Other new teachers have spoken about being placed in special education classes because of learning disabilities, having eating disorders as adolescents, or being tracked into slow classes because they were second-language learners.

Questions to Consider:

1. Which of the school experiences described in this section are most like yours? Whose experience was most different? Explain.
2. Make two lists: (a) What I liked about secondary school. (b) What I did not like about secondary school. How would your current list differ from a list you would have made as a teenager? Why?
3. Write a biographical essay, "How My Experiences as a Student Will Shape My Work as a Teacher."

SECTION D: TEACHING STORIES 1

Teaching Stories (1997) is the title of a book by a San Francisco, California, middle school teacher named Judy Logan. It is one of my favorite books about teaching, and I highly recommend it. Judy is committed to a student-centered, project-based approach to teaching social studies and literature, and she is not afraid to develop personal relationships with her students or to "rock the boat." Her students create history quilts and write poetry to celebrate the past, to draw connections between historical events and the experience of their own families, and to demonstrate their understanding of content material. They create class rituals that define membership in their tribe. They go on camping trips to build their sense of community.

Judy tries to maximize student participation in governing the classroom and the projects. She writes, "If I control the content, I try to let them control the form. If I control the form, I try to let students control the content" of projects (p. 17). She wants all of her students to be able to see themselves "mirrored in the content of the curriculum" (p. 18).

Some of my teacher education students have found her more unorthodox projects a little unnerving. Judy developed an activity she calls "Stealing Stories" where her students read and discuss stories about taking something that does not belong to you. Judy believes that sharing these and their own stories gives students a chance to "cultivate wisdom" about themselves and others and is far more effective for developing values than humiliating or punishing them for breaking rules.

My favorite story from her book is about a rite-of-passage project Judy calls "Angela's Ritual." A seventh-grade girl named Angela asked Judy to organize a menstruation ceremony to commemorate her first period. The ritual was held at Angela's home and included her parents, friends, and teachers. When we discuss this story, most of the students in my preservice class shout "Never!" They will never do anything like this; it is too risky, it is not "school-related," and it would jeopardize their careers.

I try to focus class discussion on the significance of the project rather than the professional risk. I usually ask the women in the class if they would be willing to share with the group either their own experiences as they entered puberty or the experience of a close female friend or relative. Once we start going around the room, the stories become more and more painful as the women report on their own ignorance and fear as their bodies began to change and the humiliations they suffered at the hands of the boys in their classes. Sometimes the atmosphere in class becomes so intense that the men begin to spontaneously apologize declaring, "We didn't know. We didn't understand." The point, however, is that there was no way they could know because the subject of sexual maturation was taboo in their classes. By taking menstruation out of the closet and making it a subject for discussion and celebration, Judy Logan made it possible for the young women and men in her classes to reconsider their behavior and build a classroom based on respect and gender equity.

I confess that I was rarely as brave as Judy Logan, yet I still consider some of my personal teaching stories as moments of triumph. Others, however, are so embarrassing I never discuss them. But they have all shaped me as a teacher and an individual. As you begin to teach, you will assemble your own collection of teaching stories. In the meantime, some veteran teachers have agreed to share theirs with you. As you read Maureen Murphy's story about how her childhood and educational experiences led her to become an English teacher and Rhonda Eisenberg's discussion of being a mathematics teacher and department chair in an inner-city high school, ask yourselves, "What is a teacher?"

JOIN THE CONVERSATION—JUDY LOGAN'S TEACHING STORIES

Questions to Consider:

1. What do you think of Judy Logan's approach to teaching? Why?
2. Do you having any teaching stories of your own yet? If yes, why are they important to you?

I Come From a Family of Teachers
By Maureen Murphy

Maureen Murphy is one of the assisting editors of this book and a good friend. She is the English education coordinator in the Hofstra University School of Education and Allied Human Services. She taught secondary school briefly as a young woman before going to graduate school and becoming a university professor. Her area of expertise is Irish literature and history and she edited a 1,000-page interdisciplinary curriculum guide on the Great Irish Famine for the New York State Department of Education.—Alan Singer

I come from a family of teachers. My grandmother taught in a one-room school house and my mother was an elementary school teacher and principal in the town of Valley Stream, New York. It is not surprising that my mother was actively involved in my education and that of my brothers. When we were little, we sat at the kitchen table and did our homework while our mother sat at a small picnic table nearby and did her school work. When she ironed clothes, she would read to us at the same time. My mom was a strong proponent of John Dewey's educational philosophy and always encouraged us when we worked on special projects.

Because of my mother's jobs, the boundaries between school and home virtually disappeared. She would bring kids home from school who needed extra attention. My father used to say that when he died, he would have to be buried in the backyard, because my mother would not be able to take a whole day off from school to go to the cemetery. In our house, gender roles were not clearly differentiated. My mother and father always worked together. My father cooked and cleaned when he had to and helped put us to sleep.

I attended East Rockaway high school, a very small school, where my education was both "good" and "bad." The school had a marvelous science department but terrible math teachers, so I did well in science but poorly in math. When my brother was in 12th grade, a math teacher wrote a note home saying that she did not want him to continue in the class. My father went to the school to ask what the problem was. The teacher said he was asking too many questions and taking up too much of her time. My father told her that he thought she was wrong, but that he would tell his son to drop the class because "if you feel a student who asks questions is a nuisance, I would rather he not be in your class."

For me, perhaps the most important aspect of high school was the sense of community we had there. There was always a lot going on and girls were encouraged to participate in all sorts of activities, including intramural sports. What I liked best was that I could participate in athletics without having to be good at it. As a result of those early school years, to this day I still enjoy participating in sporting events.

At East Rockaway High School, I discovered how valuable extracurricular activities can be for students. Through our participation, my friends and I learned leadership skills, improved our ability to communicate with others, and began to take responsibility. Even though I did not really apply myself academically in high school, I graduated 10th out of a class of 80 and earned a partial college scholarship. In college, once again, I was more involved in student activities than in classes. I attended Cortland State Teacher's College where I prepared to teach English and physical education. While I enjoyed studying science, history, and English, I found that I really loved Irish studies, especially Irish literature. In fact, I considered myself Irish until I visited Ireland, where I discovered I was an American.

Because of my scholarship, my parents agreed to let me study in Europe after my junior year. That trip was a major awakening for me. I traveled with students who were fluent in French and I met other students who were much better prepared academically than I was. Because of these experiences, when I returned home I got serious about my studies.

I still remember a Kappa Delta Pi picnic I attended while in college where I met a distinguished Irish historian. He encouraged me to pursue my interest in Irish studies and recommended that I apply for graduate school in the folklore department at Indiana University. I was lucky and received a resident assistantship there that made it possible for me to earn my Ph.D.

Before I went to graduate school, I decided to teach for a year in a combined middle school–high school in upstate New York and I often wonder what would have happened if I had stayed there. I was back there recently to see a friend who was ill. One evening, a guy tried to sell us some chances to support the school wrestling team. He had been one of my 10th-grade students decades ago. At the time, he was in a class of students who were considered dumb by everybody.

With these students, I was forced to become creative and learn how to engage their interests. We read biographies of sports figures and examined Shakespeare's *Hamlet* as the tale of a troubled family. Tolstoy says unhappy families are all alike. What a great topic for discussion! Here is a guy whose widowed mother quickly remarries a guy whom he hates, a guy he suspects killed his father. What should Hamlet do? Should he kill the king? The students easily related to these issues because they were real for them.

These students, of course, taught me far more about teaching and about life than I ever taught them. Many of the boys in my classes worked part-time in garages or just worked on their own cars, so we looked at car magazines and manuals. This helped them realize that they had to improve their readings skills to be more effective at their chosen work. They helped me understand what it means to connect to students.

While teaching in this school, I found a used bookstore where they sold action and adventure books for 10 cents a piece. They were horrific tales of people getting eaten by ants, and the students loved them. My students got interested in reading from these books. I also bought simplified versions of the books they were supposed to read in class. In class, we discussed books, movies, television, art, why people or things were good or bad, anything that stimulated their curiosity and got them to read. I like to use the sports cliché, "Practice makes perfect." That is how it works with reading. As teachers, we have to find material that interests and challenges students so they want to be readers. That way, as they practice, they improve.

In my English education classes for preservice teachers, I stress the importance of valuing student experiences and connecting with their lives and interests. Both teachers and students have to be comfortable with the texts they are examining. The material has to be accessible to students to be useful. This does not mean that it has to be watered down to the point that it is too easy, but it does mean directing student attention to key passages and providing help with vocabulary words. Perhaps the most difficult job of the teacher is balancing the need to connect to where students are academically while challenging students to move to a higher level.

In secondary schools, even though students should already be reading, there are areas that they have to improve. For example, students need to be active, speculating, questioning readers and learn to examine material carefully, so they can find deeply imbedded meaning. Before my student teachers have their students read a novel, I have them hold the book up so the class can look at the cover together and discuss what they expect to discover.

When I teach a novel, I have a very structured approach. We read the first page and a half together and discuss what the author is saying to us. Do you trust the author? Where do you thinking the author is going with this book? Then we finish reading the first chapter together and we talk some more. We have a lot of discussion because I believe it is important that students draw their own conclusions about a text.

As we read the book, we also watch sections from movie versions and discuss whether the directors capture our image of the characters, setting, and mood, and present accurate summaries of the plot. My grandmother always said you could teach everything with just two books, the King James Bible and the Sears catalogue. The keys are connecting with students and challenging them to think.

Many contemporary English education theorists stress the process of reading and writing over the content of what is being created or examined. I try to balance a concern with process with a commitment to exploring literary content because students need to experience both doing and appreciating. Reading quality literature helps students learn to express complex ideas clearly and stimulates them to ponder serious philosophical questions. It also helps them develop a sense of taste, of style.

Many teachers complain that students do not read alone enough because they are engrossed in television, pop culture, and the Internet. Instead of complaining, I tell student teachers to have their classes read and write in school everyday. A book that helped me think about my teaching of English is *Beat Not The Poor Desk*, by Mary Ponsot and Rosemary Deen (1982). Ponsot worked in a college with nontraditional students who had poor academic skills. While the other teachers complained that their students could not read, she inspired them to read. Her approach to teaching is wonderful.

I am also a big fan of Nancy Atwell, author of *In the Middle* (1987), a book about teaching middle school students to be readers and writers. One exercise I really like is encouraging your students to write letters—personal letters, business letters—any letters. I remember once a girl in my class was extremely sad because a friend's mother had died. I said, "How about we write a letter to this kid?" I taught the class how to write a condolence letter. We used a very structured approach to writing. In the first paragraph, the author had to express sorrow for their loss. In the second paragraph, the author discussed something they remembered about the person who had died or the mourner. My students needed the structure to get started. Structure gave them the freedom they needed to write. In fact, that is a good motto for my approach to teaching. Structure and planning give us the freedom to teach and learn.

* * *

JOIN THE CONVERSATION—A FAMILY OF TEACHERS

When she read Maureen's story about being from a "family of teachers," Robin Edwards, a New York City high school teacher, felt that it resonated with her own story in a number of ways. Robin's father was a social studies teacher and school administrator and her mother teaches mathematics. At first they discouraged her from becoming a teacher, but when they realized that it was her great love, they gave their full support. Of course they kept on fighting over which subject area she should concentrate on.

Questions to Consider:

1. What is your family's attitude about teachers and teaching? How has this shaped your own views?

2. In her classes for teachers, Maureen argues that literary content is as important as the reading and writing process. She believes that reading quality literature helps secondary students learn to express complex ideas clearly and stimulates them to ponder serious philosophical questions. Do you agree? Explain your views.

3. Maureen believes that teachers must value student experiences and connect with their lives. Do you share her belief that this is part of the job of the teacher? Explain.

How I Learned to Teach Math
By Rhonda Eisenberg

Rhonda Eisenberg, a high school math department chairperson, is one of my oldest friends. We student taught at the same time while students at the City College of New York and used to meet once a week as an informal support team. Later we worked together as camp counselors and community organizers. As beginning teachers, we continued to meet regularly as we tried to figure out how to be teachers.—Alan Singer

I have been a high school mathematics teacher for 26 years. The last 3 years I was also the math department chair in my school. In this essay I will try to explain how I learned to teach. I hope you find it useful.

I believe that a very important part of my teaching is my understanding of both math and teenagers. I feel I know my subject matter in a deep, deep way. This helps me figure out what my students are having difficulty understanding and to plan lessons with future activities in mind. I never assume my students know something. I always build on what has been presented and developed in class.

I have confidence in my students' ability to learn and I show it to them. They also know I am interested in their lives. I learn their names quickly, and, at the very beginning of the semester, I ask them what they want to do when they finish school. This helps me connect to them and show them how the study of mathematics can be essential for achieving their goals.

A major aspect of what I am as a teacher are my beliefs. I am convinced that as human beings we all have the same "brain," so we all can learn. I also really feel that people have a responsibility toward each other and that the more our society educates teenagers, the better their lives will be, and the better the world will be.

Before high school, I did well in math, but I did not consider myself anything special. When I took 9th-grade algebra, I received good grades, but in 10th-grade geometry, I truly excelled. My sister, who was a year older than I was, was a grade ahead in school. That year we took different statewide standardized final exams in math and we both scored 100. This was a relatively small high school and it was a rare phenomenon for two sisters to get 100% on the "Regents" exams. Suddenly the teachers took notice of us. When I came back to school in the fall, it seemed like they all knew my name. The math department had especially high expectations for me, and in response to attention from my teachers, I started to work in a different way. I began to deeply understand fractions, decimals, and percentages, and I realized that I could explain them to other people. I thought, "Gee, maybe I should be a math teacher." After that, I never thought of becoming anything else.

I attended the City College of New York from 1967 until 1971 during a turbulent period when it seemed as if the entire country was debating issues such as U.S. involvement in Vietnam and the future of race relations. During those 4 years the campus was shut twice for extended periods of time because of student strikes. At the time, many women were making the decision to become teachers. Some of the women in the education program chose teaching because it was the kind of work they could see themselves doing; they did not envision other possibilities. Some figured it was a nice job and they would get out by 3:00. But for me, I really thought I could make a difference in the world as a teacher. To prepare myself, I worked as a counselor in an interracial, nonsectarian, sleep-away camp sponsored by a community center in Brooklyn, New York. I also student taught at my old high school, which because of demographic changes, now had a largely Black and Latino student population. The only regret I have about my decisions at that time in my life is not entering the master's program in math education at Harvard. When I told my parents I had been accepted, they said, "Made what? You've gotta work. You've been going to school for 4 years. Go out and get a job." Sometimes I wonder what would have happened in my life if I had been able to make that other choice.

The summer camp where I worked was both an exciting and difficult place and I learned a lot there about being a teacher. One experience I especially remember was a 3-day hike along a river I took with a group of racially and ethnically mixed junior-high-school-age boys and girls. Everything you could imagine went wrong on that hike and that is what made it so great. We were eaten by bugs so badly that the kids could not sleep. One night the rain was pouring so hard that we had to huddle in a culvert. I remember one of the girls hid her underwear and the other kids were teasing her. She had started to menstruate during the hike, and she did not know what it was. When the counselors realized what was going on, we called for a group meeting and discussed with the campers what was happening to this girl and what it meant to care about each other. That remains the most amazing discussion I ever had with kids. It taught me how much was possible working with teenagers and the importance of developing a sense of community by working together to achieve a common goal.

Another really important thing I learned working at the camp is not to be punitive. You can set limits for kids without making them feel like they are trapped in a box with no way out. A teacher needs to combine firmness with caring. Kids respond to caring when you let them. I worked at this camp for many years and eventually became its program director. Over the years, my experience at camp really became part of me and helped me understand both kids and myself.

Many other things contributed to my learning how to teach as well. As far as I can remember, I always had an ability to explain things, to break down problems so other people could understand them. As a student teacher, I learned to plan, execute, and evaluate lessons, but I have to say that I do not think I was adequate as a teacher until I had 5 years of experience. By then, I had a sense of the broader picture and understood how all the lessons in the curriculum hung together. I was no longer teaching individual lessons; I was teaching a system of reasoning. It also took that long to understand where the kids were coming from, what they understood, and why they acted the ways that they did. It can be hard, but a teacher cannot take every action or statement by a student personally. You have to remember that people often act out of frustration and their behavior may have nothing to do with you.

One of the things that helped me become an effective teacher was figuring out the purpose of tests. There are people who make up tests that are "ball busters." I always ask them, "What are you trying to do? Is the purpose of a test to show students how much you know and how much they don't?" Eventually I learned to construct tests that build up kids and show them if they do the work they can learn the things they need to know. As a teacher, your mind always has to be creative. You are constantly looking for new ways to teach a topic in case someone in your class is not getting it.

As a teacher you cannot invent everything yourself and I am always willing to "borrow" from another teacher. If I observe someone and I see something interesting, I try to use it in my class. My son is in elementary school and his teacher gave him a science review sheet called "Things to Know." For example, one thing to know was the difference between a vertebrate and an invertebrate. I thought this was a great idea and I changed my review sheets so they list important ideas as well as provide practice problems. Of course, borrowing must be mutual. I lend out my handouts to other teachers and I let people use my tests.

I think a lot about why it is so difficult for many students to understand math. A major part of the problem is that students start off believing that they cannot do well. It is ingrained in them throughout school. They think you are either born with math ability or not. Because of this, they give up on themselves and end up failing. These and other problems are compounded when teachers act as if certain groups of students will never be able to learn math. When I grew up, like almost everybody else, I accepted that boys were better than girls in math. That is another notion that must be challenged.

One way to help students understand math is to draw connections between math and the world around us. I do not mean saying something like, "If you're going to be a gardener, this is the math you need to know." I think the most important part of math is learning its logic: how the whole thing fits together. The ability to solve problems that students learn in math carries through in many other areas in both school and life. In all secondary school math classes, students and teachers are really doing two things. We are learning to think logically and to see how smaller pieces fit together to form a broader picture in the mathematical world.

A good example of this approach to mathematics is the study of plane geometry. It is a system of reasoning where you accept certain postulates about the universe, and based on these postulates, you can develop and prove other ideas. But in geometry, if you change a single postulate, you change the whole system.

When we postulate that the universe is two dimensional or flat and looks like a piece of paper, if you have a point (C) that is not on a line (AB), one and only one line can be drawn through the point (C) that is parallel (II) to the line (AB). But the universe we live in is three dimensional. If we define parallel lines as two lines that never intersect, in a three-dimensional universe an infinite number of lines can pass through that point and remain paral-lel with the line because they exist on different surfaces or planes. To complicate the matter even further, scientists argue that in our universe space is really curved. What happens to parallel lines then? They do not exist!

Each of these postulates about the universe leads to a different geometry. It is incredible, but you can build a whole different system by changing one postulate. By examining this principle in geometry, we help students explore the implications of their assumptions in other fields as well. What I try to do while I teach math is have my class continually return to the basic assumptions so they can see how later ideas were determined by their initial be-liefs. I always ask my students, "How do we know something is true?" We discover that in math, truth means that something is logically derived from our initial postulates. These fun-damental ideas have profound meaning for all areas of study. They helps us understand as-sumptions we make about ourselves and about society.

As a department chair, I try to draw on my experience to help other people become better teachers. Just as with the students, some teachers resist my suggestions because they think they know better than I do or because they are afraid to examine what they do not know. I try to observe department members as frequently as possible and compliment them even when they do something different from what I would. I have learned that one per-son cannot change a school by her or himself. I depend on these people to help create a pos-itive climate for learning, where I can be an effective teacher and accomplish my goals with the students.

* * *

JOIN THE CONVERSATION—LEARNING TO TEACH

Questions to Consider:

1. Rhonda writes that "a major aspect of what I am as a teacher are my beliefs. I am con-vinced that as human beings we all have the same 'brain,' so we all can learn. I also really feel that people have a responsibility toward each other and that the more our society educates teenagers, the better their lives will be, and the better the world will be." Do you agree with these underlying beliefs? Explain your views.

2. The way Rhonda felt about school as a student was very much a reflection of how she was treated by her teachers and their expectations. Were your experiences similar to hers? Explain.

3. Rhonda relates some of the experiences that shaped her development as a teacher. Which do you consider most crucial? Why?

For Jonathan Levin, Teacher
By Alan Singer

I originally wrote this essay in 1997 in response to the murder of Jonathan Levin, a New York City high school English teacher. A slightly different version was published in a local newspaper. This was a painful essay to write and it is a painful essay to read, though I try to end it on a note of hope. You have already met the other teachers I mention in the essay.—Alan Singer

Jonathan Levin was a popular and respected English teacher at William Howard Taft High School in the Bronx, New York. Taft is a large inner-city high school with a student population that is largely Latino and African American. Many of its students are from families that live on the economic margins of our society. Levin, who came from an affluent family, chose to teach in the Bronx because he wanted to have an impact on the lives of young people. He was found dead in his apartment in New York City on Monday, June 2, 1997. A former student, with a history of drug use, criminal activity, and incarceration, was one of two men arrested and charged with his murder.

I did not know Jonathan Levin, but I feel that in many ways we were brothers. I am also a White, Jewish, middle-class professional, and I spent 15 years as a teacher in inner-city junior and senior high schools before becoming a teacher educator. From what I read about Jonathan and his work as a teacher, I believe we shared a commitment to rethink what is possible in education and to struggle, along with others, to change schools, communities, and lives. I am writing because teachers who disagree with Jonathan's expansive view of the job of the teacher as a caring and connected human being are using his death to undermine his vision. I am also concerned that new teachers, many of whom live in the suburbs, will be afraid to work in urban or minority communities because of Jonathan's death.

The week after Jonathan died, I visited schools, teachers, and students across New York City introducing preservice teachers to the world of urban education. We met with young teachers, alumni from our program, who chose to work in city schools out of a sense of mission and of possibility.

We spoke with Christina, who grew up in the suburbs, attended an Ivy League university, and currently teaches in a Bronx high school. Christina regularly stays after school with the community service club and takes her students on weekend trips to museums and the botanical gardens. Last June, she brought 35 students and their parents to Washington, D.C., for the "Stand for Children" rally. Christina could teach anywhere in the metropolitan area, but she chooses to remain with her students in the Bronx. She told the visiting preservice teachers that "my students need and value me. Working here means I can do something important with my life."

We visited Howard, a graduate of a suburban high school who teaches in an urban school. This semester one of his students was arrested and Howard posted bail. Howard believes that "people are innocent until proven guilty, and I could not allow one of my students to remain in jail just because his family is poor."

We also met Stephanie, who grew up in the city but moved to the suburbs as a youngster because "it was safer and because my mother wanted me to attend better schools." Stephanie teaches sixth graders in a middle school and wants her students to have the same opportunities that she had. On Friday afternoon at dismissal, she lined her class up in the stairwell and had each student explain the weekend assignment before they could go home. At the foot of the stairs, teachers from her carpool kept on calling her, but Stephanie would not leave until every child was finished.

Many young teachers and preservice teachers I work with were worried by the news reports about Jonathan Levin's death and the police search that targeted one of his former students. Older, discouraged colleagues continually warn new teachers that they cross some mythical line of professional propriety if they treat their students with respect and show concern for the problems in their lives. Jonathan's death was cited as final proof that teachers must remain aloof, transmit information, but never, never, show students their humanity or vulnerability. When the barrier is broken, "just look what happened to that guy."

Christina, Howard, Stephanie, and thousands of other teachers do not recognize a barrier between students and teachers and they know that Jonathan Levin did not die because he crossed it. They believe, and think Jonathan believed, that inner-city kids and teens are the victims of inequality, injustice, and abandonment by our society, and that the only way to change conditions is to empower young people, through education, to build a better world. Until that happens, our society will continue to create alienated and angry young men and women like the people suspected of killing Jonathan. According to police records, Jonathan was not their only victim, and they did not target him because he was a teacher. He was someone with money, and they needed money.

Jonathan Levin died because of the conditions in our society he was trying to change. To pull back from his struggle, to surrender to cynicism and despair, is to dishonor Jonathan and abandon the young people for whom he cared. Jonathan Levin's dream continues to live in the life of every student he affected. Jonathan Levin was a teacher.

* * *

JOIN THE CONVERSATION—JOB OF THE TEACHER

Questions to Consider:

1. What do you think of the job of the teacher as defined by Jonathan Levin and the other teachers mentioned in this essay?
2. At this point, how would you define the job of the teacher? Why?

REFERENCES AND SUGGESTIONS FOR FURTHER READING

Atwell, N. (1987). *In the middle: Writing, reading, and learning with adolescents*. Portsmouth, NH: Heinemann.

Beagle, P. (1968). *The last unicorn*. New York: Viking.

Darling-Hammond, L. (1994). Who will speak for the children? How "Teach for America" hurts urban schools and students, *Phi Delta Kappan, 76*(1), 21–34.

Darling-Hammond, L. (2000). Reforming teacher preparation and licensing: Debating the evidence, *Teachers College Record, 102*(1), 28–56.

Freire, P. (1995). *The pedagogy of hope*. New York: Continuum.

Kohl, H. (1994). *I won't learn from you and other thoughts on creative maladjustment*. New York: The New Press.

Logan, J. (1997). *Teaching stories*. New York: Kodansha America.

Marquez, G. (1993). *Chronicle of a death foretold*. New York: Knopf.

Ponsot, M., & Deen, R. (1982). *Beat not the poor desk*. Portsmouth, NH: Heinemann.

II

PRO/CLASS PRACTICES

Planning
Relationships
Organization
Community

AN INTRODUCTION TO PRO/CLASS PRACTICES

On my first day as a high school teacher, an older adult whom I did not recognize (he probably was not that old, but I was only 28) came into my classroom and yelled, "Why are students out of their seats?" He was referring to three students who were walking toward my desk to hand in assignments they had just completed. As quickly as he had entered, he left the room. The unexpected visitor turned out to be the school's principal.

Later, when I learned who he was, my stomach started to knot. I had waited a long time for this opportunity and now I was worried that I would be fired on my first day. It turned out that my transgression of school rules (students were not permitted out of their seats during instruction) was not considered that serious. The principal, who was in the middle of responding to an emergency in the building at the time he passed by my room, did not refer to the incident when we were formally introduced. Although I remained unnerved, my job was safe.

Student teachers and beginning teachers are often obsessed with the problem of classroom control. They feel they are being judged, not only by the way students perform, but also by the way they behave. Many fear they are one casual observation or parental complaint away from unemployment.

In most cases the fear is unreasonable. I tell student teachers in our program, "If we did not think you could student teach, we would not have let you." Similarly, if school administrators do not think a "beginner" has the ability to become a good teacher, they do not hire him or her. Most reasonable people do not expect anyone to be an expert on their first day. If they wanted an expert, they would have hired someone with experience.

Part of the problem with the fear of failure is that it pushes beginning teachers into self-defeating classroom practices. They frequently end up with scripted, impossibly complex lesson plans that translate into long, boring, teacher-centered lessons. Classrooms and learning become painful for students and they rebel. Teachers respond by cracking down and the cycle of boredom, resistance, and punishment escalates. As a beginning teacher, you find yourself becoming the kind of teacher you hated.

But it does not have to happen this way! Teaching and learning can be fun and exciting. You can become the teacher you want to be. It takes time and hard work, but you can do it.

JOIN THE CONVERSATION—BENE GESSERIT LITANY AGAINST FEAR

In college and while I was student teaching I was a big science fiction fan. One of my favorite books was *Dune* (New York: Berkeley Medallion, 1965) by Frank Herbert and my favorite passage was the "Bene Gesserit Litany Against Fear" (p. 8). The hero learns to recite the chant in order to calm his mind when faced by a crisis. I do not know if it will work for you, but as a student teacher and new teacher it helped me a lot.

I must not fear.

Fear is the mind-killer.

Fear is the little-death that brings total obliteration.

I will face my fear.

I will permit it to pass over and through me.

And when it has gone on past I will turn the inner eye to see its path.

Where the fear has gone there will be nothing.

Only I will remain.

Philosopher Bertrand Russell wrote, "To conquer fear is the beginning of wisdom." Deon Gordon Mitchell and Michael Pezone, whom you met earlier in this book, developed their own ways of overcoming fear and preparing for difficult situations. Deon turns to prayer, whereas Michael is a Zen aficionado. Some of his favorite Zen stories are included in chapter 10.

Question to Consider:

How do you overcome your fears and prepare for a difficult situation?

In book II, we examine ways that teachers can design lessons, develop personal connections with students, and build classroom communities. I call this approach to teaching PRO/CLASS Practices. We will not be learning foolproof formulas. They do not exist. Instead, we will look at principles of teaching and ideas about teenagers that my colleagues and I think make sense. But you need to reinterpret and refine them as you develop your own approach to teaching. As I think you have learned from the stories told by teachers in book I, there is not just one right way.

Before we go on, I have to make a confession. People always wonder how you end up with a nice acronym like PRO/CLASS Practices—*P*lanning, *R*elationships, *O*rganization, *C*ommunity, *L*iteracy, *A*ssessment, *S*upport, and *S*truggle. I confess, I cheated. I made a list of key terms and moved them around until they spelled something I thought was memorable. I really did start with "P" for Planning, "R" for Relationships, "O" for Organization, and "C" for Community, just not in that order. At any rate, these four topics will be examined in book II, chapters 3, 4, 5, and 6. As you examine the list and the explanations that follow, consider which you would give priority to in your teaching and prepare to explain why.

- **Planning:** Lessons that relate to student interests, involve students in activities, and are appropriate to their academic performance level are more likely to hold student attention and involve students in learning. They may even be fun.
- **Relationships:** Students who feel that their teacher cares about them as human beings, and is willing to respond to their needs and concerns, will be more willing to cooperate, even if they do not understand or agree with instructions. When a teacher helps one student out, or just gives a student who is having difficulty a break, somehow all the other students quickly know.
- **Organization:** As a teacher, you can structure lessons and set up a classroom to minimize conflicts and encourage student participation (e.g., use assignments to settle the class and establish a context for the lesson; shift desks for group, individual, or full class activities; limit bathroom visits so that students can be engaged by class work; involve students in developing reasonable classroom procedures).
- **Community:** As students develop a sense of relationship with each other and the teacher, an interest in the topics being explored, and confidence that they will not be put down, and as they are convinced that their ideas will be heard, they develop a commitment to the success of the class. Individuals become classroom leaders committed to the class as a democratic community of learners and draw their classmates into the community. As a group, they want to learn and they take responsibility for what goes on in their class.
- **Literacy:** Preparing students for full participation in a democratic society means empowering them through the enhancement of critical literacies. Student need to learn how to learn; find and evaluate information available in different formats; think systematically; support arguments with evidence; present ideas clearly, both orally and in writing; and evaluate their own work and the work of others.
- **Assessment:** Nobody makes good choices all of the time. The key to growth as a teacher is to think about what you are doing and make the best choices you can. Think of your classroom problems as learning experiences rather than as personal failures. Reflect on your goals and how you can achieve them with this particular group of students. Think of student examinations as tests of what you have taught. It is never too late to change what you are doing. While you spent all night (or all weekend) worrying about a particular incident and its impact on the class, the students probably haven't thought about it since they left the room. Try to relax a little bit.
- **Support:** Everybody has "bad hair days." Instead of dumping on students, give them a little space. Treat them the way you would want to be treated if you had just had a fight with your mother, were overtired, or were just plain grumpy. Instead of backing a student into a corner and provoking an explosion, try a dramatic shrug and taking it up later after everyone has calmed down. When a troublesome student or class responds, make a big deal of it. Show them that you care.
- **Struggle:** There is no magic wand. Change never happens instantaneously. Why should adolescents behave any differently from other people? Being an effective teacher means engaging in a long-term struggle to convince students that your goals for the class make sense and are worth examining.

JOIN THE CONVERSATION—PRO/CLASS PRACTICES

Question to Consider:

Which of these PRO/CLASS practices would you give priority to in your teaching? Why?

REFERENCES AND SUGGESTIONS FOR FURTHER READING

Other teachers and books on teaching emphasize similar ideas. These are books that have helped me to think about my work as a teacher and I recommend them highly.

Bigelow, B., Christenson, L., Karp, S., Miner, B., & Peterson, B. (Eds.). (1994). *Rethinking our classrooms*. Milwaukee, WI: Rethinking Schools.

Christenson, L. (2000). *Reading, writing, and rising up*. Milwaukee, WI: Rethinking Schools.

Delpit, L. (1995). *Other people's children*. New York: The New Press.

Haberman, M. (1995). *Star teachers of children in poverty*. West Lafayette, IN: Kappa Delta Pi.

Kohl, H. (1994). *I won't learn from you and other thoughts on creative maladjustment*. New York: The New Press.

Ladson-Billings, G. (1994). *The dreamkeepers, successful teachers of African American children*. San Francisco: Jossey-Bass.

Logan, J. (1993). *Teaching stories*. Plymouth, MN: Minnesota Inclusiveness Program.

Weiner, L. (1999). *Urban teaching, the essentials*. New York: Teachers College Press.

Wigginton, E. (1985). *Sometimes a shining moment: The foxfire experience*. New York: Anchor/Doubleday.

Wood, G. (1992). *Schools that work*. New York: Dutton.

3

PLANNING: HOW DO YOU
PLAN A LESSON?

In the movie musical *The Sound of Music* (1965), the Singing Nun recommends that we start to learn at the very beginning—when you read you begin with A, B, C and when you sing you begin with do, ray, me. We will begin learning about lesson planning by discussing goals, teaching strategies, and finally, lesson formats.

SECTION A: WHAT ARE YOUR GOALS?

William Shakespeare wrote a play called *Much Ado About Nothing*. I think much of the debate over education in the United States today would more appropriately be titled, "Much Ado About the Wrong Things." For example, everybody (politicians, parents, and teachers) is worried about high standards and the assessment of student learning. It seems like every educational organization has its own published list of what children should know and every political unit (city, county, or state) has its own standardized tests that students are expected to pass. But there is very little public discussion of exactly what we mean by standards. Most experienced teachers I know respond to the call for higher standards by saying, "This is the same thing we always do."

I think the general public finds the call for higher standards confusing because the term means different things in different contexts. In track and field, the standard is the record performance that other athletes try to surpass. In baseball, it is the Yankees with a century of accomplishment. In basketball and golf it is identified with one player, Michael Jordan or Tiger Woods. But everybody cannot be like Mike, Tiger, or the Yankees, and that is the problem with using the top performer as a measure or standard.

In education, standards can best be described as goals—the things we hope all students will achieve, the things we plan for them to achieve. Achieving standards is not a competition. In theory, in a well-run classroom with effective teaching strategies, every student should be able to obtain the goals.

New York State, where I work, publishes elementary, intermediate, and commencement (high school) standards in each subject area. They do not differ very much from standards developed by other states (if you do not believe me, you can look up standards from other states on the Internet). If we examine the New York State standards for English Language Arts, you can see why I describe them as goals.

The English Language Arts Standard 1 is: "Students will read, write, listen, and speak for information and understanding. As listeners and readers, students will collect data, facts, and ideas; discover relationships, concepts, and generalizations; and use knowledge generated from oral, written, and electronically produced texts. As speakers and writers, they will use oral and written language to acquire, interpret, apply, and transmit information." But the standards do not prescribe a specific calendar of lessons, instructional strategies, or transitional learning outcomes. These are left to the professional discretion of teachers who individually, and in conjunction with their subject area colleagues, must figure out the best ways for their students to acquire and develop these skills over the course of a year. As long as students perform satisfactorily on assessments, teachers are generally allowed wide latitude to determine what and how they will teach. Because of the intimate relationship between standards and assessments, we will return to this topic at greater detail in the chapter on assessing student learning.

Most of my experience in secondary schools was as a social studies teacher, but I have also taught reading, English, general science, shop, and business math, and I believe the principles for successful planning are similar. In my social studies methods classes, I recommend that teachers plan units, or packages of ten to twelve lessons at a time, and that they start by "brainstorming" a list of both long-term (unit) and lesson-specific goals. I find it useful to think in terms of four distinct types of goals—concepts, content, academic skills, and social skills (see Fig. 3.1 for a framework for unit plan design).

- *Concepts* are broad, overarching terms or principles that are continually reexamined throughout a curriculum, like democracy in social studies, character development in English, standard temperature and pressure in chemistry, or congruence in geometry. They also include *main ideas* and *understandings* that are specific to a unit or an individual lesson, for example, causal relationships in history or science, recognition of particular character traits in literature, or a rule for conjugating verbs in a foreign language class.
- *Content* refers to the factual information about a topic that will be considered during the unit or lesson, for example, the result of a chemical reaction, the procedure for solving an equation, the way a poet describes a person, or a sequence of events from the past.
- *Academic skills* include activities such as thinking critically, writing expressively, speaking clearly, and gathering and organizing information presented in different formats.

FIG. 3.1 Framework for unit plan design.

Topic: What will be taught on this day.

Goals: Where lesson fits into broader strategies for achieving standards, for example, promote literacy or critical thinking.

Concepts: Broad categories of fundamental ideas, for example, democracy, sequence, communicative principle, causality.

Main Ideas: Specific ideas, relationships, or formulas examined in this lesson.

Content: Specific information examined in this lesson.

Academic and Social Skills: Subject-related skills developed in this lesson, for example, problem-solving and social skills, e.g. cooperative learning, that will be emphasized.

Materials: Technology, activity sheets, and so on.

FIG. 3.1 *(Continued)*

Design: Full class or group, demonstration or discussion, and so on.								
	Topic	Goals	Concepts	Main Ideas	Content	Skills	Materials	Design
1								
2								
3								
4								
5								
6								
7								
8								
9								
10								
Unit Assessment:								

- *Social skills* involve learning to work effectively in a group, to take responsibility for individual work, to coach a fellow student, or to provide leadership on a class project.

Advanced planning is not unique to teaching. Anyone who has worked in the business world; played an organized team sport; competed in chess or poker; or has been in the military knows the importance of having a strategy to achieve success. A lesson plan is our strategy to achieve our goals.

Most new teachers and many experienced teachers start their planning from a textbook, following its organization of the subject and emphasizing its concept, main idea, content, and skill choices. Starting from the textbook is helpful when teachers do not feel comfortable with their own knowledge of the subject or the scope of the curriculum. It can also make it easier for students to follow the sequence of lessons. But there are potential problems with this approach. Students become overwhelmed by facts, main ideas are lost in a swirl of details, lessons are dry, and students grow bored. In addition, when teachers are dependent on packaged textbook-based units, they sacrifice much of their own creative energy. They become part of an information conveyor belt, instead of being active learners themselves.

It is often very difficult to decide in advance how much planning is enough. Certainly, unit and lesson planning is more an art than a science, and decisions become easier as a teacher gains experience. As you plan, it is useful to ask yourself some questions:

- Does this unit build on previous work and understanding?
- Does this unit lay the basis for future explorations?
- Do I understand the period, the broader issues, or the topic? Will students understand them based on these lessons?

- Is there sufficient material for students to analyze in class? Do the lessons include enough active things for students to do?
- Does the unit cover the same scope and/or information as the textbook assignments? How closely do I want them to parallel each other?
- Are my lesson designs varied and interesting?

If planning seems daunting, remember that there is no reason that supervisors, experienced teachers, and beginners should not work together to develop a curriculum. Lesson and unit planning does not have to be a private, individual experience or a competitive sport. When teachers work together, old-timers benefit from new insights and perspectives, and rookies do not have to discover every document for themselves and reinvent every teaching strategy. At a minimum, new teachers should not be afraid to borrow. That is why they invented the copying machine.

JOIN THE CONVERSATION—ADVANCED PLANNING

Questions to Consider:
1. Describe a non-teaching activity in which you have learned to plan in advance.
2. What are the crucial aspects you focused on in your advanced planning for this activity?

SECTION B: WHAT ARE TEACHING STRATEGIES?

There are as many possible strategies for teaching as there are for many other human activities. A football coach has to decide whether to emphasize the team's ground game or passing attack, taking into consideration the team's strengths and their opponent's weaknesses. When you go holiday shopping, you have to decide whether you want to visit a department store or specialty shop at the mall or perhaps go catalogue hunting or search for that elusive gift on the Internet. You weigh the trauma of traffic congestion versus the benefit of seeing products first hand.

For teachers, a key aspect of planning is deciding which approach or approaches are best suited for presenting a given subject to a specific groups of students. Teaching is not an abstract activity. It requires that teachers connect with adolescents who are not necessarily interested in making the connection. A chess champion or a football coach always goes into a match with a strategy, but the plan has to be flexible so the contestant can respond to an opponent. The need to be flexible and to respond to students is one of the things that makes it hard to discuss and plan hypothetical lessons. But every coach will tell you that you need practice, so in this section, let us try.

When I examine sample lesson plans prepared by preservice teachers in my methods classes, they often contain a phrase such as: "Students will discuss blah, blah blah and yada, yada, yada." In the margins, I always write "HWTK?" How Will They Know? What have you presented to the class that makes it possible for them to discuss this topic?

As you decide on teaching strategies, you always need to consider two things: (a) How will students know? (b) What will students do?

JOIN THE CONVERSATION—TEACHING STRATEGIES

There are different ways to provide a class with information. The approaches that follow can be mixed together in different proportions:

Readings. Teachers provide students, either in class or as a homework assignment, with something to read—a page from the textbook, a passage from a novel, or a primary source document. Students can also be asked to "read" a picture, chart, or map to uncover information.

Modeling. Teachers provide students with a model problem and solution or an example of what you want them to draw, construct, or create. Sometimes the teacher models the activity for the class (e.g., sorting lab specimens by selected traits, solving a geometry problem, tracing a route on a map).

Direct instruction. Teachers outline and explain what they want students to know. A recording, either audio or video, can be substituted to provide information.

Dramatic presentation. Students act out a story or an event, either from a script or spontaneously from a scenario (role playing). The information garnered from the reenactment becomes the basis for discussion.

Allegories and anecdotes. A brief story or comparison is sometimes sufficient to allow students to scaffold on prior knowledge.

Brainstorming. Sometimes students are unaware they know something, or sometimes different students in the class know part of the puzzle. The class compiles, sorts, and analyzes a list of potentially useful information.

Questioning. Many experienced teachers approach questioning as an art and are skilled at drawing information out of students and getting them to respond to each other. They use questions to assemble a pool of information to be further evaluated.

Questions to Consider:

1. Based on your own experience as a secondary school student, which teaching strategies did you find most effective in your own learning? Why?
2. In your opinion, would the effectiveness of a strategy depend on the group of students? Explain.

SECTION C: MY BEST TEACHERS 2: A LESSON IN HUMILITY

Many of my best teachers were my colleagues at middle schools and high schools. It can be a humbling experience to discover that you are not as good as you think you are at something you want to do well and that other people are better at it than you are. That was my experience as a young teacher, and it continues to be my experience today. But being humbled is not necessarily a bad thing.

When you work at becoming a teacher, it takes between 3 and 5 years of hard work, planning, and practicing for the things you want to happen in a lesson to happen on a consistent basis. It is easier to learn how to do these things when you appreciate the competence of other teachers, even teachers who do things differently from you do. I was a dynamo who entered teaching hoping to change the world. My lessons were fast paced; I taught with a sense of urgency. However, I soon learned that there were other ways of teaching and that caring teachers can be very effective even if they do not share my agenda.

I worked at Franklin K. Lane High School in New York City during most of the 1980s and was fortunate to work with a number of outstanding individuals. Lane could be a difficult place to work and many teachers, including myself, had trouble maintaining control and teaching our classes.

Emilie was a middle-aged White woman who was barely 5 feet tall. Her students, most of whom were Latino or African American, generally towered over her. As a teacher, Emilie can best be described as a "skilled craftsman." Her lessons and her units were carefully laid out. Students respected her because they knew they could count on her to teach them in ways that they would understand and to prepare them for standardized tests and graduation requirements. She was always responsible and never yelled, or lost her patience or her poise.

Barry was an "old school" teacher who demanded and received total attention and effort from students. In Barry's classes, students did the homework on time and they answered questions when called on. He had high expectations and no one ever said "NO!" to him. It was just the way things were.

Rozella was every student's "dream" mother, organizing special activities and every other aspect of their lives. It was usually impossible to tell what was going on in Rozella's classes, probably because so many things were going on at the same times. Students sometimes seemed confused, but they were always patient with her. They cared about her and about learning because they knew she cared about them.

After I left Lane to work as a teacher educator, I had the opportunity to return to high school, teaching for a year at Edward R. Murrow High School. At Murrow, I worked with three extraordinary colleagues. Saul, about 60 years old, was the school's principal. He was a conscientious follower of John Dewey's philosophy of education and Socrates' method of teaching. Murrow, under Saul's direction, allowed students to spend unassigned periods sitting in the halls, studying, or hanging out with friends. Saul would continually walk through the halls, stopping repeatedly to squat down and chat with students.

I do not think I ever heard Saul make either an affirmative or negative statement or raise his voice. It seemed that whatever students or faculty said, he always thought for a second and then responded with a question. Saul taught an advanced placement class that met an hour before school began in the morning. Every term it was overloaded with students, who voluntarily left home before dawn to travel to Murrow by bus or subway in order to take his class.

John, David, and I often used to plan lessons together. John was a devotee of the overhead projector and a short quote or newspaper headline. David, who shared my proclivity for extended documents and activity sheets, was always clipping articles from the newspaper. John had the ability, mid-lesson, to introduce a simple headline and use it to draw the entire class into heated discussion. Just when the discussion was dying down and everyone seemed swayed to the same position, another headline was slapped on the overhead and disagreement would erupt again.

David's handouts were detailed, with readings of different lengths, maps, pictures, graphs, cartoons, and plenty of questions. He often reproduced an entire newspaper article because he wanted students to get used to reading and evaluating complex subject matter. David's knack was discovering and organizing a wide range of material with carefully constructed questions so that even when students stumbled over a difficult reading passage, they could figure out the meaning from the questions or the other materials.

Recently, as a field supervisor for student teachers, I have had the opportunity to visit the classrooms of many of my former teacher education students who have become cooperating teachers. A number of them have their secondary school students create elaborate individual and group projects to demonstrate what they have learned about a topic and as a form of authentic assessment. The cooperating teachers enjoy ushering me through the building and, with great pride, show me what their classes have done. Inevitably, they thank me for teaching them how to do the projects. But the irony is, I really did not teach them these things. I did introduce the idea of a project approach to teaching and showed them some sample activities, but the projects were never as elaborate, and I was not as effective as they are working on projects with middle school and high school students. I shared my ideas with them, but the projects are the invention of these teachers and their students, not mine.

Frank Sinatra had a big hit song late in his career, "I Did It My Way." That song could be about any of these teachers. Each of them is or was outstanding. Each of them did it his or her own way.

JOIN THE CONVERSATION—TEACHERS YOU ENJOYED

Questions to Consider:

Think of three secondary school teachers who you really enjoyed. How were they similar and how were they different? What strategies did they use as teachers? Why did you enjoy these approaches to teaching?

SECTION D: WHAT DOES A LESSON LOOK LIKE?[1]

What Is a Lesson Plan?

- Lesson planning is part of the process of making pedagogical, intellectual, and ideological choices.
- Lesson planning is the process of figuring out the intermediate steps necessary to achieve long-term goals.
- Lesson planning includes researching information for your lesson.
- Lesson planning means deciding what are the major ideas that students need to consider during a lesson.
- Lesson planning involves translating abstract concepts into concrete examples that teenagers can critically examine, struggle to understand, decide to accept or reject, and use to reshape their own conceptions of the world.
- Lesson planning means making decisions about the most effective ways to organize classrooms and learning activities so students become involved as active learners.
- Lesson planning means thinking of creative ways to motivate students to explore topics that might not initially attract their interest and thinking of questions that help them draw connections between ideas and events.
- There are a number of different ways to organize a lesson plan. Some school districts allow teachers to use the lesson design they are most comfortable with as long as their lessons are effective. Other districts require that teachers use a specific format. In that case, teachers learn to adjust the requirements to meet their personal needs. In this chapter,

---

[1]This section expands on material originally published for social studies teachers in Singer, *Social Studies for Secondary Schools, Teaching to Learn/Learning to Teach* (LEA, 1997).

we examine four different ways to organize lessons: activity based, developmental, the Hunter model, and a streamlined format I developed for overstressed student teachers.

What Do You Need to Consider?

- Lesson plans are necessary tools for teaching. They are not works of art. They will never be perfect.
- Lesson plan formats are suggestions based on other people's experiences. They are not etched in stone. What works for one person may not work for someone else or in another setting. There are a number of different ways to plan effective lessons.
- Successful teachers, even the most experienced, always plan. Some very good veteran teachers argue that they do not need *written* plans any more because everything is in their heads. It may be possible for them to teach this way and it may be possible for you in the distant future, but it has never worked for me. The effort to involve students in a lesson is too demanding for me to just rely on my memory during a lesson.
- Lesson plans are experiments. Sometimes they get the expected results and sometimes they do not. Every teacher has lessons that did not work the way they wanted them to. I try to include three or four possible activities in each lesson. If something does not seem to be working, I go on to the next activity.
- One of my students compared a lesson plan to a recipe. She said that when she first started cooking she needed to follow all of the steps carefully. Later, as she became more experienced, she felt more comfortable varying the ingredients and experimenting with her own ideas. Lesson plans are a lot like recipes.
- It is better to overplan than underplan. An important part of teaching is making choices. You can always leave something out or decide to use it another day or in another way. As I became a more experienced teacher I overplanned on purpose.
- Lesson plans should change. If something does not work in one class, you can do it differently the next period, the next day, or the next year. At the end of a class or the day, I jot down comments on my lesson plans for future reference: what worked, what did not, what to add, drop, or change.
- Some lesson plan goals require more than one period to achieve. Just because time can be subdivided into discrete intervals does not mean that human beings think in 40-minute blocks or that every (or any) idea can be grasped in one class period.
- A structured plan makes it possible to be flexible in class. You can choose from different built-in lesson alternatives based on student involvement in the lesson. Maybe you cannot change a horse in "midstream," but you can change a lesson plan.
- Lesson plans must be adjusted to meet particular circumstances and they need to be different for different students. A lesson that makes sense for a class of 15 may not work with a class of 34. A lesson planned for a class that meets in the morning probably has to be modified for a class that tears into the room at 2:30 PM. Lessons planned for heterogeneous classes will differ from lessons planned for homogenous classes. Lessons must be planned with students in mind.
- Lessons planned for middle school students differ from lessons planned for high school classrooms. Usually middle school teachers have fewer time constraints. This makes it

possible for students to approach an idea from different directions and for teachers to plan more group activities.

- Students are not inherently interested just because the clock says it is time for my class. It is my job to interest and motivate them.

- A lesson needs a clear structure. If students cannot figure out what I want them to do, they cannot do it.

- Sample lessons (including mine) may look great on paper, but teachers need to adapt them to their classes and their own personalities.

- The things a teacher includes in a lesson plan change as a teacher becomes more experienced. A beginning teacher, knowing that he or she will be nervous, should list possible questions in advance. Preparation makes it easier to think on your feet. As I grew more experienced and confident, I became more adept at developing questions during the course of a lesson based on student questions and comments.

- Everyone can participate and learn if I organize a lesson around materials that I bring to class. If students did the homework in advance, their experience will be enriched. But even if they did not do the homework, they will be able to use the materials to participate in classroom activities and discussions.

- Whatever your individual preferences are for a lesson plan format, when you first start out, you will likely have to use the format recommended by your district or department. Beginning teachers are generally monitored closely until they establish a reputation for competence. I think you will discover that whatever format you are asked to use, you will be able to adapt it to what you believe should be included in a lesson plan.

- Personal computers were probably invented with teachers in mind. I design lessons, modify them as worksheets, rearrange them into homework assignments, and recycle homework and classroom questions when I make up tests. The next time I teach the subject, I start with a lesson plan database that I can easily reorganize. In addition, the World Wide Web is an abundant source of lesson ideas, lessons, and materials. Recommended sites are discussed in the Appendix at the end of this book.

SECTION E: FOUR SAMPLE LESSON FORMATS

I. An Activity-Based Format

This is my preference for lesson design. An activity is broadly defined. It can mean examining a document, a problem, or a specimen. It can include reading, writing, drawing, building, talking, or singing. Activities can take a few minutes, a full period, or a number of days, though every day needs to start with an introduction and end with some type of closure.

Because this approach to lesson planning is organized around activities, by its nature it is hands-on, is student centered, and promotes inquiry. I find it has other advantages as well. The activities draw on outside learning (e.g., projects and homework), but do not require prior knowledge. That means that every student has the ability to participate. Activities can be full class, group, or individual, which allows the teacher to rearrange the room around mid-lesson and keep students alert and on task. It also allows teachers time to work with individual students or student teams. Discussions, student presentations to class, and written work are incorporated into a number of activities, which allows teachers to continually assess student learning.

I.a. Ingredients for an Activity-Based Lesson

Unit: where this lesson fits in the overall conceptual sequence.

Aim: a question that a particular lesson is designed to answer or a statement or phrase introducing the topic of a lesson. Usually it is written on the board at the start of the lesson; sometimes it is elicited from students during the early stages of a lesson.

Goals/objectives (standards): the skills, concepts and content that students will learn during the lesson. They can also include social or behavioral or classroom community goals.

Main ideas/understandings: the underlying or most important ideas about a topic that inform a teacher's understanding and influence the way lessons and units are organized—the ideas that teachers want students to consider. They can be formulated as statements or as broad questions that become the basis for ongoing discussion.

Materials: the maps, documents, audio or video cassettes, and other equipment needed by teachers and students during the lesson to create the learning activities.

Activities/lesson development: the substance of the lesson—the ways that students will learn the goals and objectives. This can include discussions, document analysis, mapping, cartooning, singing, drama, research, cooperative learning, and teacher presentations.

Do now: an introductory activity that immediately involves students as they enter the room.

Motivation: a question, statement or activity that captures student interest in the topic that will be examined.

Questions: prepared questions that attempt to anticipate classroom dialogue—designed to aid examination of materials, generate class discussions, and promote deeper probing. Medial summary questions make it possible for the class to integrate ideas at the end of an activity.

Transitions: key questions that make it possible for students to draw connections between the information, concepts, or understandings developed during a particular activity with other parts of the lesson and to broader conceptual understanding.

Summary: a concluding question or questions that make it possible for the class to integrate or use the learning from this lesson and prior lessons.

Application: extra optional question(s) or activity(ies) planned for this lesson that draws on and broadens what students are learning in the unit. These can be used to review prior lessons or as transitions to future lessons.

Homework assignment: a reading, writing, research, or thinking assignment that students complete after the lesson. It can be a review of the lesson, an introduction to a future lesson, background material that enriches student understanding, an exercise that improves student skills, or part of a long-term project.

I.b. Sample Activity-Based Middle-Level English Lesson (developed by Maureen Murphy)

UNIT: Exploring Character in Literature

AIM QUESTION: How does a person's actions teach us about her or his character?

GOALS/OBJECTIVES (STANDARDS):

Explain the literal meaning of a passage, identify who was involved, what happened, where it happened, what events led up to these developments, and what consequences or outcomes followed.

Compare and contrast stories with similar themes.

View information from a variety of perspectives.

Translate images and ideas into different formats.

Participate in interpersonal and group activities.

MAIN IDEAS/UNDERSTANDINGS:

Acts of generosity to friends and strangers are important values in many cultures and religions.

Stories of hospitality are used to teach values.

Actions toward strangers, especially during hard times, reveal the character of individuals.

Hospitality stories are an important part of the cultural and literary legacy of famine-era Ireland.

MATERIALS:

Activity sheets with edited passages from "Mrs. Fitzgerald and the Milk" and "A Meal for a Stranger."

Pencils, paper, and crayons.

DO NOW ACTIVITY (Individual assignment):

Read an edited version of "Mrs. Fitzgerald and the Milk." Answer the following questions.

1. Why was Mrs. Fitzgerald well known?
2. What happened that surprised Mr. Fitzgerald?
3. What is the lesson or moral of this story?

MOTIVATION ACTIVITY (Full-class discussion):

Did you or someone you know ever do a good deed for someone else? Tell us about the good deed and why you did it. How did this act of generosity make you feel? Why?

TRANSITIONAL QUESTION:

Do you feel generosity is an important value to teach children? Explain.

LESSON ACTIVITIES (Full-class and group assignments):

- Teacher reads aloud "Mrs. Fitzgerald and the Milk."
- Students should write down words that describe Mrs. and Mr. Fitzgerald.
- Why was Mrs. Fitzgerald well known? Why did Mr. Fitzgerald want to keep all of the milk? What happened that surprised Mr. Fitzgerald?
- Make a list of terms that describe Mrs. and Mr. Fitzgerald on the board. Which of the Fitzgeralds would you rather have as a neighbor? Why?
- What is the lesson or moral of this story?
- Introduce the story "A Meal for a Stranger." It is from a time in Ireland known as the Great Hunger when the potato crop failed repeatedly and there was much starvation.
- Discuss the terms starvation and famine. Is there hunger and famine in the world today? What can we do about it? Would you share your food if you had very little but a stranger had none? Explain.
- Working in pairs or teams of four, students should read and discuss an edited version of "A Meal for a Stranger" and answer the following questions.
  1. Whom did the woman find in her kitchen?

2. What difficult decision did she make?

3. What is the lesson or moral of this story?

4. How are the two stories similar and different?

- Discuss "A Meal for a Stranger." What is the lesson or moral of this story? How are the two stories similar and different? Which story do you find more effective at showing the character of the people? Explain. Which story do you find more effective at teaching the value of generosity? Explain.

KEY QUESTIONS:

How do acts of generosity make you feel? Why?

Do you feel generosity is an important value to teach children? Explain.

Which of the Fitzgeralds would you rather have as a neighbor? Why?

Would you share your food if you had very little but a stranger had none? Explain.

Which story do you find more effective at showing the character of the people? Explain.

Which story do you find more effective at teaching the value of generosity? Explain.

SUMMARY QUESTIONS: How did these stories teach us about the character of these two women? How do they teach readers important social values?

APPLICATION:

Draw a picture illustrating characters and scenes from one of the texts that shows how actions reveal character. Be prepared to explain your drawing to the class (Note: Depending on time, drawings will be presented in this lesson or the next day).

HOMEWORK ASSIGNMENT:

- Complete drawings.
- Write a poem or brief story where someone's actions reveal their character. Be prepared to share your writing with the class.

I.c. Sample Activity Sheet

NAME: _____

AIM: How do a person's actions teach us about their character?

DO NOW: Read "Mrs. Fitzgerald and the Milk" and answers questions 1–3.

MRS. FITZGERALD AND THE MILK

Mrs. Fitzgerald lived in County Cork, Ireland. She was a good woman who never refused to give milk to the poor. Often her husband was not happy. He would blame her for giving away milk and letting their calves go hungry. One day while he was working in the fields he saw a line of poor people by the door of the house. Mrs. Fitzgerald was giving each of them a pitcher of milk. He became angry and ran home.

"You are giving away all of our milk," he shouted. "The calves will go without and we will have no money to live on. What will happen to our own children?" Then he stormed away towards the dairy barn. Mrs. Fitzgerald worried what would happen when he found the pails of milk were empty. But when he returned from the barn, he was smiling. He had had a wonderful surprise. All of the pails were filled to the brim with milk or cream. As he walked back to the field he was whistling. Never again did Mr. Fitzgerald interfere when his wife gave away milk to the poor. The more milk she gave away, the more the family seemed to prosper.

QUESTIONS:

1. Why was Mrs. Fitzgerald well known?
2. What happened that surprised Mr. Fitzgerald?
3. What is the lesson or moral of this story?

LEARNING ACTIVITY: Working in teams, read and discuss "A Meal for a Stranger" and answer questions 1–4.

A MEAL FOR A STRANGER

Near the village there lived an old woman and her husband. They lived on a small farm and were very poor. One day the husband and a friend were working in a field not far from the house. As dinner time approached, the old woman prepared a meal of porridge for them and placed three plates on the table. Soon she went outside to call the men into the house to eat.

When she returned to her kitchen, she found a stranger. He had a wild, hungry look on his face. He said that he was starving and asked the woman for something to eat. Even though she only had a little bit of porridge herself, she told him he could have a meal. He quickly ate one serving and then asked for more. She gave him another serving and he finished that one also. Then he thanked the old woman and left.

As soon as he had gone the husband and his friend entered the house. She asked them if they had seen the stranger, but they replied, "No." She was puzzled and told them what had happened. Her husband said, "You have done the right thing. One portion of porridge will be enough for the three of us." From that day on the family's luck changed. The old woman and her husband, their children and their grandchild all had plenty to eat and happy lives.

QUESTIONS:

1. Whom did the woman find in her kitchen?
2. What difficult decision did she make?
3. What is the lesson or moral of this story?
4. How are the two stories similar and different?

I.d. Outline for an Activity-Based Lesson

UNIT: _____

AIM QUESTION: _____

GOALS/OBJECTIVES (STANDARDS): _____

_____

MAIN IDEAS/UNDERSTANDINGS/CONCEPTS: _____

_____

_____

_____

MATERIALS: _____

DO NOW ACTIVITY: _____

_____

_____

MOTIVATION ACTIVITY: _____

_____

_____

TRANSITION QUESTION(S): _____

_____

_____

LESSON ACTIVITY(IES): _____

_____

_____

_____

KEY QUESTIONS: _____

_____

_____

SUMMARY QUESTION: _____

APPLICATION: _____

HOMEWORK ASSIGNMENT: _____

II. A Developmental Lesson Format

The developmental lesson is designed to teach about a major concept, event, or relationship, and it is tailored to one lesson period. A lesson has an aim, either in the form of a question or a statement, that defines the topic for the day. Sometimes a teacher will open the lesson with the aim already written on the board and sometimes the aim question or statement will be elicited from students during a motivation. Key to the developmental lesson is systematic questioning designed to achieve specific learning objectives. Carefully constructed questions are used to draw information from students in order to develop an outline of notes on the board. Generally, a model outline is available in advance. Medial summary questions are used to help students summarize learning at crucial points in the lesson. By the end of the lesson, multiple students answer the aim question or if it is a statement, a question based on it. Medial summary questions, final summary questions and applications are also used to assess student understanding.

II.a. Ingredients for a Developmental Lesson

Aim: a question that a particular lesson is designed to answer or a statement or phrase introducing the topic of a lesson. Usually it is written on the board at the start of the lesson. Sometimes it is elicited from students during the early stages of a lesson.

Performance objectives (standards): specific content and skills students are expected to master by the end of the lesson. Lessons usually have between three and five objectives.

Preparation: prior classroom instruction or homework that prepares student for this lesson.

Development: outline of the actual lesson.

Motivation: an introductory question that reviews prior preparation and establishes the topic that will be examined.

Questions: prepared in advance and narrowly focused. Designed to elicit information from students based on prior preparation.

Notes: information obtained from students is translated into a detailed outline that is placed on the board.

Medial summary questions: promote deeper probing and classroom dialogue. Used to monitor student progress toward achieving objectives during the lesson.

Final summary question(s): Based on the aim question, it integrates material from the entire lesson and allows teacher to assess student understanding and achievement of objectives.

Application: extra optional question(s) that draws on and broadens what students are learning in the unit. These can be used as review, additional assessment, or as transitions to future lessons.

Homework: independent work that scaffolds on the lesson to prepare students for the next lesson.

II.b. Sample Developmental Mathematics Lesson
(developed by Rhonda Eisenberg)

AIM QUESTION/STATEMENT: How can we use similar triangles to solve problems?

PERFORMANCE OBJECTIVES (STANDARDS):
1. Review the relationship between corresponding sides and angles of similar triangles
2. Apply the properties of similar triangles to find the heights of various figures
3. Solve the problems involving indirect measure using similar triangles

PREPARATION:
1. PREVIOUS HOMEWORK: Problems from textbook on properties of similar triangles
2. PREVIOUS LESSON: What are the properties of similar triangles?

DEVELOPMENT:
1. MOTIVATION QUESTION: In a summer camp a dead tree had to be cut down. The tree stood 16 yards from the recreation hall. Since the tree was leaning in the direction of the recreation hall, it seemed best to let it fall in that direction. Would it hit the building? What do you think? How would you figure out if the tree would hit the recreation hall?
2. QUESTIONS/NOTES/MEDIAL QUESTIONS:

QUESTIONS	NOTES (OUTLINE)
1. What mathematical principles can help solve this problem?	1. When two triangles are similar, corresponding sides are in proportion.
2. What is the relationship between similar triangles?	2. When two triangles are similar, corresponding angles are congruent.
3. Once we know that two triangles are similar, what is the relationship between corresponding sides?	3. If we have information about the sides of one of the similar triangles, we can calculate information about the second triangle.
4. What is the relationship between corresponding angles?	

MEDIAL SUMMARY	How can the properties of similar triangles help us discover the heights of very tall objects?

QUESTIONS	NOTES (OUTLINE)
1. How can we indirectly measure the height of the dead tree using a similar triangle?	1. Draw and label a diagram showing the triangles created by the girl and her shadow and the tree and its shadow.
2. If a 5 foot tall girl casts a shadow 4 feet long at the same time as the tree casts a shadow 20 feet long, how tall is the tree?	2. Translate the diagram into mathematical notation and solve the problem. $(5 : X = 4 : 20)$; $(4X = 100)$; $(X = 25)$

3. FINAL SUMMARY QUESTION	How can the properties of similar triangles help us solve the problem of the dead tree?
4. APPLICATION	Assign students additional problems to solve individually or in groups from the text book. Volunteers place additional problems on the board. Class reviews solutions.
5. HOMEWORK ASSIGNMENT	Assignment from textbook reviewing using properties of similar triangles to solve problems.

II.c. Outline for a Developmental Lesson

AIM QUESTION/STATEMENT: _____

_____

PERFORMANCE OBJECTIVES (STANDARDS):

    1._____

    2._____

    3._____

PREPARATION:

    1. PREVIOUS HOMEWORK: _____

_____

    2. PREVIOUS LESSON: _____

DEVELOPMENT:

    1. MOTIVATION QUESTION: _____

_____

2. QUESTIONS/NOTES/MEDIAL QUESTIONS

QUESTIONS 1. 2. 3.	NOTES (OUTLINE)
MEDIAL SUMMARY	
QUESTIONS 1. 2. 3.	NOTES (OUTLINE)
MEDIAL SUMMARY	
QUESTIONS 1. 2. 3.	NOTES (OUTLINE)
3. FINAL LESSON SUMMARY QUESTION(S)	
4. APPLICATION	
5. HOMEWORK ASSIGNMENT	

III. Format for Hunter's Approach to Lesson Planning

A number of school districts across the country have adopted a seven-step lesson design that is part of the "Madeline Hunter Teacher Effectiveness Training Program." This design, which is intended to be applicable in all subject areas, tries to systematize lesson planning. In theory, it makes it easier for teachers to plan and for students to follow the development of a lesson and ensures that teachers have clear learning objectives for their students that are achievable by the end of the instruction period. Each section of the lesson plan may include questions that the teacher uses to measure student understanding up until that point.

III.a. Ingredients for Hunter's Approach to Lesson Planning

Anticipatory set: a brief opening activity or a statement that focuses student attention on what they will be learning.

Objectives (standards): a detailed list of what students will know or be able to do at the end of the instruction period. It includes information that a teacher provides to students about what they will be able to do at the end of the lesson and how the lesson is relevant to their learning.

Instructional input: information that a teacher provides students so they can perform a skill or complete a process—questions that a teacher asks to insure that students understand procedures.

Modeling the information: The teacher leads the class in an activity so students understand what they are supposed to do.

Checking for understanding: Teachers ask questions and examine student work to ensure that students possess the essential information and skills necessary to achieve the instructional objective.

Guided practice: Teachers assist students as they work on assignments to ensure that student efforts are accurate and successful.

Independent practice (assessment): Students have mastered the basic skills and understandings needed to complete activities without direct teacher intervention. This is the final measure of whether lesson objectives have been achieved. This can also include a homework assignment.

III.b. Sample Hunter Approach Middle-Level Science Lesson (developed by S. Maxwell Hines)

ANTICIPATORY SET: Students will:

1. Examine a period on a page.
2. Measure the size of the period and hypothesize how many microorganisms could be contained on the period.
3. Discuss ways to confirm their hypotheses.
4. Discuss the function of a microscope.

OBJECTIVES (STANDARDS): Students will:

1. Identify the component parts of the microscope with an accuracy of 90%.
2. Produce drawings of slides viewed under the microscope with an accuracy of 90%.
3. Calculate the size of microorganisms based on the use of the microscope with an accuracy of 90%.

INSTRUCTIONAL INPUT: The teacher will:

1. Review safety rules for classroom equipment, including the proper care, transport, and storage of microscopes and slides.
2. Examine a diagram of the parts of a microscope with students.
3. Have students hypothesize the purpose of each component as it is introduced.
4. Carefully explain the concepts surrounding magnification and scale, as these concepts tend to cause confusion in novice learners.
5. Confirm or correct students' hypotheses.

MODELING: The teacher will:

1. Model the steps needed to use the microscope to identify bacteria on a period.
2. Display a list of the steps needed to use a microscope.

CHECK UNDERSTANDING: The teacher will:

1. Have students hone their basic microscopy skills by giving them a series of slides to view and draw. If students are familiar with the materials they are viewing under the microscope, have them diagram their drawings. (This provides the teacher with the initial assessment of appropriate microscopy use).
2. Circle around the room and assist each student in developing her or his microscopy skills.
3. Ask a series of questions of struggling students to identify the step at which they begin having trouble.

4. Guard against doing the work for the student. Students must be allowed to struggle a bit in order to learn proper microscopy.

5. Evaluate student drawings to make sure they know how to use the microscope before proceeding.

6. Close lesson with review of lesson and preview of next lesson.

GUIDED PRACTICE: Students will:

1. Examine an area the size of a period under low power and high power using a slide containing microorganisms.

2. Draw what they see under each power setting.

3. Count the number of organisms they see within an area the size of the period.

4. Review and integrate calculations, paying special attention to using estimation as a guide to evaluating the accuracy of answers.

INDEPENDENT PRACTICE (ASSESSMENT): Students will:

1. As a homework assignment, calculate the size of the organisms they saw using the size of the period they identified in class.

2. For additional credit, identify the specific types of organisms they saw and diagram their drawing.

III.c. Outline for Hunter's Approach to Lesson Planning

ANTICIPATORY SET	
OBJECTIVES (STANDARDS)	
INSTRUCTIONAL INPUT	
MODELING	
CHECK UNDERSTANDING	
GUIDED PRACTICE	
INDEPENDENT PRACTICE (ASSESSMENT)	

IV. Format for a Streamlined Activity-Based Lesson Plan

Student teachers are often overwhelmed by lesson planning, especially once they become responsible for a full teaching program. In our reflective practice seminar for student teachers we played around with ideas for a simplified, minimalist format for activity-based lessons. It is organized around questions that basically ask, "What do you want to achieve in this lesson?" and "How will you do it?"

IV.a. Ingredients for a Streamlined Social Studies Lesson Plan

Unit: Where does this lesson fit in the curriculum?

Lesson: What topic or skill will students learn in this lesson?

Main ideas: What are the main ideas (maximum of three) students need to know about this topic?

Materials: What materials (e.g., activity sheet, map, song) will I use to present information and teach academic skills?

Aim: What overall question am I asking the class to answer?

Do now: What activity, if any, will I use to settle students and establish a context?

Motivation: How will I open the lesson and capture student interest?

Activities: What activities will I use to help students discover what they need to learn?

Key questions: How will I summarize and assess student learning?

Homework: What must students learn on their own to reinforce what we did in this lesson or to introduce the next topic?

Follow-up: What topics come next?

IV.b. Sample Streamlined High School Social Studies Lesson Plan (developed by Alan Singer)

UNIT: The Growth of Sectionalism—the Antebellum South

LESSON: Lives and hopes of enslaved Africans in the American South

1. What are the main ideas (maximum of three) students need to know about this topic?
   1. Traditional songs are primary sources that help historians understand the lives and dreams of ordinary people.
   2. Enslaved Africans experienced slavery as oppressive and wanted freedom.
   3. Songs from the era of slavery express the dreams and aspirations of enslaved Africans.
2. What materials (e.g., activity sheet, map, song) will I present? Activity Sheet: African American Songs from the Era of Slavery; audiocassettes and tape recorder.
3. What question will I ask the class to answer (aim)? How do songs express the dreams and aspirations of Africans enslaved in the United States?
4. What activity, if any, will I use to settle students and establish a context (do now)? Read "All the Pretty Little Horses" and answer questions 1–3.
5. How will I open the lesson (motivation) and capture student interest? How can we learn about the ideas and feelings of ordinary people from the past? Brainstorm a list of ideas on the board.
6. What activities will I use to help students discover what they need to learn (activities)? Read the lyrics to the songs and listen to recordings. The first song is a do now for individuals. Groups will analyze and report on the other two songs.
7. How will we summarize and assess student learning (key questions)? What does this song tell us about the experience of enslaved Africans? What does this song tell us about the lives and hopes of enslaved Africans in the American South?
8. What must students learn on their own to reinforce what we did in this lesson or to introduce the next topic (homework)? Read pages *xxx*. Answer questions 1–4 on page *xxx*. Take one of the three songs and rewrite it as a "rap." Be prepared to perform your version in class.
9. What topics come next (follow-up)? Tomorrow: Slave resistance; After: Debate over slavery.

*IV.c. Sample Activity Sheet: African American Songs
from the Era of Slavery*

NAME:_____

AIM: How do songs express the dreams and aspirations of Africans enslaved in the United States?

DO NOW: Read "All the Pretty Little Horses" and answers questions 1–3.

All the Pretty Little Horses—The key to understanding this lullaby is that there are two babies.

Hush-a-bye, don't you cry, go to sleep my little baby,
When you wake, you shall have all the pretty little horses,
Blacks and bays, dapples and grays, all the pretty little horses.
Way down yonder, in the meadow, lies my poor little lambie,
With bees and butterflies peckin' out its eyes,
The poor little things crying Mammy.

Questions

1. Who are the two babies in this lullaby? Which baby is the woman singing to?
2. Why do you think the woman was assigned to care for this baby?
3. What does this song tell us about the experience of enslaved Africans?

ACTIVITY: Working in teams, read and discuss one of the songs and answer questions 1–3.

Go Down, Moses—This song is an African American version of Exodus from the Old Testament.

Chorus—Go down, Moses,

Way down in Egypt land.
Tell old Pharaoh to let my people go.
When Israel was in Egypt land, Let my people go.
Oppressed so hard they could not stand, Let my people go. *Chorus.*
"Thus spoke the Lord," bold Moses said, Let my people go.
"If not, I'll smite your first-born dead." Let my people go. *Chorus.*
Old Pharaoh said he'd go across, Let my people go.
But Pharaoh and his host were lost, Let my people go. *Chorus.*
No more shall they in bondage toil, Let my people go.
They shall go forth with Egypt's spoil, Let my people go. *Chorus.*

Questions

1. What does Moses say to Pharaoh?
2. Why do you think enslaved African Americans sang a song about ancient Israelites?
3. What does this song tell us about the experience of enslaved Africans?

Follow the Drinking Gourd—This song is supposed to contain an oral map of the Underground Railroad. The "drinking gourd" is the star constellation known as the Big Dipper.
Chorus—Follow the drinking gourd, follow the drinking gourd,
For the old man is awaiting for to carry you to freedom,
If you follow the drinking gourd.

When the sun comes up and the first quail calls, follow the drinking gourd,
For the old man is awaiting for to carry you to freedom, if you follow the drinking gourd.
Chorus.
The river bank will make a mighty good road, the dead trees will show you the way,
Left foot, peg foot, travelin' on, follow the drinking gourd. *Chorus.*
The river ends between two hills, follow the drinking gourd,
There's another river on the other side, follow the drinking gourd. *Chorus.*

Questions

1. Why does the song tell passengers on the Underground Railroad to follow the "drinking gourd"?
2. Why would runaway slaves prefer an oral map to a written map?
3. What does this song tell us about the experience of enslaved Africans?

IV.d. Outline for a Streamlined Lesson Plan

UNIT: Where does this lesson fit in the curriculum? _____

LESSON: What topic or skill will students learn in this lesson? _____

_____

1. What are the main ideas (maximum of three) students need to know about this topic?

   1. _____

   2. _____

   3. _____

2. What materials (e.g., ACTIVITY SHEET, MAP, SONG) will I present?

_____

_____

3. What question will I ask the class to answer (AIM)? _____

_____

_____

4. What activity, if any, will I use to settle students and establish a context (DO NOW)?

_____

_____

_____

5. How will I open the lesson (MOTIVATION) and capture student interest?

_____

_____

6. What activities will I use to help students discover what they need to learn (ACTIVITIES)?

_____

_____

7. How will we summarize and assess student learning (KEY QUESTIONS)? _____

_____

8. What must students learn on their own to reinforce what we did in this lesson or to introduce the next topic (HOMEWORK)?_____

9. What topics come next (FOLLOW-UP)?

Tomorrow _____

Day After _____

SECTION F: BECOMING A TEACHER 3: WHAT MAKES SOMEONE SUCCESSFUL AS A TEACHER?

I Will Not Let the Wheelchair Be an Excuse
By Dennis Mooney

When Dennis was 21, he broke his neck during a diving accident. Since then, he has moved around using a wheelchair. As a teenager, Dennis was an indifferent student. After he was injured, he had to relearn the ordinary tasks of daily living and figure out what he wanted to do with his life. He feels that the two things which have been his greatest assets in becoming a teacher are his memories of being an indifferent student and his experience of overcoming his disability. He remembers how other student teachers complained during seminars how hard it was to learn how to teach. Dennis never complained. For him, "teaching a classroom of teenagers is difficult," but "it is easy compared to being paralyzed." When he wrote this essay, Dennis was 34 years old and in his second year as a high school teacher.—Alan Singer

As a high school and college student I was academically strong but very lazy. I was the same way in swimming. My coach thought if I took time to do my strokes properly and practice I could be good, but I never liked to practice that much. I did not have the determination. I had attended a community college on and off for 2 years before I had my accident while diving. My dream was to make lots of money, but I was never motivated to achieve it.

After the accident, I was in the hospital for 9 months—2 weeks in an intensive care unit and the rest of the time in rehabilitation. At the start, I figured my paralysis was temporary. When I was first injured I could not move anything from my neck down. Slowly, I started to get movement back in my arms and the doctors were surprised. When you cannot move your arms up and down, and then you can, it is a big thing. My friends used to hold a soda can up for me to sip from and one day I lifted it myself; I was so excited I let go of the can and I spilt it all over my lap. I thought the progress would continue, but at a certain point it stopped. In occupational therapy they were trying to teach me how to do things differently, and I kept telling them that I did not have to learn because I was not going to be in a wheelchair for the rest of my life. I planned to take the police officers exam.

Today, many young people with paralysis wait for a miracle cure instead of going on with their lives. Part of the problem is that they are released from rehabilitation programs much too quickly. The idea is that people should resume their regular lives, but you cannot go back to who you were before. You may be physically ready for the outside world, but that does not mean you are mentally and emotionally ready. I needed 9 months to accept what had happened to me and to adjust to it. I was lucky I had a support network of friends who pushed me to try things. A year after the accident they had me back in the water.

When I got out of "rehab," I knew I had to go to school and be serious about it. A friend from college brought me to see one of our professors and he encouraged me to start school right away that summer. I was not ready yet, but I began in the fall. It was a good decision. If I had waited longer, I might not have gone back.

While I was in the hospital I discovered that I liked working with children. There were little kids in the hospital in wheelchairs who were being taught to walk. I was always amazed as they wheeled up and down the hallways laughing. Being in a wheelchair was the normal thing for them. They would cry every time adults made them get out of their chairs. I realized the medical staff did not really understand the way the children felt, so I tried to help them learn to walk by coaxing them out of their wheelchairs.

When I started at a 4-year college, I met a history teacher who kept asking questions and he got me to think about things I had never considered before. I finished an economics degree, rejected the idea of working on Wall Street and thought I might want to become a college professor. A friend reminded me how much I liked working with children and I made a spur-of-the-moment decision to enter a graduate program in teacher education.

I know I am disabled, that I am handicapped, and my solution is to overcompensate. I will not ask for any special consideration at work because I do not want people to think I cannot do the job. I will not let the wheelchair be an excuse for me. The day I went to take the teacher certification test there was an ice storm, the sidewalks were not cleared, and I could not get out of my van. Almost every person who took that test was dropped off by someone else. I would not let anyone take me, so I missed the test.

My philosophy of life and teaching is that nothing is worth freaking out over. While teaching a classroom of teenagers is difficult, it is easy compared to being paralyzed. If I have a problem in a class, I have to figure out a solution. I had to figure out how to shave, how to brush my teeth again, how to feed myself. If I can do these things, I know I can find a solution to a teaching problem.

When I started student teaching I had an entire monologue figured out about what I was going to say to students about being in a wheelchair. I began the opening lesson, "As you can see I am in a wheelchair and I can't write on the board, so we will have to work together in this class." I was so nervous, that was the end of my speech.

My first semester as a regular teacher, I told students, "This class is not about my being in a wheelchair. I am your teacher. I just happen to be in a wheelchair. If you have any questions, you are free to ask me those questions after class." During the term, only three students spoke with me about it. The next time around, I did not even bring the topic up. I figured when they walked into class, they saw I was in a wheelchair. At this point, most of the kids had seen me in the building or heard about me and they knew who I was.

There are teachers who react to my being in a chair and they have made comments that betray their prejudices, but I do not really care what others think anymore. That is their problem, not mine. After a year of teaching the school assigned me to teach the advanced placement economic classes. Obviously, my supervisors thought I was qualified to do it. I was even nominated for an award as an economics teacher.

People ask me how I adjust my teaching to being in a wheelchair. The fact is I never had to adjust because I was always in a chair. I never taught any other way. The people who have to adjust are my students so I try to find ways to help them. The big difference for students is note taking. I never use the board and I rarely use transparencies. I tell students that in my class they will learn to figure out what is important and that I will help them. I have had about 850 students since I started teaching and only 3 have complained that they were having trouble. I told each of them that I understood their problem and I would try to be more systematic and give them a signal when to take notes. Now I tell classes, "When I repeat something, that is your signal that it is important. The second time I say something you better start writing." Some classes are really good about it. In other classes, I have to repeat things three or four times.

Beginning teachers worry a lot about controlling their classes. I am not sure how I control the class. I just go in and I am who I am. I treat students with respect and I expect to be treated the same way. I tell students, "I can be your best friend or your worst enemy—I hope to be your best teacher, but that is up to you. If you do not want to do the work, I cannot force you to, but I will not allow you to disrupt the learning of others." My first term, when students were noisy, I would threaten them with a quiz. I ended up bringing home stacks of papers to read. It aggravated me when I realized the only person being punished was me. Now I sit in class and wait. I say, "Whenever you are ready," and they get quiet. My latest technique is to shake my wrist and I tell them to all shake their wrists. When they ask why, I say "You are going to be doing a lot of writing and you need to warm-up so you do not get cramps." Now, when they are not paying attention, I shake my wrist and they pay attention. Respecting students means giving them credit for being intelligent. Because I was a "65 student," I understand what is going on in class and this helps me figure out ways to get them to learn.

I do not have a lot of rules, but the ones I have, I expect to be obeyed. Once a community is established in class you can pull back, but you have to start with consistent rules. If students have too much freedom at the beginning, it is impossible to take it back. My first term, a student complained that I kept changing the rules. He said, "We don't know what you want." I got mad at him, but then I realized he was right. All teachers have to learn how to be the teacher. When you screw up, you will have to live with it. The beauty of teaching is you get to fix your mistakes when you have a new set of students. I learned in life that you can fix things and that there are things in life that are more important than who got the highest score on the test.

* * *

JOIN THE CONVERSATION—OVERCOMING DIFFICULTIES

Frank Bowe, head of the special education program at Hofstra University and a nationally renown advocate for the rights of people with disabilities, believes that what is most remarkable about Dennis is not that he teaches from a wheelchair, but that he really wants to be a teacher and it shows every day. According to Frank, "Dennis is doing what he wants to do and he is paying a high price in a lot of ways to do it. The wheelchair is secondary to this joy he derives from teaching."

Questions to Consider:

1. In your view, what qualities make Dennis a successful teacher?
2. How did he figure out how to be successful in the classroom?
3. Were his life experiences handicaps or sources of strengths as he became a teacher? Explain.
4. What aspects of his approach to teaching do you agree with or disagree with? Explain.
5. If you were on a school's hiring committee and knew about Dennis' accident, would you have interviewed him for a job or hired him? Explain.

SECTION G: TEACHING STORIES 2

How I Learned to Be a Teacher
By David Morris

Dr. David Morris is one of the teachers I wrote about in the "My Best Teachers" section earlier in this chapter. I cannot overemphasize the importance of colleagues who share your goals and approaches to education. They are partners in transforming the lives of students and schools. Since I left Edward R. Murrow High School, David and I have continued to work together. He has been a cooperating teacher for observers and student teachers, a high school assistant principal, and an adjunct assistant professor at Hofstra University.—Alan Singer

I was born in Barbados in 1958. At that time Barbados was part of the British West Indies. Today, it is an independent country with a population of about 260,000 people. I lived in Barbados until I was 19, when I immigrated to the United States and settled with family members in Brooklyn, New York. The neighborhood where I lived was largely West Indian.

While I was a child in Barbados, my father was a minister. Because of his vocation, my family moved every 2 to 3 years. My mother was as religious as my father. Schooling was important to my parents, but as a young child I was never interested in learning. I loved playing outside, building things, doing all sort of different things. I was not bad. I just did not want to do school work. As a result, I was always being punished.

The public schools we attended as children were very, very crowded, so it was easy not to do the work. They did not have enough books to go around. Just the teacher and the board. The common entrance exam at age 10 or 11 determined your life. If you passed the first two parts, you moved on. If you did not pass, you stayed in elementary school until age 16. My older brothers and sister scored high on the exams and went to the top public high schools. Because of my poor performance on the common entrance exams, I would have been denied admission to these programs, so my mother decided I would attend a private school.

In Barbados, teaching meant lecturing to the class, and students who did not pay attention faced physical punishment. The teacher told you a story and you wrote everything down. If you did not do well on tests, you got lashes. If you did not do the homework, you got lashes. In the early grades, I occasionally got lashes. However, in high school I was a better student and was always at the top of my class.

My father died when I was 9 years old and this was a major turning point in my life. We moved closer to the city and I joined the Boy Scouts. I gained a lot of confidence in myself from my experience in the Boy Scouts: marching at parades, recruiting other boys, and taking responsibility This helped me in school. I began to pay attention. By the time I finished high school, I was the top performer in my school on the Cambridge University O'Level examinations.

My mother moved to the United States in 1973, but I stayed behind in Barbados with my four brothers and two sisters. There is a tradition in the Caribbean that an older sibling takes care of the younger children because parents are often forced to migrate to find work.

When I came to the United States, I worked in a coat factory. The factory was started by two Polish Jewish brothers. They were survivors of the World War II concentration camps. Half of the people who worked at the factory were Holocaust survivors and most of the others were Dominicans or Puerto Ricans.

I worked at the factory for about 9 months until I got laid off; then, I started school at Hunter College in the City University of New York. At that time, I thought of my stay in the United States as temporary, so I wanted to study something I could use when I returned to Barbados. Because I was considering a career in law, I majored in both Political Science and Communications, and minored in history.

When I graduated from college, I got a job at the public library and entered the New York University School of Education's doctoral program in communications. But life takes funny bounces. My mother knew someone who worked at the New York City Board of Education, and she was able to get me a teaching position. Because of my background in communications, I was assigned to teach at Edward R. Murrow High School, a special theme magnet school. When I started at Murrow, I had no educational credentials. I decided to kill two birds with one stone and used electives in the New York University doctoral program to take the courses I needed for teacher certification.

When I started teaching, I took a crash course in classroom management from a veteran teacher, and this helped me become much better organized. Because of my own experience as a beginning teacher, I focus on the importance of providing students with a structured environment and developing organizational skills in my teaching methods classes. I especially remember one education professor whose lessons and readings gave me a broader understanding of what it means to be a teacher. He had an interesting, student-oriented style and he made the philosophy of educators like John Dewey seem both concrete and alive. The introduction to Dewey was important for me because the approach to teaching used at Murrow High School was based on Dewey's ideas.

The special thing about Murrow High School is that it is a public school in New York City with a very diverse student body that emphasizes that teenagers need to experience freedom. Students have independent time built into their schedules when they can sit in the hall reading or talking with friends, can go to the library, or can work in an office. I think kids need freedom so they can learn to take responsibility. Of course, there are problems. Some students don't deal well with freedom, and they actually mess themselves up. Murrow is a pretty middle-class school, and I am not convinced its practices would work in a more troubled school or a school with a high concentration of students with weak academic skills. In communities like the one I teach in now, students have high aspirations, but they do not have role models who have been successful in school. They often do not understand the work that is necessary to perform at a high academic level. They need teachers and administrators to provide greater structure. But I think as kids adapt and perform better in school, increasing freedom and individual responsibility is an important goal.

The most important part of my education as a teacher was getting an opportunity to teach and getting feedback from my students. At the beginning I taught only communications classes, but at the end of my first year I was assigned to teach social studies as well. In the communications classes, I had my students work in groups and produce projects, but in social studies I tended to tell the kids what I wanted them to know. My students finally asked me, "How come downstairs with communications your classes are so exciting and upstairs in social studies you are so boring?" So I said to myself, "Let me change." I was teaching about the industrial revolution at the time. Instead of just telling students about the period, I had them act as factory owners and workers and they loved it.

I learned how to be a teacher by discovery and reflection, by acting as a teacher in school, and by discussing ideas about teaching with my supervisors and in my education classes. It made sense that my students would also learn through this process. Instead of telling them information, I gave them things to examine as historians and I asked them questions to guide them through the process of analyzing and understanding the past.

Later, I became a more effective teacher when I studied teaching and supervision techniques at Bank Street College. I learned how to organize groups and make learning fun, but more important, I realized that being a successful teacher means always learning yourself. Teaching is something you have to work hard at all the time. Many young teachers say I can do this or that already so I do not have more to learn. "I'm good already." But there is no such thing as being a finished product as a teacher. At a minimum, you always have to work at being good because your students are always changing and challenging you.

My approach as a teacher today is to set up situations for students to examine, individually, in groups, or as a class, so they can learn from experience. As a teacher educator, I try to model what I do as a high school teacher. Sometimes my teacher education students get frustrated because they want me to tell them what to do or what to think. I always participate in class discussions, but I refuse to intervene to settle disagreements or lecture to them. They have to figure things out for themselves. I will not be in their secondary school classrooms with them to give them answers.

My communication background was a definite advantage as I learned to define my pedagogy as a teacher. Creating videos, television programs, and promotional campaigns requires putting things together into an integrated package that makes sense. My approach to teaching means helping students draw connections and put together their own intellectual packages.

Growing up, I loved to hear stories. History is my hobby. I love the story part. But I consider myself a teacher, rather than an historian or a history teacher. For me, teaching is teaching. Give me a package to present and I will find a way to teach it. I taught math, English, and science in evening high school equivalency programs. I know many educators argue that content knowledge is fundamental to effective teaching. But I consider it more important to focus on the process of learning. When I prepare lessons, I spend more time developing exciting ways to present material in class, ways that will make it more likely for students to remember the content information. I also focus on designing activities that will help students develop their thinking skills and literacy within the academic discipline. For me, the activities and skills, the package, are more important than the content. Without the package, students will never remember the content.

When I start planning new lessons or a new unit in any subject area, I pick out books and articles on the topic and try to figure out the key narrative to present in class. Once I figure out the story, I look for documents, maps, cartoons, pictures, and other materials that complete the "package." My goal is to organize the material in such a way that the students, working in groups, individually, or as a full class, can analyze the material and discover the story for themselves. I organize each lesson around four or five documents that illustrate main ideas. The kids have to find the components of the story in the material. I continually ask them, "What is the story here?"

Another aspect of successful teaching is connecting with students. I have had a lot of success with immigrant students from different parts of the world—Russia, the Caribbean, China, and Central America—because they realize that I experienced many of the same things they are going through. At Murrow High School we had a number of Russian students and I learned to say simple things like "hello" in Russian. They saw this as a sign of interest in their lives. Eventually, I learned a little of their language and this helped us get along. Sometimes, I shocked new Russian kids. They wondered, "How does this Black guy know Russian?" Clearly, you do not have to be an immigrant yourself to make these kinds of connections.

As an assistant principal, I see a lot of students when they are in trouble. One of the first things I ask a student is where they are from. If they say "Grenada," I talk to them about Grenada. Some of the teachers get upset because this kid just cursed out a teacher and now I am talking with him about his home country. What I am doing is building a connection between us. Later in the discussion, I might ask him, "Would you say the same things to teachers back home?"

I think it is important that I learned to connect with students from a wide variety of cultures. Some people say that I do well with students because I am Black or Caribbean, or because I am an immigrant. But some of the most devoted teachers I have worked with were White and I have worked with Black teachers who grew up in British school systems who never learn to work with kids. Being from Barbados is not the same as growing up Black in an inner-city community in the United States. In the Caribbean, you know you can be a doctor, lawyer, or accountant, or open a business if you choose, because in our society, 95% of the people are Black. Since the abolition of slavery in the 19th century, people have had the opportunity to go to school or learn a trade. Although most Whites in Barbados are well off, they are a small minority. Black people do most of the white collar and blue collar jobs. Black people in the United States have had much greater obstacles because inequality continued into the contemporary era and because this is still a racially divided society that favors Whites.

I actually consider myself a conservative person. I take a practical approach to teaching. The things I do are not revolutionary. I am a successful teacher because I worked hard to learn how and because I am still working at it!

* * *

JOIN THE CONVERSATION—TEACHING IS TEACHING

1. David Morris writes that he considers himself a teacher, rather than an historian or a history teacher. "For me, teaching is teaching. Give me a package to present and I will find a way to teach it. I taught math, English, and science in evening high school equivalency programs. I know many educators argue that content knowledge is fundamental to effective teaching. But I consider it more important to focus on the process of learning." Do you agree or disagree with his position? Explain your views.

2. Charles Cronin is a preservice teacher who helped to review this book. Following discussion of David Morris's "Teaching Story" in class, Charles sent the following e-mail message: "Dr. Morris is saying that we have to try and find things that we have in common with our students. These connections can help to establish a trusting relationship. He uses his experience as an immigrant from Barbados to establish connections with the high school students he teaches. I have taken his methods class and he also used incidents from his daily life to make similar connections with us. I am looking forward to student teaching in the spring. It is my belief that if I can hold on long enough, that I will be able to build the bonds of trust and experience needed to make me a successful teacher."

Question to Consider:

Do you believe it is possible to develop "bonds of trust" with students from backgrounds different from your own? Explain.

SECTION H: WHAT IS THEMATIC TEACHING (IN SOCIAL STUDIES, BIOLOGY, AND EVERYTHING ELSE)?

In his essay, David Morris spoke about presenting a "package" that allows students to discover the underlying "story." I like to call this idea *thematic teaching*. As a high school social studies teacher, I used the first few lessons of the new school year to establish themes classes would be exploring throughout the curriculum. Although I did this in different ways over the years, my favorite way involved getting students to define the *essential questions* they wanted to study, questions that I would then integrate into units, projects, and lessons.

To start, I distributed newspapers and news magazines to teams of students who were assigned to select articles that they believed signaled important issues facing the contemporary world. Teams had to write down the headlines of the articles and their reasons for selecting them. At the end of day 1, I asked at least one group to report on their deliberations, then listed the topics of their articles on poster paper.

On the second day, the rest of the groups reported and we listed the topics of every article. After the presentations, students categorized the issues, identified underlying problems raised by the news articles, and discussed questions they wanted to answer during the year. Articles on racial discrimination, sexual harassment, and police brutality led to questions such as, "Can the United States become a more just society?" Topics such as welfare reform, health care, unemployment, tax breaks, and crime prompted students to ask, "What is the responsibility (or job) of government?" Other questions developed by students have included, "Should the United States be the world's police force?" and "Is technology making the world a better place?" These essential questions were placed on poster boards and hung prominently around the room. Students took pride in the questions they came up with, and the activity increased their willingness to participate in class and furthered our exploration of social studies and history.

Preservice teachers I work with in general methods classes and new teachers in the Hofstra New Teachers Network often accept that this type of thematic teaching can work in social studies, but doubt whether it is possible in other disciplines, especially when teachers are confronted with the requirement that they prepare their students for end-of-the-year standardized assessment tests. The idea that follows developed out of a conversation among Robyn Tornabene, a second-year biology teacher at Long Beach High School on Long Island, New York; S. Maxwell Hines, the science coordinator at Hofstra University; and myself at a New Teachers Network meeting.

The final two paragraphs of Charles Darwin's *Origin of Species* (1859/1964) summarizes what he calls "this view of life." Harvard paleontologist and evolutionary biologist Stephen J. Gould used an exploration of Darwin's view of life as the basis for essays written for the general reader and published in *Natural History* magazine from 1974 through January 2001.

Most secondary school biology teachers I have talked with teach biology as a series of semiautonomous units with a tremendous amount of hard-to-remember detail. They find some students lap it up, whereas others, the majority, either struggle with memorization of seemingly random facts or else give up trying and just muddle through the year.

I believe that Darwin's ideas on the evolution of life on earth, as explored by Gould, provide fundamental themes that pervade the biology curriculum and can help teachers and students make sense out what they are studying. I propose that the entire biology curriculum be used to establish and test Darwin's view of the fundamental relationship between all living things, what Gould calls the "fact of evolution," and the mechanisms for change over time, what Gould identifies as theories that explain evolutionary development. Every unit in the curriculum can address the question, "How does this topic (e.g., the human circulatory system, the nervous system of a frog, environmental problems, the origin of disease) support or challenge Darwin's view of life?" As they approach each new field of study, students explore fundamental similarities and differences between living things in the past and present, the basis for ordering information (taxonomy), and the scientific method for establishing knowledge.

As a final assessment project for "this view of biology," classes can create their own natural history museum. Individual students or student teams would prepare exhibits and reports that question or support Darwin and Gould and elaborate on their own understanding of the science of life.

Some teachers are concerned that placing Darwin and evolution at the center of the biology curriculum will subject them to challenge by religious opponents of evolution and by supervisors worried about test results. The best answer I can come up with is that we do not expect students to understand geometry without understanding its basic axioms, the physical universe without understanding its underlying laws, chemistry without the periodic table, music without notation and scales, or language without grammatical structure. These are fundamental for understanding the entire structure of the discipline. In the same way, evolution explains biology.

JOIN THE CONVERSATION—CHARLES DARWIN'S *ORIGIN OF SPECIES*

To help you consider this idea for a thematic approach to biology (or any subject area), carefully examine the passage from the conclusion to Charles Darwin's 1859 book, *Origin of Species* (Cambridge, MA: Harvard University Press, 1964, pp. 488–490).

> When I view all beings not as special creations, but as the lineal descendants of some few beings, . . . they seem to me to become ennobled. Judging from the past, we may safely infer that not one living species will transmit its unaltered likeness to a distant futurity. And of the species now living very few will transmit progeny of any kind to a far distant futurity; for the manner in which all organic beings are grouped, shows that the greater number of species of each genus, and all the species of many genera, have left no descendants, but have become utterly extinct. We can so far take a prophetic glance into futurity as to foretell that it will be the common and widely-spread species, belonging to the larger and dominant groups, which will ultimately prevail and procreate new and dominant species. As all the living forms of life are the lineal descendants of those which lived long before, . . . we may feel certain that the ordinary succession by generation has never once been broken, and that no cataclysm has desolated the whole world. Hence we may look with some confidence to a secure future of equally inappreciable length. And as natural selection works solely by and for the good of each being, all corporeal and mental endowments will tend to progress towards perfection.
>
> It is interesting to contemplate an entangled bank, clothed with many plants of many kinds, with birds singing on the bushes, with various insects flitting about, and with worms crawling through the damp earth, and to reflect that these elaborately constructed forms, so different from each other, and dependent on each other in so complex a manner, have all been produced by laws acting around us. These laws, taken in the largest sense, being Growth with Reproduction; inheritance which is almost implied by reproduction; Variability from the indirect and direct action of the external conditions of life, and from use and disuse; a Ratio of Increase so high as to lead to a Struggle for Life, and as a consequence to Natural Selection, entailing Divergence of Character and the Extinction of less-improved forms. Thus, from the war of nature, from famine and death, the most exalted object which we are capable of conceiving, namely, the production of the higher animals, directly follows.
>
> There is grandeur in this view of life, with its several powers, having been originally breathed into a few forms or into one; and that, whilst this planet has gone cycling on according to the fixed law of gravity, from so simple a beginning endless forms most beautiful and most wonderful have been, and are being, evolved.

Questions to Consider:

1. Make a list of what you consider the main ideas presented in the passage. Explain whether you agree or disagree with each of these ideas. Note that contemporary scientists do not embrace all of Darwin's conceptions about the mechanism of evolution.

2. Discuss whether Darwin's "view of life" helps you better understand the study of biology.

3. Discuss whether, in your view, thematic teaching offers a useful alternative to listing and explaining relatively unrelated topics and information in your own field.

4. A picture can be worth a thousand words, or at least illustrate what you think you know. Draw a picture of Darwin's view of life as you understand it. Compare it with others. Are differences in the pictures reflections of your views or Darwin's?

This is my list of Darwin's main ideas.

- "I view all beings not as special creations, but as the lineal descendants of some few beings."
- "The greater number of species of each genus, and all the species of many genera, have left no descendants, but have become utterly extinct."
- "It will be the common and widely-spread species, . . . which will ultimately prevail and procreate new and dominant species."
- "Natural selection works solely by and for the good of each being, all corporeal and mental endowments will tend to progress towards perfection."
- "Elaborately constructed forms, so different from each other, and dependent on each other in so complex a manner, have all been produced by laws acting around us."
- "From so simple a beginning endless forms most beautiful and most wonderful have been, and are being, evolved.

SECTION I: SOME USEFUL IDEAS FOR ORGANIZING LESSONS

FIG. 3.2   What does a lesson look like?

Some students are "visual learners." They need a concrete object or an image to help them understand what is usually described using words. Teachers can also be "visual learners" as well. I like to use the following pictures to represent the structure of a lesson.

A. Newspaper Story—The Inverted Pyramid

In basic journalism classes, a newspaper article is described as an "inverted pyramid." An introductory paragraph summarizes the major points of the story. In the rest of the paragraphs, information is presented in descending order of importance. Stories are written this way so that editors, or at the last minute, word processors (they used to be called typesetters), can eliminate material from the bottom up depending on the space available for the article.

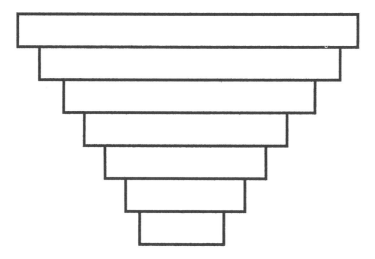

FIG. 3.2   *(Continued)*

B. Regular Lesson Pyramid

Try to picture a lesson as a "modified pyramid." An introductory activity establishes the context for the lesson. The first or primary activities introduce the major points students will be learning. Secondary activities introduce supportive information organized in descending order of importance. If a lesson proceeds quickly, they get included. When time gets tight, these activities can be eliminated from the bottom up. Unlike the inverted pyramid, the summary activity is crucial because it allows students to summarize major points. Wherever you are in the lesson, at the "2-minute warning" you move to your final activity.

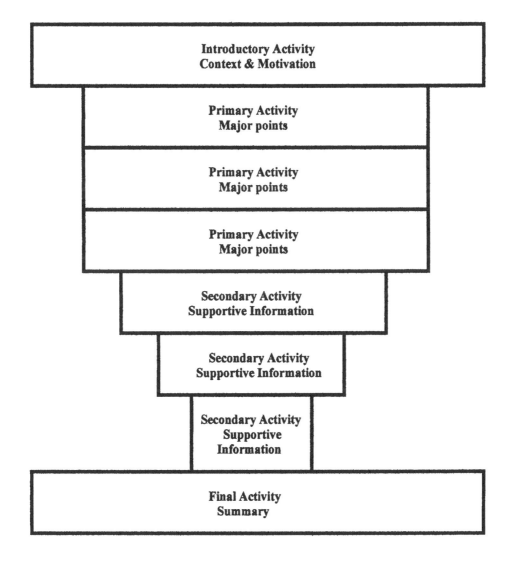

FIG. 3.2 *(Continued)*

C. Modified Lesson Pyramid

No two classes are alike. Life always manages to intervene in the classroom. If you have an early morning class or one just after lunch or gym, students are going to wander in late. If you wait for them to arrive, more of them will just come late, so you have to start teaching at the bell. So latecomers know what the class is doing, I change the "picture." Instead of starting the lesson at the beginning, I start in the "middle" with an extended introductory activity using supportive information. When enough students arrive, I swing into the primary activities, establishing the context of the lesson and introducing the major points. Once again we proceed to secondary activities, and at the "2-minute warning," move to the final activity.

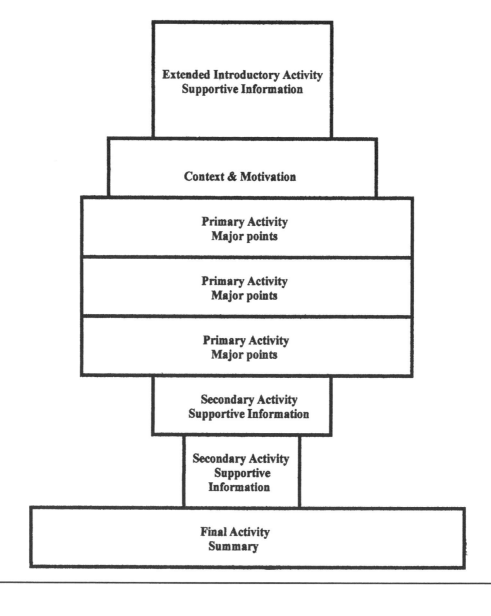

FIG. 3.3   The perfect "brain" storm.

In the sample streamlined high school social studies lesson plan on the lives and hopes of enslaved Africans in the American South, I suggest having students brainstorm a list of ideas on the front board about ways we can we learn about the ideas and feelings of ordinary people from the past.

Many teachers like to begin a lesson by having students "brain storm" or list what they already know, or think they know. The "K-W-L approach" provides a useful structure for organizing brainstorming. After students list "what we know," they evaluate the list for missing pieces and contradictory statements, and then construct a new list, "what we want to know." At the conclusion of a lesson (final activity) or a unit, students return to their initial lists and construct a final list, "what we learned."

What We Know	What We Want to Know	What We Learned

FIG. 3.4   Planning high school-level mini-lessons.

Cliches usually contain an element of truth. There is always a first time. Everyone starts as a beginner. No one improves without practice.

While you try to figure out what will work and to develop your own particular classroom style, it is helpful to build lessons up from their component parts and practice presenting mini-lessons either for colleagues in secondary education classes or for small groups of students. Essentially, a mini-lesson is a piece of a lesson, usually consisting of only one activity. Working on one part of a lesson, a particular idea, teaching skill, or approach, allows you to focus in on an area you need to strengthen or something you want to experiment with.

However, even though you will be designing and teaching only a part of a lesson, you need to keep in mind a vision of the lesson as a whole and where this piece fits in. As you prepare a mini-lesson the following are some things you need to continually consider:

- **Who are my students** (both socially and academically)?
- **What are my goals** (short-term goals for this activity and lesson and long-term goals for an entire unit and curriculum)?
- **What are my strategies** to help this particular group of students achieve these short-term and long-term goals?
- **What materials** do I have available?
- **How will I assess** the success of my strategies in achieving my goals?

SUBJECT: _____ GRADE LEVEL: _____

LESSON AIM OR TOPIC:_____

GOALS (Concepts, content, and/or skills developed in this mini-lesson):_____

- _____
- _____
- _____

MATERIALS: _____

INTRODUCTORY ACTIVITY (To establish context and motivate student interest): __

_____

_____

TRANSITION (Shift from the introductory activity to the body of the lesson): _____

_____

_____

ASSESSMENT (Criteria I will use to evaluate the mini-lesson): _____

_____

FIG. 3.5   Sample high school mini-lessons.

SUBJECT: Science/Physics   GRADE: High School, 11 or 12

LESSON AIM: Can "something" be both "mass" and "energy"?

CONCEPT(S): Change of state, complexity, multiple perspectives, physical properties of matter.

MATERIALS: Hot plate, beaker, water and ice; headline on overhead projector.

INTRODUCTORY ACTIVITY:

A) Project headline: "Room in the Universe for Ancient Beliefs and Modern Physics." Explain that the article claims that traditional Buddhist philosophy makes it easier for Japanese scientists to understand complicated physical principles such as duality and transformation. Can someone give me an example of something that is a duality? What makes something a duality? How do things transform?

B) Boil water. Insert ice cube. What happens to the ice? the water? Which is really "water"—solid, liquid, or gas?

TRANSITION: Why does water appear to have three very different forms? Can anyone suggest other examples of physical dualities and transformations? Can anyone suggest other simple experiments that demonstrate duality and transformation?

ASSESSMENT: Was I comfortable and fluid in front of the class? Was I able to respond to student questions? Did the depth and breadth of student participation in discussion demonstrate interest in and understanding of the subject matter?

Excerpt from The New York Times, June 9, 1998, F.4.

**Room in the Universe for Ancient Beliefs and Modern Physics
by Malcolm W. Brown**

Hilda Village, Japan, June 7—Everywhere in this restored 17th century village, old wayside shrines remind visitors of the belief that Buddha could assume several manifestations, each representing one of the deep tenets of Buddhist teaching.

Barely a mile away from the old wood houses of this village is the modern provincial town of Takayama, where trailblazing physics is coming to light at an international conference on neutrino particles.

Despite the contrast between the carefully tended icons of Hilda (which bespeaks ancient religious mysticism) and the research that has been unveiled nearby during the past week, many Asian scientists view the two worlds as complimentary rather than conflicting.

"We say that the Buddhist tradition makes it easier for us to grasp the dualities and transformations of particle physics," said one of the Japanese scientists here, who spoke on the condition he not be identified.

"For example, the duality of particles and waves manifested in all the ingredients of matter has long been known, but although everyone accepts this duality intellectually, the idea may be hard to feel in your heart unless you are Asian," he said.

The announcement last Friday that a coalition of Japanese and American scientists had found strong evidence that neutrinos undergo transformation from one type to another (and therefore have mass) also evokes comparisons with Buddhist traditions.

FIG. 3.5   (Continued)

SUBJECT: Introductory Italian   GRADE: High School, 9
(developed by Maria Tartaro Musacchia)

LESSON AIM: Che tempo fa? (What is the weather like?)

CONCEPT(S): Il Tempo (weather); useful vocabulary; oral expression.

MATERIALS: Vocabulary sheet, flashcards, cotton balls, spray bottle, sunglasses, scarf and gloves, hand fan, stickers.

INTRODUCTORY ACTIVITY:

A) Model weather expressions while using cotton balls (as snow), spray bottle, sunglasses, scarf and gloves, and hand fan for dramatic effect.

B) Ask students, "Che tempo fa?" Hold up visual flash cards and ask volunteers to identify the weather in Italian. Go through the cards again and call on nonvolunteers. Sprinkle students with cotton balls to simulate snow. Spray with water to simulate rain. Put on sunglasses to act out a sunny day and gloves and scarf when it is cold. Flicker classroom lights for lightning and bang on a desk for thunder.

C) Students are given a vocabulary sheet with weather expressions. Working individually, they have 3 minutes to identify as many expressions as they can. Next, they share their answers with a partner.

TRANSITION: Repeat until every student is able to identify the weather in Italian and to pronounce words correctly

ASSESSMENT: Was I comfortable and fluid in front of the class? Was I able to respond to student questions? Did the depth and breadth of student participation in discussion demonstrate interest in and understanding of the subject matter?

SUBJECT: English/Shakespeare   GRADE: High School, 10 or 11

LESSON AIM: Why does Shakespeare have a witches' chorus in *Macbeth*?

CONCEPT(S): Dramatic structure (scenes), complexity, multiple perspectives, narrative.

MATERIALS: Handout (or overhead projection) of an excerpt from *Macbeth*.

INTRODUCTORY ACTIVITY:

A) Students read handout on *Macbeth* and answer questions. What is the setting? Who are Graymalkin and Paddock?

B) Volunteers act out scene.

C) Do you believe in witches? Why? Why not?

TRANSITION: In your opinion, what do the following lines mean: "When the battle's lost and won" and "Fair is foul, and foul is fair"? Why does Shakespeare have the witches' chorus recite these lines?

ASSESSMENT: Was I comfortable and fluid in front of the class? Was I able to respond to student questions? Did the depth and breadth of student participation in discussion demonstrate interest in and understanding of the subject matter?

FIG. 3.5 *(Continued)*

ACTIVITY SHEET: Why does Shakespeare have a witches' chorus in Macbeth?

Do Now: Read the opening scene from *Macbeth* and answer questions 1–3.

1. What is the setting for the play *Macbeth* by William Shakespeare?
2. Who are Graymalkin and Paddock?
3. In your opinion, what do the following lines means:
   a. "When the battle's lost and won."
   b. "Fair is foul, and foul is fair"?

Scene I. Scotland. An open place.

Thunder and lightening. Enter three witches.

Witch 1—When shall we three meet again,

  In thunder, lightening or in rain?

Witch 2—When the hurlyburly's done,

  When the battle's lost and won.

Witch 3—That will be ere the set of sun.

Witch 1—Where the place?

Witch 2—Upon the heath

Witch 3—There to meet with Macbeth.

Witch 1—I come, Graymalkin!

Witch 2—Paddock calls.

Witch 3—Anon!

All—Fair is foul, and foul is fair.

Hover through the fog and filthy air.

SUBJECT: Math/Algebra   **GRADE: High School, 9**

LESSON AIM: What is Algebra?

CONCEPT(S): Algebra, unknown, and balance and equality.

MATERIAL: Balance scale.

INTRODUCTORY ACTIVITY:

A) Students should attempt to solve the following equations (from the board):

   a. $7 + 8 = X$ $X =$

   b. $10 + 5 = X$ $X =$

   c. $21 - 6 = X$ $X =$

   d. $27 - 12 = X$ $X =$

B) Examine a balance scale. How does it work?

C) What does the equal sign mean in math? In arithmetic, where do we usually place the "balance scale"?

TRANSITION: In algebra, we move the unknown. ($10 + 5 = 7 + X$ $X =$) What do we have to do to maintain balance?

ASSESSMENT: Was I comfortable and fluid in front of the class? Was I able to respond to student questions? Did the depth and breadth of student participation in discussion demonstrate interest in and understanding of the subject matter?

FIG. 3.5   *(Continued)*

SUBJECT: Social Studies/Global History   GRADE: High School, 9 or 10

LESSON AIM: Can violent revolutions improve the world?

CONCEPT(S): Revolution, complexity, multiple perspectives, impact of revolution on people and society.

MATERIALS: Cassette recorder and tapes of Bob Marley and the Wailers, "Get Up, Stand Up" and The Beatles, "Revolution."

INTRODUCTORY ACTIVITY:

A) Explain that today we are going to examine the debate between two famous philosophers about the value of violent revolutions. I am going to play statements by them and then we will discuss their ideas.

B) Listen to songs by Bob Marley and the Wailers, "Get Up, Stand Up" and John Lennon and The Beatles, "Revolution."

C) What are they saying about revolution? Whose philosophy comes closer to your views? Why?

TRANSITION: What criteria should historians use to evaluate whether violent revolutions improve the world?

ASSESSMENT: Was I comfortable and fluid in front of the class? Was I able to respond to student questions? Did the depth and breadth of student participation in discussion demonstrate interest in and understanding of the subject matter?

SUBJECT: Music   GRADE: Middle School or High School
(developed by Dean Bacigalupo)

LESSON AIM: What is the message in this music?

CONCEPT(S): Musical imagery, content, context.

MATERIALS: Cassette recorder or CD player and a sample piece of music.

INTRODUCTORY ACTIVITY:

A) Explain that we are going to listen to sample piece of music. Our goals are to learn how to listen carefully, how to describe what we hear, and how to discover the ways that music makes us feel and stimulates us to think.

B) Listen to a sample piece of music.

C) Describe the musical content (speed, volume, voices, or instruments). Who do you imagine is listening to this piece of music? Why? Where and when do you think it is being played? Explain.

TRANSITION: How does the music make you feel? What does it make you think? How do the composer and musicians use the music to present a message?

ASSESSMENT: Was I comfortable and fluid in front of the class? Was I able to respond to student questions? Did the depth and breadth of student participation in discussion demonstrate interest in and understanding of the subject matter?

4

RELATIONSHIPS: WHY ARE RELATIONSHIPS WITH STUDENTS CRUCIAL TO SUCCESSFUL TEACHING?

This chapter explores supportive teacher–student relationships that are part of a general approach to teaching. Gloria Ladson-Billings, Lisa Delpit, Michelle Fine, and Nel Noddings are among a number of educators who have written about the importance of emotional connections between teachers and students. In *The Dreamkeepers: Successful Teachers of African American Children*, Ladson-Billings (1994) studied the qualities that made a multiracial group of teachers successful working with African American students. A key element of what she describes as "culturally relevant pedagogy" is the ability of these teachers to care about and connect to their students. Delpit (1995) is concerned that teachers reject working-class, poor, and minority youth because their perceptions of proper behavior and ways of learning are based on their own class and cultural backgrounds. Fine (1991) argues that in an irrational world where students are sometimes demeaned by school authorities, dropping out may be the only rational choice some students can make. Noddings (1984, 1992) offers a philosophy of education based on an "ethic of caring."

In "My Best Teachers 3," I describe how I learned to be a teacher from relationships with my students. Other sections examine ways of "seeing" students, what schools mean by gifted education, and a project that helped remedial students experience success in school and develop a sense of self-worth.

An essay by S. Maxwell Hines, the science educator at Hofstra University and a faculty advisor to the New Teachers Network, discusses her experience as a student who was rejected by teachers and schools. She explains how the idea of culturally relevant pedagogy makes it possible for teachers to connect with and scaffold on the life experiences of their students. A concluding section examines a statement about education by James Baldwin, a noted African American author, who invited teachers to participate in a movement to transform the world.

SECTION A: HOW IMPORTANT ARE RELATIONSHIPS BETWEEN A TEACHER AND STUDENTS?

In May 2001, Johanna Grussner took 24 members of an elementary school gospel choir to perform in her hometown in Finland. The fifth and sixth graders were from an inner-city American neighborhood with a large immigrant population. Many of the children had histories of academic and behavioral problems in school. The trip, which was reported in the national press, was the culmination of 2 years of hard work by both the students and their teachers.

The consensus among parents, teachers, administrators, and the children themselves was that their experience in the chorus had transformed students. Yet transformation can be a fragile thing. Soon after the trip, Ms. Grussner announced she had a chronic illness and would leave the school and her chorus to return home permanently. Threatened by the loss of their relationship with Ms. Grussner, old patterns of school behavior reemerged among some of the children and at least one of the lead performers was threatened with being held over (Hartocollis, 2001a, 2001b).

The story of Johanna Grussner and the gospel choir is not a unique story. The impact of caring relationships on students and the frailty of transformation if these relationships falter have been described in popular movies such as *Blackboard Jungle* (1955), *The King and I* (1956), *Stand and Deliver* (1988), *Dead Poets Society* (1989), *Dangerous Minds* (1995), and *Playing from the Heart* (2000). Each of these movies tells the story of a teacher who connected with students emotionally and was able to build on the connection to change the way they functioned in school and the world.

Perhaps the leading proponent of the importance of relationship in teaching is the feminist philosopher and psychologist Nel Noddings. In the conclusion to *Caring, A Feminine Approach to Ethics and Moral Education* (1984, p. 197), Noddings argues for reorganizing schools based on an "ethic of caring" and a "maternal attitude." In such a school, "rules are not sacred, ... what matters is the student" (p. 178), and the most important task of the teacher is to model what it means to be a moral caring human being.

Noddings explains that "[a] teacher cannot 'talk' this ethic. She must live it, and that implies establishing a relation with the student" (1984, p. 179). Noddings' approach is similar to John Dewey's idea, discussed in chapter 1, that effective teachers connect subject matter to the lived experience of their students and create classrooms where experience is a crucial element of curriculum. It is also consistent with Michael Apple's ideas about "hidden curriculum." Apple (1979) believes that in every school and classroom there is a basic set of unstated and unexamined assumptions about right and wrong, what and who is valued, and the way people should be related. Usually the hidden curriculum pits students into competition for limited teacher attention and scarce academic awards. Noddings wants the hidden or underlying curriculum brought out into the open and changed. Education would be based on caring human relationships, not on formality and rules that act as barriers between people.

The importance of caring relationships for improving education is a cornerstone of the movement to create smaller, less depersonalized secondary schools. In *Chartering Urban School Reform* (1994), Michelle Fine discusses efforts "to dismantle the urban high school as we know it—large, anonymous, and filled with more cracks than safety nets—and to nourish, in its place, many small, intellectually intimate communities of learners" (p. 2). The most important aspect of this approach to education is that it ends student anonymity and combats alienation by fostering relationship and community. Smaller schools and the process of community classroom building are discussed more fully in chapters 5 and 6.

In my experience, some teachers develop caring relationships with students even in large, traditional secondary schools. We all know teachers who put in extra time working with teams and clubs where they develop very close and supportive relationships with their students. Judy Logan, whom we met in chapter 2, writes about sharing "stealing stories" in her class without making moral judgments about each other. Presenting their stories of wrongdoing to people who care about them allows Logan's students to expose their vulnerability to each other, learn from their errors, and retain their humanity. Herbert Kohl (1994), who wrote about "creative maladjustment," also discusses the idea of "willful not learning." Kohl believes that many students decide not to learn the standard school curriculum as an act of defiance against arbitrary rules and unfair actions by teachers. He argues that the key to reaching students who are "willfully not learning" is developing mutual relationships of caring and trust. He agrees with Noddings that teachers must "walk the walk."

How important are relationships between a teacher and his or her students? Adeola Tella is a second-year teacher working in a troubled inner-city middle school (it was placed on a state list for reorganization). When students in her classes misbehaved or failed to complete assignments she required them to attend lunch detention or remain after school. After a while her room was packed with students doing detention. Adeola realized that the students wanted to be with her and were competing to be "kept in." She decided to build on her relationship with her students and make detention a reward rather than a punishment.

JOIN THE CONVERSATION—A TEACHER WHO CARED ABOUT ME

When I was in middle school I joined the school's math team, even though I was not particularly interested in math. The reason was my official teacher, Brenda Berkowitz. My friends and I joined the math team because we liked the way she treated us and we wanted the relationship with her.

Questions to Consider:

1. As a student, did you ever have a special relationship with a teacher that inspired you to do well in school? Explain.

2. In your opinion, how important are relationships between a teacher and her or his students? Explain.

SECTION B: MY BEST TEACHERS 3: LEARNING FROM MY STUDENTS

In "My Best Teachers 1," I describe Camp Hurley, a summer sleep-away camp in the Catskill Mountains of New York State. The children and teenagers who attended the camp were primarily from inner-city neighborhoods and between the ages of 6 and 17. Most were African American, but there were significant European American and Latino minorities.

The camp's philosophy stressed the richness of difference and the ability of people from diverse backgrounds to work together for common goals. The campers worked together on construction projects and dramatic presentations. They participated in sports, dance, and hiking. But the most important aspect of the camp's curriculum was reflecting on the conflicts that arose among people during the day-to-day experience of living at Camp Hurley.

I worked summers at this camp between the ages of 19 and 24 and I continued to volunteer on weekends and vacations into my 30s. As I mention in chapter 2, it is here that I learned how to teach. Most of my best teachers at Camp Hurley were the children. In this section I want to share some of my most powerful learning experiences as children and teenagers struggled to help me understand what it means to be a teacher.

Lesson 1. It is possible to develop a diverse community based on mutual respect. At the beginning of the summer of 1973, I worked with the preteen group, boys and girls ages 12, 13, and 14. In early July, we went on a 20-mile, 3-day hike along the Rondout Creek to the point where it flows into the Hudson River; to the best of my memory, about 16 campers and three staff members made the trip. One of the campers, a young girl I will call Joan, had cerebral palsy. She walked with difficulty and it was often hard for the other children to understand her when she spoke. She was also one of the few European American children in this group.

Before the hike, the group decided that Joan would walk in front and set the pace for the others. It also discussed why she would not be able to carry a backpack. It was a difficult hike and at one point we walked most of the night in a downpour. At first there was some grumbling that Joan was not carrying anything. But as we hiked on, complaints about fairness turned into admiration for the doggedness and courage of this young woman who led by example. By the end of the hike, the staff and campers were helping each other as we sang, talked, and played. On this hike I learned what young people are capable of if they are respected, given a chance to work out their conflicts, and allowed to show their best side.

Lesson 2. It is not what you say, but how students experience what they hear. Later that summer, I learned a very painful lesson from the preteen boys groups. The youngsters were all African American. We were preparing a dramatic presentation on slavery and I explained that some Southerners used the Bible to defend the enslavement of Black people. They thought I believed these proslavery views and they were furious with me; it took weeks to reestablish a relationship of trust. I learned that a teacher has to be concerned with who students are and how they feel. As a teacher, it is not what you say, but how students experience what they hear.

Lesson 3. When people work together they can achieve their goals. During the final three weeks of 1973, I was working with the 10-year-old boys group and we were having a very good time together. The summer was ending with a Medieval Guild Fair and my group was making ceramic chess pieces and a wooden board and performing at the fair as tumblers. The only problem was that the boys wanted to go on an overnight hike and the program director felt the schedule was too crowded to permit it.

At the last Friday evening staff meeting of the season, we heard shouting and the sound of general mayhem coming from my cabin. The program director and I went up to investigate, but as we approached the lights went out and everything quieted down. Nevertheless we rushed into the cabin, flicked on the light, and the program director, determined to punish the malefactors, shouted: "This group is going on a night hike." Simultaneously, nine 10-year-old boys leaped out of bed fully dressed and ready to go.

Lesson 4. Building a relationship requires time, patience, and trust. During the summer of 1974, my nine-year-old boys group was put in charge of repairing a roadside drainage ditch. It was an important task: Unless the drains were repaired, the edges of the dirt road washed away during rainstorms.

Some of the boys were not enthusiastic about the assignment. I spent 2 days trying to get the campers interested in the job and one boy was particularly resistant. The group could not persuade him to work and I could not make him. His holdout was beginning to threaten the entire project so the group met and decided that only people who wanted to learn how to repair the ditch were allowed to help. The only condition was that people who decided not to work had to remain within sight of the group. At first, two other boys joined him and they meandered a short way off into the woods. However, the second day they decided to join the rest of the group.

The third day, the program director came by while eight of the nine-year-old boys were working hard clearing the drains of leaves, roots, and rocks; mixing cement; and lining the ditch with slate slabs. He asked if I knew that one of the boys was in the woods. When I said that I did, he wanted to know why I had not gone after him. I explained that the boy did not want to work on the project and I had left the decision up to him. The program director was a little skeptical about what would happen, but the next day the boy decided to join us.

A couple of days later, I was working with the camp newspaper committee and a substitute counselor was with my group. Suddenly we were hit with the first big rain of the season. About 15 minutes into the storm, the counselor came to get me. The entire group ran away and he had no idea where they were. I started to laugh and we set off to find them. We located them on the road at the spot where we were fixing the drain. The boys wanted to see how their work was holding up. When the counselor decided not to let them go because it was raining, they decided to go without him. After all, it was their work.

Lesson 5. Learn to laugh at yourself. In my first year at camp, I had an 11-year-old group of boys. One of the campers had been abused as a child and was living in a group foster home. To ingratiate himself with the other children, he would imitate the camp staff, principally me. I was new on the job, stressed out, and the imitations drove me crazy. I thought he was out to humiliate me in front of the other campers and I could not take it. I started screaming at the group and lost control of myself and of them. It was a horrible 3 weeks.

Three years later I was assigned to work with the 14-year-old boys, including this same young man. He immediately started doing imitations of me. Some of the other campers knew him and me from previous years and they wondered what would happen. Before the tension could mount, I laughed, gave him a high five and said something like, "Man, you are good. You do me better than I do." Then we gave each other a hello hug and the group began to discuss all the things we wanted to do that summer.

Lesson 6. Use the "think" method. Playing softball with 8- to 10-year-olds can be an annoying experience. Most of the children find the sport too difficult. They get frustrated, the games become long and boring, the field is hot and dry, and tempers are short. Finally, I borrowed ideas from two popular movies, *The Karate Kid* (1984) and *The Music Man* (1962), to teach campers how to play.

In *The Karate Kid*, the martial arts master has his young apprentice paint a fence and wax a car using precise, repetitive motions. Once the apprentice can duplicate the motions, he is ready to practice karate. In *The Music Man*, a con artist convinces a town that its children can learn to play musical instruments by imagining that they are playing them (hence, the "think" method).

I decided to break softball down into a few basic movements used for hitting, catching, and throwing the ball. Campers practiced the movements without any equipment, kind of like a baseball ballet. Then they would come to bat, without a bat, and learned to "see" the pitch instead of guessing at its location and lunging at it. After a few days of the think method, they were able to play softball.

Lesson 7. Ask them. Many of the younger children were homesick and a little scared, especially at night. At "lights out," I walked from bed to bed, tucking in some of the children, giving a few a peck on the forehead and a little hug, and just saying "good night" to others. One of the counselors asked me how I decided which children got tucked in, who got hugged and kissed, and who got a simple "good night." I reflected for a few seconds and responded, "I ask them."

Lesson 8. Given an opportunity, young people do amazing things. In 1971, the entire camp held a 1-day "conference of struggle." Each group of campers did a presentation on ways that different groups of people struggled for freedom. Some of the presentations were in the form of dance or drama. Other groups led songs or created artistic displays. At the end of the conference, everyone (from children age 6 to adults in their 50s) participated in a discussion on the meaning of freedom. Given an opportunity, young people do amazing things.

SECTION C: HOW IMPORTANT IS IT TO "SEE" AND "HEAR" STUDENTS?

Patricia Carini and the Prospect Center (Himley, with Carini, 2000) developed an approach to teaching that includes a "descriptive review" of students. It involves teams of teachers in careful observation of children and a "disciplined" review of their ideas and work. The purposes of the process are "to make the child more visible by coming to understand him or her more fully and completely as a particular thinker and learner" and to develop in teachers "the habits of mind—*the stance*—of careful observation and description" (p. 127). Close and disciplined observation and review allows teachers to relate to children as human beings with a world of potential, rather than as problems to be solved. Teachers discover student academic and character strengths, see the connections students make between ideas, and learn how they make meaning of their world. The process supports the caring environment described by Noddings and makes it possible for teachers to scaffold on the strengths of individual students as they plan instruction.

Another advantage of careful observation of students by teams of teachers is that it helps us examine exactly what we are doing. Teachers are human, and I know I have made quick and unfair judgments about students and classes. When you talk issues over with other teachers, you get to see a different side of students and events. I have also reviewed videotapes of my own teaching and the work of other teachers, and discovered that what we thought had happened in the class was quite different from what had taken place. The research team of Sadker and Sadker (1994) has prepared videotapes of exemplary teachers, who unconsciously were providing more attention to the boys in their classes than to the girls. After reviewing the tapes, the teachers were able to change the way they related to students.

Relationship is fundamental to instruction. Maxine Greene, a major 20th-century American educational philosopher, argues that to create democratic classrooms, teachers must learn to listen to student voices. Listening allows teachers to discover what students are thinking, what concerns them, and what has meaning to them. When teachers learn to listen, it is possible for teachers and students to collectively search for metaphors that make knowledge of the world accessible to us.

Attention to individual students takes time, but if Noddings, Greene, and Carini are correct, it is fundamental to transforming schools and classrooms and reaching all children. I think it is significant that when a child has recognized special needs, this kind of personal attention to the way they learn is mandated by law. Teachers, counselors, and psychologists develop an individualized education program (IEP) for each student that is reevaluated on a regular basis.

Close attention to the needs and learning styles of individual students is also a goal in middle schools where teachers are organized as interdisciplinary teams who have the same classes, rather than into academic departments. In these schools, teachers and counselors meet daily and engage in an ongoing review of individual student progress. This helps team members to better know individual students and allows them to intervene before a minor upset grows into a major problem.

Mentoring is another way to foster relationships between teachers and students. A number of high schools are experimenting with student-created interdisciplinary portfolios or projects that are periodically examined by teams of teachers. These reviews provide the opportunity for teachers and students to get to know each other and for teachers to offer academic support and guidance. Portfolio assessment is discussed in greater depth in chapter 8.

In order to learn about her students, Susan Soitiriades, whom we met in chapter 2, has them write personal essays about themselves and their backgrounds that are shared in class. Another way to learn about students is to ask them to complete a voluntary "student profile." A sample follows in Fig. 4.1.

JOIN THE CONVERSATION—ONE SIZE FITS FEW

Susan Ohanian is a leading critic of national standards and standardized tests. In her book, *One Size Fits Few* (1999), Ohanian argues in favor of personalizing instruction and individualizing assessment as the best way to meet the needs of students and to really understand what they have learned.

Questions to Consider:

1. In your view, what are the advantages and disadvantages of careful observation of students and a "disciplined" review of the ideas and work of individual children?

2. Do you think asking students to complete a student profile like this sample would help you as a teacher? Explain.

3. If you used this sample profile, which questions would you eliminate? What questions would you add? Why?

4. Where do you stand in the debate over national standards and testing versus personalizing instruction and individualizing assessment? Explain your views.

SECTION D: WHAT DOES IT MEAN TO BE "GIFTED"?

The next two essays examine the school experiences of different sets of students. The first essay discusses "gifted" programs and their impact on students who are placed in these classes. The second essay is about a special project involving students in a remedial reading program. I suspect that most teachers, and most people who are reading this book, would prefer to work with students labeled "gifted." We see them as an easier and more interesting group to relate with and teach. These are the students that most frequently have special relationships with teachers. They assist in offices, are members of school clubs, and produce the yearbook and the play. This group of students generally feels comfortable with teachers; they probably had positive experiences earlier in their school careers and know teachers from their families or communities. But being placed in the "gifted" class carries a burden, which the essay explores.

The second group of students are the students that most teachers try to avoid because they can be difficult to handle. They often have serious academic and social problems and are resistant to the goals of school. I think this essay shows how important positive relationships with teachers and other adults are for these students.

Most new students in teacher education programs (and unfortunately many teachers as well) tend to *universalize* from their own experience as secondary school students. They believe there is only one right way to learn, one right way to act, and that is the way that they

FIG. 4.1

Student Profile

Name: _____ Class: _____ Age: _____

Special Academic Needs:_____

Overall GPA: _____ Grades in Subject Area: _____

Performance on Standardized Assessments: _____

_____

School Extracurricular Activities: _____

_____

School Awards: _____

_____

Other Extracurricular Activities: _____

_____

Other Awards: _____

_____

Caretaker(s): _____

Caretakers' Occupation(s): _____

Neighborhood: _____

Housing: _____

Languages Spoken: _____

Siblings/Ages: _____

Special Family Responsibilities: _____

Afterschool work: _____

Organizational Memberships: _____

Hobbies/Interests: _____

Favorite Book: _____

Favorite TV program: _____

Favorite Movie: _____

Favorite Music Group: _____

Favorite Sport/Team: _____

Best Friends: _____

Problems I Should Know About: _____

_____

Other Comments: _____

---

think they did in school (I italicized *think they did* because I am not convinced that it really happened that way).

As I mentioned earlier, Lisa Delpit has challenged this approach to teaching because when teachers act based on their own class and cultural assumptions, they fail to see the strengths and the needs of their students and are unable to relate with them. The idea that teachers should respond to individual differences in the ways that students learn is also a crucial component of Howard Gardner's theory of multiple intelligences (Gardner, 1987, 1993). Gardner disputed the ideas that human intelligence can be accurately summarized with one reference point, and that all people learn in essentially the same fashion. He suggests nine types of intelligence possessed by students in a variety of combinations: linguistic, logical-mathematical, spatial, body-kinesthetic, musical, interpersonal (social), intrapersonal (reflective), naturalistic (characterized by interest in the natural environment), and ritualistic (exhibited through a deep understanding of connectedness and ritual). Gardner (1987) argues that curricula and teachers must "recognize and nurture all of the varied human intelligences, and all of the combinations of intelligences" (p. 193) so that schools and societies are able to appropriately address "the many problems that we face in the world." Although I think that Gardner fractures intelligence into too many distinct pieces, his basic idea is very valuable. If teachers accept that students have cultural and conceptual differences, it will not only improve instruction, but also bonds of relationship.

As you read the essays, I hope you reconsider some of your assumptions about how schools should be organized, whom you would prefer to work with, and the impact of this kind of grouping on students. I wrote a version of the first essay for a local newspaper (Singer, 1999); the second essay was written with one of my research partners, Judith Y. Singer, who is also my wife. Judi was formerly the director of the day-care center discussed in the essay. A version of this article appeared in the magazine *Multicultural Perspectives* (Singer & Singer, 2000).

JOIN THE CONVERSATION—WERE YOU GIFTED?

Questions to Consider:

Before reading the essays, please answer the following questions:

1. What was your experience with "gifted" or advanced placement programs as a student?

2. In your opinion, what does it mean to be "gifted"?

Were the Mystery Men Gifted?
By Alan Singer

Mystery Men (1999) was a movie about a band of super-hero wannabes with pretty unusual powers. They included a character who used flatulence as a weapon and who emerged as the favorite of junior high school age students. Although the movie did not win any Academy Award nominations, it did raise a significant question: What does it mean to be gifted?

Part of the difficulty in discussing programs for "gifted children" is that there is not a consensus on the criteria for being selected. Albert Einstein and Thomas Edison were considered slow learners and many child prodigies have had unhappy lives and unsuccessful careers. I do not think it is an accident that children from the most affluent families in a community tend to predominate in its "gifted classes." What school districts may actually be doing is selecting children who have had the most advantages at home and then providing them with the most advantages at school.

The designation "gifted" is arbitrary. Children who score high enough on standardized examinations or an individualized assessment to be placed in a gifted program in one district are sometimes denied access to a program in another, either because there are children who have higher scores or because of enrollment caps due to budgetary concerns. Families that move from middle-class districts to more affluent communities often discover that their children are no longer considered "gifted." For a youngster, this can be a traumatic experience.

Segregating students based on academic performance also reinforces stereotypes. Children are taught that some people are better than others and deserve special rewards, even if they did not do anything observable to earn them. For some children, it encourages their sense of entitlement, that they are better than other people and should get more from life. Other children worry they will lose their friends or that they will be thrown out of the select group if they ever make a mistake. Meanwhile, children left in the drill-and-skill club get the message that they are academic failures. Many give up trying to learn, setting the stage for future failure in life.

Another problem is that a variety of programs claim to serve the needs of "gifted children." In urban areas, students in "gifted" classes are generally from middle-class families that constitute a diminishing percentage of the public school population. These children, who are from all racial and ethnic backgrounds, are segregated into special classes and magnet schools that receive extra resources. These so-called "gifted" classes function as oases in a troubled school system. Often they are the only classes and schools where children receive a sound basic education. John Obgu (1994) reports that African American youth in these classes, especially if they are from poor communities, carry an especially heavy burden. Pressure is placed on them to be positive representatives of their race. At the same time, performing well in school often means alienation from their peers. This phenomenon was effectively explored in the movie *Finding Forrester* (2000).

Many elementary school gifted programs are pull-out programs: Children who are designated as "gifted" spend most of the day or week with a regular class and are "pulled out" for special enrichment. This type of program is justified in two ways. Parents and school officials claim that without enrichment the "gifted" children will be bored in school and their performance will suffer. In addition, pulling them out of the classroom is supposed to enable teachers to provide individualized attention to students who are having difficulty learning the basic material.

I have serious reservations about organizing educational instruction this way. Pull-out programs generally employ a project approach to teaching that encourages kids, working individually and in groups, to explore computers, science, literature, and history. The reality is that this type of teaching makes learning exciting and benefits every child. Educational researchers have repeatedly demonstrated that it can be done in mixed ability groupings with sufficient teacher support. Although repeated drilling of students who are having difficulty in the basics has a long history of failing to improve their performance, stimulating them to want to learn through enrichment programs has the potential to change their attitude toward learning and their performance in school.

In middle schools and high schools, the gifted program is usually called the honors program, the advanced placement class, or a class that prepares students to compete in a program such as the Intel Science competition. I have the same concerns with these programs that I do with elementary school gifted programs, and I have two other concerns as well.

In middle school and high school, students feel pressured to be chosen for selective programs with limited enrollments because their parents see this as an avenue for entry into elite colleges. Instead of learning how to learn, how to enjoy learning, and how to work socially with groups of diverse people, teenagers learn to compete for limited rewards. This leaves them ill prepared for a world where they will need to work cooperatively with people from many different backgrounds. In addition, pressure to get into advanced classes and the hierarchies these programs help create contribute to the stress and social division that have exploded into violence in schools around the country. In Japan, the intense pressure to excel has led to a high suicide rate among young adolescents; it is a worry in the United States as well.

The irony is that students are often poorly served by the advanced classes. Many use advanced placement credit to earn exemptions from subjects instead of using them to qualify for elective courses in these subject areas. As a result, they can go through college without ever taking a history or a science class. Because of this, Ivy League colleges generally offer advanced standing in a field instead of course exemptions. They want students to take college-level courses in a broad range of subject areas as part of a college learning community.

As *Mystery Men* shows, the question of who is "gifted" is a complicated one to answer. Unfortunately, in most cases, the primary qualification for being considered "gifted" is having parents who are educated and know how to play the system. We need to ask ourselves what kind of society we have when the students most likely to have a computer at home are also the ones most likely to have access to one in school. Does being considered gifted simply mean you come from an affluent family that can provide you with more of the gifts?

* * *

Promoting Relationship, Literacy, and Responsibility
By Judith Y. Singer and Alan Singer

The 2-, 3-, and 4-year-old children cheered for Cabree the goat and his friend Teegra. They squealed with excitement when the 6-foot tall tiger puppets fled across the stage. The play was *The Banza*, a Haitian tale. The performers, all dressed up in white shirts and blue pants or skirts, were seventh graders from a local middle school. After performances of *The Banza* (Wolkstein, 1981) and *The Enormous Turnip* (Parkinson, 1987), an Eastern European folk tale, the seventh graders from class 7-71 were paired with children in the 4-year-old group called the Rabbits. They sat down at tables, in chairs, or stretched out on the floor, and the teenagers read folk tales from children's books to their young friends.

While Charles read *The Adventures of Connie and Diego* (Garcia, 1992), a Mexican story, 4-year-old Jamel sat on his lap. Later, during the 15-minute walk back to their intermediate school, Charles excitedly said to his teacher, "This was special. They really looked up to us."

Initially, Diamond did not want to visit the preschool program or read with the younger children. When class 7-71 discussed the idea, he strenuously objected, claiming, "The books we read are for kids." He wanted to know, "Is this a 'special ed' class?" In the end, however, he agreed to be a narrator in *The Banza*, and on the way back to school, his misgivings forgotten, he told a teacher, "The little boy I read to was so excited he just wanted to hold the book."

The Multicultural Literacy and Citizenship Project is a partnership between the MLE Learning Center in East New York, Brooklyn; its sponsoring agency, the United Community Centers; and Intermediate School 292 in New York City's Community School District 19. Its most important partners are the 13- and 14-year-olds in class 7-71 and the 4-year-olds at the Learning Center. Together, maybe, these young people can build a new, multicultural, more literate, caring world.

Part of the strength of the Multicultural Literacy and Citizenship Project is that it speaks to the needs of two groups of learners at the same time. It exposes both groups to interesting, accessible, multicultural children's literature. While the younger children are provided with role models of older children who like to read stories, the older children feel encouraged when they realize that they can be role models. The middle school students also have the opportunity to read literature they can successfully navigate without feeling stigmatized as slow readers.

At I.S. 292, students were introduced to the Multicultural Literacy and Citizenship Project during a discussion where they were asked to define "multicultural," "literacy," and "citizenship." Outside observers might look at class 7-71 and only see a room full of black and brown faces. But the seventh graders quickly identified their cultural similarities and differences. They all live in East New York, Brooklyn, and they each speak either English or English and Spanish. They also have relatives from many different parts of the world, including the U.S. South, South and Central America, the United Kingdom, Jamaica, Puerto Rico, the Dominican Republic, and Haiti.

Although defining "multicultural" was not hard for these students, understanding the relationship between citizenship and the literacy project was a problem. Most of the students were native-born citizens of the United States. They all could identify themselves as citizens of I.S. 292 and class 7-71; however, for them, citizenship means membership and obeying rules. The idea of taking responsibility for others was something they reserved for their families. Some of the students initially insisted that "we should be paid to volunteer," but they each eventually decided that they were willing to volunteer "to do something important" and 100% of the class returned signed permission slips allowing them to visit the preschool program.

The students in class 7-71 know that they do not perform very well in school, so what they had the greatest difficulty understanding was why their class was being asked to participate in the project. When they found out that their job as literacy volunteers was to help young children in a local day-care center learn to read, their collective reaction was, "Why are you asking us?" The answers they arrived at through discussion were that "this is something we can do well," "the young children need our help," and "practicing reading and writing can help us, too."

Some of the teachers in the school also could not understand why this group of students was invited to participate in the project. One staff member told organizers, "If you realized how bad these children are, you would never trust them with the little ones."

The Multicultural Literacy and Citizenship Project supports many important educational goals. It encourages student interest in understanding the culturally diverse nature of our world and uses their interest to stimulate literacy. Working as literacy volunteers with young children promotes an interest in reading and writing among middle school students, and the relationship with the older students increases the desire of the younger children to learn to read and write. It has also helped "discouraged" youngsters develop personal and supportive relationships with teachers and other adults in their community.

* * *

JOIN THE CONVERSATION—WHAT IS GIFTED EDUCATION?

Questions to Consider:

Now that you have read the essays, please answer the following questions.

1. Do the benefits of "gifted" programs outweigh the problems they create?
2. Should programs like this be reserved for the "gifted" class? Explain.
3. In your opinion, were the children at I.S. 292 "gifted"? Explain.
4. What steps would a teacher need to take to create a project like the one implemented with the students from I.S. 292?

SECTION E: TEACHING STORIES 3

Reflections on Race, Democracy, and Education:
What Kind of Teacher Do You Want to Be?
By S. Maxwell Hines

S. Maxwell Hines or "Max" is one of the assisting editors of this book and a good friend. She is the science education coordinator in the Hofstra University School of Education and Allied Human Services. As a young African American girl, she was one of those students who was alternately ignored by some teachers and promoted by others as a model Black student. In graduate school, she stopped using her first name because she felt her work as a scientist was devalued because she was a woman. An important question to consider as you read her story is whether her experience should be considered an exception or as a suggestion of possibility.—Alan Singer

Before I discuss my ideas about teaching, let me first tell you a bit about myself. I am an African American woman, a teacher educator in a university near New York City, a scientist, a wife, and a mother of twin boys. My husband is a junior high school math teacher.

Being African American has been significant in everything that I have done my entire life. If African Americans do not take charge of our lives and take care of each other, I fear we will slide into a situation that will be untenable for us. We have to be academically prepared, and not just concentrate on areas society pushes us into like sports and music. I decided to focus on science because nobody thought I could do it. They said, "Why science honey? It's so hard." or "Why don't you try nursing? That's a better idea." Of course, they left out the rest of what they were thinking: "for a Black woman." But I said to myself, "I have the same amount of brains that anyone else has, and if they can be scientists, so can I." I believe that people have to resist stereotypes and do things that they are not expected to do.

My childhood experiences played an important role in who I am as a person and as a teacher. I was their only child, so my parents gave me a girl's first name and a boy's middle name. I started calling myself S. Maxwell Hines when I was a young woman and I was studying immunology. I found that it was much easier to get recognition and to get items published if my name did not sound female. Using my first initial and my male middle name simply worked better. Today, my friends and family call me "Max."

I was born in Brooklyn in the early 1960s and I grew up in Queens, another borough of New York City. My father, who was born and raised in Brooklyn, was a jack of all trades, but mostly he made a living as a presser in a cleaning plant. My mother was a teacher, a guidance counselor, and a school librarian. I guess I got the idea of becoming a teacher from her. My father, who was adopted, had had a very hard time growing up. He was not educated, but he was a very well-read and articulate man.

My mother was a small-town girl from a rural part of North Carolina. Wherever she went during her life, she was an activist. She was involved in the civil rights movement before she came north, she remained involved in New York City, and she is an activist now back in North Carolina. Both of my parents valued character, education, family, and community. These were much more important than color or credentials.

When I started school we lived in St. Albans, Queens, a middle-class Black community with a lot of municipal employees, teachers, and other professionals. I attended the local public school until one of the teachers told my mother that I was outpacing the other students. She recommended that I enter a special program in another district that would provide me with more of a challenge and greater opportunity. My mother decided to move me across town into an experimental school located at a local college. It was convenient because it was located near the high school where she was working.

I got an excellent education at that school, a very different education from what my peers received at our neighborhood school. We were taught how to chart stocks and bonds. I was part of the debate team, and I played in orchestra. The population of the school was approximately 80% White, mostly Jewish, and maybe 20% Black. The first orchestral piece that I learned to play was an Israeli song, "Havanagilah."

Most of the Black students at this school were bussed from a poorer neighborhood called South Jamaica. The teachers at the school tended to see all Black children as the same, but I was some kind of anomaly. I was far advanced in reading and pretty articulate for a kid. I came there already playing a musical instrument. I did not fit any of the stereotypes, and I think it made them uncomfortable. At school, I did a lot more challenging of authority than they thought I should do. I took my cues from White children who did it all the time. However, what was acceptable from them was not acceptable from me.

As a student, I felt a lot of pressure in elementary school, both because I was considered different from the other Black children and because the staff knew my mother was a teacher and a community activist. Someone was always looking at me. I think a lot of them were looking and watching for me to fail. I remember watching civil rights demonstrations on television and thinking, "Why do people hate me just because I have black skin?" It was hard to be a person who loved to read and write and play an instrument and have people judge me because of the prejudices they had against my people.

When I think back to that time, I do not remember having any problems with the White children at school. I was invited to the birthday parties and bar mitzvahs, though I was usually the only Black child there. I met a lot of families and I learned that we were a lot more alike than we were different. The Black children were often much more difficult for me to deal with. My mother dropped me off at school so I was not riding the bus with them every morning. I did not come from their neighborhood or have the same experiences as they did. They saw me as a token Black who was being held up in front of them as the way Black people could be and they resented me because of it. I was trying to take advantage of the opportunity the school provided, but they felt I was acting White so I would be accepted by the White teachers and students. These young Black children were so used to being put down in school that they banded together and developed a form of cultural resistance to the way they were treated. Now I can also understand how difficult it was for those Black students in South Jamaica. They were being made to squeeze into a structure that did not want them or care about who they were and how they felt.

As a middle-class girl whose mother was a teacher, I was taught not to fight, and to talk about disagreements and work them out. I was always a tall child, a lot taller than most of the children in my school, so I was usually left alone. I had a problem with one particular girl who wanted to fight me. It bothered me that I could not make this girl a friend or at least benign. After she had cajoled me for weeks, I finally spoke with my mother who told me I would have to make her stop. She surprised me by saying, "After school, when she starts to harass you, you knock her head off." I said fighting was against everything she had taught me, but my mother said, "If one thing doesn't work, you have to try something else. Now if you don't do it, when you get home. I'm gonna whip you. I'm not going to let you become a victim." I still remember that day very clearly. That girl started to pick on me and I thought, "If my mom drives up, I'm really in trouble." So we fought and I won. Later I looked down the block and there was my mom sitting in her car watching to make sure that I was okay.

From my mother I learned to do what I had to do to succeed, and if one thing did not work, to try something else. Another valuable thing that my mother taught me early on was that you have to work and live in a number of "different skins" and in a number of different communities. I like that advice. In school I learned things I needed to become an educated and successful person. In our neighborhood, at meetings, and in church, I learned about building community, respect, and getting along with people, things I did not learn about in school.

In high school, I hung out with a mixed group of Black and White students. They were from a range of backgrounds, including upper middle-class and working-class families. The year I entered high school was the first year that it was racially integrated. I describe my high school as racially integrated because that is what the board of education called it; however, it remained segregated inside the school. The Black students and some White working-class youth were in one set of classes. The top classes were reserved for students from affluent families, and they were all White. School officials claimed that tracking was done based on ability. Every year they put me in the lowest math class, but each time my mother went to school and she had them transfer me into the honors or advanced placement class. Of course, I was the only African American student in these classes. The other Black parents trusted the school system and figured their children were being placed in the classes where they belonged. It was not until I aced the SAT exams that the guidance counselors stopped trying to track me back into the lowest group.

In high school I started to follow in my mother's footsteps and I became an activist. The social studies textbook in 10th grade was called something like *Our European Heritage*. I got up in class and said, "Excuse me, but my heritage is not European and I find this book offensive. Why are we using a book that does not discuss the accomplishments of my people?" I refused to read the book and the argument continued until a compromise was reached. The school said I would not have to take the class, and if I passed the standardized state examination at the end of the year, I would get credit. Of course, I passed the test.

During my senior year in high school, while everyone was applying to college, the guidance department invited the Army into school and I was one of the students they tested to discover my aptitudes. They decided I would make a great truck driver! They took a bunch of us over to Fort Dix where they tried to convince us how great the army would be. I was suspicious because I thought the high school was trying to find a way to keep the Black students from graduating from their school. As it turned out, from my neighborhood, I was the only one of more than a dozen Black students that graduated.

I remember that my parents received a letter from school that said, "Congratulations, your child has been selected to go into the satellite program." It explained in glowing terms that I would have an opportunity to finish high school early by earning a GED. Most of my Black friends' parents were honored that their children were selected. When I told my mother that I wanted to enter the program, she said, "Go to school tomorrow; talk to some of your White friends; ask them how many were sent that letter." When I canvassed around, I discovered that none of them had received the letter. When I told her, she asked me, "If it is such a good thing, wouldn't more White students be involved?"

I lived on a block in St. Albans where there were approximately 70 houses. Out of all of these families, I was the only teenage girl who did not end up pregnant while in high school. When I was a high school student, I did not have many dates and I thought something was wrong with me. Later I learned that the older guys on the block, guys in their 20s, would run off anybody who was interested in me. I was their "sister," and they were trying to help me make it. They believed that I was special, and I know that I would not be where I am today without them and the other people in the neighborhood who cared about me and gave me support. A lot of them have had tragic lives. But they made it possible for me to be here and I cannot ever forget that.

When I went to get my master's I was originally pursuing a degree in biology. I was the only American Black in the master's program, and I ran up against much opposition. I remember when my father died. I had to go home and bury him, and I missed a week of classes. One professor told me that missing classes demonstrated that I was not qualified to become a scientist.

At the time I was taking some classes with medical students, and I kept thinking "This is not how I understand science." The attitude of the teachers was that only special people could understand the material. I really felt like it could be taught so that it would make sense to everybody. Part of Albert Einstein's genius was that he could explain the theory of relativity to ordinary people. He had the ability to make the complex seem so simple. He did not worry whether he sounded erudite.

I had always felt that I had the ability to explain. I tutored lots of friends and helped people get through their courses. I learned how to translate academic science into something that made sense in my life and was relevant to my experience, and I figured out ways to translate it back on tests. I called my mother up and said, "I think I'm going to transfer into education." She said, "You know, I could have saved you 10 years. That's where I thought you should go anyway."

A major reason I decided to become a teacher, and then a teacher educator, is that I believe I owe something to the people from my neighborhood and to the Black students who never graduated from my high school. I know I was not the most talented or the brightest of the bunch, but others were systematically pushed out until they could not stand it anymore and quit. Maybe I am more pigheaded than the rest. I managed to learn in spite of the teachers. I decided my mission was to go back to high school as a science teacher and say to students you can have a good experience because of me. You do not have to learn in spite of me. It is possible to achieve and I will help you do it.

At my first secondary school teaching job I worked with students who had always been low achievers, and they began to be successful. I knew some of my students were interested in dancing, so I used it as a hook to get them involved in science. I was teaching them about cilia and how these hair-like projections move cells around. At the time there was a dance called the body wave. I brought the music to school and we got up and did the body wave. That's how students learned how cilia beat. My principal was not necessarily all that happy. He looked in and wondered what was going on. I said let me try and teach them this way. If they do not respond, I will go back to the traditional methods. But my students did just as well, or better, than the other classes.

Another time, I had a student who was very artistic but did not want to learn. The other teachers let him sit in the back of the room and draw in his notebook as long as he did not bother anyone else. They warned me that if I tried to engage him in class he would become very disruptive, but I could not stand having him sit back there and not learn anything. I told him that his job was to draw all of my diagrams on the board. I bought him the most expensive chalk I could find because he was an artist and was going to help me teach science. He drew the most beautiful diagrams and carefully labeled each one. By the end of the year, this young man was talking about becoming a science teacher.

As a young teacher I learned that if I worked at teaching, and figured out what made my students "tick," something would get through to them. I know it gets through. This is a far more effective way of teaching than boring students, punishing them, and feeding into the resistance culture that alienates them from school. It is the right thing to do and it makes your life in the classroom much easier.

As a result of these experiences, I was invited to lead in-service workshops to show other teachers how to make the material more accessible to students. Later, I ran a program at the

University of North Carolina at Chapel Hill that taught students who were not doing well in science and mathematics how to think about science and mathematics in different ways. At that point I had my master's degree, and I decided to work toward my doctorate. I never really made a planned decision to go into teacher education, but opportunity, and my belief that everyone can learn science, led me in that direction.

As a high school teacher, I was determined to make science available to Black students like myself. However, as a teacher educator, I find that I generally work with White preservice teachers. Too many Black and Latino youngsters still do not make it into college, and amongst those who do, few currently see themselves becoming secondary school science teachers. That means if I am going to change science education for Black and Latino kids, I am going to have to prepare teachers to work with students whose cultures they do not share, in a society where working with these students is not valued.

Most of the White undergraduate and graduate preservice teachers who enter our teacher education program start out with a "deficit model" that they use to explain inadequate student performance, especially among minority youth. They look at what children do not know and what they cannot do, and they blame students, their families, their cultures and their communities for these perceived deficits. They talk about "why Johnny can't read," instead of the cultural richness, network of social relationships, and intelligence, nurtured in homes, communities, and churches, that children bring with them to school. I try to help preservice teachers see these strengths and figure out how to make them the basis for effective teaching and successful learning.

In my teacher education methods classes we examine case studies and discuss how different teachers handle situations in their classrooms and possible alternatives. We try to understand the same events through the eyes of both a teacher and of students. There is always some diversity in a classroom, and we spend a lot of time exploring each other's culture and heritage and how they shape who we are and the way we see the world. The more diverse a class is, the better. That way, when someone issues a pronouncement, "This is how it is!" someone else can respond, "That's not how it was for me." Sometimes people grow up in such a narrow segregated world that they never realize that other people do not have the same opportunities and experiences that they have. In a lot of ways, the class becomes an epiphany for them. I try to remind students that they are the success stories of the school system, but that everybody did not share their success.

I am a strong believer in the idea that teachers are professionals and must be educational leaders. To me, that means that teachers must find ways to relate to all children, not just the students who are quite capable of learning by themselves. And classroom teachers should not pretend they are sheep, followers who just do their jobs. Being a professional teacher requires a commitment to constantly learning new methods about presenting material, new ideas in your subject areas, and about your students. It means challenging things and people that do not make sense. Sometimes I hear teachers say, "Well, these kids today, they don't study like they used to. They never take the books home." That may be true. But all it means is that a different student population requires different teaching strategies. We can all sit at the bar and cry in our beer about how terrible it is, but if we are professional educators, we have to be willing to change what we do and change our schools to ensure that our students learn. Sometimes it means that teachers must surrender some of their control over the classroom and the curriculum in order to validate the life experiences of students. I like the slogan, "Think of yourself as the guide on the side, rather than as the sage on the stage."

One of the things I do in both my general methods classes and in my science curriculum classes is require preservice teachers to interview other people. They need to learn how to talk with people, how to ask them questions, and how to listen to their answers. I think one of the greatest things about growing up in a multicultural environment is that I learned how to talk with different kinds of people and I grew to respect their cultures and traditions.

My approach to teaching is actually a lot like my approach to science. My goal in both is to always ask questions. When you ask questions, you discover answers about people, science, the world, or teaching. You learn new information to integrate into your world view.

Being a woman has influenced my work as a teacher. I feel free to express love, compassion, and concern for students. I think that men feel like they lose their authority by reaching out to students. When I was teaching high school I inherited a class at midyear that was not doing very well. I was forced to double up on assignments so they would be ready for the test at the end of the year. One day they complained, "Ms. Hines, why are you making us do this?" I gave them 10 minutes to vent their frustrations and then replied, "Because I love you and know how important this will be in helping you choose what you want to do with your life. I put up with all your belly-aching because I love you."

The only thing that I would like to add is that teaching is truly a difficult job. But when you see the "light bulb" go on over a student's head, when you know that they "get it," all your hard work becomes worth it.

JOIN THE CONVERSATION—EXCEPTION OR POSSIBILITY?

Questions to Consider:

1. Max describes being stereotyped as a woman and as an African American pushed to go in a direction she did not want to take. Have you, or someone you know, had a similar experience? Describe the experience and explain how the person responded.

2. Max attributes many of the problems she faced in school to attitudes about race in the United States. Do you agree with the way she sees this issue? Explain your views.

3. As a young teacher, Max came to believe that if she "figured out what made my students 'tick,' something would get through to them." Do believe this is the obligation of a teacher? Explain.

4. In the introduction to this essay I asked you to consider whether Max's experience should be considered an exception or a suggestion of possibility. What do you think? Why?

SECTION F: SHOULD TEACHERS SEE RACE AND DISCUSS INJUSTICE?

In 1963, James Baldwin (1998), a well-known African American author, wrote a powerful essay that he directed toward teachers. After acknowledging that he was not a teacher, Baldwin asked his audience to hear out his ideas about the problems confronting schools, teachers, and students. Baldwin argued:

> The whole process of education occurs within a social framework and is designed to perpetuate the aims of society. Thus for example, the boys and girls who were born during the era of the Third Reich, when educated to the purposes of the Third Reich, became barbarians. The paradox of education is precisely this—that as one begins to become conscious one begins to examine the society in which he is being educated. The purpose of education, finally, is to create in a person the ability to look at the world for himself, to make his own decisions, to say to himself this is black or this is white, to decide for himself whether there is a God in heaven or not. To ask questions of the universe, and then learn to live with those questions, is the way he achieves his

own identity. But no society is really anxious to have that kind of person around. What societies really, ideally, want is a citizenry which will simply obey the rules of society. (pp. 678–679)

According to Baldwin, "The obligation of anyone who thinks of himself as responsible is to examine society and try to change it and to fight it—at no matter what risk. This is the only hope society has. This is the only way societies change" (p. 679). He believed he was speaking in a dangerous time and he was especially concerned with teachers who were working with African American youth. He said that if he were a teacher working with this group of students:

I would try to teach them—I would try to make them know—that those streets, those houses, those dangers, those agonies, by which they are surrounded, are criminal. I would try to make each child know that these things are the results of a criminal conspiracy to destroy him. I would teach him that if he intends to get to be a man, he must at once decide that he is stronger than this conspiracy and that he must never make his peace with it. . . . I would teach him that there are currently very few standards in this country which are worth a man's respect. That it is up to him to begin to change these standards for the sake of the life and health of the country. (p. 685)

He concluded: "One of the paradoxes of education was that precisely at the point when you begin to develop a conscience, you must find yourself at war with your society. It is your responsibility to change society if you think of yourself as an educated person" (p. 685). He adds, "If this country does not find a way to use that energy, it will be destroyed by that energy" (p. 686).

Each time I reread this essay, I am struck by its currency, yet I know it was written nearly 40 years ago. I think we have to ask ourselves why it still rings so true, and how we respond to it as teachers and prospective teachers.

Should we dismiss Baldwin as an echo of another era or as a prophet whose message is only intended for people planning to teach in "the city" or "the ghetto"? If we teach in those inner-city urban schools, do we expose ourselves to criticism by colleagues, administrators, and politicians by inviting students to stand up against injustice and demand "standards" that are "worth a man's respect"? Can we do this knowing that when students learn to challenge unfair practices, they will also be questioning our attitudes and behavior in class?

If we are working in suburban schools, do we have a responsibility to teach about race and upset the comforting myths held by many White students, parents, and colleagues? Or, do we allow them to continue to live with blinders on, culturally challenged, in the middle of a world of diversity and oppression beyond their wildest imaginations?

Should privileged students learn that their bounty comes at the expense and suffering of others, or is it safer to just let them compartmentalize, stereotype, and believe that I have what I have because my family, my ancestors, my people, and so on worked hard, while "they" are poor, sick, without because of some flaw in their individual or group character and culture?

JOIN THE CONVERSATION—RACE AND INJUSTICE

Question to Consider:

Should teachers see race and discuss injustice? Explain.

REFERENCES AND SUGGESTIONS FOR FURTHER READING

Apple, M. (1979). *Ideology and curriculum*. New York: Routledge.

Baldwin, J. (1998). *Collected essays*. New York: The Library of America, pp. 678–686.

Delpit, L. (1995).*Other people's children*. New York: The New Press.

Fine, M. (1991). *Framing dropouts*. Albany, NY: State University of New York Press.

Fine, M. (Ed.). (1994). *Chartering urban school reform*. New York: Teachers College Press.

Garcia, M. (1992). *The adventures of Connie and Diego*. Danbury, CT: Children's Press.

Gardner, H. (1987). Beyond IQ: Education and human development. *Harvard Educational Review, 57*(2), 187–193.

Gardner, H. (1993). *Multiple intelligences: The theory in practice*. New York: Basic Books.

Greene, M. (1993). Diversity and inclusion: Towards a curriculum for human beings. *Teachers College Record, 95*(2), 211–221.

Hartocollis, A. (2001a, May 11). Teacher takes chorus students to her eager Finland home. *The New York Times*, p. B1.

Hartocollis, A. (2001b, June 5). A chorus of hallelujahs and tears for a teacher. *The New York Times*, p. B8.

Himley, M., with Carini, P. (Eds.). (2000). *From another angle: Children's strengths and school standards*. New York: Teachers College Press.

Kohl, H. (1994). *I won't learn from you and other thoughts on creative maladjustment*. New York: The New Press.

Ladson-Billings, G. (1994). *The dreamkeepers: Successful teachers of African American children*. San Francisco: Jossey-Bass.

Logan, J. (1997). *Teaching stories*. New York: Kodansha America.

Lottridge, C. (1990). *The name of the tree*. Old Tappan, NJ: Simon & Schuster Children's.

Noddings, N. (1984). *Caring, a feminine approach to ethics and moral education*. Berkeley: University of California.

Noddings, N. (1992). *The challenge to care in schools*. New York: Teachers College Press.

Ogbu, J. (1994). From cultural differences to differences in cultural frame of reference. In P. Greenfield & R. Cocking (Eds.), *Cross cultural roots of minority child development* (pp. 365–391). Hillsdale, NJ: Lawrence Erlbaum Associates.

Parkinson, K. (1987). *The enormous turnip*. Morton Grove, IL: Albert Whitman.

Sadker, M., & Sadker, D. (1994). *Failing at fairness, how our schools cheat girls*. New York: Simon & Schuster.

Singer, A. (1999, September 5). Do programs for "gifted" kids leave other students behind. *Newsday*, p. B7.

Singer, J., & Singer, A. (2000). The multicultural literacy and citizenship project. *Multicultural Perspectives, 2*(2), 32–34.

Wolkstein, D. (1981). *The banza*. New York: Dial Books for Young Readers.

5

ORGANIZATION: HOW ARE CLASSROOMS AND SCHOOLS ORGANIZED?

Teacher education students and beginning teachers rarely think about the different ways that schools are organized. For most, their own experience as a secondary school student is the primary model they are familiar with and what they assume is the norm. But there are a number of things you need to consider as you try to figure out the type of teacher you want to be and where you would prefer to work. I emphasize prefer, because as a new teacher you may not have much of a choice.

For most of my career, I was a nontraditional teacher working within a traditional school setting. I needed to find a way to fit in and hold a job and to establish space where I was comfortable with my ability to relate with and influence students. As I grew older (and hopefully wiser), I realized there were some things I could change and other things or people I would have to accept (at least temporarily), work with, through, or around. As a new teacher you will be able to make some choices about how you want to organize your classroom, but generally you must comply with the way a school is organized or leave. In my experience, as you establish competence and your ability to work successfully with students, you will be allowed greater freedom in decision making, but the bottom line is that schools are not organized for the benefit of teachers or to help a young and idealistic social activist achieve his or her personal vision for education. You may be the world's best teacher; however, if you cannot hold a job, you will not change anyone.

I know that at this point in your "career" it is difficult to imagine, but there are schools where you may not be willing to work. Twice I said "No, thank you" to positions. While I was still searching for a permanent appointment, I was offered a job at a middle school where the principal prided himself on centralized control over everything that took place in "his" building. This extended to dictating to teachers what they taught and what their students read and wrote every lesson. With the arrogance of youth, I explained I did not think it was a good system and left the interview. On another occasion, I was offered a transfer to a newly established elite academic high school that wanted me to set up a Westinghouse (now Intel) social science research program for its top students. I disagreed with their desire to make individual research by a select few the school's educational priority and declined the offer.

Although this chapter starts with the way schools are organized, its primary focus is on classrooms. I prefer the term organization to either management or control because in the end, I think the only one you can control is yourself. Other people, especially adolescents, must be convinced that what you are saying and doing makes sense and they should go along. To paraphrase a quote by Abraham Lincoln, you can control all of the students some of the time, some of the students all of the time, but you cannot control all of the students all of the time. The effort to control everyone either promotes rebellion or teaches students to accept dictatorship. I do not think either of these ends is a worthy goal.

My experience is that the combination of relationships with students and effective organization eliminates 90% of the classroom problems new teachers anticipate and fear. This allows you to concentrate on your primary task, which is teaching students. As a teacher, you must learn how to structure lessons and set up a classroom to minimize conflicts and encourage student participation. But effective classroom organization is difficult, especially for young and inexperienced teachers. I find that this is an area in which people who have had other work experience usually have a decided advantage. As you start your career, experienced teachers, including myself, will give you a lot of conflicting suggestions about how to be successful as a teacher. Take all advice "with a grain of salt," and see what makes sense to you.

The rest of this chapter examines ways that high schools and middle schools are organized, including the tracking of students. I offer suggestions on how to adapt enough to find and hold onto a job in a traditional school setting, tips for organizing a classroom and developing class rules, and approaches to inclusive teaching. The chapter concludes with essays by four new teachers. Laura Pearson talks about the first day of the school year, Nichole Williams discusses her experience adjusting to life in a traditional school, Ken Dwyer compares being a student in a rural school with his experience teaching urban children and adults in rural Africa and in an affluent suburban community, and Kate Simons Smith describes teaching in public and parochial schools in different areas of the United States.

SECTION A: IF YOU COULD BUILD A SECONDARY SCHOOL FROM SCRATCH, WHAT WOULD IT LOOK LIKE?

In October 2000, a highly regarded magazine for teachers and school administrators, *Educational Leadership*, selected Raymond Callahan's 1962 classic *Education and the Cult of Efficiency* as one of the 100 most influential books on education written during the 20th century. Callahan studied the period between 1900 and 1940 when the modern American school system emerged. It is an era when the goals and practices of industry were widely celebrated, so it is not surprising that business and industrial management philosophies shaped the development of public schools. The assembly line was the model; economy, the ideal; efficiency, the goal.

Two other powerful forces shaping the American secondary school at the same time were Christian religious beliefs and opposition to immigration. Between 1880 and 1924, more than 26 million immigrants, the largest number from Eastern and Southern Europe and either Roman Catholics or Jews, arrived in the United States. This new population changed the face of the country and threatened to transform its culture and politics. The response of traditional elites, industrialists, established ethnic groups, and political and religious leaders was forced assimilation. New laws prohibited the manufacture and sale of alcoholic beverages and virtually barred new immigration between 1924 and 1965. Political radicals were arrested and deported, and schools were specifically designed to control, process, assimilate, and sort the new Americans and prepare them for manual labor and factory work. Progressive education, education for understanding and leadership, was reserved for the economic, social, and academic elite. Leonard Covello (with D'Agostino, 1958), an Italian immigrant who later became a high school principal, wrote in his memoir how working-class and immigrant youth who could not fit into this system dropped out of school and entered the workforce at the lowest end of the wage and skill scale.

In the second half of the 20th century, this system received a series of shocks that forced it to adapt, but not to fundamentally change. The Cold War between the United States and the Soviet Union, especially the Soviet's launching of a Sputnik satellite in 1957, increased the urgency for upgrading technical and scientific education and extending it to a larger number of students. As a result of the African American civil rights movement of the 1950s and 1960s, and the post–World War II women's rights movement, entire groups of people were no longer systematically relegated to second-class status and denied the right to a quality education. Technological change and the deindustrialization of the United States since the 1960s has meant an end to many factory jobs and pressure to keep students in school longer.

However, despite the powerful socioeconomic forces at work in the past 50 years, most secondary schools in the United States continue to be organized on the old fashioned business-industrial model. They have a rigid hierarchical chain of command, administrators are middle managers who enforce directives rather than team leaders who model successful teaching, teachers are required to achieve clearly operationalized and discrete outputs, and students are continuously tested to maintain quality control. Those who fail to meet standards are discarded.

Because of legal concerns, tracking has become more subtle, but it continues. The wealthiest families send their children to elite and expensive private schools. Affluent suburban districts provide a level of services parents, students, and teachers in other areas can barely imagine. Cities offer the select few special magnet programs. The more academically able of those who do not qualify frequently end up in parochial schools. The vast majority of inner-city youth and a large proportion of students in rural areas are still controlled, processed, assimilated, and sorted.

I recently visited a large urban high school that reminded me of the movie, *Demolition Man* (1993), starring Sylvester Stallone, Sandra Bullock, and Wesley Snipes. It was two schools in one: One school was clean, shiny, and above ground; the other was seething with activity, received little in the way of resources, and was hidden away. At a meeting with the principal of these "schools," he told a group of teacher education students about the approximately 200 students in the Scholar's Institute, the college scholarships they have earned, their advanced placement courses, and the number of awards the school has received because of this program. He distributed issues of the school's newspaper that recorded every one of their achievements. Yet the school had an official population of more than 2,500 students. Outside the window of his office we could see hundreds of students lined up, late for school, waiting to pass through metal detectors and be patted down by security guards. None of them was in the newspaper and the principal spoke as if they did not even exist.

There are some hopeful signs that these situations will change in the future, especially if teachers and their representatives have more of a say in school organization.

- An important force for changing the way schools are organized are legal campaigns being waged in state courts to require equalized school funding. In 1990, the New Jersey Supreme Court ruled that the funding of public schools primarily through local property taxes had produced a system in which "the poorer the district and the greater its need, the less the money available, and the worse the education." By 1994, 28 states were involved in cases dealing with the financing of education and eleven were reviewing the use of local property taxes as the major source of revenue for public education. If these campaigns are successful, schools in poorer communities, especially urban and rural areas, should have significantly more money available for education.

- School-based management offers real possibilities for reforming the way schools operate. This approach to running schools usually involves teams of administrators, teachers, parents, and sometimes student and community participants in collective decision making about issues as diverse as spending on supplies, curriculum, school lunches, discipline codes, and construction priorities. This approach has been tried in many communities and has received strong support from teacher unions.

- What has come to be called the *middle school model* is organized so that interdisciplinary teams of subject teachers who have the same classes meet on a daily basis with counselors, inclusion teachers, classroom aides, and administrators to plan instruction, coordinate projects and trips, and review the progress of individual students. Not only does this approach improve instruction, but it builds morale among staff members and tears down some of the barriers that exist between teachers and administrators.

- Many large buildings housing thousands of high school students and hundreds of teachers have been subdivided into mini-schools of a few hundred students. This reform is similar to some of the innovations of the middle school movement. It is designed to combat youthful alienation and anonymity. Mini-schools provide a family atmosphere in which small groups of teachers know students on a personal level. They also allow for closer cooperation between teachers and site administrators.

JOIN THE CONVERSATION—MODELS FOR ORGANIZING SCHOOLS

Traditional Model	Alternative Model
Clear hierarchy of authority among staff members, between staff and students.	Teachers and administrators are a team; decisions are collective; students are involved in the decision-making process.
Tight uniform schedule.	Flexible schedule based on activities.
Distinct academic departments.	Interdisciplinary collaboration.
Priority is *control* through enforcement of rules and punishment.	Priority is *relationship* through positive reinforcement and struggle.
Teacher-centered lectures.	Student-centered activities.
Competitive atmosphere. Homogenous, tracked classrooms.	Cooperative atmosphere. Heterogeneous, untracked classrooms.

Questions to Consider:

1. Which school would you rather attend as a student? Explain.
2. Where would you rather work as a teacher? Explain.
3. Do you think the "detracking" of schools is a legitimate goal? Can it work? Explain.
4. If you could build a secondary school from scratch, which of these models would it more closely resemble? Why?

SECTION B: HOW CAN YOU FIND (AND HOLD ONTO) A JOB IN A TRADITIONAL SCHOOL SETTING?

If you need to show off your great tattoos, insist on orange highlights in your hair, and just "can't go out" without your metal body piercings, I do not know if I can help you. But if you are willing to tone down a bit so you can find and hold onto a job in a traditional school setting, I have some tips that might not stretch your integrity too far.

I am a product of the 1960s, which is a polite way of saying that my appearance is a bit disheveled and I am a prone to fits of self-righteous indignation. I have a 5 o'clock shadow by 10 in the morning on days I do shave, my shirt is never stuck in my pants, I do not own a hair brush, and I like comfortable shoes. Stylish, I am not; professional looking, just barely.

I am starting with appearance because I think it is symbolic of your willingness to compromise in order to fit in and to discover flexibility in what can appear to be a rigid school system. The way you deal with appearance gives some clue to how successful you can be navigating a school.

School administrators tend to wear formal clothing: suits and ties for men, professional suits for women, and leather shoes. I think they learn this dress code in administrator classes. Rarely is someone promoted who does not fit this model; however, in most schools, teachers are not expected to dress this way. I certainly did not. On the other hand, I think it is a sign of respect to students to dress appropriately. I do not wear jeans, sneakers, or T-shirts to class. It also helps establish that school is a serious place where we are all expected to work hard and act in a responsible way.

I learned early in life that I hate ironing. I wear drip dry shirts and add a tie to cover most of the remaining wrinkles. A discreet tie is also important because it shows you are willing to try to fit in. Some of my ties are geared to lessons—a "Unicorn Tapestry" tie for studying about the Middle Ages, an "Australopithecus" tie from the Smithsonian Museum for human evolution, and maps of different parts of the world. I also fancy the "Save the Children" series. I did have a problem once when an administrator mistook a hammer and saw tie (from the PBS carpentry program) for a hammer and sickle (a symbol for communism), so you need to be careful.

Dry cleaning can be expensive, so I try to keep my wardrobe simple. I limit my school clothes to shades of blue and brown so pretty much everything goes together. I wear "Dockers" and corduroy pants and in the winter add a sleeveless vest. Stay away from wool because it is a magnet for chalk dust. Because I am on my feet all day, I prefer lightweight leather walking shoes. I am a big fan of the Eddie Bauer, L.L. Bean, and Land's End catalogs. The Lands End canvas briefcase is inexpensive, durable, stretches to hold everything, is easy to sort through, and always looks presentable. And remember, if you go to an interview and set off the metal detectors, you are wearing too much jewelry.

JOIN THE CONVERSATION—RACHEL GAGLIONE'S TIPS FOR WOMEN ON DRESSING FOR TEACHING AND TENURE

Rachel Gaglione is a middle school teacher and a mentor teacher in the Hofstra New Teacher Network. You will meet her again in chapter 6.—Alan Singer

What should a young female teacher wear to ensure that students and staff see her as an intelligent and respectable adult? Before you use the excuse of your first teaching job to shop for an entirely new wardrobe, here are a few things to keep in mind. This is a job you want to keep. In order to pave your way, move up the ladder, and, hopefully, get tenure, you need to project a certain image to supervisors, colleagues, parents and students. Believe it or not, when you were a student in high school, no one ever paid as much attention to what you wore as your students will pay to what you are wearing now.

1. How short is too short? If you look at yourself in the mirror and wonder if your skirt is too short or if the slit is too high, then it probably is. Ditto for V-neck tops.

2. A student once asked a colleague if she knew she had on "hooker" boots. If students are telling you how sexy you look, then you need to stop at the mall and buy different outfits. Remember, it is really hard to run around a classroom in high heels everyday, and those pants that sit low on your waist may be great for a night out, but what happens when you bend over to talk with a student or write on the board? Your job is to help students stay focused on the lesson, not on your outfit.

3. I worked at my school for 2 years before anyone found out that I have a tattoo. Was I embarrassed by my youthful decisions? No. I just realized that I came of age in a different time from many of my colleagues who view tattoos and other forms of body art as "irresponsible" and "reckless." I wanted to make sure that I would be evaluated on my teaching, not my "cover." The same goes for nose rings (yes, I had one too), belly button rings, and all the other piercings that are common today. Not everyone understands why you choose to decorate your body. In addition, children are impressionable. Some student might want to be just like you and run home and ask Mom for a butterfly tattoo on her ankle. This is not the phone call the district superintendent wants to receive. If you feel strongly about your right to self-expression, make sure you work in an environment in which it is accepted.

4. "Casual Friday" is for office workers who have to wear business suits every day of the week. As a teacher, you have a lot of "clothing" freedom everyday. However, jeans and sneakers do not a pedagogue make! Denim skirts and tops can also be questionable. Check with coworkers whom you respect. They are always the best source of information at a new place of employment.

5. Dressing professionally and neatly is a lot more important than dressing expensively. I have seen teachers of all shapes, sizes, styles, and ages mesmerize their students. The common factor is not how trendy or stylish they are, but rather how professional and respectful they are. Look at yourself in the mirror before you go to work and ask yourself, "Is the way I am dressed going to command respect?" If you dress like you deserve respect, then you will act respectfully, you will treat others with respect, and you will get respect.

Questions to Consider:

Rachel Gaglione recommends a relatively conservative approach to clothing and accessories.

1. What do you think of her views on appropriate school dress? Why?
2. How are they similar or different from yours?

Dealing with my streak of self-righteous indignation has been a little more difficult. Lois Weiner, a former New York City high school teacher and author of *Urban Teaching, The Essentials* (1999), believes it is possible to maintain cordial relations with all colleagues, and suggests smoothing over potential conflicts. When someone says something about students that she finds offensive, she replies, "I know you don't believe that so you shouldn't say it" (p. 34). I respect Lois a lot, but I was never willing or able to follow her advice. Sometimes you must take a stand on an issue and cannot avoid making enemies. Everyone in the school will not be your friend. When colleagues openly and publicly talk about individuals or groups of students in ways that I find unacceptable, I acknowledge their right to their opinion but challenge what they have to say and their right to say it in an unprofessional manner. If they continue, I inform them that I will not hesitate to report our conversation to appropriate supervisors. Over the years, many teachers have supported my response. They are upset when colleagues disparage or demean students and are glad when these teachers are confronted.

On the other hand, you will need allies if you want to affect the lives of students and even possibly help change schools. Over the years, I have found many colleagues, mentors, union officials, and school administrators whom I was privileged to work with. You were introduced to some of them in the chapter 3 section on "My Best Teachers." Others have contributed to this book. I have concentrated my efforts as a teacher on building these relationships, though I have battled with my share of "dinosaurs" along the way.

I have also learned a few valuable lessons that I would like to share.

1. When you do well with students, advocate for their rights and education, and are a positive force in the building, people who disagree with you will still respect you and you will earn the space you need to be the kind of teacher that you want to be. In the early 1980s, I tried to persuade my school principal to give us a MacIntosh computer (advanced for that time) for the social studies magazine. He said there was none available, but that students could use the machine in his office whenever it was necessary. For a week, I scheduled students to be there every period of the day. On Friday, he gave us the computer to get them out of his office.

2. As an activist, I often made waves that unsettled school administrators. When students in my government class organized to go to Washington D.C., to participate in a demonstration, the district office, fearing political opposition, questioned its educational validity. My department chair intervened and worked out a compromise that I accepted. An assistant principal joined us as a chaperone to ensure that the students were safe and that it was a legitimate learning experience. In this case, district officials were prepared to be flexible, but I had to be flexible as well.

3. If you champion every issue, people will soon either stop listening to you or resent it when you speak out. At school and department meetings, I try to be selective about my participation in discussion. I listen while others present their ideas, write down my thoughts, edit them, and only speak once or twice.

4. Teachers are swamped with paperwork and it is sometimes hard to tell which circular is important and which was issued so an administrator can claim everyone was notified (These are technically known in teaching as CYA notices, or "Cover Your Rear"). In general, attendance reports, grades, and anything else that directly affects students should get priority. For everything else I use the "third notice" rule. If a deadline is important, they will send you a third notice or contact you individually.

5. Teachers are fortunate to have union representation. Most of the time, your relationship with supervisors will be congenial, but not always. They often have outside pressures on them. If there is a point of contention, and you have a good working relationship with your supervisor, you can usually have an "off-the-record" conversation that will help clarify issues. But if an off-the-record conversation is not possible and there is a union in the school, you should consult your representative. What you are obsessing about is probably not such a big deal and has happened to many people in the past. If it is a real problem, the union representative will advise you how to proceed. In some circumstances, if it is allowed under the union contract or by law, your representative can be present at formal meetings with supervisory personnel.

6. Many senior teachers will recommend that you take a low profile until you get tenure, then you can "rock the boat" if you choose. In my experience, teachers who remain silent while untenured will continue to remain silent later, because administrators always have ways of re-

warding the compliant and punishing opposition. Assignments to special programs, classes, clubs, or teams can be offered or withheld. As a new teacher you need to decide what kind of compromises you are prepared to make. Some school settings may be the wrong ones for you.

JOIN THE CONVERSATION—"VALUABLE LESSONS"

Questions to Consider:

1. Earlier I warned you to take the advice of senior teachers with "a grain of salt." However, in this section I offered six "valuable lessons" that I learned as a teacher. Which of the lessons do you agree with? Why?
2. In your opinion, does compromise mean selling out your values? Explain.

SECTION C: IF YOU COULD DESIGN A SECONDARY SCHOOL CLASSROOM, WHAT WOULD IT LOOK LIKE?

In *Hard Times* (1854/1973), English novelist Charles Dickens introduces us to Thomas Gradgrind, an industrialist and the headmaster of a school where the goal is to take "little pitchers" and fill them "full of facts." Gradgrind's school is in an English mill town during the industrial revolution of the mid-1800s and his students are destined to become cogs in the machinery of the new society. In the second chapter, titled "Murdering the Innocents," he demonstrates his scientific method of teaching to a new instructor, Mr. M'Choakumchild:

> "Girl number twenty," said Mr. Gradgrind, squarely pointing with his square forefinger, "I don't know that girl. Who is that girl?"
>
> "Sissy Jupe, sir," explained number twenty, blushing, standing up, and curtseying.
>
> "Sissy is not a name," said Mr. Gradgrind. "Don't call yourself Sissy. Call yourself Cecilia."
>
> "It's father as calls me Sissy, sir," returned the young girl in a trembling voice, and with another curtsey.
>
> "Then he has no business to do it," said Mr. Gradgrind. "Tell him he mustn't. Cecilia Jupe. Let me see. What is your father?"
>
> "He belongs to the horse-riding, if you please, sir."
>
> Mr. Gradgrind frowned, and waved off the objectionable calling with his hand.
>
> "We don't want to know anything about that, here. You mustn't tell us about that, here. Your father breaks horses, don't he?"
>
> "If you please, sir, when they can get any to break, they do break horses in the ring, sir."
>
> "You mustn't tell us about the ring, here. Very well, then. Describe your father as a horse-breaker. He doctors sick horses, I dare say?"
>
> "Oh yes, sir."
>
> "Very well, then. He is a veterinary surgeon, a farrier and horsebreaker. Give me your definition of a horse."
>
> (Sissy Jupe thrown into the greatest alarm by this demand.)
>
> "Girl number twenty unable to define horse!" said Mr. Gradgrind, for the general behoof of all the little pitchers. "Girl number twenty possessed of no facts, in reference to one of the commonest of animals! Some boy's definition of a horse. Bitzer, yours." (pp. 8–9)

Later in the chapter, we learn that Mr. M'Choakumchild, "and some one hundred and forty other schoolmasters, had been lately turned at the same time, in the same factory, on the same principles, like so many pianoforte legs. He had been put through an immense variety of paces, and had answered volumes of headbreaking questions." Dickens wearily suggests that "if he had only learnt a little less, how infinitely better he might have taught much more!" (p. 12).

If this kind of classroom was a thing of past, it would be bad enough. Sadly however, many of us have witnessed, or experienced as students, schools in which teachers still use these approaches to teaching, where boredom and humiliation are wielded as weapons to keep students in line.

As a new teacher you have to decide on the kind of classroom you want to have, a decision that reflects your broader philosophy of teaching, standards established by your school or district, what your students are accustomed to from earlier experiences, what you have planned, and the materials you have to work with. Generally, I favor a flexible approach to organizing the classroom. I prefer moveable chairs with arms, but if I have to, I can adjust to tables and even fixed row seating. Even when I use cooperative learning with a class, I usually start every lesson with the room organized into rows. It makes it easier for me to perform clerical tasks (e.g., take attendance, check homework) and for students to get started with the lesson. From there, we switch the room around depending on what we are going to do that day. Students can work individually or with a partner in the next row, or four chairs can be made into a pinwheel that allows student cooperative learning teams to work together. If there is a student or teacher presentation, if we are watching a video, or if something needs to be copied off the board, we can keep the desks in rows. For a full-class discussion, in a large enough room, we "circle up."

I decorate rooms with colorful subject-appropriate posters, student work, and plants. Once we had a class parakeet named Thomas Jefferson, whose cage was lined with photocopies of a picture of Jefferson's archenemy, Alexander Hamilton. When possible, I got free posters from airlines, video stores, book publishers, and at teacher conferences. When necessary, I bought them. I had to live in these rooms a large part of my day, so I wanted them to look and feel welcoming. One year, my room was so decrepit that I enlisted a group of students and we painted it. Steve Marlowe, a mentor teacher in the New Teachers Network, has a room full of hanging plants and plays music as students enter his class.

Other ideas for organizing the classroom to help achieve your educational goals (assuming you are not committed to the Gradgrind approach) and to convince students you know what you are doing include the following:

- Come in early in the morning and put greetings and instructions for each of your classes on the board. This makes it possible to greet students at the door at the start of the period. If you share a room with another teacher, you can arrange to use a side board and cover assignments with a roll-down map or a poster. If you are a "traveling man (or woman)," put notices on poster paper. Avoid using the overhead projector at the start of a period before the class is set up. If you turn out the lights, you invite trouble.

- Seating arrangements are important. Most students like to have their own designated space. When you do not assign seats there is sorting at the start of every period. Bullies grab the prime spots (e.g., in the back, next to a talkative, attractive, or flirtatious person). It is harder for you to learn student names and there is a general sense of disorder. On the first day of class I assign students to seats alphabetically and then we shift around a little so that a 6-foot 4, 250-pound football player is not squeezed into a chair in the front, blocking everyone behind him, and so that everyone can see and hear. I also inform students of three procedural rules. First, "I take attendance from the seat, so if the seat is empty, you are marked absent." Second, "I do not like empty seats in the front. If you are absent a lot, I will move other people up." Third, "There is no such thing as a permanent seat. If there are problems, someone may have to move so we can all work more effectively. We will also change some seating assignments once we form cooperative learning teams." Many new teachers seat "disruptive children" in front and middle of the classroom so they can "ride herd" on them. But if the student could be controlled in this simple fashion, neither the teacher nor the student would have the problem in the first place. This can also be counterproductive because it makes the student the center of attention. In my experience, students who are "wired" would rather not be that way and they certainly do not want to be embarrassed by teachers. I recommend letting a student who needs more space sit on the side of the room by the window so he or she does not feel so hemmed in.

- I used to live in terror that I would lose my record book. I wrote my name, classroom, department, home phone number, and home address on the inside cover. Then I discovered the spread sheet. I am a "MacPerson" and use Microsoft Excel. I prepare a spread sheet for each class and recruit a monitor to enter names, official classes, ID numbers, and phone numbers for each student. Columns are designated for attendance, homework, projects, and tests. I write on a printout for a week, update the data bank, reprint, and sleep better at nights. The program can even calculate student grades.

- Use your voice and posture to get attention, but once you have it, speak softer so they have to listen. If you habitually yell over the class, they will only get louder. Do not flick the lights on and off. It is demeaning to secondary school students and makes you look silly.

- My homework policy is very simple. You must do every assignment to pass the class. Homework is due the day assigned, but late homework is always accepted. I believe every excuse, but students still must make up the work. I encourage students to do homework by putting questions from the homework on tests and by giving failing grades on report cards to students when they are missing work. Once students make up the work, I remove the homework penalty. I have been known to give incompletes (not enter a grade) or negotiate, but privately and only under extreme circumstances.

- Most new teachers collect, read, and grade too much student work. They become bookkeepers instead of teachers. Eventually they get swamped, frazzled, and burned out. They walk around the building with piles of loose-leaf scribbles and spend nights pushing paper instead of planning. Assignments are for the students so that they learn. I usually spot check homework while they are working individually or in groups and only collect what I actually want to read. Another helpful idea is pairing each student with a "writing buddy" who edits written work before it is submitted for evaluation.

- To free you up from clerical responsibilities and allow you to concentrate on teaching, have student monitors take attendance; check homework; and distribute books, supplies, and activity sheets.

JOIN THE CONVERSATION—MODELS FOR ORGANIZING CLASSROOMS

Traditional (or Gradgrind) Model	Alternative (Inclusive) Model
Fixed desks. Students sit in rows.	Moveable furniture. Room arranged based on activities.
Focus is on the teacher.	Focus on interaction and community.
Fixed time schedule and curriculum.	Flexible schedule and calendar based on activities.
Priority is *control* through punishment and boredom.	Priority is *relationship* through positive reinforcement and struggle.
Teacher-centered lectures.	Student-centered activities.
Competitive atmosphere. Homogenous, tracked classrooms.	Cooperative atmosphere. Heterogeneous, untracked classrooms.

Questions to Consider:

1. Which classroom would you have preferred as a student? Explain.
2. Where would you rather work as a teacher? Explain.
3. If you could organize your classroom your own way, what would it look like? Why?

SECTION D: NUTS AND BOLTS OF TEACHING 2: HOW DO YOU ESTABLISH CLASSROOM RULES?

I smile on the first day of class. Why not? I like being a teacher and I like working with teenagers. I find you can be caring and still be efficient and demanding. When students know you are willing to smile, a disappointed or disapproving "teacher's look" carries much greater weight. If you always frown, it does not make a difference.

In January 2001, the New York State edition of a teachers' union newspaper reported that the winner of the Disney American Teacher of the Year Award winner had five "rules" and 50 "procedures" that students were obligated to follow in class. It seems to me that this was far too many procedures and substitutes control for community. I prefer a more minimalist approach to rules that encourages student freedom and responsibility. However, I also recognize that some classrooms need greater structure than others. I would sometimes tell a more rambunctious group (the class at the end of the day or right after lunch), "I know how to teach the fun way and the boring way. I prefer the fun way, but by your response you will decide the way that I will teach this class."

When I taught at schools that were relatively well organized and where students had an expectation of doing work and behaving in class, I had only two class rules. I introduced them with selections from songs performed by "Professor" Aretha Franklin: R-E-S-P-E-C-T and THINK. On the first day we discussed having a classroom where students and teachers respected each other and thought about the implications of our behavior on classroom community before we acted. We also discussed some procedures for resolving conflicts and my expectations for them.

In schools that tended to be disorganized and where procedures were less firmly established, I distributed "Singer's Ten Commandments" and we went over them on the first day. Some of the commandments were a restatement of school rules (no hats in class) and some were tailored for my class. However, even in this case, I tried to keep the classroom atmosphere relaxed. I did not post rules or require that students sign contracts where they promised on the pain of death to always be good. I always warned students, "If you sit with your head down I will figure the problem is that your wicked stepmother keeps you up all night chopping wood for the fireplace and scrubbing pots and pans. If it keeps happening, I will have to report her for child abuse, so don't give me the wrong message."

JOIN THE CONVERSATION—SINGER'S TEN COMMANDMENTS

An important idea in this class is the connection between freedom and responsibility. The more responsibility students take in class, the more freedom you will have to learn. A few basic procedures will help the class run more smoothly.

1. Be a serious student. Respect yourself and others. Raise your hand before speaking and listen to your classmates. Let's learn from each other.
2. Come to class on time. Sit with your assigned team.
3. When you enter the room, copy the AIM, the DO NOW, and the HOMEWORK.

4. If you have to go to the bathroom, go to the bathroom. Take the pass from the front of the room. Unfortunately, only one person can go at a time. Don't leave for the first 10 minutes or the last 10 minutes of the period because you won't know how the lesson began or ended.

5. Please don't eat in class, play a radio, or sit with your head down. Please remove hats in class.

6. If you are absent, bring a note. Cutters will be penalized. I take cutting as a personal insult.

7. Be prepared with a pen and notebook everyday.

8. Class participation, homework, and preparation are all part of your grade.

9. Number all homework assignments. Keep them in a separate section of your notebook.

10. Homework is due when assigned, but can be made up late. You must compete **all** homework assignments to pass the class. Answer all questions in complete sentences.

Questions to Consider:

What do you think of my recommendations on class rules? Why?

There are many ways to present rules in class. Henry Dircks, a social studies teacher in the New Teachers Network, has three posters hanging in his room. Each poster includes a picture of a former U.S. president and a slightly modified "quote." Franklin D. Roosevelt says: The only thing we have to fear is fear itself; . . . that and being late to class. Thomas Jefferson explains: All men are created equal, . . . but people who participate in class get better grades. Abraham Lincoln suggests: With malice towards none; with charity for all . . . let us strive to finish the work we are in . . . and study hard for unit tests.

Every society, community, and school has unofficial as well as official rules. These rules are not written down but definitely exist in practice. For example, what should your students call you? Most schools expect students to address teachers as Ms., Miss, Mrs., Mr., or Dr. So-and-So. But the rule is rarely written down anywhere. When I was young and just beginning, I needed to have students call me Mr. Singer to help me to establish myself as an adult and their teacher. On a couple of occasions I had students whom I knew from camp or the neighborhood, where they called me Alan. I told them that "outside I would always be Alan, but in class, they had to call me Mr. Singer."

Eventually, when I became more comfortable with my role as a teacher, I changed the unwritten rule and introduced myself to new classes as Alan. The sun continued to shine, the Earth did not tremble, no administrator ever reprimanded me (though some teachers were unhappy), and I did not lose the respect of my students. Members of the New Teachers Network who have tried this report similar results.

The advantage of unofficial rules, such as giving students incompletes, is that they are less likely to cause a problem with school authorities, and if they do, the situation can be "massaged." Once I was called to the assistant principal's office because I had too many missing grades on my grade sheets. I looked puzzled and said "it must be a computer error." Some of my unwritten class rules, that I convey to students orally, include the following:

- If you have trouble with another teacher or the dean, come see me before it escalates. As long as you are honest with me, I will help you as best as I can. But if you ever lie to me, I will not be able to trust and support you.

- Nobody in my class is allowed to fight in school. If anyone is picking on you or wants to fight with you, tell them they must fight me first. I am not worried because I know you and your friends are my "back."
- If you want to tell me something, I cannot promise in advance to keep it a secret. You are telling me because you know I care about you and you trust my judgment that I would not intentionally hurt you.

In chapter 2, I introduced a guide for teachers developed by the U.S. Army Air Corps during World War II. Although their students were generally adults, some were not much older than the teenagers in your classes and I suspect many were not enthusiastic about being either students or soldiers. The guide offers 14 suggestions to help teachers reduce discipline problems. Its basic premise is that "in a class of mature students who are kept busy in worthwhile activities which are of interest and value, there is little or no disciplinary difficulty. If students have a real motive for studying, if the class work gives them something useful and important, and if they are kept busy thinking or doing, problems of discipline will be rare indeed." In general, I agree with its approach. What do you think? At the end of book II, chapter 6, I have a series of case studies that will let you test out your own ideas on dealing with classroom and other professional problems.

JOIN THE CONVERSATION—THE ARMY AIR CORPS MANUAL'S RECOMMENDATIONS ON CLASSROOM DISCIPLINE

1. Be the master of the situation from the start.
2. Begin each lesson promptly, vigorously, and interestingly.
3. Plan each lesson carefully so that there is enough to keep the entire class busy to the end of the period.
4. Don't worry about being too severe or strict during the first lesson. Your class will "size you up" quickly as a good disciplinarian, or as a weak one. It is easier to relax a tight rein than to get control again after the class has run away with you. This does not mean that you must be a martinet. Be fair and human even though you set high standards.
5. Deal promptly and effectively with the first infraction of discipline, however small. A class does not object to a strict instructor if he is fair and efficient.
6. Don't use a loud voice or threatening language.
7. Drive home the idea that your students and you are working together in a great cause, the preparation of our nation's defense.
8. Keep everyone busy, and there will be little opportunity for trouble.
9. Distribute your questions to all the members of the class and hold all accountable.
10. Follow no set order in asking questions. Keep all the class alert and attentive.
11. Stand while you teach so that you can see what is going on all the time, as well as being able to serve more efficiently as an instructor.
12. Make your teaching lively and interesting.
13. Don't make threats of punishment that you cannot or do not intend to carry out.
14. Make your students enjoy your class; let them learn that you know your job and that by working with you they can achieve much that will be of great value to them. Take a personal interest in them. Help them with their difficulties and problems, and you should have little or no trouble with discipline.

Questions to Consider:

1. What are your concerns about student discipline as you prepare to become a teacher? Why?
2. Do you agree or disagree with the philosophy that underlies this approach to classroom discipline?
3. Do you think an approach to discipline intended for "mature students" in the military is appropriate in a middle school or high school classroom? Explain.
4. What formal rules would you want in your classroom? Why?

SECTION E: HOW DO YOU ORGANIZE AN INCLUSIVE CLASSROOM?

Increasingly, teachers are grappling with ways to adapt teaching strategies to inclusive classrooms containing students from different social and economic backgrounds and with different levels of preparation and interest, and including students who had previously been programmed for separate remedial or special education classes. Inclusive classes can be models for heterogeneous grouping and multicultural education.

Some of the students previously assigned to separate classes have physical difficulties whereas others are labeled learning disabled, ADHD (with an attention deficit and hyperactive), or emotionally disturbed. Many youths were classified as special needs students and placed in separate restricted classrooms because teachers and evaluators considered them unable to adjust to the discipline demanded of students in regular classroom settings. This is the group of children classroom teachers have the greatest reservations about reassigning to inclusive classrooms. Significantly, in many school districts, this group of students is disproportionately African American, male, and from lower income families.

Under law, every student assigned to special education programs has a specific defined "disability" or special need and an IEP intended to help him or her succeed in school. Many special education programs have unnecessarily isolated special needs students, contributing to stereotyping and high rates of academic failure. The issue should be how the educational and social needs of these students are best addressed.

An additional problem is what schools and teachers mean by disability and ability. We tend to think of these categories as universal, distinct, and unbiased. However, this model may be arbitrarily squeezing a wide spectrum of normal human activity into a narrow band deemed acceptable.

As a teacher, instead of discussing ability and disability, I prefer to talk about performance level. Performance level is temporary, not permanent, and more easily measurable. More important, teachers can develop strategies to help a range of students improve their performance levels. As you will discover as you read the following suggestions, I believe the same approaches for organizing inclusive classrooms are applicable in every classroom.

Some teachers are uncomfortable with the idea of inclusive classrooms because they often mean that more than one teacher will be in the room and planning instruction. It requires a level of teamwork that can be enticing in theory but difficult to implement in practice.

General Classroom Suggestions for Inclusive Classrooms

- *Structure*—Organize lessons and set up the classroom to minimize conflicts and distractions and to encourage student participation. All students need structure. In an inclusive classroom with a diverse student population, a clear structure becomes even more important.

- *Relationship*—Students who feel that their teachers care about them as human beings and are willing to respond to their needs and concerns will be more willing to cooperate, even if they do not understand, disagree with, or have difficulty following instructions. Students want you to be demanding but must believe you are caring and fair.
- *Classroom community*—As students develop a sense of relationship with each other and the teacher, an interest in the topics being explored, confidence that they will be treated fairly, and the conviction that their ideas will be heard, they develop a commitment to the success of the class as a whole and all its members. As a group, they want to learn and they take responsibility for what goes on in their class. They develop the collective mentality that "we learn as a TEAM!" A sense of classroom community is essential if inclusive classrooms are going to be successful.
- *Curriculum and instruction*—In traditional, tracked classrooms, teachers aim curriculum and materials at a hypothetical class average. Sometimes difficult material is used to challenge the more advanced students; sometimes easier material is used to help everyone keep up, but the goal generally is to target the middle. A different model for inclusive classrooms is the use of differentiated texts and assignments. Everyone in class studies and discusses the same topics, but working individually or in either homogenous or heterogeneous groups, students use reading material adapted for their current performance level.
- *Assessment*—Tests should not be a contest for the highest grades. I use the same rule for all students. Everyone receives the time and the help they need to demonstrate what they have learned on exams. Students who need to can take tests in a resource room. This is discussed further in chapter 8.

Co-teaching Suggestions for Classroom and Inclusion Teachers

- Plan together. The classroom teacher, as content specialist, develops initial lessons. The inclusion teacher designs adapted materials.
- Work together. It is almost impossible to teach a full class lesson while someone else is moving around the room talking with individual students or collecting material. Necessary individualized teacher–student interactions have to be planned in advance.
- Teach the class together. Take turns teaching the full class or have the inclusion teacher step in during individual work and group activities.
- Have a study center in a quiet corner where the inclusion teacher can provide extra help during individual assignments. Every student in the class should have the right to use the study center. This will enhance classroom community.
- Inclusion teachers can take groups of students to the library or computer center to work on individual reports and study for tests. Again, every student in the class should have the right to use this resource.
- Do not put all the inclusion students in the same group. It undermines community and defeats the purpose of inclusion. Academically high performing students will benefit from the opportunity to explain ideas to students who are performing at an academically lower level. We all learn from teaching.
- People are good at different things. Inclusion students will be group leaders and peer teachers on some projects.

- Sometimes teachers can organize groups that are able to function with minimal teacher involvement so both teachers can concentrate on helping the other groups.
- When students are in groups, the inclusion teacher (and the classroom teacher) should work with the entire group, not just the inclusion students.
- Individual students within groups can use material appropriate to their individual performance levels (differentiated texts) and contribute to team learning.
- Even in a team relationship, someone has to have ultimate responsibility for the class and make final decisions about policies, curriculum, and timing. Someone has to be in charge. I believe it should be the classroom teacher, who must teach a subject to the full class, rather than the inclusion teacher, whose primary responsibility is the performance of an individual student or a small group of students. Disagreements between teachers should be openly discussed in team meetings or, if necessary, mediated with supervisors.

JOIN THE CONVERSATION

1. Many school districts are moving toward an inclusion model for secondary schools. Do you believe these classes can be successful for all students?
2. Laura Peterson, a member of the New Teachers Network, is an inclusion social studies teacher in a 7–12 school. Laura helped me with this section, but disagrees with my idea that one teacher must be in charge of the class. She feels they can be co-equals. What do you think? Why?

SECTION F: BECOMING A TEACHER 4: RESPONDING TO DIFFERENT SCHOOL SETTINGS

In this section, you will meet four young teachers who have worked in a range of different school settings. The question you need to consider is whether successful teaching differs significantly from community to community or has a fundamental universality.

The First Day of the School Year
By Laura Pearson

Laura Pearson is a middle school teacher in a suburban school district. She remembers how much she loved school as a child and that is her starting point as a teacher. She recommends that teachers keep the classroom rules simple and concentrate on building an inclusive and caring community from "day 1."—Alan Singer

Teachers need to spend the first couple of weeks really getting to know students. For some of my students, it is not only the first day of the school year, but their first day in middle school. They are both excited and very nervous. It is important from "day 1" that they know I am happy to be there, organized, ready for action, and a caring individual who is interested in them. That means you have to S-M-I-L-E.

On day 1, I . . .

. . . greet each student at the door.

. . . hand each child a course outline.

... direct students toward preassigned seats (in either alphabetical or reverse alphabetical order).

... welcome students to class and introduce myself with a personal anecdote about who I am and why I teach.

... explain clearly how to read and follow instructions written on the board (each day when you enter the room you need to copy the date, aim question, and homework assignment and start the "do now" assignment).

... review procedures for arriving and leaving the classroom (no one packs up until I say, "Have a great day"); completing, collecting, and grading homework, projects, and tests; and implementing our class "discipline plan." Students are expected to be respectful of each other. Misbehavior is not tolerated. Every situation is different and students are treated individually.

... send home a letter introducing myself and the course of study to parents.

... ask the students to complete a class census.

On day 1 (time permitting) we also ...

... make a "top five list" of their likes and dislikes about school (I type it up and hand it out the following day).

... discuss what they will be learning about in class this year.

... look at sample projects from previous years.

FIG. 5.1 Welcome to Ms. Pearson's class.

Please complete the following census form about yourself and your family.

Name: _____ Class period: _____ Lunch period: _____

Home address (Number/Street/Town/ZIP): _____

_____

Home phone number(s): _____

E-mail address and Web site: _____

Parents' names: _____

Best phone numbers to reach your parents: _____

Names of other members of your immediate family (brothers and sisters and other people you live with): _____

Previous year's teacher(s): _____

After-school activities you are interested in: _____

_____

An interesting fact about you summer: _____

_____

An interesting fact about yourself: _____

_____

. . . answer any questions students have about class, school, and life.

I find the following are seven things most students want to know on the first day of school:

1. Am I in the right room?
2. Where am I supposed to sit?
3. What will I be doing this year?
4. How will I be graded?
5. What are the rules in this classroom?
6. Will the teacher treat me as a human being?
7. Who is the teacher as a person?

JOIN THE CONVERSATION—MS. PEARSON'S CLASS

Questions to Consider:

1. Laura liked school and believes that most students also like school. Do you agree? Do you think this is related to who students are and their life experiences? Explain.
2. Laura is willing to share a personal anecdote with her students. Do you think this is advisable? Explain.
3. Laura has few class rules. She believes that "every situation is different" and that students should be "treated individually." Do you agree? Explain.
4. Knowing Laura from this essay, if you were a parent, would you want her to teach your children? Why?

A New Teacher's Difficult Journey
By Nichole Williams

Nichole Willams is now a mentor teacher in the Hofstra New Teachers Network and a cooperating teacher. Despite the problems she faced in her first year of teaching, she decided to earn an advanced certificate in school administration so that she can try to change her school from within. In this essay, she says, "I know some people think that I have an advantage being successful with my students because I am African American. I think it gives me a head start; I admit that. I have an edge because I can relate more to their lives. . . . But that is only the beginning. . . . If you are boring students to death, if you do not respect them, it does not make a difference if you are Black or White."—Alan Singer

The first year of teaching is a mind-numbing experience. Schools of education can give you all the academic training in the world, but they cannot prepare you for the barrage of paperwork, discipline issues, and the delicate politics involved in working with parents, administrators, and veteran colleagues. Added to this, I had the special situation of returning to live and work in the school district where I was raised.

When I started working in the district, I was excited for many reasons. There was a special feeling knowing that I could give something back to a community that I had been a part of and was a major part of my life. I also looked forward to working with teachers who had encouraged me to join their profession.

Once the school year began, however, I was struck by some serious realizations. What I had studied about educational philosophy did not easily correlate with what I actually experienced in the classroom. The pedestal that I put my former teachers on turned out to be much too high. Finally, I had to find a way to redefine my relationship with my students. Although we related in a lot of ways, there were big social, political, economic, and academic holes in their lives that I had to address, even when they were unwilling to cooperate. Suddenly, somehow, I had to find a way to integrate into one cohesive mission my personal dreams about being a teacher and working with young people, all I had learned and had adapted into my educational philosophy, and the reality I was experiencing trying to get along with colleagues and motivate students. I discovered that my mission, to educate students to the best of my ability, in the most creative ways possible, so they could achieve to the best of their ability, is a profound joy for me, but also an overwhelming challenge.

I made the decision to teach in my old high school despite reservations because my experience there as a teenager was so important to me. I actually turned down a higher paying job in another district. The interview process was odd because the committee included my 9th-, 10th-, and 12th-grade social studies teachers, and they remembered me because I had been very active in school programs as a student.

When I did a demonstration lesson, I knew a number of the students from the neighborhood and they kept calling me Nichole instead of Miss Williams and telling me they hoped I would become a teacher there. There was also tension because when I was offered the job, a young White woman, who was a substitute teacher at the school and who was also an alumna, was passed over. The rumor was that I got the job because I was Black. Despite everything, or because of it, I accepted the position.

I remembered it as a very small community, and a small high school, where they really nurtured teenagers, but very quickly I learned that things would not be like my memories. At the first meeting in August, the teachers started talking about the students, saying nasty, negative things like, "It's time for the animals to come back." I said to myself, "Is this how they referred to me?" Others would joke, "Thirty-five years until retirement," and they would laugh. Were they all laughing at me?

When the school year started I felt undermined a lot of the time, even by teachers who tried to be nice. They would not stop telling the students that they had me in class when I was a student. Here I was, trying to get my class to see me as an adult, which is hard enough because I am a young Black woman who lives in the neighborhood, and these teachers kept on reminding everyone that I used to be their student. One teacher, who did not know me, even stopped me in the hall and demanded to know where I was going. I had to tell him that I was a teacher. While this was only one teacher, I think his reaction to me because I am young and Black is indicative of the atmosphere in the school.

When I went into the faculty room, what I thought was the faculty room, you know, lots of smoke and coffee, I felt like the other teachers were trying to turn me into something I did not want to become, somebody like them. When they talked to me about the students, they would say, "When you were here, it was so much different. These aren't the same kind of kids as you." But I kept thinking to myself, "What could have possibly changed in 8 years?" The same stupid stuff that kids are doing now, we were doing then. I do not see the intelligence of the students as less than it was 8 years ago.

I finally concluded that it is not so much that the kids have changed, it is the teachers who have changed. They have gotten older; less patient with teenagers, especially Black, Latino, and immigrant teenagers; and they reject the more open ways of teaching and relating to students. Educational practice and theory have changed, but unfortunately they have not. When I try something different or interesting in my classes, they always respond, "That is all well and good, but what about the Regents (state) exam?"

I like to have a relaxed atmosphere in the classroom, and I do not keep the desks in rows; we usually sit in a circle and I let students choose their own seats. I am also lenient as far as homework goes. I think my whole approach to the classroom gets the students to think, "Oh, she's cool, she's not like one of them."

So far, this approach is working for me for some reason. All of my observations have been good, but after my last one, the chairperson said that I need to have the students see me as more of an authority figure. While he was speaking, I kept thinking that if he keeps treating me as if I am still a child whenever he sees me in the building, how does he expect the students to react to me?

A problem I face with the older students is that they have spent 2 or 3 years in high school doing the bare minimum, and I am trying to get them to do more. I had a fight with my 11th-grade class because they told me how the rule was that three paragraphs make an essay. Well, I changed the rule. I said that in my class four paragraphs make an essay and I struggled with them to learn how to write more. When they ask what to write, I say, "Write what you learned. Write what you think." I tell them that writing is not about what the final exam requires; it is about what you need for life.

I feel that the things I was taught to do in high school, these students are not taught to do. The high school is different from what it was 8 years ago, not because of the students, but because some teachers have just given up and the climate of the school is different. I am sure the situation is similar at most minority and inner-city schools. As a young teacher, I find this sense of surrender is scary and disheartening. When one of these teachers moans, "Oh, these kids," I think to myself that I am one of these kids. What they are saying is insulting to students and to me. The teenagers in my classes are as intelligent as I was and they have so much potential, but how can you expect young people to respond in school when their teachers have no faith in them?

I know some people think that I have an advantage being successful with my students because I am African American. I think it gives me a head start; I admit that. I have an edge because I can relate more to their lives and I am familiar with their music, the magazines they read, and the television shows they watch that I watch. They are glad to see me and I think they are more willing to trust me. But that is only the beginning. There are African American teachers who are out of touch with their students and White teachers who find ways to connect. If you are boring students to death, if you do not respect them, it does not make a difference if you are Black or White.

My biggest thrill as a first-year teacher is the response I get from students. In the school I am known as the Pied Piper. I really love to be with them and they like to hang out with me. I go to every football and basketball game. They see me there and know that I care, but you do not have to be Black to do these things with your students. One young White woman teacher wore African clothing in the school fashion show and the students loved her for it.

A big issue we have to face as educators is the way that schools replicate injustice. I do not accept it. Partly that is because I am Black, but you do not have to be Black to think that injustice is wrong. At my high school there are a small number of White students, and most of them are in the higher academic and honors classes. These classes have a mixture of White and Black students, Chinese, and Latinos. All of the high-achieving students travel together; they have traveled together since they were sorted out in third grade and they are kept separate from the rest of the student body. They are the students whose parents are professionals or active in the Parents Association. In retrospect, my feelings about being nurtured here may well have been because I was in this special group. What I am discovering now is that this experience is not available to everyone, and it can be. I took my regular track classes on a trip to the Metropolitan Museum of Art in New York City to see an Egyptian exhibit. It was the first time a teacher had taken a class to the city in 3 years. Other teachers told me: "Don't take those kids into the city," "They are going to leave you," and "Someone will break something." I told my class that if they screw up this time, they will be the group that screws it up for everybody. You know, we went to the museum, had a great time, and they were so great.

I want to end with some advice I try to keep in mind for myself.

1. When students are doing something wrong in class, I do not just let it go. They need to have demands made on them if they are going to rise to expectations. But on the other hand, I do not just sit there and admonish them. I take them out of the room and we talk. The key is to treat students with respect.

2. I did some cooperative learning and it did not work. Instead of blaming the students, I tried to figure out what I did wrong. I decided to make the activity more structured so the students would learn how to work in cooperative groups. Rule 2 is do not blame the students when the problem is the way you are organizing the class.

3. Sometimes, I find myself getting into a preaching mode in class and I have to stop myself from talking too much. Anytime I get thirsty, I know I am talking too much and I stop myself. I always try to figure out ways to get them involved in the lesson. When they are involved, that is when they are learning.

I guess this final point means it is time for all of you to get involved in discussion, because that is when we are really learning.

JOIN THE CONVERSATION—NICHOLE'S JOURNEY

Questions to Consider:

1. Do you think Nichole made a mistake teaching in the school she attended as a teenager? Explain.

2. Nichole believes that she has an advantage being successful with her students because she is African American; however, she emphasizes that that is only the beginning. "If you are boring students to death, if you do not respect them, it does not make a difference if you are Black or white." Do you agree or disagree with Nichole's view? Explain.

3. At the end of the essay, Nichole offers three lessons she learned during her first year of teaching. Which lesson do you consider most important? Why?

4. Knowing Nichole from this essay, if you were a parent, would you want her to teach your children? Why?

I Know I Can Get My Message Across
By Ken Dwyer

Ken Dwyer grew up and attended school in a small, rural farm community in New York State. He has taught in urban settings, programs for "at-risk" youth, a rural African village, and an affluent suburban community. Ken believes that a teacher's ability to know students and earn their re-

spect, no matter what the locality, is the universal key to successful teaching. I find his discussion of earning the respect of African masons through a sharing of expertise reminiscent of Paulo Freire's ideas, which were discussed in chapter 1. In a Freirean classroom, and Ken's, everyone has a recognized area of expertise that includes understanding and explaining their own life. Sharing this expertise is an essential element in the classroom curriculum.—Alan Singer

I grew up in Chateaugay, New York, about 45 minutes west of Vermont and 3 miles from Canada. My ancestors were famine-era Irish immigrants to the United States, and members of my family have been dairy farmers since the American Civil War. I started helping on the farm when I was in second grade and was involved in all aspects of farming until my father retired and sold the farm while I was a senior in high school.

There was one school in Chateaugay for grades kindergarten through 12. There were two classes per grade, but students were not "tracked" academically before high school, when we were divided according to the difficulty of math and science courses. Chateaugay was overwhelmingly White. In my 13 years in school, there were only three African American students.

I believe growing up in a town like Chateaugay and attending a small school has a number of benefits for children. A lot of our teachers were from the area. Everyone knew everyone else so students did not get lost in the shuffle. There was little truancy and delinquency in school, but there was a relatively high dropout rate. When teens turned 16, those who were having difficulty in school often left to work on the farms.

There was realization in the 1980s that family farming was not going to survive, so people needed to get a higher education. Since I graduated from high school, a lot of the family farms have gone out of business and unemployment is becoming a problem. I am the youngest of seven siblings and we all went to college. My mother was a nurse, so higher education was important in our family.

I attended a small college because it was less intimidating for me coming from a rural community. In college, I was a sociology major and had an internship at the Martin Luther King Institute for Non-Violence in Albany, New York. I later taught in their summer school program. All of the students and most of the staff were African American. This was my first significant experience working with people who were different from myself. I do not remember making a conscious decision to work with minority youth, but I know that I was very interested in learning about difference in our world. After college, I worked at a Boys and Girls Club Outreach Center in a public housing project in Connecticut that had many minority youngsters.

A lot of people join the Peace Corps with the idea of saving the world, but I joined for the personal challenge. I knew I would learn much more than I would be able to give to others. I was assigned to Niger, in equatorial West Africa, where I taught masons to build woodless domes and vaults using traditional techniques. After learning the Hausa language during a 10-week in-country training program, I was sent to live in a village of about 700 people.

While working in this African village, I learned how important it is not to judge people and their values and the importance of community relationships. I also learned not to give up just because something is difficult or I am confused. As a teacher, I had to get around the problem that I did not truly understand the language and culture, yet I was there as an expert on a particular subject. I learned that once you have the respect of students, whether they are teenagers or adults, it is much easier to present ideas. An important part of teaching was showing that I was willing to learn from the African masons as much as I was willing to teach them. Because we were working with their traditional materials, we had to learn from each other. For example, I knew the consistency of the mud that we needed but had no idea how to achieve that consistency. That was their area of expertise; they had been doing this all of their lives. I am proud that I was accepted as a Hausa person, given a Hausa name, and later asked to stay an extra year to help with the building project.

When I returned to the United States, I had a great deal of nontraditional teaching experience, but I had been out of a regular classroom since student teaching. I found a 1-year position in a suburban county that operated satellite programs for students with drug and alcohol abuse problems and other students who were considered "at risk." We also taught in a special program for young people who are gifted in the arts. While working there, I made contacts with people in the area and was hired to teach global history in a relatively affluent suburban school district.

In the suburbs, I have been confronted by a new set of problems that have helped me grow as a teacher. Students who are affluent and attend schools that are overwhelming White often have misconceptions about the world. My responsibility is to open up their minds to people they do not otherwise see and issues they usually do not consider. Part of the reason I decided to teach was because I enjoyed high school as a teenager. I like the school atmosphere, not just the classroom, but the whole setting. I coach and work in the after-school activities. I do not just teach history; I teach young people about life.

The greatest lessons I have learned about being a teacher are that you have to understand the population you are working with and that wherever the classroom, a teacher has to earn the respect of students. This requires listening more than talking so you can learn about who they are. This is universal to successful teaching. One of my biggest strengths as a teacher is my ability to evaluate a situation without making value judgments about people and to adjust my approach according to their needs. I feel I have been successful at this whether I was working with inner-city youth, African masons, at-risk teenagers, or advanced placement students. Once rapport is established, I know I can get my message across.

* * *

JOIN THE CONVERSATION—KEN'S CHOICES

Questions to Consider:

1. Many of Ken's career decisions have been based on his desire to learn about differences in the world. Would you be willing to make similar choices? Explain.

2. Ken explains that an important part of his teaching while in the Peace Corps was showing that "I was willing to learn from the African masons as much as I was willing to teach them. Because we were working with their traditional materials, we had to learn from each other." Ken believes that this approach is equally valid in school settings. Do you agree or disagree? Explain.

3. Ken believes the qualities of successful teaching are universal. Do you agree? Explain.

4. Knowing Ken from this essay, if you were a parent, would you want him to teach your children? Why?

My Students Call Me the "Math Geek"
By Kathleen Simons Smith

Kathleen Simons Smith is a European American young woman who grew up in a suburban community where she attended parochial schools. Both of her parents are currently university-based teachers. Kate was an outstanding student who majored in mathematics in college. She decided to become a teacher while working as a house manager in a psychiatric treatment facility for teenag-

ers. After teaching in a suburban minority community for 3 years, Kate and her husband relocated to another part of the United States where she got a job teaching math in an all-girls Roman Catholic high school. In this essay, Kate discusses her goals as a teacher and compares her experiences in these schools.—Alan Singer

In my short career as a high school mathematics teacher I have had the opportunity to teach in two very different schools. My first position was at a public coeducational high school with large Hispanic and Caribbean student populations. The school was located in a suburban community abutting New York City. Many of my students were immigrants or the children of immigrants, and the district had a number of problems usually associated with inner-city schools. My current position is at an all-girls, largely White, Roman Catholic high school in Portland, Maine. In many ways it is similar to the school I attended as a teenager.

The training I received in my teacher education program and at my first school has definitely made it possible for me to be successful in my second position. In both schools, I have had kids dealing with divorce, death, drugs, and alcohol, and pressure to have sex, to be cool, and to drive fast. I have had to be teacher, social worker, friend, and parent substitute. In my new school, I find I am more teacher than social worker, but I still do both. Although the lives of the two groups of students outside of school may be different, in the classroom the issues they face as math students, especially problems related to motivation and anxiety, are largely the same.

I am very gifted at math and some of my students call me the "math geek." Where I have had to work hard is reteaching myself topics as if I were learning them for the first time—which is what my students are doing. I had my mother as my eighth-grade algebra teacher and she was a wonderful role model. I also watched her help neighborhood kids with math. She always experimented with different ways of explaining something until she found the one that worked for a particular student.

My primary goal in teaching at both schools has been to help students think mathematically and reason logically. At my first position, there was considerable pressure to prepare students for the state's standardized final exam, so I tried to present as much information as possible. Without the pressure of the exam, my emphasis has shifted from teaching a large number of concepts to helping students think through problems with greater depth. One of my goals now is to teach fewer things, so I can concentrate on helping students develop a deeper understanding of mathematical thinking.

I do not believe students have to like every class they take, and I certainly do not believe that every lesson has to be fun and entertaining. However, I want my students to appreciate math. I also try to share my love of mathematics with them. Eventually, someone in my classes always says, "You really like this stuff, don't you?" I get tremendous pleasure when one of them says that they want to be a math teacher, "just like you."

A major goal since I started to teach is getting to know the students in my classes. I like to watch them play sports, act in plays, and perform in talent shows. When students know that you care about them, it makes them care about your class and about doing well in your subject area. This was true in both high schools.

My biggest headache at my first school (actually for me it was a stomachache) was caused by the rigidity of some administrators. Teachers were expected to have the aim, do now assignment and homework assignment on the board before the lesson, and to greet students at the door. I did not have my own classroom for 2 years, so I arrived at the room after some of the students. By the time I put my stuff down, raced to write the previous night's homework questions on the board (to avoid utter chaos when the rest of the students arrived), and assigned students to put up their solutions, the bell would ring before I could make it back to the door to greet the stragglers. I do not like being given impossible tasks! Now I have my own room and this stress no longer exists.

The diversity at school 1 was actually amazing and I miss it. Students came from more than 90 countries, but mainly from Haiti, Jamaica, India, and South America. I felt the principal and teachers did a wonderful job creating opportunities for expressions of individual culture while maintaining the necessary communal culture of school. Our diversity was considered a bonus, not a handicap.

The main problem I had in my classes was overcoming many students' lack of either internal or external motivation for learning. As a student, I certainly had external motivation from my parents, but mostly I had the internal motivation to do well (though I must admit learning may not have always been as important to me as the grades). Motivation to learn was an acute problem because many students came from single-parent or non-English-speaking families with little or no formal education. In addition, the adults in their families were all working so they were not supervised after school. Mostly, I found that their motivation to learn had to come from me.

At my current school, parents pay money to send their children, so there tends to be more external motivation to do well. However, my goal in September is still to motivate students to put in the effort on homework, come for extra help when needed, and ask questions and take risks in class. I love teaching math to girls because many believe that success in math is beyond them. Often it is their parents who give them excuses for not being good at math by saying, "Oh, I was never very good at math either." Students start off acting as if mathematical understanding is based on your genes or your gender. But by the end of the school year, they learn they can do math and do it well.

I still am challenged by the need to keep better math students interested while I go slow enough to keep everyone together. Group work helps but I am still trying new ways to keep everyone involved. I am rather strict and the refusal to do work or displaying disruptive behavior means a student is sent out of the room, but I always try to give students a way out of the situation and time to try to get themselves calm and orderly.

Sophomores and juniors in honors classes are my favorite students to teach. They have already adjusted to high school and tend to be more motivated to learn than seniors. In honors classes I can start to develop an idea and have students fly ahead of me as they realize where they must go next mathematically. It is exciting to see them make connections on their own. Another plus is that in honors classes, you spend more time teaching and less time reminding students to take out their books and supplies.

I get a different kind of satisfaction teaching nonhonors classes. Some students who have never done well in math before "click" with geometry. With a little (or a lot of) extra help, students who think they will never understand math, are suddenly successful. It is always satisfying for me to help a student learn something they never thought they would understand.

I have three tips I want to share with new teachers, regardless of the setting where you are teaching.

- Do not assign work that you cannot grade in a reasonable amount of time. I always return things the next day unless there is an unforeseen problem. When assignments are returned promptly, the topic is fresh in their minds and students are more interested in figuring out what they did wrong. If you take too long to return work, students tend to read their grade and shove it into a book.

- Always stick up for a student. If I think another teacher is underestimating a student's ability, honesty, or potential, I try to talk with the teacher. I find I can change someone's ideas about a specific student, but I confess that challenging negative attitudes about teaching is a battle I do not wish to start.

- Learn as much as possible. In math, it is important to cover different types of problems. That means preparing in advance. Be willing to admit if you do not know something. You can always tell students that you will have an answer tomorrow and you can assign them to discover an answer as well.

* * *

JOIN THE CONVERSATION—KATE'S ADVICE

Questions to Consider:

1. Kate believes that "although the lives of the two groups of students outside of school may be different, in the classroom the issues they face as math students, especially problems related to motivation and anxiety, are largely the same." Do you agree or disagree? Explain.

2. Because she is such a strong math student, Kate finds that her greatest difficult is "reteaching myself topics as if I were learning them for the first time—which is what my students are doing." Is this a potential problem in your subject area? Explain.

3. Kate advises: "Learn as much as possible. . . . Be willing to admit if you do not know something. You can always tell students that you will have an answer tomorrow and you can assign them to discover an answer as well." Do you agree or disagree? Explain.

4. Knowing Kate from this essay, if you were a parent, would you want her to teach your children? Why?

REFERENCES AND SUGGESTIONS FOR FURTHER READING

On the history and purpose of schools:

Bowles, S., & Gintis, H. (1976). *Schooling in capitalist America: Educational reform and the contradictions of economic life.* New York: Basic Books.

Callahan, R. (1962). *Education and the cult of efficiency.* Chicago: University of Chicago Press.

Covello, L., with D'Agostino, G. (1958). *The Heart is the Teacher.* New York: McGraw-Hill.

Dickens, C. (1973). *Hard times.* New York: Penguin. (Original work published 1854)

Katznelson, I., & Weir, M. (1985). *Schooling for all.* New York: Basic Books.

Perkinson, H. (1991). *The imperfect panacea: American faith in education, 1865–1990.* New York: McGraw-Hill.

Spring, J. (2002). *American education* (10th ed.). New York: McGraw-Hill.

On classroom organization:

Atwell, N. (1987). *In the middle: Writing, reading, and learning with adolescents.* Portsmouth, NH: Heinemann.

Bigelow, B., Christensen, L., Karp, S., Miner, B., & Peterson, B. (Eds.). (1994). *Rethinking our classrooms: Teaching for equity and social justice.* Milwaukee, WI: Rethinking Schools.

Bigelow, B., Harvey, B., Karp, S., & Miller, L. (Eds.). (2001). *Rethinking our classrooms, volume 2.* Milwaukee, WI: Rethinking Schools.

Haberman, M. (1995). *Star teachers of children in poverty*. West Lafayette, IN: Kappa Delta Pi.

Kohl, H. (1994). *I won't learn from you and other thoughts on creative maladjustment*. New York: The New Press.

Meier, D. (1995). *The power of their ideas: Lessons for America from a small school in Harlem*. Boston: Beacon.

Weiner, L. (1999). *Urban teaching, the essentials*. New York: Teachers College Press.

Wood, G. (1992). *Schools that work*. New York: Dutton.

Zemelman, S., Daniels, H., & Hyde, A. (1993). *Best practice: New standards for teaching and learning in America's schools*. Portsmouth, NH: Heinemann.

6

COMMUNITY: HOW DO YOU BUILD CLASSROOM COMMUNITIES COMMITTED TO EDUCATIONAL GOALS?

How do you build classroom communities committed to educational goals? It takes time, attention to broad goals, and concern with the details of daily living. In chapter 4, I discuss experiences at Camp Hurley that helped me understand the importance of relationships between students and teachers and their impact on young people. One of the things I learned as a counselor and young teacher is that communities always exist, but they do not always include the people in nominal authority (teachers) or a commitment to the goals of dominant institutions (educational achievement). When a group or class appears chaotic, it is often because adolescents have coalesced around their own agenda and leadership, like the group that ran away to see what the rain was doing to their drainage ditch. The struggle for teachers is not just to build classroom communities, but to build communities committed to educational achievement. I believe this requires the creation of democratic communities with student leaders and community members who feel they are part of the decision-making process.

In my experience, as students develop relationships with each other and their teachers, interest in the topics being explored, confidence that they will not be put down, and are convinced that their ideas will be heard, they develop a commitment to the success of the class, to questioning and knowing. They take responsibility for themselves and each other and become a community of learners. As an increasing number of students become committed to the class as a democratic community, they draw their classmates in with them. Students who initially were suspicious or aloof follow the leadership of their peers and get swept up in the maelstrom.

On the surface, some of the things that build classroom community seem like minor things. Yet, they are the things that ordinary people do for each other. When a teacher gives a student a break or helps them out of a jam, all the other students seem to know and care about what happened. When a teacher lends out pens, treats students with respect, loans someone money for lunch or the bus, plays ball with students after school, attends a school play or game, or visits a family struck by a tragedy, the teacher is saying to his or her students that we are all human, we are all family, and we must stand together. By example, the teacher is modeling for students what it means to be a community member and inviting students to join. One of the defining moments in the movie *Stand and Deliver* (1988) is when Jaime Escalante, the math teacher, visits a restaurant to persuade its owner to allow his daughter to return to school.

Community can become contagious and empowering. One year, when I was teaching an honors class in an inner-city high school with a weak academic reputation, students pledged that every member of their study team would pass the state's standardized exam, or none of them should pass the class. Before the test, we all put our hands in the middle of the room, like at a football rally, and shouted. When the papers were graded, one student had failed and she and her study team came to meet with me. I told them I knew they all worked hard and would not hold them to their pledge. But they insisted and only agreed to accept passing grades if I let them prepare her for a retest and promised to reverse all of their grades if she failed again. On the second try, she passed with flying colors.

This chapter begins with the story of Linda Christensen, a high school English teacher from Portland, Oregon. I read a number of articles by Linda in a newspaper for teachers, *Rethinking Schools*, where she discusses her efforts to build classroom community. The "nuts and bolts" sections describe classroom practices that promote student community, and an extended essay examines cooperative learning in the classroom. Rachel Gaglione of the New Teachers Network explains how she tries to develop community in her middle school classroom, and a final essay discusses developing community and student leadership during a high school social action campaign.

SECTION A: CAN COMMUNITY EMERGE FROM CHAOS?

Educational philosopher Maxine Greene (whom I have had the good fortune to know as a friend and mentor) believes that the human mind provides us with powerful tools for knowing ourselves and others. She encourages teachers and students to combine critical thinking with creative imagination in an effort to empathize with and understand the lives, minds, and consciousness of human beings from the past and our contemporaries in the present. Greene sees the goal of learning as discovering new questions about ourselves and the world. This leads her to examine events from different perspectives, to value the art, literature, and ideas of different peoples. For Greene, learning about the world and democratic community building are part of the same process.

Greene (1995) argues:

> Teaching and learning are matters of breaking through barriers—of expectation, of boredom, of predefinition. To teach . . . is to provide persons with the knacks and know-how they need in order to teach themselves. No teacher, for example, can simply lecture youngsters on playing basketball or writing poetry or experimenting with metals in a chemistry lab, and expect them to meet the requirements or standards she or he had in mind for that activity. Teachers must communicate modes of proceeding, ways of complying with rules and norms, and a variety of what have been called "open capacities," so that learners can put into practice in their own fashion what they need to join a game, shape a sonnet, or devise a chemical test. (p. 14)

But how do you persuade teachers and students to do these things?

The most honest answers I have ever read were by Linda Christensen. Many of the articles she has written for the newspaper *Rethinking Schools* have been collected in her book, *Reading, Writing, and Rising Up* (Christensen, 2000). Three that I find especially helpful to me as a teacher are "Building Community from Chaos," "Discipline: No Quick Fix," and "Writing the Word and the World."

Linda begins "Building Community from Chaos" by explaining to readers that "I read a book on teaching that left me feeling desolate because the writer's vision of a joyful, productive classroom did not match the chaos I face daily. My students straggle in, still munching on Popeye's chicken, wearing Walkmen, and generally acting surly because of some incident in the hall during break. . . . Too often, they were suffering from pains much bigger than I could deal with: homelessness, pregnancy, the death of a brother, sister, friend, cousin due to street violence."

Each new school year, Linda starts with the "misconception that I'm going to create a compassionate, warm, safe place for students in the first days of class." But new students quickly remind her that community is created out of shared relationships that develop over time and that before she can build a classroom community, she must find ways to connect with her students and for them to connect with each other.

Linda calls her collected essays *Reading, Writing, and Rising Up* because in her classroom, reading and writing are fundamental to community building and human empowerment. Linda has her students "plumb their lives for stories," stories that they share with each other. This process helps them discover common themes. "Students who stung privately with humiliation discovered that they weren't alone." Common themes, shared understandings, and the experience of reading and writing together become the building blocks for classroom community.

Another valuable teaching activity used by Linda and her co-teacher Bill Bigelow "to promote student empathy with other human beings" is the interior monologue. For an interior monologue, students imagine the thoughts of a character in history, literature, or life during an event that they are studying. Linda believes that this activity develops social imagination (a variation of what Greene called creative imagination), which allows students to connect with the lives of people "with whom, on the surface, they may appear to have little in common." Students read their dialogues out loud in class, which allows the entire group to discuss their observations and arrive at new understandings about people. Again, sharing builds understanding, respect, and community.

Linda believes that it is a mistake for teachers to ignore "the toll the outside world" exacts on students. She begins the semester by having students interview each other, to establish that their identities and questions are at the center of the curriculum. Readings are selected to explore the issues that students raise.

One semester, when Jefferson High School students were caught up in a storm of violence, she had her class read *Thousand Pieces of Gold* by Ruthanne Lum McCunn (1991). The novel includes an uprising by Chinese peasants who rampage through the countryside. Some of the outlawed peasants organize into bandit gangs, where they re-create relationships that were lost when their families were destroyed. As her students read about these Chinese rebels, they discussed conditions in their own communities. As they better understood their own lives, they began to recognize what was happening in the Chinese society they were studying.

One of the things I enjoy about Linda is her willingness to discuss the difficulties she has as a secondary school teacher. In "Discipline: No Quick Fix," she describes how she struggles along with her students to become intellectually and emotionally aware of her own choices and prejudices as she tries to develop a classroom community each year. Linda recognizes the difficulties for a teacher to relinquish her or his control over the curriculum, her uncertainties when student decisions push classes into uncharted waters, and her concern that after all of their efforts, a cohesive classroom community might not emerge.

Despite my enthusiasm for Linda's classroom, I have gotten mixed reviews from teacher education students when discussing her stories with them. A math student teacher wrote in her journal, "Sharing power and passion are important experiences for students, young people, everyone. But how do you bring this stuff up in a classroom with a curriculum that does-n't involve these topics? Especially for me, where the topic is actually math. What can I do to get my students' attention?"

Another student wrote, "Linda shares with students her stories about a hard life, her fa-ther's alcoholism, lack of education, not being a good student. This helped her open up with her students. I do not know the direct effects of gang war or gunfights. I do not have a wealthy family but we live a comfortable life and are close knit. If I have nothing in common with my students, will they trust me?"

I decided to address these issues by borrowing a page from Linda's book on teaching. I asked these students and others to read their comments about Linda's classroom and ques-tions about teaching to our class. As students read and spoke, common themes emerged, and it quickly became apparent that students in my class were not really writing about Linda and her classroom, but about themselves, their concerns about relating to their students, and their apprehensions about becoming teachers. And just as Linda described, "Students who stung privately with humiliation discovered that they weren't alone," and common themes, shared understandings, and the experience of reading and writing together become the building blocks of our classroom community.

For me, Linda's approach to community building seems valid no matter what your subject area. It means that teachers must continually seek out ways to connect lessons to the lives of their students, be willing to allow students an arena of choices, and not be afraid to go off on tangents. Learning and community building are usually not done in straight lines.

JOIN THE CONVERSATION—"DO WE NEED A SICHA?"

(From a handout distributed in a seminar for student teachers)

On an Israeli collective farm (kibbutz), important decisions are made at a community meeting called a *Sicha*. Last week we established three simply stated, yet profound, rules for our classroom community. We based them on two songs performed by Aretha Frank-lin, "Respect" and "Think."

1. **Respect.** Respect yourself. Respect others.
2. **Think.** Think about the implications of the things that you say and do and their im-pact on other people.
3. **Freedom.** Maximizing the freedom of individuals to participate, learn, and grow from student teaching and this seminar requires individual and group responsibility and a commitment to rules 1 and 2 (respect and think).

We also had a serious discussion about whether attitudes expressed in the "sanctity" of the teachers' room or privately held prejudices and beliefs affect the way teachers func-tion in their classes and treat students. Part of this discussion included whether student teachers, or other teachers, should respond to people who make derogatory remarks about student intelligence or racial and ethnic groups.

While we were having these discussions, I noticed four things.

1. Some members of our community were sitting with friends, talking with them while other people were speaking to the class, and passing notes back and forth.
2. Two leaflets were being circulated around the room during community discussion.
3. While members of our community were speaking, other people held their arm up to attract my attention.

4. Some members of our community freely volunteer to discuss their experiences whereas other community members only speak when called on.

Do we need a *Sicha*? Should we discuss these issues today? Yes? No? Why or why not? Please vote and then write the reason for your ballot. Be prepared to share your reasons with the class.

Questions to Consider:

1. What is your opinion of the issues and process for community decision making raised in this handout? Explain.
2. The handout and the ensuing discussion took place in a teacher education class. Do you believe this process could be effective in a middle school or high school classroom? Explain.
3. Do you believe that Linda Christensen's ideas for building community from chaos could work in your content area? Would you be willing to try her approach in your classroom? Explain.

SECTION B: HOW "TEACHER TRICKS" CAN HELP BUILD COMMUNITY

As I said earlier, small things can make a big difference. Here are a few basic rules from "Alan's big bag of teacher tricks." I call them teacher tricks because I want to emphasize that these are not innate qualities of master teachers. They are skills that anyone can learn.

Learning Student Names

One of the most important things you can do is to learn student names—quickly. People, and students are people, like when you know their names. It is a sign of respect and a statement that they belong. But learning new names is not always easy.

You learn names by using them. The first few days, take attendance and keep referring to students by their names. Some students have a way of "sticking out" on the first day. Learn their names immediately. They will be more inclined to cooperate as you establish procedures, and when you refer to them by name, it will seem to the class as if you know all of their names.

Assigned seats help. I think I have "relational memory." I see a face in a familiar spot and I remember a name.

The top line on every handout should have space for a student to place his or her name. Over the first few weeks, as you grapple with 150 or so new names and faces, this will help you remember who people are. As students work, walk up and down rows, chat with them, get to know them, and learn those names.

Do not be afraid to forget some names. I tell students, "Next year when I see you in the hall, I will smile, but probably not remember your name. I have to delete old files to create space in my memory for new names." I do not know if this is technically true, but students like the computer analogy and do not seem to mind when I forget their names.

I have had students whose families were from all over the world, and the names that gave me the most difficulty were Hindi names from India. They seemed to consist of a long string of consonants and few, if any, vowels. Usually students had abbreviated Anglicized versions of their names that they used in school, but they appreciated that I tried to learn their real name, no matter how much I butchered it.

I am notoriously poor at language acquisition, but I also try to learn a few words from each of the languages spoken in class—even if only to say hello to parents on "open school night." As with names, students forgive a lot if they believe that you tried.

The Memo Pad

In discussions with family, friends, and colleagues, I have a tendency to get anxious and interrupt people while they are speaking or trying to organize their ideas. I have the same problem with students in my classes, especially when I am nervous about getting a point "just right." I learned to carry a memo pad and pen and jot down my ideas, rather than blurting them out. I find that as a result, I am better able to hear people through to completion and more selective about my comments.

I started to use the memo pad as a regular part of my teaching and it became an important tool in building classroom community through directed discussion. As students work independently or in groups, I circulate around the room and write down notes about the ideas of individuals. I also tell students when the connections they are making are very good and encourage them to present their discoveries to the class. During full-class discussion, I use the notes in my memo pad to call on students who I know will introduce specific ideas into the discourse. I also know who disagrees with them, so I can call on those students, if necessary, to generate student-to-student interaction and discussion. When it is going well, discussion takes off and I can withdraw into the background, occasionally asking a student for further clarification, settling the class if arguments get too heated, or calling on students who are having trouble breaking in and adding their ideas to the mix.

Discipline Problems

I do not write disciplinary referrals on students in my classes. If we are a community, or hope to become one, we have to handle these things as a community. This is fundamental, because it makes the idea of community real for students. For example, I allow students to use the bathroom without permission as long as the room pass is available. If one student goes for extended walks and monopolizes the pass on a regular basis, it is the community's problem and the community must address it.

Please note that this does not mean I neglect to document problems in writing or keep counselors up to date on developments. But it does mean that involving outside disciplinary authorities is a last resort only used under extreme circumstances. If you have a serious confrontation with a student, you can always shrug your shoulders, roll your eyes, suck your teeth, and BACK OFF. Remember, you are the adult.

Smiley Faces

I know this seems ridiculous, but high school students like "smiley faces," rubber stamps, and stickers. One marking period, I started to give every student in my ninth-grade class a smiley face if he or she passed every subject on their report card. A student who had passed every subject but one asked if she could have a smiley face, too. I explained that I could not give her one, but I assured her she was a good student and would get one on her next report card.

For reports and homework assignments, I use cartoon rubber stamps that say, "Brrrrr-iliant," "Terrific!" "You will make a world of difference," "Needs Work—Please Fix," "Keep Trying," and "Please See Me." The absolute best reports receive a turtle sticker.

Although the stickers and stamps may be a little silly, students do appreciate getting positive feedback. The stickers and stamps also become part of our class's special rituals.

Contact With Parents

I make home visits for a number of reasons. A student is sick or in the hospital and misses a lot of work and time, there was a family tragedy, or I am having trouble connecting with a student and I think personal attention will help. On occasion, I ride my bicycle or walk around the community meeting students and family members. Once, I was riding my bicycle home from school on a lovely fall day when I bumped into a student who had cut my class. I said, "What gives? I want you in class." The next day, not only was the student present, but everyone in class had heard the legendary story about how I had tracked him down in the neighborhood and made him go to school.

I find that phone calls to parents at home or work, especially when a student has a history of trouble in school, are really impersonal and often unwelcome. They say to a parent, "Something is wrong with your kid. They need to be punished." Although parents should know what is going on and be a partner in the education of their children, the reality is that once a student is a teenager, problems at home are not so different from problems at school, and parents have limited coercive power. An option is to try calling home when you have good news to share. It is guaranteed to put parents in a more cooperative frame of mind and to win you friends among your students.

At a minimum, I try to open any home contact or open-school visit with a positive statement. "I like your son." "Your daughter has done good work." "Your child has a lot of potential." If possible, I prefer three-way conversations, at home, over the phone, or in school, so students know I am not just "dumping" on them, and so I can ask them how they see the situation.

Before open school night I organize a special project in class and videotape students at work, presenting or performing. I play the tapes for parents while they are waiting for conferences. The tapes are tangible examples of what their son or daughter has achieved. And if their child is missing from the tape, it is evidence that something is wrong.

SECTION C: BECOMING A TEACHER 5: WHAT DOES COMMUNITY BUILDING LOOK LIKE?

I Struggle for My Students, Not Against Them
By Rachel Gaglione

Rachel Gaglione believes that her experiences growing up have been fundamental in shaping her work as a teacher. She was a smart student but did not like school and often cut classes. She dropped out of a regular high school in ninth grade because she felt that the rules were too constricting and the teachers did not really care about her. Eventually, Rachel entered and graduated from an alternative program. Today, she believes that part of her problem was tension at home. Both of her parents were police officers, and job-related stress was a source of conflict between them and between her and her parents.

Reflecting on what was happening as she grew up has helped Rachel to understand what is going on in the life of her adolescent students. Currently, she teaches in a junior high school but hopes eventually to work at an alternative high school. "I want to go back into that environment and help young people who are like me when I was their age. Many teachers can be successful working where I work now. But those students really need me. Because I came from there, I feel a sense of responsibility to return."—Alan Singer

A teacher's most important job is to pay attention to what is going on with students and to care about what happens to them. I am not afraid to show students that I care. Caring puts the majority of them on your side, which helps you with everything you have to do as a teacher. Your feelings show through if you are genuine and students respond.

Because I pay attention to them, I have been able to help students work through problems that would have interfered with their schoolwork if allowed to continue. I had a boy in my class who never purchased the loose-leaf binder that is required in my school. I knew this was a signal of other problems in his life. I wrote a note on his homework and told him that I had an extra binder he could have. About a month later he asked me, "Could I have that loose-leaf you talked about?" I said, "Sure. Tomorrow." I did not really have an extra one in school. I meant to pick one up, never did, and that night I forgot about it. The next morning when I was already at school I remembered. I tore my room up before I found a 1-inch black binder, just the kind this boy would like. When I gave it to him, he was in shock. He said, "For me?" like he could not believe it. It was a great moment for both of us. I think it made the difference in the year for him.

I get tremendous satisfaction when a student responds to me. Once a student from the previous year left a four-page letter in my mailbox telling me how much she missed my smile every morning and how much she appreciated my caring. I saw her later on and gave her a big hug and let her know I was always here for her if she needed anything, even if it was just a smile.

I try to create a sense of community in my classroom by building on the idea that we are a union. We cannot succeed as individuals. We need to help each other, speak to each other and listen to each other. One student asked me why I always make them listen to each other. I told him, "We can learn from everyone, not just the teacher." I believe a lot of the world's problem's would be resolved if we would just take the time to listen to others.

I find that most students like my approach to classroom community and they work hard to achieve our class goals. We set rules and procedures as a class. If we need to address a problem, I ask them how they would like to address it. This gives them a strong sense of what it is like to take responsibility for themselves and others and what it means to work together.

I deal with conflict between students or between myself and a student by trying to calm the situation down, not aggravate it. If a student is angry with me, I am the one who needs to turn the situation around. If a problem is getting too heated, no learning will take place for the student. I try to avoid fighting or arguing because I know kids want to have the last word. I know I always did. But if I allow that to happen, it can undermine our class community. So it is often better to just let the conflict fizzle out. Nothing is so important that it cannot wait until later.

Conflicts between students are more difficult to resolve because two student egos are involved, not just one. Although many teachers claim you need to address bad behavior or put-downs as they arise, I do not do it that way. If one student calls another a name, even a racial name, I tend just to say, "That's enough." I am not sure this is completely appropriate, but I believe that handling something on the spot often makes the situation worse. We can get back to the issue and deal with it as a community when the tension has eased off. I do not like to throw anyone out of the room, but I confess that sometimes I will suggest that a student go for a walk with the pass for a little while.

Nothing about teaching is easy and sometimes I have to remind myself that they are just "kids" and that many things are going on in their lives. My motto is: "I struggle for my students, not against them." Fortunately, I have not had to handle a physical conflict in my classroom, but I believe a teacher has to be willing to break it up. That is part of showing that you care about the individuals involved and the classroom community.

It is important to establish patterns for community relationships and conflict resolution at the beginning of the school year. But even then, students must continually be reminded about the decisions we reached on how we will relate to each other. Instead of lecturing the class about behavior when I do not like the way they are acting, I use group work activities and projects to reinforce my ideas about working together and caring about each other. I continually experiment with new student-centered group activities. I find that when school is fun and relevant for them, students will be more willing to cooperate with each other and they will learn more. I put a lot of effort and time into figuring out how to be interesting and motivating. It is worth it to me because it eliminates many of the problems that otherwise come up in class.

I advise people who are thinking of becoming teachers to spend a lot of time with children and talk with them about what they like and do not like. Teachers need to be up to date on the realities of teenage life including movies, music, styles, books, and television shows and should be familiar with the neighborhood where they plan to teach. I also recommend eating right and getting plenty of exercise because the job requires a lot of energy if you are going to do it right! But the most important part of teaching, at least for me, is the struggle to show kids that you really care about them.

* * *

JOIN THE CONVERSATION—A SUCCESSFUL TEACHER

Questions to Consider:

1. In your view, what qualities make Rachel a successful teacher?
2. How did she figure out how to be successful in the classroom?
3. Were her life experiences handicaps or sources of strengths as she became a teacher?
4. What aspects of her approach to teaching do you agree with or disagree with? Explain.
5. If you were on a school's hiring committee and knew about Rachel's history as a student, would you have interviewed her for a job or hired her? Explain.

SECTION D: HOW DO "CORNY TEACHER JOKES" HELP YOU TO BE "REAL"?

I used to tell "corny teacher" jokes to my own children during dinner. If I got a pause followed by a groan, I knew I had hit it just right. The purpose of the corny teacher joke is not to get a belly laugh or to have your audience rolling in the aisles. That would be too distracting and interfere with the flow of a lesson.

The corny teacher joke is like a change-up pitch in baseball. It succeeds because it is unexpected. It catches the attention of students who are "drifting off" with a statement that is incongruous, and by catching their attention, it brings them back into the lesson. It also helps relieve tension.

I like to frame my corny teacher jokes as questions, but they can be slightly ridiculous statements or implausible instructions as well. Try to include one in every lesson plan (that was a corny teacher joke).

Stu Stein, a high school teacher and a member of the Hofstra New Teachers Network, is a former stand-up comedian. When he finds that a class is drifting or if things are getting dull, he likes to toss out a quick one-liner. In his case, however, he is convinced that his jokes are not corny.

Stu argues that the most important thing for connecting with students, or any audience, is being "real." He uses mock laughter at his own "bad" jokes and pretends to look around in surprise when the class laughs at something he says. According to Stu, "If students know you are apt to make irreverent comments, they are far more likely to pay attention. They do not want to miss the next joke. The trick is finding the balance between irreverence and education." He also thinks I need a new comedy writer.

Some Warnings

1. If you use the same corny teacher joke too often, it becomes a class mantra. When you say the opening, they respond with the punch line, and soon it will get on everyone's nerves—so try to be judicious.
2. Your goal is not to make anyone feel bad. Apologize if you overstep the "line." I have had students answer my jokes with their own wisecracks. My response is, "I guess I deserved that."
3. Avoid sexual innuendo. No matter how funny, it is not appropriate in school.

Some of Alan's Worst

"Do you have to take a make-up test to become a beautician?"

"If you get detention, should you take de-aspirin?"

"Is it a coincidence that dogs and teachers both are licensed?"

"Why did the rabbit fail math? It could multiply but not divide."

"Oh, no! The computer ate your dog."

"There is no such thing as a stupid question; (pause) this is just the wrong time."

"Don't think of it as homework, think of it as quality time with your computer."

"What do you get if you cross a teacher with . . .

. . . an anteater? Someone who can't keep their nose out of your business."

. . . a lawyer? A teacher with a suit."

. . . an elephant? A teacher you can never forget."

. . . a donkey? My seventh-grade math teacher."

. . . a pit bull? A riot as students run for their lives."

Middle School Students Love Bathroom Humor

Alan: "Don't cut! I had a student who cut my class to go to lunch everyday. The only thing he passed was gas."

Eighth-grade student: "That joke stinks."

Alan: "So did the gas."

JOIN THE CONVERSATION—CORNY TEACHER JOKES

Educational researchers have actually studied the use of humor in the classroom. According to an article in the Association for Supervision and Curriculum Development's *Education Update* 43(5), "Make Me Laugh: Using Humor in the Classroom," a 1991 study found that teachers use humor to put students at ease, get their attention, demonstrate their humanity, and reduce the psychological distance between teachers and students.

Questions to Consider:

1. When you were a student, how did you and your friends react to teachers who thought they were funny? Why?
2. Do you think humor is an important part of a teacher's repertoire? Explain.

SECTION E: HOW DOES COOPERATIVE LEARNING BUILD COMMUNITY WHILE PROMOTING STUDENT ACHIEVEMENT?

Cooperative learning is not completely new. Students taught and learned from each other in colonial and frontier America; fans of author Laura Ingalls Wilder know that cooperative learning was used in her one-room prairie school house. As a result of the ideas of educators such as John Dewey and Francis Parker, cooperative learning was popular in the late 19th and early 20th centuries, and many teachers continue to use elements of cooperative learning in group work, projects, and reports.

As with any other educational "innovation," advocates of cooperative learning frequently disagree with each other about the best approaches and the most important goals. However, some common points do emerge in the educational literature and in teacher discussions:

1. Cooperative learning enhances student interest because it gives them a greater stake in what is happening in their class and in their education. In large classes, it provides students with more individual attention because they are involved in helping each other. Students at all academic levels, including students in need of remediation and academically advanced students, seem to learn more and to learn more effectively, in cooperative learning teams.
2. Cooperative learning enhances the social skills and values that are important for future academic and economic success, and that are essential for participation in multicultural, democratic communities.
3. Teachers must be able to define their own classroom goals and experiment with the approach or approaches that are successful in involving their students in learning.

I used cooperative learning teams in large high school classes with more than 30 students, and I consistently found four major benefits. First, there is significant improvement in the willingness of students to write and the quality of their writing. Working in cooperative learning teams, students are able to stimulate and support each other and to edit each other's work. Second, participation in discussions in their cooperative learning teams gave students an opportunity to test their ideas before presenting them to the full class and in front of me. It enabled students who generally did not participate in class discussions to participate more freely, either presenting their own ideas or representing their teams. As a result, class discussions were enriched by the addition of diverse viewpoints. Third, class attendance and punctuality in handing in assignments improved because students were able to make demands on their team members and follow up on each other. People having difficulty were less likely to get lost in the shuffle. Fourth, all of these benefits contributed to, and were accelerated by, the growth of a positive, academically directed, classroom community.

Before you experiment with cooperative learning in your classroom, I recommend reading additional resource material, participating in workshops sponsored by school districts, union-sponsored teacher centers, or local colleges. You should also talk with your colleagues. Teachers may already be using cooperative learning in your school and someone might want to work with you. Teachers can also cooperate, and it is easier to experiment with something new when you have a support group.

Once you are committed to using cooperative learning in your classroom, the first step is defining your goals. What do you want to achieve? Do you want to focus on content or skills learning? Do you want to concentrate on group process and developing democratic values? Do you want to address intergroup tensions in your class? It makes sense to involve students in discussions about cooperative learning goals and the process from the start. Listening to their ideas can be helpful, and it gives them a sense of ownership and responsibility from the beginning.

How you organize teams depends on your goals. In general, a teacher has to make two basic decisions: Will students be permitted to choose their groups or will they be assigned to groups? Will groups be homogenous (students are more alike) or heterogeneous (students are more different)? If students choose their own cooperative learning groups, the groups will most likely be based on friendships or shared interests.

Advantages of student choice are: (a) group members will more likely have prior experience working together; (b) group members will share more interests in common; (c) there may be fewer intragroup conflicts for the teacher, the group, and the class to deal with; and (d) students may have a greater sense of identification with the process if they feel that they selected their own groups. Disadvantages of student choice are: (a) groups will more likely be segregated by race, ethnicity, gender, class, or academic achievement levels; (b) friendship bonds can be socially constraining as students try to learn and experiment; (c) some students will feel left out because they do not have a group of friends in the class; (d) teams based on friendship groups may tend to compete with each other in destructive ways; and (e) students will not have the opportunity to work with a new and diverse team of people where they all start out on an equal footing.

Students should discuss the advantages and disadvantages of choosing their own cooperative learning teams, and of heterogeneous versus homogenous groupings. After discussion, a teacher has the option of allowing the class to make a decision or making the decision for the class. Often after a discussion of the goals of cooperative learning, a class will reach consensus that it wants teams to be heterogeneous, and that the fairest way is for the teacher to set them up. There is also no reason that groups cannot be organized one way for some activities and a different way for others.

Some parents and educators have questioned whether heterogeneous cooperative learning teams penalize "high-achieving" students. Studies conducted by cooperative learning specialists from the University of Minnesota show that high achievers working in heterogeneous cooperative learning teams do at least as well on standardized academic tests as high achievers who work in competitive individualized settings. "Low-level achievers" and "middle-level achievers" who are involved in heterogeneous cooperative learning teams almost always do better on these types of tests. Meanwhile, all groups of students benefit from the important social skills they develop by working in cooperative learning teams.

Cooperative learning teams are not just a group of students who are given an assignment and left alone to complete it. In our society, young people, as well as adults, need to learn how to work cooperatively. For cooperative learning teams to work successfully, teachers and students must have clear group process goals. There must be a clear structure for democratic group decision making, and there must be a sense of shared group responsibility for the team. In *Circles of Learning* (1993), David Johnson, Roger Johnson, Edythe Johnson Holubec, and Patricia Roy suggest that the following should be built into the cooperative learning process:

1. Teams need to depend on all of their team members to achieve the team's goals; students have to work together.
2. Team members must be held collectively and individually accountable for learning by group members; everyone is responsible for the group.
3. Responsibilities are divided up so that all team members have the opportunity to play both leadership and supporting roles.
4. Teams are concerned with learning and maintaining cooperative group relations.
5. Team members need to learn how to run meetings, make decisions, organize projects, divide responsibilities, and evaluate progress. Teachers cannot assume that students already have social and organizational group work skills.
6. Teams must evaluate themselves and be evaluated as teams by teachers, on both group process and the completed team product.

Responsibilities can be divided up among students and then rotated on a regular schedule or when a team finishes a project. Team members will need to learn how to perform all of these important assignments. Sometimes a student will assume more than one of these responsibilities. When team responsibilities are divided up, possible tasks include the following:

- *Chairperson/facilitator*—the person responsible for leading team meetings.
- *Recorder*—the person who keeps a record of what is said at meetings and team decisions.
- *Reflector*—a person assigned to listen carefully during discussions so they can be summarized at the end of meetings.
- *Reporter*—a person who reports on the team's problems and progress when the class meets as a whole.
- *Liaison*—a person who meets with representatives of other teams to share ideas.
- *Organizer*—a person who makes sure that work is completed on schedule and is ready to be presented or submitted.
- *Mediator*—a person who attempts to resolve internal conflicts between team members.

While students are working, teachers are busy as ex officio members of each cooperative learning team: You may (a) stick your head in a team meeting, listen for a while, say and do nothing, and then move on to another team; (b) ask a team a question or give it direction, helping a team solve an especially difficult academic problem; or (c) have questions about how a team is working together. A team may need a teacher to mediate a problem, the entire class to get involved, or only to hear the suggestion that they reflect on what they are doing so they can work it out by themselves.

Some teachers have expressed concern with grading policies for students working in cooperative learning teams. Just as organization of the teams can change depending on the activity, so can grading systems. For some activities, students may only receive a group grade. For others, they may be evaluated based on both individual and group performance.

JOIN THE CONVERSATION—GOALS FOR COOPERATIVE LEARNING

In classrooms using cooperative learning teams, students will learn to do the following:

- Work cooperatively in small groups.
- Work as part of a broader classroom community.
- Work cooperatively with students from other racial, ethnic, and religious backgrounds, and across differences created by gender, class, interest, and academic achievement level.
- Give leadership to and accept leadership from others.
- Respect the abilities and contributions of others.
- Understand the roles of cooperation, compromise, and consensus in democratic decision making.
- Participate in group and class activities with greater confidence in their individual abilities.
- Explain their ideas orally and in writing more effectively.
- Score higher on class and standardized tests.

Questions to Consider:

1. Based on your experience as a student and your knowledge about the way that you and other people learn, how do you evaluate cooperative learning as a teaching strategy?
2. Many claims are made about the importance of cooperative learning. Which of these objectives would you consider most important in your classrooms? Why?

SECTION F: HOW CAN TEACHERS DEVELOP STUDENT LEADERSHIP?

Sean Brown (not his actual name) was a tough young man who returned to class midway through the semester after 2 weeks in a juvenile detention center. Sean had failed 10th-grade social studies once before and was assigned to a "repeater" class with about 20 other difficult students, each with his or her own issues, but with a shared "school phobia." I cannot honestly say I missed Sean when he was not there.

On his return to school, Sean asked, in an off-handed way, if there was anything he could do to make up missed work. The class was about to examine folk dancing as a form of cultural expression and an example of parallel development. I asked him if he could dance. Puzzled, he said, "Of course, what do you think I am?"

I offered Sean a proposition. He would have to make up missed assignments, but in addition, I wanted him to work with me to get students up and teach them dances from South Africa, Romania, Japan, and Israel. Sean looked at me like I was crazy, but I insisted that that was the deal. Finally, he said, "I have to tell them you are making me." "Fine," I replied. "Tell them I threatened to break you legs."

We met during a free period and he picked up the folk dances very quickly. The next day, I announced Sean would be teaching international folk dances and told everyone to get up and push their chairs to the side and back. No one moved until Sean came to the center of the room and announced: "He's making me do this. Said he would break my legs if I didn't dance. NOW, EVERYBODY, GET UP AND MOVE YOUR CHAIRS." At which point everyone did.

I want to emphasize that there were no real threats being made here. I was the least physically intimidating male in the room, and there were other young men who dwarfed Sean. At any rate, these were not students who would have responded well to threats. If unhappy they would have just walked out of the room.

I believe the students in this class responded to three things: first, my willingness to work out with Sean a way that would make it possible for him to pass the class; second, the novelty of one of their own being the teacher; and third, and most important, they valued internal or peer leadership. Sean was respected by the group, and students who would not dance with me would dance with him.

In the 1920s, an Italian revolutionary named Antonio Gramsci was grappling with how to change the dominant, or hegemonic, ideas of a society. Gramsci argued that the key people for promoting change were "organic intellectuals," members of oppressed communities who had a broader vision of possibility and were able to convey their vision to other community members. I believe Gramsci was writing about leadership imbedded in community, similar to the leadership displayed by Sean Brown.

Student leadership that builds classroom community can be expressed in small ways, such as what happened in this class and on a larger scale. Community is enhanced when a member of a cooperative learning team presses other team members to get their assignments in and helps them complete their work. It grows when a student tells classmates to get to class on time because she or he is interested in what we are studying. It flourishes when students challenge stereotypes or demand that classmates respect each other, listen to diverse views, and constructively respond to disagreements.

I had what I consider my greatest success as a teacher because of schoolwide leadership taken by students in my 12th-grade civics class one year. Until 1990, I was a high school social studies teacher in a working-class poor minority New York City neighborhood, and the faculty advisor to the school's "Forum Club." The club, an extension of my classes, brought speakers to the high school to discuss controversial issues and it encouraged students to be active participants in our democratic society. In 1989, the club organized students in civics classes to join the debate over abortion rights and condom availability in schools. It sponsored afterschool discussions with representatives of advocacy groups that involved hundreds of students; held meetings with parent groups; circulated petitions; wrote and presented position papers, editorials for local newspapers, and speeches; prepared video material and posters; and participated in political rallies. Their activities energized the entire school and succeeded in having a public health clinic placed in the building.

I would like to share excerpts from two speeches written and delivered by members of the Forum Club. They are examples of how young people can grapple with complex moral and political issues and develop essential academic skills while providing leadership in class, school, and society.

One young woman represented the Forum Club at a New York City Hall rally against parental consent laws. She told the audience:

> I am a strong believer in freedom of choice. A woman must have the freedom to choose an abortion and this includes teenage women. It was not easy for me to decide to be pro-choice. I come from a religious Hispanic family. My father is the pastor of my church. I attend church every Friday night and every Sunday morning. My father is not happy with my positions on these issues because he opposes the idea of abortion. But regardless of his personal feelings, my father has understood and supported my right to choose my own beliefs. He realizes that my life is my own. I consider myself lucky because I have support from my parents. I think a teenage woman

who gets pregnant should discuss her choices with her parents. . . . I believe that if I were pregnant, I would be able to tell my parents and get their support whatever my choice. But just because I am able to talk to my parents doesn't mean that I think that informing someone's parents should be the law. . . . Often teenagers have bad relationships with their parents and they are unable to talk with them about anything. A law that required parental consent before an abortion would only make things worse in these families. It would not create a better relationship. It would only lead to explosions.

A second young woman represented the Forum Club at a board of education public hearing on condom availability in high schools. She told the board:

It is certainly not a secret that many high school students are sexually active today. While some are very conscious and practice "safe sex," many do not. Many teenagers . . . deny that they can be victims of sexually transmitted diseases. They think that they are invulnerable. Condom availability in the schools, when combined with a comprehensive program of sex education, would help teenagers become more sexually responsible. This would lead to less teenage pregnancies and less sexually transmitted disease. My advice is "Save a Life—Use a Condom!"

These young women and the other members of the Forum Club represent the kind of thoughtful, committed high school students and leaders that educators hope schools will produce. Not only did they transform themselves socially and intellectually through their activism, but they elevated the interest and performance levels of every student they worked with in class and in the school. What is interesting is that they, and Sean Brown, became student leaders in similar ways. They were given an opportunity and encouragement and they responded.

REFERENCES AND SUGGESTIONS FOR FURTHER READING

Christensen, L. (2000). *Reading, writing, and rising up*. Milwaukee, WI: Rethinking Schools.
Greene, M. (1995). *Releasing the imagination, essays on education, the arts, and social change*. San Francisco: Jossey-Bass.
Johnson, D., Johnson, R., Holubec, E., & Roy, P. (1993). *Circles of learning: Cooperation in the classroom* (5th ed.). Minneapolis, MN: Burgess Publishing Company.
McCunn, R. (1991). *Thousand pieces of gold: A biographical novel*. Boston, MA: Beacon Press.

Concluding Thoughts for Book II: A PRO/CLASS Practices Approach to Dealing With Classroom and Other Professional Problems

I usually do not like to use case studies to talk about dealing with classroom or other professional problems. I think case studies give you a false sense of preparedness. In the abstract, it is much easier to be reasonable in a case study because you have little at stake. In the classroom, dealing with real people and under the pressure of making decisions on the spur of the moment, it is much more difficult. Your feelings, and those of the other people involved, tend to get in the way. Responses to case studies can lend themselves to scripted conversations and, in my experience, the situations that arise in classrooms are anything but scripted. More important than having a script are your ideas, your goals, and your concern for students. Every situation is unique and every student needs to be treated as an individual. As with clothing and shoes, one size never fits all.

An added problem is that each school or district has its own guidelines and administrative procedures for guidance and for disciplinary action. Many schools practice what they call "zero tolerance" toward infractions or have a very strict and detailed code, which allows teachers little leeway once a problem is reported. In some of these cases, conflicts that could easily be handled as educational or counseling issues are handed over to the police for adjudication. Although I have not worked under these dire circumstances, I have taught in schools with what I considered punitive approaches to student discipline problems.

My approach, as we have spoken about already, is based on building relationships of trust and responsibility between students and between students and teachers within a classroom community. My general policy about discipline is that when possible it should be handled within the classroom community. It also involves "creative maladjustment," which includes bending the rules to make them work for my students and myself. I always tell students that if they are honest with me, I will support them if they have conflicts with school authorities or other teachers. At a minimum, I can attest to their honesty in our relationship. But if they lie to me, and I cannot trust them, I cannot offer them support.

My first recommendation to every student teacher and new teacher is to find out what supervisors and parents expect from teachers when there are classroom problems, to learn guidelines established by both the school and the law, and then to figure out how you can satisfy the school and legal expectations while remaining faithful to your goals for teaching and beliefs about teenagers. Veteran teachers, mentors, and union representatives can be very helpful here. In my experience, supervisors, parents, and students respect teachers with integrity, especially when they have a record of success with students. Usually you will find room for teacher judgment even under the strictest regime. However, sometimes a particular school or district may be the wrong place for you to work.

When student teachers and new teachers are extremely nervous about managing classroom problems, I have a couple of "props" that I offer them for help. Remember, by the time they are in your secondary school class, students have been in school for between 7 and 12 years. They know the rules for proper classroom behavior. In fact, the only one who is uncertain about the rules is probably you. That is why teenagers are sometimes "playing you" for all it is worth. It is an entertaining part of the schoolhouse game. What the props do is help you to remember that you are the teacher and in charge of the class. You decide what happens. The best weapons in your arsenal are your teacher voice and body language. **You have to learn how to say it like you mean it.**

My three best props for building up your confidence are a jar of "M" or "mean" pills, to help build up your fortitude (really M & Ms); an Incredible Hulk T-shirt that warns students, "Don't Make Me Angry, You Won't Like Me When I'm Angry"; and a silver wand, topped by a star and covered by glitter (à la Harry Potter) that you can wave around the room to get attention. Very few student teachers or new teachers have ever borrowed the props, but I think just the idea of them help people gain perspective on what is happening in classes.

With all of these reservations in mind, I will present school situations that happened either to me or to members of the New Teachers Network and my ideas for responding. Rachel Gaglione (*whose responses are in italics*) also offers ideas on some of the situations from her perspective as a younger female teacher working in a middle school classroom. Please remember that these situations and responses involve **choices** and **judgments**. We are not offering rules for behavior.

I divided the examples into four categories: classroom problems, guidance-related issues, relationships with colleagues, and conflicts with school policies. I recommend writing down your own ideas before comparing them with ours. After finishing, you need to JOIN THE CONVERSATION and discuss what you remember about your own experience as a student and adolescent, and your approach to "classroom and other professional problems."

JOIN THE CONVERSATION—THINGS TO REMEMBER
FROM ALAN'S BIG BAG OF TEACHER TRICKS

- The only one you can control is you.
- Never take what students do "personally."
- You can be both firm and caring.
- Remember the Bene Gesserit Litany Against Fear or your own variant.
- If you can, wait before deciding what to do. Give yourself a chance to relax and think.
- To quote Mary Poppins, "A spoonful of sugar helps the medicine go down."
- Once you have their attention, get softer.
- You can always suck your teeth or shrug your shoulders, and walk away from a situation.
- Try to ease up a bit. Laugh at yourself. There is always tomorrow (Oh no!)

Questions to Consider:

1. By this point you have read a long way into this book and thought quite a bit about your own views on teaching practice. How do you react to these tips? Why?
2. What would you add to the list? What would you take away? Explain.

SECTION A: SOME COMPLICATED BUT PRETTY STANDARD "CLASSROOM PROBLEMS"

1. A student sits with his head down. Other students are talking with neighbors. Even though the school rule is "no hats in class," several students ignore you when you ask them to take theirs off. How should you respond?

There is a broader problem in this room and I do not think a "quick fix" is likely. The issue is not the behavior of individual students, but the overall class tone and the ability of the teacher to give direction. As a beginning teacher I took this kind of situation as a sign of personal failure and I used to get very frustrated. Later I learned that it takes time, hard work, and a systematic approach to build classroom community. In this class, I would try to develop a core of students committed to learning and interested in the lessons and use them to win over the others. When you have most of the students, it is easier to deal with the problems that come up. Then you can speak with "Mr. Head Down" privately, while other students are working on an assignment or after class. Ask him if there is a problem you can help with. Tell him you really want him involved in class. Ask what signal you can give him in the future to "bring him back into the fold" before he drifts too far off. Humor helps, whereas confrontation only escalates the situation. Whisper in his ear. Tickle his hand with a feather. Cover the body with a coat. Sometimes my "class rules" included threats to report "evil stepmothers" to child abuse authorities for not allowing students to get enough sleep at night or "recidivist hat wearers" to the health department for endangering public safety (rules on hat wearing appear to date from an earlier historical period when head lice was a big problem in schools). When students complain they are too embarrassed to uncover their heads, I point to my unruly mop and welcome them to the bad-hair-day club. The thing is, if a class is going badly, these things cannot be dealt with effectively on an individual basis, and if a class is going well, it is not worth spending too much time or effort on something like this. If a student still balks after your best efforts, you can always throw up your hands, shrug your shoulders, and suggest they do their hair before they come to class next time. Everyone will laugh and the situation will be less likely to be repeated. The key things to remember are that it does not help to get angry, it will take time to change the classroom tone, and relationships with students will win you allies. In addition, if students are behaving this way in your classroom, other teachers in the school are probably facing similar problems. You should not be afraid to seek the advance of colleagues whom you respect on how they are addressing these issues in their classes.

Rachel Gaglione—I have NEVER grabbed a hat off of a student's head. How would you like it if someone did that to you? I ask, "Can you please take your hat off for me?" Usually a simple and polite request works. Sometimes, if it is a student I do not know, he or she will look at me strangely in shock that someone asked them nicely to take the hat off. The few times when this does not work, I say something to bond us together like, "Look, it's a groovy hat. I dig the Mets too, but Mr. Rosen says we can't wear hats in school. You know he always pops into the room and, if he sees you with it on, he's going to try to take it from you and he's going to get mad at me. Just please take it off for me. If you think someone might snag it from you, I'll hold it and make sure no one touches it." I do not think this has ever failed to work. It requires a commitment to mutual respect and trust.

2. A student teacher was having difficulty settling a seventh-grade class right after their lunch period. After playing outside, students would run into the room shouting and pushing each other. No work was getting done. How should she handle the situation?

This student teacher was on the verge of giving up. She had started yelling at the students, but instead of quieting, they got noisier. This one class was sending her home with a headache every day and souring her entire experience. Finally, we met and came up with a strategy that worked. She placed an aim question and instructions on the board before the class so she would not be preoccupied with other tasks. She met students at the door and blocked their path to force them to slow down. When a student was calm, they were given an assignment sheet, told to start their work, and allowed to enter the room. Really rambunctious students were required to remain on the side in the hall until they had "their act together." After a couple of days, she had established that students were expected to enter the room quietly and begin their work. She was also able to talk with them about the kind of class they wanted to have. The students still roughhoused in the yard and the student teacher had to meet them at the door, but they settled down much more quickly and learning was taking place in the classroom.

Rachel Gaglione—I always have a class like this line up in the hall and calm down a bit before they enter the room. Usually, they just need some time to wind down. In addition, I would start the lesson with a quiet individual activity, not group work.

3. It is springtime. It is getting warm outside and the thoughts of young men and women turn away from school. Cutting is increasing, especially at the end of the day, at the same time you are trying to prepare students for standardized end-of-the-year tests. What should you do?

The tendency in most schools is to tighten the screws and get punitive, but I found punishment counterproductive. Many students simply stopped coming to class at all. The strategy I found most successful was being more of a "presence" in the building by wandering around during my free periods. Once I had spotted a student during the day, they were much more reluctant to cut a class later on. Once I went down to the gym after school to say good-bye to students going on the senior trip. I met three students who had cut my class that day lining up for the bus. If I had fingered them, their trip was over. I only nodded and said I would see them when they got back. Embarrassment and good faith seemed to work. None of them cut my class again.

Rachel Gaglione—The only way I can see to beat this one is to make the reviews and classes even more fun than normal. Incorporate a game such as Trivial Pursuit, Jeopardy or, the new favorite, Who Wants to be a Millionaire? This is definitely the scenario for a learning project that touches on many things, without having quiet time. Sitting and reading is the last thing they want to do. This is a good time of year to experiment. One June my class made "human" physical maps. Some of the students were rivers; others were mountains. One was the Continental Divide. Students had to dress appropriately. Lakes, for example, wore blue,. It got a little crazy in the room, but they all came to class!

4. A member of the New Teachers Network refused to admit a student who was chronically late coming to class. He stopped her at the door and requested an explanation. A young man whom he did not know, but who was evidently a friend of hers, came up to them and started cursing at the teacher. The young man threatened to "hurt" the teacher if he did not stop bothering his "woman." The incident was observed by another teacher who reported it to the dean. How should the teacher respond?

This is a very difficult situation and a lot depends on school policy. If the teacher files a formal complaint with school authorities, both the young man and young woman would probably be suspended and the young man would have faced arrest. The teacher decided to take a guidance, rather than a disciplinary, approach and declined to file a complaint. Instead, after speaking informally with the dean and apprising him of the situation, he got the young woman's schedule from the program office, found her later in the day, and they walked through the halls talking. The young woman responded to the attention and concern and they agreed on the following plan. They decided that if she came to class on time in the future and was able to change her attitude, the teacher would not make a formal complaint about the incident to school authorities. However, the teacher would call her home and speak with a parent. He would tell them that she had been doing well up until this point, but he was concerned about a pattern of lateness to class. She could then discuss her own concerns about school with her parent. The teacher also offered to speak with the young man about what had happened, but did not make this a condition for resolving the situation. Although he never spoke with the young man, the situation with the young woman improved. The teacher is also convinced that his decision not to be punitive improved relationships between him and the class and contributed to a generally enhanced class tone.

5. Students in a first-period class are chronically late. If the teacher starts the lesson at the beginning of the period, the late arrivals have no idea what the class is doing. When the teacher decides to wait before starting lessons, even fewer students arrive on time. What should the teacher do?

This one always drives me nuts. It seems you are damned if you do and damned if you do not. If you do not start the lesson at the beginning of the period, you are telling students that they do not have to be there. I tried to address this problem (not always successfully) by reorganizing my lesson and starting "at the bell" with something that was not crucial. As soon as students arrived they went directly to work, but I would not launch into the main point of the lesson until we had a sizable crowd. At the end of the period, we would discuss my concerns that some members of the community were hurting our efforts by coming to class late and ask them all to make a special effort to arrive on time. I would also offer to call the home of students with "irresponsible parents" who were not getting them up on time. This would usually solve the problem for students who were hanging out outside with friends. Some students have real problems that are not handled so easily. They may have to take a younger sibling, or their own child, to school or day care. I try to meet with these students individually and find a way to address their problem that keeps them coming to school. They may need a program change that allows them to start the day at a later period.

Rachel Gaglione—Take a walk to the local food mart before homeroom—that is usually where you will find them. If students are eating breakfast, consider letting them eat in your room. Start class with a really fun activity so those who miss it are jealous.

6. A member of the New Teachers Network has a student who just cannot sit still. He fidgets, gets out of his seat, talks to students sitting next to him, and shouts out answers or questions. The student is distracting her and disrupting the entire class. What should she do?

I was that child and I remember being punished by teachers for things I could not control. I try to approach the situation by thinking about things that would have helped me. Often teachers seat "disruptive children" in front and in the middle of the classroom, so they can ride herd on them. But if the student could be controlled in this simple fashion, neither the teacher nor the student would have this problem in the first place. I recommended that the teacher talk with the student about what was happening in class and ask him where he wanted to sit and what kind of rules would help him to behave in a different way. She and the student eventually arrived at the following accommodation that allowed them both to function in class: She agreed to place the student in a seat at the side of the room by the window so he could look out when he felt the need, look through a book or draw, stretch without bothering other people, and even stand up without being disruptive. She also agreed to let him go to the bathroom (really for a walk) when he asked. For his part of the bargain, he agreed to do all of his work, to pay attention when something was important, to try not to talk with neighbors or shout out during class, and to return quickly from the bathroom. They even worked out a signal so she could get his attention without embarrassing him in front of the class. She would walk by his desk and without saying anything, just tap on it quietly.

Rachel Gaglione—This student needs to be kept busy. Make him or her a monitor giving out supplies, books, or homework. You can also let students know it is okay to get out of their seats to go to the garbage can. Many students grow antsy when they are not allowed to get up. If they know they can get up if they need to, they may be more able to relax. However, teachers need to emphasize that if a student disturbs other people, they lose the right to leave their seat.

7. A member of the New Teachers Network had an especially unruly class. Trying to establish some control over the class, she instituted lunchtime detention. Instead of calming some of the students, the threat of detention seemed to make their behavior worse. What should she do?

The problem with lunchtime detention was that students wanted to be there. The atmosphere was much nicer than in the cafeteria where students tended to push and shove each other and the adults were always screaming. At lunchtime detention you could read, talk with your friends, or play on the computers. We discussed the situation at a New Teachers Network meeting and a number of members explained that they had "turned the problem on its head." Instead of having lunchtime detention, they made lunchtime an optional free period for students who wanted to stay in the classroom. They established rules for behaving during the lunch period, which students eagerly followed (and enforced), and stated that students could not stay for lunch if they misbehaved during the regular class period. The lunch period gave teachers a chance to develop relationships with students that supported positive class leaders, calmed disruptive ones, and, by enhancing classroom community, spilled over into the regular class periods.

8. As a younger teacher, I liked to play basketball with students during lunch or after school. Sometimes students would curse at each other or use racial epithets. Should I respond and if so, what should I do?

I decided to use the basketball games as teaching opportunities. Because the students wanted me to play, they were prepared to listen to what I had to say. They also liked the idea that, because we were not technically in school, they were not required to do what the teacher said. The games helped me teach students how to work cooperatively, how to care about and include others, how to work within rules, and how to control their tempers when disappointed or upset. They also established contexts for discussions in class about use of language and the impact of racial epithets on participants, communities, and the broader society.

9. Students were asked to read an excerpt from George Washington's Farewell Address that discussed domestic issues confronting the new nation, summarize its main ideas, and explain the historical context of the document. The previous year I had given a similar assignment based on the Farewell Address, only the excerpt focused on foreign policy concerns. One student handed in a paper based on the previous year's excerpt. What should I do?

Although the problem of cheating on reports has been exacerbated by the ability of students to download material from the Internet, it basically remains the same. I caught this student because the assignment had been tailored in a particular way. When an assignment is unstructured or open-ended it is much easier to copy someone else's work. I always warn students, "I do not want to turn on my computer and find your report." Sometimes, however, the warning is to no avail. In this case, I decided to meet with the student and discuss what I had found, but not the issue of cheating. If I accused her of cheating it would become a disciplinary matter and referred to the department chair for further investigation and potential punishment. I got the student's schedule from the program office, found her later in the day, and we walked through the halls talking. I explained that she had done the wrong assignment and I was concerned because what she handed in had been assigned the previous year. I did not ask her to explain or confess, but did ask what she thought she should do. She asked for the opportunity to do the paper again without penalty. I agreed under the condition that something like this did not happen in the future. Although I did not tell other students about our discussion, many students from my class saw me come to the room and speak with her. I suspect word that she had been caught but given a second chance quickly spread. I hope this demonstrated to students that I was both vigilant and fair.

10. I suspected that a student in my class was cheating on multiple-choice tests, but I had not caught him cheating. I did not want to make the atmosphere during tests uncomfortable for all students because of my suspicions about one of them. What should I do?

I often warn students not to copy because the person sitting in the next row might not have the same test. Sometimes I reproduce one test with two different cover pages, one labeled form A and the other form B. Sometimes I place questions on the first page in a different order. I rarely do more than that. In this case, I was sure the other students "knew" what was going on and decided to set a trap. On the next test, I gave the "suspect" his own test. It had the exact same questions as everyone else's, but the choices were arranged in a different order. When I gave the test back, he had the nerve to raise his hand and complain that he had the same answers as the person sitting next to him, but his were marked wrong. I reminded him that they probably had different tests, and the entire class started to laugh. I spoke with the student later and confronted him about cheating. He confessed that "maybe he copied some things." We agreed to discount both his earlier scores on multiple-choice tests and his failing grade on this examination, if he kept "his nose clean" for the rest of the school year.

SECTION B: GUIDANCE-RELATED ISSUES CAN BE VERY THORNY AND CAN RAISE LEGAL QUESTIONS

1. I have often been approached by students in my classes who want to discuss a personal or school-related problem, but before they will talk about it, they ask me to "promise not to tell anyone."

The first thing you need to tell the student is that you can never promise in advance "not to tell anyone." As a teacher you are professionally and legally responsible to report certain disclosures, especially physical or substance abuse and threats of violence. If a student decides to tell you something that is personal, they are trusting your judgment as a concerned and caring adult. But they must be aware that you may have to report what they say, either to a parent or to a school official. The next thing I ask is if there is a friend they would like present while we talk. I do this for two reasons. It may make it easier for the student, and it provides a witness to what took place. We live in a very complicated world and a teacher must protect himself or herself from accusations made later by a disturbed student or a distressed parent. I often find students just need a friendly ear, a chance to cry, or a warm hug. Unfortunately, as a male teacher, my actions may be misconstrued. Again, because of the complications of the world, I have developed professional relationships with female counselors or teachers in my schools, and when necessary and as quickly as possible, I involve them in the discussion. I have also faced more serious issues. I have had young women tell me they are pregnant and do not know what to do or that they are being sexually harassed. I have had students report friends who they fear are on drugs or suicidal. Students have also come to me with legal problems, especially involving immigration. In most cases the school has crisis intervention counselors and I have persuaded students to speak with them. Sometimes I have succeeded in getting the student to speak with their parents. In other cases, especially when they need legal assistance, I have referred them to outside community agencies.

2. There is an undercurrent in a class of boys teasing and poking girls. None of the girls have said anything.

In 2001, New York City reported a surge in student-on-student sexual harassment incidents. Most school authorities simply attributed it to more systematic reporting. I believe it was actually a combination of two other factors. Instead of treating inappropriate behavior by boys toward girls as a teaching opportunity, school officials are wiping their hands of the matter and either punishing students internally or turning them over to the police. I find this policy misguided and irresponsible. The second factor is that the definition of acceptable behavior by boys toward girls has changed since I was in junior high school. The boys back then were horrible. If we were punished according to the standard in effect today, I think we all would have been arrested for teasing and touching. New attitudes toward gender equity and appropriate behavior are overwhelming improvements, but violations should be treated as learning issues and community concerns, not as punishable offenses. The girls need to talk to the group about how they feel when a boy snaps their bra or makes fun of the size of their bosom and the boys need to understand the pain they cause when they target or demean someone. If schools and teachers address the teasing and poking before they escalates, most problems can be avoided, relations can be improved, and students, both males and females, do not have to be marked for life.

3. A student speaks, dresses, or behaves in ways that suggest a possible homosexual orientation. Other students are gossiping about or teasing the student.

The first question is, what is the problem here? Too many teachers and school officials act as if the problem is the student who is being victimized. But that student has the right to be the way he or she is, whatever that happens to be, and the student does not have an obligation to answer to anyone for his or her sexual orientation or sense of style. For me the difficult issue is how to address the biases of the overall student population without stigmatizing students who are perceived as different. It is the same issue whether students are teased or gossiped about because of their ethnicity, race, disability, social class, academic performance, or interests. In this case I would be preemptive and press for a school policy and curriculum that respects diversity, tolerates all forms of difference, and challenges oppressive or discriminatory behavior. I think the school must be prepared to meet with parents or students who reject homosexuality because of religious beliefs. However, in our society, these parents and students are legally responsible to respect the rights of others. In addition, given the pressure on people who experience being different in our society, schools should provide a range of counseling services and support groups.

4. A student's personality appears to change. He or she becomes sullen and his or her performance in school is deteriorating.

When students appear to change personality, especially when they become sullen and their performance in school is deteriorating, they are sending out a signal that they need help. Our job as teachers is to recognize the signals, show concern, and provide support. As a teacher, I try to reach out to students and ask them, "What's happening?" Students who feel connections to adults rarely hurt themselves or others. Again, schools should provide a range of counseling services and support groups. We need to address problems before they become emergencies.

SECTION C: RELATIONSHIPS WITH COLLEAGUES CAN BE TRICKY

1. A student who does well in your class is constantly in trouble with one of the other teachers.

When a student is failing one class or keeps getting referred to the dean by one teacher, it can affect their performance in every subject. They miss class time because of hearings and suspensions, may give up trying to learn, or disappear from school altogether. My first action is to recommend to the student that he or she talk with the teacher about the problem. If the student feels he or she cannot, or if the results of such a talk are unsatisfactory, I try to mediate the dispute. I ask the student what he or she thinks the problem is and if he or she would like me to speak with the other teacher to help find a solution. I try to be careful not to blame the teacher, no matter how upset, or seemingly justified, the student is. There are always multiple sides to a story and the student's behavior in response to the teacher was certainly counterproductive. Usually both student and colleague are glad to have the intervention because it offers the possibility that the situation will improve. On occasion, we arranged for an especially upset and disruptive student to sit in my room and do work for the other teacher, instead of attending the regular class. This gave both the student and teacher time and space and allowed the conflict to defuse. In many middle schools, teachers who have the same students meet as teams and this facilitates this kind of networking. I have had colleagues who tell me to get lost. In these situations, I generally back off. However, in extreme cases, I have raised the problem with department chairs or informed the dean that I had another view of the problem. An additional reason for becoming involved, though a bit self-serving, is that it helps me to develop a relationship with the student and with the rest of the class.

2. Students complain to you about the way they are treated by another teacher or the way that another teacher teaches.

This is a slightly different case from the previous one because the students have taken the initiative. My initial response is that the students need to learn how to work with many different kinds of people and that the first step is to talk with the teacher about the problem. If the students feel they cannot, or if the results are unsatisfactory, I have a decision to make. If it is a cooperative colleague that I am comfortable with, I will speak with them about the problem, trying not to identify the specific student(s). If the colleague and I do not have a good working relationship, I can speak with my supervisor or with the other teacher's supervisor about the student complaints. If there is a history of similar complaints and the students are in danger of failing or exploding, I might go with students to their guidance counselor and try to facilitate a transfer to another class. I have to confess, I have not always handled this sensitive situation with sufficient diplomacy and I have made enemies.

3. Colleagues are openly and publicly talking about individuals or groups of students in ways that you find unacceptable.

A lot of my friends recommend staying away from the teachers' lounge in order to avoid these kinds of confrontations. They find responding is useless at best, aggravating at worst. Lois Weiner, whom I mentioned earlier, believes it is possible to maintain cordial relations with all colleagues and suggests smoothing over potential conflicts. I was never willing or able to follow her advice. Sometimes you must take a stand on an issue and cannot avoid making enemies. When colleagues openly and publicly talk about individuals or groups of students in ways that I find unacceptable, I acknowledge their right to their opinion but challenge what they have to say and their right to say it in an unprofessional manner. If they continue, I inform them that I will not hesitate to report our conversation to appropriate supervisors. Over the years, many teachers have supported my response. They are upset when colleagues disparage or demean students and are glad when these teachers are confronted.

SECTION D: DISAGREEMENTS WITH SCHOOL POLICIES

1. Senior teachers recommend that you contact parents when students are either misbehaving or falling behind in their work. You are uncertain when should you call, what tone you should take, and what you should say to parents.

As a parent, I have been on the other end of calls home. I got upset when a teacher was officious with me, disparaging about my children, or just read from a long list of grievances. I sometimes asked teachers, "How would you feel if you were on my end of the phone?" or, "What exactly do you want me to do?" When a student is acting up or slacking off in school, there are generally other things going on in their life. Their parents are also probably having difficulty getting them to respond and act appropriately. By the time most students are teenagers, parents can rarely force a difficult student to behave. A conversation will be much more fruitful if you talk about a student as a human being, rather than as a "problem," show parents that you are genuinely concerned, and respect the parents as people who would like their children to do well in school and life. Ask them if they can tell you something that will help you be more effective as their child's teacher and ask if there is something you can do to support what they are already doing. If at all possible, try to find something positive to say, at least that you look forward to meeting them and working with them in the future.

Rachel Gaglione—I like to make "good conduct" calls to tell parents when their child is doing well. Students like the idea and will come up to you and ask if they can get a "good conduct" call as well. If you call about a student who is misbehaving, pay attention to the response of the parent. If the parent is standoffish, just tell them you wanted them to be aware of the situation, say "thank you" and "good-bye." If the parent is angry, try to calm them down and do not call them again. Word gets out among students when you make either type of phone calls.

2. Some of my students are fooling around in the hall during a change of period and refuse to identify themselves to a security guard. The security guard asks me for their names so she can report them to the school administration and have them suspended. What should I do?

This happened to me on more than one occasion and it can be a difficult situation to resolve. If you identify the students, no matter what they did, they will dismiss you as a "rat" and an adult who just wants to "get them." It will jeopardize your ability to reach them and other students in the future. On the other hand, you do not want to undermine a coworker. Most school security guards are concerned about students and act professionally. If you tell the security guard that you will take care of the situation, they are usually glad to leave it up to you, especially if you have treated them with respect in the past. If you and the security guard still disagree on what to do, suggest that you go to the appropriate school authority together and try to work it out. It is crucial, however, that if you promised to speak with the students, you do it. Word travels quickly around a school. If you do not follow through, the security guards, administrators, and students will not believe you in the future.

3. In many districts, if a student is found with a knife or any other weapon, they are suspended and often arrested, expelled from school, or both. In the middle of a lesson, you witness a student picking at his nails with a pocket knife. What should you do?

This is a difficult situation because it involves student trust, school policy, and legal issues. I faced it a couple of times a year. I am not making a general recommendation. You must use your own judgment and decide based on the situation and based on your conscience, ability to take risks, and goals. If I know the student and have confidence in his or her judgment, I will approach quietly and explain that if I report seeing him or her with a knife he or she risks suspension and arrest. However, if I report that I found a knife on the floor and turn it in to school authorities, no further action will be taken. The student has to make an immediate decision. If the knife is on the floor, the situation is over. Twice, over the years, the knife was not found on the floor. On both of those occasions I notified security personnel and the student was removed from class.

Rachel Gaglione—My response depends on who else knows and what else is happening. You can get into serious work trouble for not reporting an incident like this, especially if students have made threats. I have had two experiences similar to this one and handled it differently each time. We went on a senior class trip to Washington, D.C., and a few students bought souvenir knives from a street vendor. A parent chaperone witnessed this and informed staff. Later, one of the students set off a metal detector while entering a building. We asked students for the knives, but no one turned one in. When we returned to the school, the teachers decided to report the entire incident. The second time I was involved in a situation with a knife, I was escorting a class out of school at dismissal time. A boy pulled out a small knife and started cutting his nails. I spoke with him, realized he meant no harm, walked him home and told him never to bring it back to school. Although the safer thing to do in these cases is to report it, that may not be the right thing to do.

4. Your school has a zero tolerance policy toward fighting. You witness a fight in the hall and know the participants. If you report them they will be suspended. Should you break it up, report the students to school authorities, or both?

I do not condone fighting, but I also know that sometimes conflicts between students go too far and confrontations become physical. As a preteen and teenager I was involved in some fights in school and in the street. My policy is to give combatants and their friends a chance to resolve the situation. If I know the students, I step between them. If they are grabbing or hitting each other, I try to pull away the student who is getting the worst of the encounter. While I have him or her, I turn to the crowd and give their friends a choice. If they can calm them down, get them out of there, and prevent a reoccurrence, everything is over and done with and we can all walk away. If their friends cannot stop the fight or if it starts again later, the entire incident gets reported to school authorities and everyone gets suspended.

5. What if what I say or do turns out to be the wrong decision? Should I report a poor judgment or an inappropriate action to school authorities?

No one said life or teaching is easy. When I started working as a bus operator at the New York City Transit Authority, the union shop steward recommended that we admit nothing, avoid putting statements in writing, and, if pressed for a formal report, ask for time to think about what we wanted to say. I think it was good advice. In the work world I learned not to lie, but also not to offer more information than was requested. I found that lesson made sense in schools also. Sometimes, however, you need to talk about an incident or a question with someone. If you have a good relationship with a senior colleague or with a supervisor, you can often have an "off-the-record" conversation that will help clarify issues. That is probably your best bet. If an off-the-record conversation is not possible and there is a union in the school, you should consult your representative. What you are obsessing about is probably not such a big deal and has happened to many people in the past. If it is a real problem, the union representative will advise you how to proceed. In some circumstances, if it is allowed under the union contract or by law, your representative can be present at formal meetings with supervisory personnel.

Rachel Gaglione—No two people will handle a situation the exact same way. However, one thing is universally true: Cover-ups never work. If you are a new teacher, ask for advice from a trusted colleague. You do not want to lose your job, but more important, you do not want anyone to get hurt as a result of your decision.

III

PRO/CLASS PRACTICES—LITERACY, ASSESSMENT, SUPPORT, STRUGGLE

Book III focuses on special topics: *literacy,* including technological literacy; *assessment* of student learning and teacher performance; *support* for students with social or psychological problems; and the *struggle,* as a student teacher and beginning teacher, to be the best teacher that you can be. It includes an appendix with an annotated list of Web sites useful for teachers.

7

LITERACY: HOW CAN TEACHERS ENCOURAGE STUDENT LITERACIES?

What skills and knowledge does someone need to fully participate in a modern, technological, and democratic society? Efforts to answer this question are a major part of the national debate over educational standards and the performance of schools. It is a difficult question to answer because what people need to know is constantly changing. For example, I joke with students that when I was in high school in the 1960s, we were not allowed to use pocket calculators in math class. This was not because teachers were stricter or educational standards were higher, but because miniature calculators had not yet been invented. As recently as 1983, when my in-laws offered to purchase a personal computer for my family, my wife and I did not know what we would do with one. Today we each have our own computer at home and at work and do not know how we would manage without them. Technological development has fundamentally altered what we mean by minimum competency skills.

An additional problem is that minimum competency is not everyone's goal. Few of the people reading this book would accept it as the standard for themselves or their own children. Why should it be an acceptable standard for anyone in our society?

To actively participate in today's world, a citizen must be able to gather, sort, and evaluate information on a number of topics, from a variety of sources, using different technologies. For example, to effectively select candidates for office, citizens should have at least some information about other countries, the workings of the nation's economy, educational programs, and environmental concerns. If they want to influence the ideas of their neighbors, they must be able to express ideas orally and in writing as well as know how to interact with and organize diverse groups of people. Because each citizen will probably also need to earn a living, maintain a home, and raise a family, they must be comfortable with basic math, familiar with new technologies, and even conversant in more than one dialect or language. The 21st century is certainly a complicated place. A number of commentators have made the point that the technology of literacy has probably changed more in the last 20 years than it did in the previous 2 millennia.

A useful definition of *literacy* is the ability to participate in a conversation with a level of competence and confidence. This requires both skills and knowledge. In the early 1980s, public television produced a documentary on nuclear weapons called *Nuclear Strategy for Beginners*. A scientist from the Massachusetts Institute for Technology who was interviewed for the project explained that concerned citizens did not need to know technical information such as "the size of the screw you put in the nuclear warhead," but they should understand "something about what it does, ... about the effects of nuclear war, ... about the possibility of trying to control such a war." This would enable citizens to be involved in discussion and democratic decision making about nuclear policy. I think this is a good example of literacy in a particular academic area. Because every subject has its own competencies, and different aspects of a culture require distinct knowledge and skills, it is helpful to talk about *multiple literacies.*

A traditional distinction between elementary and secondary schools is that in early grades students "learn to read," whereas in middle school and high school they "read to learn." Many secondary school teachers still insist that their primary job should be to teach content to students who already possess the required skills. However, the rapid pace of change means that people are continually learning new skills or enhancing old ones throughout their lives. Teachers must prepare students to live in a world that we can barely envision.

For me, the best way to prepare students for this new and complex world is by promoting *critical literacy,* which means teaching students how to think, organize ideas, and express them. No matter what academic discipline you are preparing to teach, your students need to learn how to learn, to find and evaluate information available in different formats, to think systematically, to support arguments with evidence, to present ideas clearly, and to evaluate their own work and the work of others so they can participate in conversations within the subject discipline.

Under the broad umbrella of literacy this chapter examines concepts such as *critical literacy, multiple literacies,* and *literacy standards.* There are also separate sections on the use of differentiated texts and instruction in classrooms, using multicultural literature to challenge student understanding of the world, using questions that promote higher order thinking skills, and promoting technological competencies among both students and teachers. It includes an essay by Gary Benenson that defines *technological literacy* and its importance in education and life.

JOIN THE CONVERSATION—LOOKING BACKWARD

A number of authors have written books in which they try, usually without success, to predict the future. In *Looking Backward,* first published in 1888, Edward Bellamy described the world in the year 2000. It would be a place without war, greed, hypocrisy, and apathy, and people would no longer struggle to survive. Part of the problem with predicting the future is that in recent decades technology has changed so rapidly and in unanticipated directions. I was born in 1950—before CDs, video and audio cassettes, transistor radios, color television, and of course, personal computers.

Questions to Consider:

1. How has technology changed the world since you first entered school?
2. How were you able to adapt to these changes?
3. In your opinion, how can teachers prepare students for a rapidly changing world when we do not know which direction it will take?

SECTION A: WHAT IS CRITICAL LITERACY?

When most teachers, parents, and nonspecialists think about literacy, we think of proficiency in reading, writing, and arithmetic—the classical 3 Rs traditionally taught through repetitive practice. This view of literacy, as skills to be acquired through constant practice, is supported by radio and television advertisements selling phonetic drills that supposedly boost reading scores. Many of us remember going to schools where a major activity was reciting spelling lists or the multiplication tables.

Linda Christensen, a high school English teacher whom we met in chapter 6, has a significantly different view. In *Reading, Writing and Rising Up* (2000), a collection of writings by herself and her students, Christensen discusses literacy as part of community building in the classroom and the struggle for social justice in the broader society. Christensen introduces her students to the power of language as a form of creative expression that allows them to discover themselves and share with others. But it is also vital for shaping, critiquing, and communicating ideas, and it empowers them, as global citizens, to influence and reshape the world. In Christensen's classroom, literacy means expression, communication, and social transformation. Her vision of literacy reminds me of a labor union song from the 1913 textile workers' strike in Lawrence, Massachusetts. As young women marched in protest against low wages, long hours, and unfair working conditions, they demanded "bread and roses"— higher pay and decent living conditions (bread) and an opportunity to experience the joy and beauty of life (roses). In Christensen's classrooms, students read, write, and speak for both "bread and roses."

Paulo Freire, whose philosophy of education was introduced in chapter 1, argues that literacy should not be viewed as a technical skill, but as a necessary action for freedom (Freire & Macedo, 1987). According to Freire, *critical literacy* requires reading and understanding both the *world* and the *word* so that people have the ability to use words to change the world. He feels that interest in and the ability to "read the world" naturally precedes the ability to "read the word." Based on his perspective, in order to enhance traditional "pen-and-paper" literacy, teachers must engage students as activists.

As a high school social studies teacher committed to promoting this kind of critical literacy, I helped students in my government classes organize a club to encourage student political activism. The club sponsored speakers on controversial topics such as abortion rights and apartheid, lobbied government agencies for increased school funding, and participated in political rallies. As these students read the world, they were forced by the momentum of their actions to improve their ability to read the word. Members researched issues and wrote reports, speeches, press releases, leaflets, and opinion essays for newspapers. They created posters, buttons, political cartoons, charts, and graphs, and they edited video reports on their activities.

A similar approach to teaching and literacy has found a powerful advocate in Robert Moses, a mathematics teacher who is also a civil rights activist. According to Moses (1994), "The main goal of the Algebra Project is to impact the struggle for citizenship and equality by assisting students in inner city and rural areas to achieve mathematics literacy. Higher order thinking and problem solving skills are necessary for entry into the economic mainstream.... Without these skills children will be tracked into an economic underclass."

The Algebra Project (Moses & Cobb, 2001) helps students build an understanding of mathematical concepts through a five-step process that moves them from familiar concrete experiences (reading the world) to abstract mathematics (reading the word).

1. Students participate in a *physical experience,* such as a trip, in which they see examples of what they are studying (e.g., arches, geometric shapes, suspension bridges).
2. Following the trip, students draw *pictorial representations* or construct models of what they have observed.
3. Next, they discuss and write about the event in their everyday dialect or intuitive language. Moses calls this stage *"People Talk."*

4. Their oral and written reports are then translated into the standard dialect or structured language as part of *"Feature Talk."*

5. In the last step, students develop *symbolic or Algebraic representations* that describe what they have learned. They present these representations in class and explore how they can be used to describe other phenomena.

What I especially like about Moses's work is that he extends critical literacy from social studies and English into the mathematics classroom. His ideas on empowering students through a structured learning process that uses their lived experience and home dialects to engage them in learning complex material is applicable in language acquisition, science, or any other area of academic study.

JOIN THE CONVERSATION—DECIPHERING OR READING?

When I was a preteenager, I learned to pray in Hebrew in preparation for my bar mitzvah at age 13. A bar mitzvah is a ceremony in which a Jewish boy is accepted as an adult member of the religious community. My friends and I used to joke that we had to pray in Hebrew because "God does not understand English." Of course we did not understand Hebrew. We simply deciphered meaningless sounds and recited them aloud. Later, as an adult, I learned that many Roman Catholic youth had a similar experience studying Latin.

I have been in many classrooms where students decipher and recite text the same way. When questioned, they have no idea what they have just read. The students possess technical skill, but they are not reading, which, according to Freire, "always involves critical perception, interpretation, and rewriting of what is read."

Questions to Consider:

1. How did you learn to make meaning of what you read?
2. What motivated you to grapple with difficult text?
3. Do you agree with the idea of critical literacy? Explain.

SECTION B: HOW MANY KINDS OF LITERACY ARE THERE?

This broader notion of critical literacy advocated by Freire, Christensen, and Moses is closer to the ideas of contemporary literacy specialists than the older version of simply mastering the three Rs. Because they view literacy as fundamental to the processes of thinking, understanding, and acting, literacy specialists are the imperialists of the educational world. For them, everything is a form of literacy and there are numerous overlapping and interwoven varieties. One book, published by the International Reading Association (IRA), listed 38 types, including academic literacy, community literacy, critical literacy, cultural literacy, media literacy, pragmatic literacy, and workplace literacy (Harris & Hodges, 1995).

Let me use an example from the world of sports to illustrate my understanding of what literacy specialists mean by literacy. One of the most difficult positions to master in any team sport is quarterback, in football. Not only must a player have the requisite physical skills, but the quarterback must be able to read and respond to a series of defensive strategies employed by the other team and to quickly communicate new plans to teammates. Quarterbacks are assisted in doing this by viewing videotape of earlier games, studying charts of opposition tendencies, reviewing their own team's playbook, and running countless simulations during practice sessions. In addition, they continually receive new information via radio, by signals from coaches scattered around the field, and orally from teammates when they huddle before a play. Each of these activities involves a different form of literacy because the quarterback is continuously gathering, evaluating, and communicating information. But in addition, the quarterback is engrossed in a cultural context, the game of football, with its own goals and rules, goals and rules that it took years to master. Football requires its own areas of competence or literacy in order to engage in the conversation (or play the game).

An appreciation of *context* is crucial for understanding this modern concept of literacy. A word means different things in different contexts. For example, if a teacher said that a middle school student's report was "bad," the student who received this evaluation would probably get upset. But if a fellow student declared that the same report was "B-A-D," it would be cause for celebration. The word *bad* clearly means different things in these different cultural contexts. As noted earlier, even the word *literacy* means one thing in standard usage and something very different to educational theorists.

Some educators are trying to reconcile traditional and contemporary ideas about literacy. The October 1999 theme issue of the highly regarded magazine *Educational Leadership* argued that teachers and school policymakers needed to promote "learning the basics of reading and writing, grammar and spelling" as well as the ability of students to participate in conversations in different arenas and use information garnered from diverse sources (Tell, 1999, p. 5).

Articles in this theme issue discussed programs for improving student performance in reading and writing, and the importance of mastering specialized literacies, including numeracy, science literacy, arts literacy, media literacy, information literacy, and technology literacy. Numeracy, or quantitative literacy, involves the ability to comfortably use basic arithmetical skills, but also includes competency with complex statistical, computer, interpretive, and technical communication skills. A person with numerical literacy must understand as well as calculate; she or he must be able to draw inferences from numbers and use them to make judgments. Science literacy requires knowledge of scientific facts, concepts, and theories and an understanding of the scientific approach to evaluating hypotheses using reason and experimentation. Information literacy, media literacy, and technology literacy, although they start from a different focus, are clearly intertwined, involving students in acquiring and evaluating sources of information. Similarly, art literacy shares much in common with music and literature.

So, how many literacies are there? By some definitions, there is at least one for each area of study and academic skill. However, I think it is more useful to limit ourselves to two general categories of literacy: *critical literacy* (which involves thinking, understanding, and acting on the world) and *multiple literacies* (which include finding, processing, and using information from different media and fields of study).

JOIN THE CONVERSATION—DO YOU SPEAK MATH?

Before looking at the questions that follow, carefully observe the room around you. Then write a paragraph describing the room.

Questions to Consider:

1. What are the key descriptors you used in the paragraph to describe the room?

2. Compare your description with those written by other students. Do you use the same kind of descriptors?

3. In my teacher education classes, I find that some students use numbers and focus on quantities and measurements in their descriptions. Other students write about colors and shapes or about how the room makes them feel. In your opinion, why do people take such different approaches?

4. I find it helpful to think of mathematics as a language that allows for precise descriptions of quantities and certain relationships, but is not as useful as other languages for poetic or metaphoric representation. In your opinion, is it useful to think of mathematics as a language? Explain.

SECTION C: WHAT ARE LITERACY STANDARDS?

A number of national organizations have adopted lists of standards (goals) designed to help teachers and schools develop strategies promoting student literacy. The National Council of Teachers of English (NCTE) and the IRA offer a joint list that includes 12 interrelated educational goals. Teachers from different academic disciplines are rarely familiar with standards from other subject areas. However, given our shared mission of enhancing student literacies, it is important that all teachers be familiar with these language arts literacy standards.

1. Students read a wide range of print and nonprint texts to build an understanding of texts, of themselves, and of the cultures of the United States and the world; to acquire new information; to respond to the needs and demands of society and the workplace; and to achieve personal fulfillment. Among these texts are fiction and nonfiction, classic and contemporary works.

2. Students read a wide range of literature from many periods in many genres to build an understanding of the many dimensions (e.g., philosophical, ethical, aesthetic) of human experience.

3. Students apply a wide range of strategies to comprehend, interpret, evaluate, and appreciate texts. They draw on their prior experience, their interactions with other readers and writers, their knowledge of word meaning and of other texts, their word identification strategies, and their understanding of textual features (e.g., sound–letter correspondence, sentence structure, context, graphics).

4. Students adjust their use of spoken, written, and visual language (e.g., conventions, style, vocabulary) to communicate effectively with a variety of audiences and for different purposes.

5. Students employ a wide range of strategies as they write and use different writing process elements appropriately to communicate with different audiences for a variety of purposes.

6. Students apply knowledge of language structure, language conventions (e.g., spelling and punctuation), media techniques, figurative language, and genre to create, critique, and discuss print and nonprint texts.

7. Students conduct research on issues and interests by generating ideas and questions, and by posing problems. They gather, evaluate, and synthesize data from a variety of sources (e.g., print and nonprint texts, artifacts, people) to communicate their discoveries in ways that suit their purpose and audience.

8. Students use a variety of technological and information resources (e.g., libraries, data-bases, computer networks, video) to gather and synthesize information and to create and communicate knowledge.

9. Students develop an understanding of and respect for diversity in language use, pat-terns, and dialects across cultures, ethnic groups, geographic regions, and social roles.

10. Students whose first language is not English make use of their first language to develop competency in the English language arts and to develop understanding of content across the curriculum.

11. Students participate as knowledgeable, reflective, creative, and critical members of a variety of literacy communities.

12. Students use spoken, written, and visual language to accomplish their own purposes (e.g., for learning, enjoyment, persuasion, and the exchange of information).

In chapter 3, I emphasize that standards should be seen as goals, rather than as a measur-ing rod of performance. I think the NCTE–IRA literacy standards underscore that point. I also think they help us define what we mean by a literate or educated person. Based on these 12 standards, a literate person is able to use print and nonprint resources to acquire informa-tion and conduct independent research, communicates effectively with a range of audiences using different media, has the ability and background to understand the diverse dimensions of human experience, and actively and thoughtfully participates in broader communities.

JOIN THE CONVERSATION—LITERACY STANDARDS

Questions to Consider:

1. Which of these literacy standards is applicable in your academic subject area? Explain.

2. Discuss three lesson ideas in your subject area that would promote student literacies.

3. How do you define a literate or educated person? Would you consider yourself a mem-ber of this group based on your definition? Why?

SECTION D: HOW CAN STUDENTS LEARN COMPLEX MATERIAL WHILE STILL STRUGGLING TO IMPROVE THEIR READING SKILLS?

Maureen Murphy and I (MacCurtain et al., 2001) recently completed a multiyear project de-veloping interdisciplinary activities, lessons, and units for teaching about the Great Irish Famine in grades 4–12. Our initial plan was to prepare separate high school (9–12) and upper elementary/middle-level (4–8) packages. High school material would be minimally *edited*, whereas the middle-level package would include documents that were *adapted* for class-room use.

Through field-testing the lessons in classrooms, participation in and observation of group work, and follow-up discussions with students, we discovered that our distinction between the two levels did not take into account the full range of student performance. Many high school students were more comfortable with the adapted documents, whereas some middle-level students were capable of reading with understanding the minimally edited text. In addition, in both middle and high school classes, some students with a record of poor academic performance could not read either set of material. Teachers working with these students recommended that documents be completely *rewritten*. As a result of this input, the final curriculum guide offers teachers the option of using differentiated edited, adapted, and rewritten text with major language revisions, either with an entire class on any grade level or with selected students.

While field-testing the curriculum, we also learned that the way material was presented to students was fundamental for capturing their interest and promoting learning. When teachers engaged students in activities, used references that had meaning to a particular group of students, reviewed vocabulary and provided a context for language, provided readings that were accessible, and encouraged freewheeling discussions, every group of students responded enthusiastically to the curriculum. Inner-city and suburban students, immigrants and native born, and students from different ethnic backgrounds were all fascinated by events before, during, and after the Great Irish Famine.

Some of our most successful lessons about the Irish were taught in low-performing inner-city middle schools, with students who were largely African American, Caribbean, and Latino. The keys to these lessons were our ability to create a context for literacy and learning, as well as to provide students with differentiated text. Students sang traditional songs such as "Paddy on the Railway" and "No Irish Need Apply," examined political cartoons and newspaper illustrations downloaded from the Internet, and compared the experience of the Irish with their own experiences with discrimination and inequality. Our experience in these classes is consistent with Maxine Greene's idea that learning is a search for "situated understanding" that places ideas and events in their social, historical, and cultural contexts.

I sometimes compare learning to read with weightlifting. If your goal is to bench press 200 pounds, you start with a lower weight and build up your skill and muscle over time. If you were given a bar with 200 pounds on the first day and told to lift, you would probably just give up. Using differentiated texts offers teachers a strategy to maintain student interest while helping them gradually reach a higher standard.

JOIN THE CONVERSATION—DEOXYRIBOSE NUCLEIC ACID

Our work on the Great Irish Famine curriculum guide points up the crucial importance of accessible text and appropriate context when teachers present complex material to students who are struggling to improve their literacy skills. These are not only concerns for social studies and English teachers. Below you will find three versions of the same passage from an article published in *Nature* magazine in 1953 explaining the molecular structure of DNA. The first version is slightly edited from the original. The second version has been adapted and the third version is completely rewritten.

Questions to Consider:

1. Read the first version and write a paragraph explaining what it means.
2. How did you feel as you read this version of the article? Why?
3. After reading all three versions, explain which version you think should be used in a high school biology class? Why?
4. In your view, how can differentiated text be used to promote student understanding of complex material while literacy skills are still developing?

FIG. 7.1   Using differentiated text in a science class.

A) A Structure for Deoxyribose Nucleic Acid (Edited)
J. D. Watson and F. H. C. Crick (1953). *Nature, 171*, 737.

We wish to suggest a structure for the salt of deoxyribose nucleic acid (D.N.A.). This structure has novel features which are of considerable biological interest. . . .

This structure has two helical chains each coiled round the same axis. We have made the usual chemical assumptions, namely, that each chain consists of phosphate diester groups joining β-D-deoxyribofuranose residues with 3',5' linkages. The two chains (but not their bases) are related by a dyad perpendicular to the fibre axis. Both chains follow right-handed helices, but owing to the dyad the sequences of the atoms in the two chains run in opposite directions. Each chain loosely resembles Furberg's model no. 1; that is, the bases are on the inside of the helix and the phosphates on the outside. The configuration of the sugar and the atoms near it is close to Furberg's "standard configuration," the sugar being roughly perpendicular to the attached base. There is a residue on each every 3.4 A. in the z-direction. We have assumed an angle of 36° between adjacent residues in the same chain, so that the structure repeats after 10 residues on each chain, that is, after 34 A. The distance of a phosphorus atom from the fibre axis is 10 A. As the phosphates are on the outside, cations have easy access to them. The structure is an open one, and its water content is rather high. At lower water contents we would expect the bases to tilt so that the structure could become more compact.

The novel feature of the structure is the manner in which the two chains are held together by the purine and pyrimidine bases. The planes of the bases are perpendicular to the fibre axis. The are joined together in pairs, a single base from the other chain, so that the two lie side by side with identical z-coordinates. One of the pair must be a purine and the other pyrimidine for bonding to occur. The hydrogen bonds are made as follows: purine position 1 to pyrimidine position 1; purine position 6 to pyrimidine position 6. . . .

It is probably impossible to build this structure with a ribose sugar in place of the deoxyribose, as the extra oxygen atom would make too close a van der Waals contact. The previously published X-ray data on deoxyribose nucleic acid are insufficient for a rigorous test of our structure. So far as we can tell, it is roughly compatible with the experimental data, but it must be regarded as unproved until it has been checked against more exact results. Some of these are given in the following communications. We were not aware of the details of the results presented there when we devised our structure, which rests mainly though not entirely on published experimental data and stereochemical arguments.

It has not escaped our notice that the specific pairing we have postulated immediately suggests a possible copying mechanism for the genetic material.

Full details of the structure, . . . together with a set of coordinates for the atoms, will be published elsewhere.

B) Molecular Structure of D.N.A. (Adapted)
by J. D. Watson and F. H. C. Crick. (1953). *Nature, 171*, 737.

We wish to suggest a structure for . . . D.N.A. This structure has novel features of considerable biological interest.

We wish to put forward a radically different structure for D.N.A. This structure has two helical chains each coiled round the same axis. We have made the usual chemical assumptions. . . . The novel feature of the structure is the manner in which the two chains are held together.

The previously published X-ray data on D.N.A. are insufficient for a rigorous test of our structure. So far as we can tell, it is roughly compatible with the experimental data, but it must be regarded as unproved until it has been checked against more exact results.

It has not escaped our notice that the specific pairing we have postulated immediately suggests a possible copying mechanism for the genetic materials.

Full details of the structure, including the conditions assumed in building it, together with a set of coordinates for the atoms, will be published elsewhere.

FIG. 7.1 *(Continued)*

C) Scientists Solve a Mystery (Rewritten)

Do you look like your parents? Do you know why?

For many years scientists tried to understand how living things create new living things that look a lot like them. We call this process reproduction. Tall parents usually have children who grow tall. Dark-skinned parents generally have dark-skinned children. If parents have big feet, their children probably also will have big feet when they become adults.

Some scientists believed that the key to reproduction was a molecule they called D.N.A. The problem was that the D.N.A. molecule is so small that the scientists did not know what it looked like. The shape of D.N.A. was a real scientific mystery.

Teams of scientists guessed different shapes for D.N.A. They tried to fit different chemicals into a complicated puzzle. Finally scientists named Watson and Crick drew the picture shown above. The beauty of their picture was that it used all the chemical pieces and it showed how D.N.A. could reproduce by splitting. When scientists did more tests, it turned out that Watson and Crick were right. They had solved the mystery of D.N.A.

SECTION E: HOW CAN THE SAME TEXT HAVE MULTIPLE MEANINGS?

Using Multicultural Literature to Understand Self and World
By Judith Y. Singer and Sally Smith

Judith Singer, whom you met in chapter 4, and Sally Smith, another Hofstra colleague, conducted a series of research projects that illustrate an additional problem with texts that teachers should be aware of as they prepare instruction. When students read a text, they construct meaning differently because they come from a variety of cultural contexts with differing sets of assumptions. Judi and Sally conclude that teachers cannot simply rely on texts, even interesting texts, to promote student understanding of complex issues, but must direct student attention and challenge preconceptions. In this essay, they suggest some ways that this can be done. Although they write about teacher education students, their ideas are applicable in any classroom.—Alan Singer

We are teacher educators who use multicultural children's literature to help teachers better understand themselves and the world. For us, multiculturalism is a form of both critical and cultural literacy. Multicultural literature has the potential to challenge biases about diversities like race and sexual orientation. It can also affirm the lives of marginalized readers. However, these experiences are never guaranteed. Creating them requires that teachers sensitively and with determination prod students to reconsider some of their fundamental beliefs.

Reader response to multicultural literature frequently depends on the context provided by a reader's life and whether dissonance precipitates new understandings. Dissonance, or discomfort with new ideas and experiences, can engage students in rethinking their ideas or it can be a cause of distancing that interferes with learning.

A book we frequently discuss with teachers is a young adult novel by Jacqueline Woodson (1995), *From the Notebooks of Melanin Sun.* A work of realistic fiction, it is narrated by a 14-year-old African American boy named Melanin Sun. Through its main character, the book confronts readers with incidents of racial tension and homophobia. Melanin Sun describes an incident at the beach where he is taunted by a group of White boys. He also shares his hostile reactions when he learns that his mother's new love interest is a White woman.

Reader reactions to the book illustrate the importance of context for establishing meaning. Although race is an active and potent issue for Black readers, most Whites see it as incidental to what is taking place in the book. Black teachers in our classes generally speak of how the book reminds them of their own experiences with discrimination and of a pervasive societal unfairness directed at people like themselves. Whites express sympathy for Melanin, but usually do not identify racism in his experiences. Class discussion of the name Melanin Sun also shows the importance of context. Black readers are generally pleased that Melanin's mother gave him a name that celebrates his dark pigmentation. Whites tend to be confused by the name and unaware of color prejudice within the Black community. Black and White students read the same book, but because of social context they read it very differently.

The dissonance generated by the book, caused by the disparity between the world as viewed by most White readers and the story told by its Black author and narrator, can either become a productive force in the classroom or obstruct multicultural understanding. White readers who are engaged by the novel and class discussion discover that other people experience the world in ways that they do not. They also learn that they are capable of empathizing with a character who is always conscious of color and speaks of alienation from White people. We believe this discovery, by introducing them to new perspectives on reality, expands their sense of who they are, their ability to work with others, and helps them become more responsive teachers.

Dissonance can also obstruct multicultural understanding. The revelation that Melanin's mother was a lesbian confronted Black and White readers with difference in new ways. In our classes, readers often distance themselves from her sexuality and focus their concern on Melanin's turmoil. In this case, the contrast between the response of Black and White readers tends to be the intensity of their feelings. Readers from both groups express sympathy with Melanin, but some Blacks communicate deep anger and disappointment with his mother, feeling betrayed by a strong, caring Black woman whom they had admired because of her eloquence on the subject of skin color. Neither group of readers is comfortable with this development in the novel or anxious to introduce the topic into discussions with adolescents.

In some of our classes, with our encouragement, readers with gay relatives have spoken out in response to the book and comments by their classmates. This has led to the creation of a counterdiscourse in class that establishes the legitimacy of Melanin's mother's life and the importance of opening this topic up for discussion with students in their classrooms.

Responses to *From the Notebooks of Melanin Sun* by both Black and White readers demonstrate the importance of multicultural literature and literacy, and their potential for self-affirmation and for promoting an appreciation of diversity. However, the novel does not always generate the productive dissonance that enables readers to reevaluate their views about racial tension and homophobia. That kind of critical literacy requires that teachers actively engage readers in examining the dissonance they experience and in the creation of new experiences for students.

JOIN THE CONVERSATION—MULTICULTURAL LITERATURE

Questions to Consider:

1. In your opinion, is *From the Notebooks of Melanin Sun* an appropriate book to read with middle school students? Explain.
2. Judi Singer and Sally Smith argue that teachers should create dissonance in order to motivate students to reconsider some of their fundamental beliefs. Do you agree with this idea? Explain.
3. Respond to the statement: "Multiculturalism is a form of both critical and cultural literacy."

SECTION F: HOW CAN CLASSROOM PRACTICE PROMOTE STUDENT LITERACIES?

I have already called literacy specialists the imperialists of the educational world. But they are not the first to claim this title. When I was taking teacher education classes as an undergraduate college student, instead of developing student literacies, teachers were expected to promote critical thinking skills using higher order questions. The core of this approach to teaching was Bloom's taxonomy (explained further at the end of this section), a system that classifies questions based on whether they encourage critical thinking by students. The lowest level of questions ask students to recall information, whereas the highest level requires them to exercise judgment. Bloom's system is useful to teachers because it emphasizes that students should be learning to use information to formulate and support their ideas.

A problem with broadly defined literacy standards is that it is often difficult for new teachers to imagine what they look like in ordinary classroom practice. We can always include reading and writing activities in lesson plans, but by themselves this is not enough for students to achieve the level of literacy that is required in our society.

A crucial part of a teacher's literacy arsenal is his or her ability to develop and ask effective higher order questions that capture the interest of students, stimulate discussions, and challenge students to examine and understand complicated text and ideas. When I design an activity sheet for a lesson, every reading passage, illustration, or chart is followed by three or four questions that scaffold on each other and require increasingly complex answers. The first question asks students to find or describe a piece of information; the second question is more interpretative; and the final question(s) asks students to draw a conclusion, explain a new understanding, or make a judgment based on information they have learned.

For example, an activity sheet with the edited passage on the "Molecular Structure of D.N.A." (from section D) would include the following questions:

1. What are the authors describing in this passage?
2. Why do they believe they offer a better model?
3. What do we learn about the scientific method from this paper?
4. In your opinion, why is their discovery a significant scientific achievement?

A middle school social studies lesson on the American Revolution might start with a picture of Washington crossing the Delaware River downloaded from the Internet with the following more or less generic questions.

1. What scene is depicted in this picture?
2. What information does this picture tell us about the "historical" period?
3. In your opinion, why is this happening?
4. Based on information in this picture and your other knowledge of the period, what proposals would you make to address this problem? Why?

Later in class, as we go over the passage or the picture, I would ask students to discuss their answers to the questions. Whatever their responses, I would follow up with one of three new questions: What evidence do you have for your answer? What do you think of responses by other students? And the most important question of all higher order thinking questions—WHY?

Using questions to promote critical literacy is also a major component of Grant Wiggins's approach to teaching methods, which he calls "Understanding by Design." Wiggins argues that teachers should present students with "essential questions" without simple answers that are reintroduced over and over throughout the curriculum. For social studies, he suggest questions such as: "Is there enough to go around (e.g., food, clothes, water)?" "Is history a story of progress?" "When is law unjust?" "Who owns what and why?" A language arts class could explore questions such as: "Must a story have a moral?" "What qualities make someone a hero (or villain)?" "Do we always mean what we say and say what we mean?" A biology curriculum could be organized to answer the question: "How does an organism's structure enable it to survive in its environment?" or "Is biology destiny?"

JOIN THE CONVERSATION—BLOOM'S TAXONOMY

Benjamin Bloom's classification system organizes questions into six categories based on the "level of thought" required from students. They are ranked here from lower level to higher level thinking.

Knowledge: Students are asked to recall or describe information that they have been provided in an assignment or by the teacher.

Comprehension: Students are asked to interpret or explain information.

Application: Students use information to explain other related events, solve a problem, or speculate about broader causes or issues.

Analysis: Students use information to draw conclusions.

Synthesis: Students use information to arrive at a new understanding.

Evaluation: Students use information and established criteria to make a judgment or support an opinion.

Questions to Consider:

1. Do you think teachers should think of questions in advance and include them in their lesson plans? Explain.
2. Do you agree with Bloom's idea of a hierarchy of questions? Explain.
3. Design three to five high-order analysis, synthesis, or evaluation questions in your subject area.
4. In your opinion, can higher order thinking questions be used to enhance critical literacy? Explain.

SECTION G: HOW CAN TEACHERS LEARN AND TEACH ABOUT TECHNOLOGY IN A UNIVERSE WHERE TECHNOLOGY IS CONTINUALLY CHANGING?

When it comes to technology, I always seem to be three steps behind everyone else. It took me years to figure out how to use a VCR for teaching. I still listen to vinyl records and cassettes (though I recently purchased a sound system with a CD player). By the time I learned how to use a computer as a word processor, other people were into graphic design. Now that I have a modem for e-mail and Web access, my son insists the only way to go is a "high-speed," always accessible, cable connection. I even have a Web site, maintained by one of my former students, that I do not know how to update.

I am not sure that I am so unique. It is not easy for teachers, even those who are willing and interested, to learn or teach about technology in a universe where technology is continually changing. Before my youngest child grew up and moved out, I learned most of what I know about computers by looking over his shoulder. I eventually realized I could adapt that strategy to learn from my students (both in high school and teacher education classes) as they become technology experts and teachers in my classes. In chapter 6, I discuss different cooperative learning approaches. To teach technology in the content area, I recommend meeting regularly with an expert group of students that can help you figure out what needs to be done and is able to master the appropriate skills, and then work within their own cooperative learning teams to ensure that all students in the class develop necessary competencies. I know this sounds a little like cheating, but it is the best way I know to keep up with the students.

Technological literacy is another literacy that has broad implications in all secondary school content areas, and it is useful to examine the standards developed by national educational organizations. The National Council for Accreditation of Teacher Education (NCATE) and the International Society for Technology in Education (ISTE) recommend the following 10 performance indicators for technology literate students before completion of grade 12.

1. Students will identify capabilities and limitations of contemporary and emerging technology resources and assess the potential of these systems and services to address personal, lifelong learning, and workplace needs.

2. Students will make informed choices among technology systems, resources, and services.

3. Students will analyze advantages and disadvantages of widespread use and reliance on technology in the workplace and in society as a whole.

4. Students will demonstrate and advocate for legal and ethical behaviors among peers, family, and community regarding the use of technology and information.

5. Students will use technology tools and resources for managing and communicating personal and professional information (e.g., finances, schedules, addresses, purchases, correspondence).

6. Students will evaluate technology-based options, including distance and distributed education, for lifelong learning.

7. Students will routinely and efficiently use online information resources to meet needs for collaboration, research, publications, communications, and productivity.

8. Students will select and apply technology tools for research, information analysis, problem solving, and decision making in content learning.

9. Students will investigate and apply expert systems, intelligent agents, and simulations in real-world situations.

10. Students will collaborate with peers, experts, and others to contribute to a content-related knowledge base by using technology to compile, synthesize, produce, and disseminate information, models, and other creative works.

I think it is significant that these technological literacy goals are similar to the other literacy goals discussed earlier in this chapter. They emphasize the need to identify the capabilities and limitations of technologies; make informed, ethical choices; and communicate and collaborate with others. The use of a particular form of hardware or software is a secondary consideration because they will quickly become outdated (along with my Apple 2E, the mimeograph machine, and 8-mm film projectors).

I know it can seem silly when someone who probably knows less than you do about a topic offers suggestions on how to teach it, but remember, 20 years from now, you will be the one behind the times and struggling to keep up. These are my suggestions on how to keep on top of the situation.

- Do not be afraid to learn from your students. Every year, you get older and fall farther behind, but they stay young and cutting edge.
- Student expert groups will not only help you and the class develop technological competencies, but will enhance classroom community.
- My mother-in-law went online in her late 70s and is an avid user of the Internet and e-mail. It is never too late to take a class or workshop and develop your own skills.
- Use your computer for lesson preparation as much as you can. Once a lesson is in your database, it is easy to modify. Activity sheets and homework assignment questions can quickly be reorganized into tests. The Web is a great source of lesson ideas with material that can be downloaded and adapted to classroom use. Spreadsheets are also a good way to keep track of student grades, homework, and attendance.
- Develop your own Web site. It helps build classroom community and makes it possible for students and parents to keep track of regular assignments and special projects. A number of teachers link their Web sites with sites they want students to use for research. This helps eliminate problems such as students getting "lost in cyberspace" during endless searches or using inappropriate or inaccurate material.
- Computers and the Internet make it easier for students to "sample" other people's work and "borrow" assignments. There is no foolproof way to prevent this. However, if you focus on the research process, checking student notes, outlines, resource material, and drafts, it is more likely they will do their own work. You do not have to accept polished final reports that are not supported by interim work.

JOIN THE CONVERSATION—MRSTEINGLOBAL

Stu Stein is a high school social studies teacher who "talks" with his students online using instant messages. He set up a separate screen name with his Internet provider (MrSteinGlobal) and told students he would be online Tuesdays and Thursday evenings from 7 to 8 p.m. Any student who has a questions can reach him then. At other times, they can send him an e-mail and he responds as soon as possible. At the beginning of the semester, most students shy away from contacting him, so he uses the time looking for materials for lessons. However, as the semester goes on and students begin to realize they can actually reach him with their questions or just talk with an adult, it gets busy. A lot of time is spent helping students with Internet research, especially sorting out credible from inappropriate sites. He also uses the Internet to post weekly homework assignments and other class announcements. However, Stu finds the best thing about MrSteinGlobal is that it gives him an opportunity to get to know his students in an informal atmosphere and develop a bond with them.

Questions to Consider:

1. Many teachers are concerned about "drawing a line" between themselves and their students. Do you think "MrSteinGlobal" is an appropriate or inappropriate use of technology?
2. Do you have confidence in your own ability to use technology in the classroom and in lesson preparation? Explain.

SECTION H: WHAT IS TECHNOLOGICAL LITERACY?

Technology Is All Around You
By Gary Benenson

As a young college graduate, Gary Benenson worked in maintenance at Camp Hurley with Jerry Harris (chap. 2), where he received some of his initial training in technology trying to understand, maintain, and repair the camp's antique plumbing system. Gary later became a mechanical engineer and a teacher at the City College of New York School of Engineering. He is the project director of "Stuff That Works," a series of curriculum guides designed for use by elementary school teachers. This essay is based on the curriculum guides, which were partly funded by a grant from the National Science Foundation.—Alan Singer

Technology has become a "buzzword" in our society and buzzwords can be hard to rescue from their sudden fame and fortune. We constantly hear phrases such as "getting on board with technology in the classroom," "technology alters the way we communicate," and "the explosion of technology stocks." In a recent speech, Federal Reserve Chair Alan Greenspan identified "technology education" with teaching students how to navigate the Internet. With all of the discussion of technology, it is vital that teachers have a clear sense of both what technology means and how students learn it.

Despite their larger-than-life aura, computers represent only a small piece of the story of technology. Equally valid examples of technology include:

- The table the computer sits on.
- The box and the Styrofoam packing material it came in.
- The tape used to seal the box.
- The symbols that identify its contents and destination.
- The pencil and paper you fall back on when the computer does not work!

The first step in achieving technological literacy is to become aware of the myriad forms of technology that surround us in our everyday lives. Technology includes all of the artifacts, systems, and environments created by humans to solve the problems they perceive.

Because every example of technology is designed to solve a set of problems, there are some basic questions we can ask about each example:

- What problems was it designed to solve?
- How well does it address each of these problems?
- What additional problems does it pose?
- Under what circumstances could it fail?
- How could it be redesigned to make it work better?

Each of these questions involves a form of critical thinking, and none of the questions is easy to answer, even though the technology itself may seem simple.

For example, the tape that seals the computer box is intended to keep the box from opening in transit. It may also be designed to prevent the labels from coming off, or to keep the ink from smearing. However, the tape may make it hard to open the box, and the tape that remains stuck to the cardboard may make the box useless afterward. The tape could come undone if it gets wet, or even if it is too hot or too humid. Maybe the tape should be replaced by string, which would be waterproof and might make the box easier to reuse. Also, string could serve as the base for a handle, which would make the box easier to carry. But there are problems with using string as well. It could get caught on something and create a safety hazard. Technological literacy means the ability to critically evaluate the purposes and effects of a form of technology. It also includes a willingness to make suggestions for how the technology can be changed to make it work better. The first of these activities is called analysis; the second is design or redesign.

Analysis and design are generally not included in discussions about learning technology. When students "learn computers," they nearly always do so as users, rather than as analyzers or designers. There are few adults who really know how computers work, let alone how to design them. Learning to use a computer does not mean learning computer technology any more than learning to drive a car implies an understanding of automotive technology. On the other hand, there are many simple technologies, such as tape and string, that nearly everyone can think about and evaluate, and even test for themselves to see which one works better.

Technological literacy is not only about figuring things out for yourself. As in any other subject, there are a host of big ideas, which are best learned for and through activities, in this case analysis and design. Some of the organizing concepts of technology are inputs, outputs, systems, materials, information, energy, environments, controls, constraints, trade-offs, side effects, and failure. The most important processes in technology include brainstorming, scavenger hunts, classifying, sorting, data collection, data analysis, modeling, identifying needs, setting design goals, establishing design criteria, evaluation, troubleshooting, maintenance, repair, reuse, redesign, and communication.

Technology education is a broad undertaking that can provide a context for all of the other disciplines. To compare competing technologies, one has to set up a "fair test," which is one of the basic processes of science. Collecting data, organizing it, and finding a pattern all require mathematical thinking. Negotiating solutions and presenting them are exercises in written, oral, and graphic communication. The problems students solve can and should be their own problems, such as how to reduce the interruptions in a classroom or improve the traffic flow in the cafeteria. As students analyze and design solutions to these sorts of problems, they engage in democratic decision making, which is a basic goal of social studies education. When viewed this way, technology can support critical thinking throughout the curriculum.

* * *

JOIN THE CONVERSATION—TECHNOLOGICAL LITERACY

Questions to Consider:

1. Gary Benenson defines technology and technological literacy in a very different way from people who identify them with the ability to use a computer. Do you agree or disagree with his position? Why or why not?

2. How do Gary's ideas influence the way you think about promoting technological literacy in your content area?

Using Modern Educational Technology Makes
Your Lessons More Exciting
By Jason Noone

Jason Noone was born in Chechon, Korea, a small town about 4 hours north of Seoul. He was adopted by an American family and came to the United States when he was $2\frac{1}{2}$ years old. He is 5 feet 3 inches tall, which makes him the shortest male in his classroom, and shorter than many of the female students. For most of his students, who are African American, Latino, and Caribbean American, he is the only person of Korean or Asian ancestry that they know. In this essay he discusses his background, his experience as a teacher, and ways that he uses modern technology in his classroom.—Alan Singer

In 1998, I had the opportunity to go back to Korea for the first time since I left as a young child. I visited the ophanage where I came from and met the Christian missionary who took care of me when I was born. At that time, Korea was going through extremely difficult economic woes. I was abandoned in a public place. The missionaries believe I was left with the hope that I would be taken to the orphanage and have a chance for survival and a decent life. My American parents made all of the arrangements to adopt me through the mail. I guess you could say that I was a mail-order baby.

I was raised in a middle-class, overwhelmingly White, suburban community. My parents, who are both of European background, were activists who participated in the civil rights movement of the 1960s. They always tried to give their children a broad vision of the world. I chose to teach at a high school in a minority community because I want to make a difference in the world and I feel I can do this as a teacher. My school has a bad reputation and it is undeserved. I received a warm welcome by students and staff when I student taught here and was pleased to be offered a regular position.

I have had students say to me, "You are picking on me because I am Black." I respond, "Most of the students in this school are Black. I am the minority here. How do you think I feel when you say things like that?" I always challenge stereotypes and have had a lot of success getting students to think about their assumptions about people. In our society, many students learn to hate other groups of people. I understand why some of my students are angry, but if they are going to succeed in our world they will have to change these views. Friends ask how I am able to relate to students who are so different from me. They do not understand that teaching is like being on a stage where you perform. If your performance is good, students are engaged and respond. It does not make a difference who they are or who you are.

As a teacher I have a reputation for overplanning my lessons. I even write down my questions. I especially like to use technology in the classroom. I find PowerPoint is a great interactive tool. I use it to make presentations and I teach students to use it to present their reports. For a recent observation lesson, I used a television and VCR, the overhead projector, PowerPoint, and music all in one period. I was a little surprised that I finished everything, but I have no question that modern educational technology makes your lessons more exciting.

I maintain a Web site with my classes that I update weekly (socialstudiesgenie.50megs. com). I post homework and extra-credit assignments. Students like to use the site to do public opinion surveys. Last year we polled everyone about their views on downloading music from Napster. I also am the Web master for our department Web site, which we use to post messages for staff and parents.

FIG. 7.2 Jason's 10 steps to set up a PowerPoint presentation.

(Using PowerPoint 98 or an updated version)

1. Select a template you are going to use (auto, design, blank).
2. Select a layout. If you want to design your own layout, choose the blank one.
3. Add text or pictures anywhere you want them to show from the clip art/file.
4. Now it is time to make your presentation flashy with animation. Move the mouse to the star icon. If it is not in your tools, then add it. If it is there, click it. You can also find it in **Tools** under **Customize**.
5. Highlight the section you want to animate. Unless you manually change the order of your animation, it will be presented in the order it was created. To change the order, go to **Custom Animation** under the **Slide Show** menu.
6. Go to the **View** menu and select **Slide Sorter** to preview your presentation.
7. **Slide Sorter** also allows you to reorganize your presentation.
8. Go to the **Slide Show** menu and click **View Show**. Right click your mouse to advance animation and slides.
9. Rehearse the timing of your presentation.
10. Make sure you save periodically because you never know when your computer may crash.

Recommendations: PowerPoint lends itself to unit review lessons and is wonderful for student presentations to class.

Any Questions: E-mail Jason Noone at grampasimpson12@aol.com or instant message him at grampasimpson12 (both MSN or AOL). Jason is willing to walk you through design of a PowerPoint presentation or help you build your own Web site.

REFERENCES AND SUGGESTIONS FOR FURTHER READING

Bellamy, E. (1997). *Looking backward.* Mineola, NY: Dover Publications.

Christensen, L. (2000). *Reading, writing and rising up.* Milwaukee, WI: Rethinking Schools.

Freire, P., & Macedo, D. (1987). *Literacy, reading the word and the world.* South Hadley, MA: Bergin & Garvey.

Harris, T. L., & Hodges, R. E. (Eds.). (1995). *The literacy dictionary: The vocabulary of reading and writing.* Newark, DE: International Reading Association.

MacCurtain, M., Murphy, M., Singer, A., Costello, L., Gaglione, R., Miller, S., et al. (2001). Text and context: Field-testing the NYS Great Irish Famine curriculum. *Theory and Research in Social Education, 29*(2), 238–260.

Moses, R. (1994). Remarks on the struggle for citizenship and math/sciences literacy. *Journal of Mathematical Behavior, 13,* 107–111. (http://www.algebra.org/apinfo/welcome2.html)

Moses, R., & Cobb, C., Jr. (2001). *Radical equations: Math literacy and civil rights.* Boston: Beacon.

Tell, C. (1999). Literacy—The pressure is on. *Educational Leadership, 57*(2), 5.

Wiggins, G., & McTighe, J. (1998). *Understanding by design.* Alexandria, VA: Association for Supervision and Curriculum Development.

Woodson, J. (1995). *From the notebooks of Melanin Sun.* New York: Scholastic.

8

ASSESSMENT: HOW SHOULD TEACHERS ASSESS STUDENT LEARNING AND THEIR OWN PERFORMANCE?

Former New York City Mayor Ed Koch had a way of springing up all over the city, continually asking constituents, "How am I doing?" However, in recent years the phrase has been associated with elected officials who seem to reappear shortly before election day to solicit support for their campaigns. Whatever you think of politicians, it is a fair question that needs to be asked by officeholders as well as by schools and teachers. The problems in both cases are, "What criteria should we use to assess performance?" and "How accurate are measuring instruments?" In addressing these questions, I am going to use sports metaphors. If you are someone who hates sports, please bear with me.

Cuba Gooding Jr.'s character in the movie *Jerry Maguire* (1996) offers us a clue in his well-known refrain, "Show me the money!" As a football player seeking a new contract, Gooding evaluates his agent, while the team evaluates Gooding, based on performance standards. How well did Gooding's character perform compared with similar athletes? Is he receiving a commensurate salary? Both the athlete and the agent may seek additional rewards based on effort or potential, but in general, the bottom line in sports today is, "What have you done for me lately?"

Even among elite athletes establishing criteria for performance assessment is difficult. During the 2002 Winter Olympics, a major international controversy erupted when a gold medal in figure skating was awarded to the Russian team. Eventually the medal was shared with Canadian competitors; however, the underlying problem, that evaluation is based on inexact and often arbitrary judgments, remained.

School systems like to pretend that the evaluation of students and teachers is more or less an exact science, like comparing the numerical statistics of quarterbacks rather than the hard-to-measure performance of offensive tackles or ice-skaters. But there are so many intangibles in sports that even a comparison of quarterbacks is difficult. Which should count the most: completion percentage, yardage gained, touchdown passes, team victories, or performance in big games such as the Super Bowl? For example, Hall of Famer Joe Montana did not always have the best numbers, but he seemed to star in the biggest games. The fact is, arguing about who is a better player is a big part of the fun of being a sports fan.

Supposedly objective rules can also be surprisingly arbitrary, so that small changes significantly alter the performance of key participants. During the 2001 baseball season, a redefined "strike zone" (higher and narrower) contributed to a 10% decline in the number of runs scored, home runs, and walks. Power pitchers with rising fastballs benefited the most from the change, whereas many control pitchers, who liked to "nibble" at the corners of the plate, could not consistently get batters out. Among hitters, Barry Bonds of the San Francisco Giants, who no longer had to chase outside pitches, went on a record-setting home-run tear, whereas Chuck Knoblauch of the New York Yankees, who had a tendency to "pop up" high strikes, was mired in a season-long batting slump. The rule changes affected players in different ways and had nothing to do with how hard they worked or their skills or their moral qualities as individuals. People who had honed their games to the old rules, and were unable to adjust, had their careers threatened.

There is a comparable phenomenon of assessments influencing results in gymnastics. Have you ever wondered why the highest scoring competitors among the men are in their middle to late 20s, whereas the best performers among the "women" are teenage girls? It is not because of a law of nature, but because of the way performances are evaluated. In men's gymnastics, the highest scores go to routines that emphasize strength, so older, stronger, and more experienced men score higher. In women's gymnastics, the highest points are awarded to routines that emphasize balance and flexibility, so younger, but not necessarily more talented, women win the events. If women were graded using the same scale and routines as men are, there would be different medal winners.

Arbitrary rules and assessments play a similar role in educational evaluation. For example, in September 2001, the incoming freshman class at the University of California differed demographically in significant ways from the previous year (Holmes, 2001). Part of the change was caused by the university's decision to count scores on the verbal and math knowledge parts of the Scholastic Aptitude Test less, while giving heavier weight to student performance on subject-specific tests, including foreign language examinations. As a result of the new criteria, native speakers of Chinese, Spanish, and Korean earned admission to the university at a higher rate than in the past. A fair change? Maybe. An objective law of nature? No way!

The point I am making is that assessment is nearly always arbitrary and often unreliable. The question for us as teachers then becomes: "Can we design assessments that facilitate the ability of students to demonstrate what they have actually learned?" I believe the answer is a qualified "yes."

An additional problem with assessment has been described by Claude Steele (1999), a psychologist from Stanford University in California. Steele has conducted a number of experiments in an effort to explain the "performance gap" (the difference between expected and actual scores) of African Americans and women on certain types of standardized assessments and sometimes on school performance in general.

Steele (1999) argues that all people are members of some group about which negative stereotypes exist and that they experience "stereotype threat" as a result—"the threat of being viewed through the lens of a negative stereotype, or the fear of doing something that would inadvertently confirm that stereotype" (p. 44). His research shows that as a result of the additional stress caused by stereotypes that claim that African Americans are not as smart as Whites or that women cannot do complex math, even top African American and women students score significantly below expectations on specific tests.

Steele's studies suggest that repeated poor performance on tests and failure in school feeds into student resistance to learning. As they seek to avoid uncomfortable situations that provoke stereotype threats, they refuse to do work, do not study for exams, and may even disrupt classes. The most important and hopeful aspect of Steele's work is that he found that when teachers were able to reduce the stereotype threat felt by students, the "performance gap" virtually disappeared.

This chapter explores the very inexact science of assessing student learning and teacher performance. Sections examine different approaches to the assessment of student work, the way to design fair assessments, the debate over national standards and standardized tests, and an examination of why teachers should continually reassess their own practice. It includes sample rubrics for grading student work, ideas for assessing your own performance as a teacher, and suggestions for creating a professional portfolio.

FIG. 8.1   Key terms for understanding student assessment.

ASSESSMENT: The ways students demonstrate understanding of concepts, mastery of skills, and knowledge of and ability to use information. Assessment devices include, but are not limited to, teacher-designed and standardized tests. Assessments are used to evaluate student performance, teacher effectiveness, and the success of curricula and programs.

STANDARDS: Formal content acquisition and skill development goals for student achievement developed by state education departments, school districts, and national educational organizations. Sometimes they are coupled with instructional strategies for teachers and assessment tools.

STANDARDIZED ASSESSMENT: Standardized assessment devices, especially multiple-choice tests, measure narrow areas of competence. Advocates for this type of assessment argue that results on these tests accurately and objectively measure a student's general level of achievement.

PERFORMANCE ASSESSMENT: Direct evaluation of student competence in different areas using various assessment devices, including standardized tests. Performance assessment attempts to directly measure a student's ability to think critically, write clearly, express ideas orally, and work cooperatively.

AUTHENTIC ASSESSMENT: A form of performance assessment that minimizes the use of tests and encourages the direct assessment of student performance during learning activities and through the evaluation of student work.

PORTFOLIO ASSESSMENT: Students' performance is evaluated based on a collection of their work assembled over an extended period. The portfolio demonstrates growth as well as final achievement.

REFLECTIVE PRACTICE: The idea that teachers, individually and collectively, need to constantly reevaluate their performance in order to assess whether they are achieving their goals.

JOIN THE CONVERSATION—AUTHENTIC ASSESSMENT

Authentic assessment is not an easy task. As a high school teacher, I continually found myself sweating over grades and offering students other opportunities to demonstrate what they learned and what I taught.

Questions to Consider:

1. What are your views about standards, testing, and assessment?

2. What were your experiences as a student? How do these shape your views as a teacher?

SECTION A: HOW SHOULD TEACHERS ASSESS STUDENT LEARNING?

Emphasis on expanding student content knowledge and improving basic academic skills is often coupled with the demand for more rigorous assessment of both students and teachers. The current push for standardized testing across the United States had its origins in the 1983 report, *A Nation at Risk*. The report charged that the country was threatened by a "rising tide of mediocrity" in public schools and unleashed a movement for test-driven curriculum change that, in theory, promotes academic excellence. By 2000, every state but Iowa had established statewide academic standards and 27 states had implemented high-stakes testing programs. For more about these developments and responses by critics, I recommend a book edited by Kathy Swope and Barbara Miner (2000), *Failing Our Kids: Why the Testing Craze Won't Fix Our Schools*.

For people who support standardized assessments, testing serves multiple functions. Tests direct classroom curricula and measure student knowledge, the competence of teachers, and the performance of schools and districts. In general, the "standards movement" relies on fact-based multiple-choice exams as the most cost-efficient objective measures of student achievement.

Educators who are skeptical about this approach to teaching and learning often raise the following questions:

- What do fact-based multiple-choice examinations actually tell us about student understanding?
- Is there a correlation between more rigorous testing and the expansion of content knowledge and critical understanding or a commitment to active citizenship?
- Will pressure on teachers to have their students score higher on standardized tests force them to emphasize drilling basic skills and the memorization of facts at the expense of more interesting and valuable types of classroom instruction?
- Does "prepping" students for tests enhance their learning or simply invalidate the tests as meaningful measurements?

As an education student in college and a beginning teacher, I was taught techniques to design supposedly "fair" tests with "good" questions. At the end of the marking period, we were supposed to average up test scores; add or subtract a few points based on factors such as class participation, attendance, and handing in assignments punctually; and then assign a scientifically precise numerical grade that summarized a student's performance in class. In theory, teachers did not evaluate students; our job was to calculate and record the grade they had earned—a task now made easier by computer programs such as Microsoft Excel.

We were also advised to do the following:

- Encourage competition between students for higher grades. This would ensure that they studied.
- Make all of the choices on multiple-choice tests the same length. Unequal length would tip off students to the right answer.
- Avoid letting "B" be the right answer too often. It is the most popular "wild guess" answer.

- Be careful not to make "All of the above" a choice only when the answer we want is "All of the above."
- Use different types of questions (e.g., fill-ins, matching, multiple choice, short description, and longer essays) so students cannot anticipate the kinds of questions you would ask. If they do, they will not study as hard.
- Throw in a few questions about really obscure points. This rewards students who do all of the homework, encourages the others to work harder, and gives you a spread of grades.

Although some of this advice is useful, I believe that something is seriously wrong with an approach to testing and grading that is only indirectly related to instruction and the assessment of learning. When the purpose of testing is to assign grades, tests and grades become weapons to control classes and make students do the work through extrinsic rewards and punishments. Students who try, but do not do very well, are offered extra help, but ultimately are put in "slower" classes where they can "experience success." Those who failed the tests because they did not seem to care are cajoled with threats, calls, or letters home; low grades; or failure for the course. Students who do well on tests are rewarded with high grades, certificates, and recommendations for better high schools and colleges.

On the other hand, I believe there are also good reasons for testing and evaluating students. Students have a right to know how they are doing compared with other people doing similar work. This makes it possible for them to assess their activities, make decisions about their priorities, and evaluate their goals. In addition, as teachers, there are things we need to know so we can do our jobs effectively. Assessing student learning helps us evaluate our performance. *As a rule of thumb, if students did not learn something, you did not teach it.*

Some important questions that assessment helps us think about include the following:

- Does the curriculum make sense to the students? Does it connect with who they are? Does it take into account their level of academic skills and help to improve them?
- Am I teaching effectively? Is the class as a whole learning? Are the books and materials appropriate? What do I need to change?
- Do individual students understand what they are studying? How can I respond to their specific needs and motivate them to try again or try harder? How do I help students assess their own learning so they can use this knowledge as a way to expand their understanding? What will make it possible for every individual to succeed in class?
- Are students doing the classroom and homework assignments? Are the assignments reasonable and interesting? Which assignments should be kept? Which ones should be modified? Which ones should be dropped?
- Are my assessment tools accurate measures of what I am trying to assess? Am I testing recall, the ability of students to read and write, or higher order skills such as understanding and the ability of students to use ideas?
- Can I assign students composite grades at the end of marking periods and semesters that have meaning to them and will encourage them, rather than just reward or punish them?

In John Dewey's view, assessing (comparing, analyzing, sorting, organizing, exploring, experimenting) is how human beings learn. What teachers need to assess is not the information that students know, but how effectively students are integrating information into their world view. A significant question is whether teachers can effectively measure this type of learning using standard assessment devices: short answer tests, essays, written reports, and classroom presentations.

Grant Wiggins (1998), a major advocate of performance assessment, is critical of most testing, which he argues only measures the least complex levels of human thought. Wiggins challenges educators to assess student performance on the higher order thinking skills identified in Bloom's taxonomy. For example, a student's ability to synthesize information and create a new understanding requires creativity and judgment. This kind of thinking stimulates diverse and unexpected responses that are not easily measured on a multiple-choice exam.

Wiggins argues that the key to employing Deweyan ideas is to view assessment as an ongoing part of a learning process, in which people repeatedly test their knowledge and their skills, and adjust what they do and how they do it based on what they discover. This is very different from creating tests that measure a limited form of knowledge at a particular point. Wiggins suggests that teachers think of their students as workers (e.g., historians, writers, or mathematicians) who are continually enhancing their skills as they create increasingly more complex products. The difficult task for teachers is establishing criteria for evaluating these products during the process of creation and after they are completed.

I believe that certain principles can guide teachers as we work to discover more authentic ways of assessing student understanding. These principles include the following:

- Assessment of student performance should be on the full range of what is being taught in class. That includes content knowledge and academic skills. It also includes the acquisition of social skills; an understanding of key concepts; the ability to gather, organize, present, integrate, and use information; and the ability to explore values and ideas and use new understandings to reconsider the way we understand and appreciate a particular subject and the broader world.

- Assessment should be part of the learning process. It should be continuous so that students have feedback on how they are doing.

- We should use tests to discover what students know, not what they do not know. A reasonable assumption is that when students are excited about what they are learning and do well on tests, they will want to learn more.

- If test scores are going to reflect what students are learning, they need to be designed for specific classes. Prepackaged and standardized tests are based on the assumption that the same things are happening in widely diverse settings.

- Although the criteria for assessment should be clear to students, they should also be flexible. Assessment is relative, not absolute. It involves judgments where people can legitimately disagree.

- Assessment is most effective when it includes individual self-assessment.

- Authentic assessment of student learning requires examining a number of types of activities at a series of points in the learning process and using different criteria and assessment devices to evaluate student performance. We do not measure temperature with a speedometer. How can a matching quiz measure a student's understanding of democratic values?

- The goal of assessment is to encourage and assist learning. Tests and projects should not be used to punish or sort students. Everyone who works hard and does well should be able to receive the highest evaluation.

- If the ability to work hard in an organized and disciplined fashion is one of the things we want students to learn, effort should count in an evaluation of students' work.

- If we want students to learn how to work collectively, take responsibility for group activities, respect the value and contributions of other people, and play leadership roles, performance on group activities should be factored into an evaluation of a student's work.

- Students with limited academic skills should be able to demonstrate their knowledge and understanding of a subject in ways that are appropriate to their skills. Imagine you are a chef being tested on your ability to cook a new dish, but the recipe is written in a language you cannot read. Would this be a fair assessment of your ability or knowledge?

- We are assessing knowledge and understanding of a subject and academic and social skills, not a student's qualities as a human being.

JOIN THE CONVERSATION—STANDARDIZED TESTING

Questions to Consider:

1. Where do you stand on the national debate over standardized assessments? Why?

2. What are your views on the following questions asked earlier in this section?

   * What do fact-based, multiple-choice examinations actually tell us about student understanding?

   * Is there a correlation between more rigorous testing and the expansion of content knowledge and critical understanding or a commitment to active citizenship?

   * Will pressure on teachers to have their students score higher on standardized tests force them to emphasize drilling basic skills and the memorization of facts at the expense of more interesting and valuable types of classroom instruction?

   * Does "prepping" students for tests enhance their learning or simply invalidate the tests as meaningful measurements?

SECTION B: HOW CAN TEACHERS DESIGN FAIR ASSESSMENTS?

As a high school teacher, I used multiple forms of assessment in my classes, including standard short-answer and essay tests geared to the academic level of my students. Most students found my tests challenging, but not tricky. There is no simple rule for the frequency of tests, the number of questions on a test, the type of questions, the vocabulary level used in questions, the time allocated for a test, or the weight assigned to different kinds of questions. A lot of test design is based on a teacher's judgments about her or his class and the points and skills they are stressing in a particular unit. I tended to give short tests on a more frequent basis to classes in which students had greater academic difficulty. I found that this gave more structure to their studying and allowed me to target specific academic skills. Otherwise, I gave full-period exams at the end of a unit as part of the process of pulling together what we had been learning.

In subjects such as music, art, language arts, and second-language acquisition, tests primarily include performance-based assessments. In social studies, math, and science, teachers need to be more imaginative when designing tests so that they focus on problem-solving skills, laboratory experiments, or primary source document analysis.

The following are my suggestions for the design of effective and fair tests:

- Test what you taught. That was what you presented to students as the more important things to learn. When I was a student we hated teachers who filled tests with obscure points from the textbook. This practice only increases competition, undermines community, feeds student resistance, and encourages marginal students to give up.

- Test what students know. When students fail miserably, teachers have no way to evaluate what they learned and we taught. I take questions and activities directly from class activity sheets, homework assignment questions, and class notes.

- I am looking for mastery, not perfection. If the vocabulary and skill level required by every question is designed to be very difficult, a student who basically understands the work will end up performing poorly on the test. If questions have different levels of difficulty, it makes it easier for teachers to learn what students can actually do.

- Students do better when presented with a variety of learning activities. It makes sense to use a variety of question formats.

- Evaluating essay answers requires a grading strategy. The three major approaches are "holistic" grading of entire essays, assigning a specific number of points for each section of an essay, or using assessment rubrics that give students credit for including different types of evidence and arguments and for the effectiveness of their writing. I have used all three strategies, and I do not think there is one correct approach. However, whatever approach you take, a teacher needs to be as consistent as possible so students know what to expect when they write essays.

- Discuss test design and grading criteria with students in advance. Involving students in assessment can, but does not necessarily, mean they participate in deciding their own grades. It definitely means that students are involved in developing the parameters for class projects and deciding the criteria for assessing their performance in these activities. The benefits of this student involvement include: a deeper understanding of research methods, insight into the design and implementation of projects, a greater stake in the satisfactory completion of assignments, and a sense of empowerment because assessment decisions are based on rules that the classroom community has helped to shape.

- Students do not do their best when anxious. In order to relax students, Steve Marlow of the New Teachers Network plays soft music while students take exams. Another alternative is to allow students who perform poorly an opportunity to take a retest.

- Time pressure should not be a major factor. Everybody should be able to finish the test. If students need more time, let them come back later in the day, during lunch or a free period. This takes some of the pressure off students who score poorly because they get anxious or because of academic difficulties.

- Even when tests are "fair" assessment devices, teachers have to decide how much to weigh different parts of a test and how to evaluate student answers on essay questions. Try assigning point values to questions after you see how students perform on a test. If many students do poorly on one part, assume the problem was either your teaching or the test itself, and count those questions less. By being flexible, you get a more accurate measure of what students understand, avoid demoralizing students with low test scores, and eliminate the practice of having to curve grades.

- Grades should not be rationed. Our goal is for everyone to do well. There is no reason that every student cannot receive an "A".

JOIN THE CONVERSATION—FAIR ASSESSMENT

Question to Consider:

I think the preceding ideas provide for effective and fair assessment. Do you agree? Explain.

SECTION C: SAMPLE ASSESSMENT RUBRICS

FIG. 8.2 Rubric for assessing an essay by Christina Agosti-Dircks.

15 points total	Weak	Satisfactory	Strong
Introduction 3 pts.	0–1: Confused and incomplete.	2: A clear but brief statement.	3: A clear and well-developed statement.
Use of evidence to support argument 6 pts.	1–2: Insufficient or inaccurate evidence.	3–4: Sufficient evidence, but not well developed. (or) Well developed, but in need of additional evidence.	5–6: Sufficient information that strongly supports the position taken in the introductory statement.
Conclusion 3 pts.	0–1: Insufficient, unclear. Not based on the evidence.	2: Some problems with either the clarity or logic of the argument.	3: A clear concluding statement that follows from the introduction and the evidence.
Quality of writing 3 pts.	0–1: Serious problems with clarity, spelling, grammar, and paragraph structure.	2: Some problems with clarity, spelling, grammar, and paragraph structure.	3: A well-written essay with minimal problems.

FIG. 8.3 Rubric for assessing a written analysis or critique paper.

	Weak (0–1)	Satisfactory (2–3)	Strong (4–5)
1. Clear, interesting, and informative introduction, summary, and conclusion.			
2. Each paragraph has a main idea.			
3. Identifies and explains social forces.			
4. Explains different perspectives.			
5. Author's views are clearly identified.			
6. Appropriate information.			
7. Effective use of details and examples.			
8. Connections with current issues.			
9. Satisfies writing requirements.			
10. Satisfies project requirements.			

Total Points _____ × 2 = Assignment Grade _____

FIG. 8.4 Rubric for assessing oral presentations/demonstrations by Lynda Costello-Herrara.

Content (55%)	Poor 0–3 pts.	Average 4–6 pts.	Good 7–9 pts.	Excellent 10–11 pts.
1. Worthwhile and relevant information.				
2. Information is sufficient.				
3. Ideas clearly explained.				
4. Ideas logically explained.				
5. Effective organization.				
Delivery (35%)	0–1 pts.	2–3 pts.	4 pts.	5 pts.
1. Contact with audience.				
2. Effective use of notes.				
3. Confidence.				
4. Articulation.				
5. Projection.				
6. Enthusiasm.				
7. Avoids distractions.				
Overall (10%)	0–4 pts.	5–6 pts.	7–8 pts.	9–10 pts.
1. Coordination with group.				

Comments: _____

_____ Grade (100%): _____

FIG. 8.5 Rubric for assessing student projects by Rachel Gaglione.

	Needs Improvement	Satisfactory	Excellent
1. The project shows evidence of understanding key content and concepts.			
2. All work is written to standard, which includes engaging the reader, an organizing structure, appropriate facts, voice, a conclusion, as well as excluding extraneous information and proper use of conventions.			
3. Project shows care, effort, thoughtfulness, and evidence of revision.			
4. Presentation shows ability to communicate effectively.			

General Comments: _____

_____ Grade _____

SECTION D: IDEAS FOR DESIGNING FAIR TESTS THAT AUTHENTICALLY ASSESS STUDENT UNDERSTANDING

The kind of questions teachers ask on tests depend on what they are trying to assess. Standard question formats include short answer or fill in, matching, true–false, multiple choice, short or extended essays, and document-based short-answer or essay questions.

Short-answer or fill-in, matching, and true–false questions generally test whether students *recall* specific factual information. Multiple-choice questions can be used to test *factual recall* or *conceptial understanding*. Short or extended essays and problem-solving and document-based short answer or essay questions are usually used to assess *conceptual understanding* and *academic skills*.

A. Sample Social Studies Questioning Alternatives (11th-Grade U.S. History)

The Battle of Saratoga (1777) is considered a major turning point in the American Revolution because a victory by American forces persuaded France and Spain to enter the war as its allies. Alternatives A–D are *fact-based* questions requiring *recall* of a specific piece of information. Alternative A offers students the least information to start with so it is the most difficult to answer.

A. (Short answer/fill in) Identify the Battle of Saratoga (1777).

B. (Matching) Battle of Saratoga (1777) *and* major turning point in the American Revolution

C. (True–false) The Battle of Saratoga (1777) was a major turning point in the American Revolution.

D. (Multiple choice) Which battle was a major turning point in the American Revolution?
   a. Quebec (1759) b. Boston Massacre (1770) c. Saratoga (1777) d. Yorktown (1781)
   e. Gettysburg (1863)

Alternatives E and F are *concept-based* questions requiring an understanding of main ideas about the American Revolution. The questions contain the information and students are asked to explain the significance of the event. Alternative E asks students to select from possible explanations. Alternative F is a more difficult question because it requires that students provide the explanation.

E. (Multiple choice) Why was the Battle of Saratoga (1777) a major turning point in the American Revolution?
   a. A victory by General Washington persuaded the Continental Congress to continue the war.
   b. Victorious American forces ended slavery in the northern states.
   c. A victory by American forces persuaded France and Spain to enter the war as its allies.
   d. British victory at Saratoga ended all hope that Canada would join the colonial uprising.

F. (Short essay) Write a paragraph explaining why the Battle of Saratoga (1777) is considered a major turning point in the American Revolution.

B. Sample Science Questioning Alternatives
(9th-Grade Geology or 10th-Grade Biology)

The Burgess Shale are metamorphized sedimentary rocks in the Canadian Rockies that contain extremely rare 500-million-year-old soft-body fossils of aquatic animal life from the Cambrian era. They are of major evolutionary significance because of their age, because they help illustrate the impact of geological change on evolution, and because some of the fossilized animals are from phyla with no surviving species. Alternatives A–D are *fact-based* questions requiring *recall* of a specific piece of information. Alternative A offers students the least information to start with so it is the most difficult to answer.

  A. (Short answer/fill in) Identify the Burgess Shale.
  B. (Matching) Burgess Shale *and* metamorphized sedimentary rocks in the Canadian Rockies that contain extremely rare 500-million-year-old soft-body fossils from the Cambrian era.
  C. (True–false) The Burgess Shale *are* metamorphized sedimentary deposits in the Canadian Rockies that contain extremely rare 500-million-year-old soft-body fossils from the Cambrian era.
  D. (Multiple choice) How old are the fossils discovered in the Burgess Shale?
     a. Cambrian (500 million years ago) b. Carboniferous (350 million years ago)
     c. Jurassic (200 million years ago) d. Tertiary (50 million years ago) e. Unknown

Alternatives E and F are *concept-based* questions requiring an understanding of main ideas about the importance of the Burgess Shale, evolution, and geology. The questions contain the information and students are asked to explain the significance of the event. Alternative E asks students to select from possible explanations (in this case the best answer is "All of the above"). Alternative F is a more difficult question because it requires that students provide the explanation.

  E. (Multiple choice) Why are fossils contained in the Burgess Shale considered of major evolutionary significance?
     a. Some of the fossilized animals are from phyla with no surviving species.
     b. They are from the Cambrian era, which makes them amongst the oldest fossils on earth.
     c. They contain rare impressions of soft-body parts.
     d. They are imprints of aquatic animal life found at high altitudes in the Canadian Rockies.
     e. All of the above.

  F. (Short essay) Write a paragraph explaining why Cambrian era fossils contained in the Burgess Shale are considered of major evolutionary significance.

C. Sample Middle-Level Math Problem Solving

This format provides students with a context for understanding and the information they need to solve the problem. They are assessed on their ability to find a solution, present the information, and explain their solution.

You are on a trip to Canada during summer vacation. In the morning you turn on the news to hear projections for the the day's weather. When the weather forecaster announces that the temperature is 28 degrees, you quickly realize that she is reporting the temperature using the Celsius scale. You remember from school that on the Celsius scale water freezers at 0 degrees and boils at 100 degrees. On the Fahrenheit scale water freezes at 32 degrees and boils at 212 degrees.

1. Write a paragraph explaining your strategy for translating Celsius temperatures into Fahrenheit temperatures.
2. Present a mathematical formula for translating Celsius temperatures into Fahrenheit temperatures.
3. Create a chart showing the Fahrenheit equivalents for the temperatures 20–30 degrees Celsius.

D. Sample Middle-Level General Science Problem Solving

This activity assesses student understanding of the process of scientific exploration. It encourages students to observe closely and systematically, establish criteria, evaluate similarities and differences, and draw conclusions based on recorded observations.

- Provide an individual or team of students with a bag containing 12 assorted items (e.g., metal nails, bones, crayons, coins, plastic spoon, rock, screwdriver, ceramic cup, dried beans, rubber band, CD, stick).
- Students must write descriptions of each item, create categories (e.g., shape, color, function, whether it is part of something else, whether it was made by people, etc.) that allow them to sort the items, divide the items into the different categories, and then write explanations for their choice of categories and their assignment of the items.

E. Sample Middle-Level Written Response Question for English or Social Studies

This format provides students with information orally and in writing. It requires them to use the information to take and support a position and present it in written form. Teachers can change or modify the reading passage depending on their experience with the academic performance of students in a class, topics being discussed in a unit, or student interest. Possible speeches include Sojourner Truth, "Ain't I a Woman"; Abraham Lincoln, "Gettysburg Address"; Margaret Chase Smith, "Republican Declaration of Conscience"; John F. Kennedy, "First Inaugural Address"; Martin Luther King Jr., "I Have a Dream"; Malcolm X, "Message to the Grass Roots"; Ronald Reagan, "The Evil Empire." As an alternative, students can write letters in response to an article in the local newspaper on a controversial issue. Students can share their letters and selected pieces can be submitted to the editors for publication.

Directions to students: You are on a committee trying to decide which speech from U.S. history will be reprinted in the eighth-grade yearbook. I will read a speech aloud to the class and then you will have an opportunity to read it to yourselves. After I read it aloud a second time, you must write a letter to the eighth-grade advisor explaining why you believe this speech should or should not be selected. In your answer, explain the criteria you are using to select a speech. Provide specific examples from the speech that show how it either meets or fails to meet your criteria. Your letter should be between three and five paragraphs long.

F. Sample Document-Based Questions

I define documents very broadly. They can be pictures, cartoons, songs, poems, charts, graphs, maps, and written material.

- Provide students with a historical picture or photograph and ask them to either answer questions or write a description of the visual image in prose, poetry, or song.
- Provide students with a speech, newspaper article, song, poem, or a passage from a novel and have them draw a picture or poster or create a diorama illustrating or explaining the document.
- Provide students with a chart or table of information and ask them either to answer questions or to create a bar or circle graph using the data.
- Provide students with a bar or circle graph and ask them either to answer questions or to create a chart or table using information from the graph.
- Have students write a paragraph or an essay comparing or integrating information from a series of documents.

FIG. 8.6.

THE EJECTMENT.

Source: Reprinted with permission from the New York State Great Irish Famine Curriculum (2001) and the National Library of Ireland.

From Picture to Paragraph

During the Great Irish Famine (1845–1851), newspapers had artists draw pictures to accompany news stories. The following drawing shows a family being evicted from their home during the famine. Write a paragraph describing people and events in the drawing.

From Paragraph to Picture

In the passage that follows, Olaudah Equiano (also known as Gustavus Vassa), an enslaved African, describes the "middle passage" from Africa to the Americas. Read this excerpt from his autobiography and draw a picture (or create a diorama) to illustrate the text (Gates, 1987).

The Life of Olaudah Equiano

I was soon put down under the decks, and there I received such a salutation (greeting) in my nostrils as I had never experienced in my life: so that, with the loathsomeness of the stench, and crying together, I became so sick and low that I was not able to eat, nor had I the least desire to taste any thing. I now wished for the last friend, death, to relieve me; but soon, to my grief,

Two of the white men offered me eatables; and, on my refusing to eat, one of them held me fast by the hands, and tied my feet, while the other flogged me severely. I would have jumped over the side, but I could not; and, besides, the crew used to watch us very closely who were not chained down to the decks, lest we should leap into the water: and I have seen some of these poor African prisoners most severely cut for attempting to do so, and hourly whipped for not eating.

The closeness of the place, and the heat of the climate, added to the number in the ship, which was so crowded that each had scarcely room to turn himself, almost suffocated us. The air soon became unfit for respiration, from a variety of loathsome smells, and brought on a sickness among the slaves, of which many died.

I was soon reduced so low here that it was thought necessary to keep me almost always on deck; and from my extreme youth I was not put in fetters (chains). In this situation I expected every hour to share the fate of my companions, some of whom were almost daily brought upon deck at the point of death, which I began to hope would soon put an end to my miseries.

One day, when we had a smooth sea and moderate wind, two of my wearied countrymen who were chained together, preferring death to such a life of misery, somehow made through the nettings and jumped into the sea; and I believe many more would very soon have done the same if they had not been prevented by the ship's crew, who were instantly alarmed. In this manner we continued to undergo more hardships than I can now relate, hardships which are inseparable from this accursed trade. Many a time we were near suffocation from the want of fresh air, which we were often without for whole days together.

From Chart to Graph

Graphs provide dramatic visual images and help us compare information from different categories. Use the information from the chart, "Animal Species Threatened With Extinction in the United States, 1991" to create a vertical bar graph.

Animal Species Threatened With Extinction in the United States, 1991

Animal	Threatened	Endangered	Total
Mammals	8	55	63
Birds	12	73	85
Reptiles	18	16	34
Amphibians	5	6	11
Fish	34	54	88
Shell Fish	10	55	65
Insects and Spiders	9	16	25

From Graph to Chart

Whereas graphs provide dramatic visual images, charts make it easier to use numbers. Use the information from the graph, "Some Animals That Run Faster Than Human Beings," to create a chart and calculate the average speed in miles per hour for these animals.

Some Animals That Run Faster Than Human Beings

(numbers are in miles per hour)

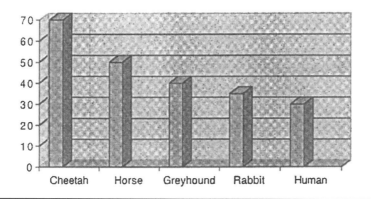

JOIN THE CONVERSATION—NEW YORK STATE SKILLS AND CONTENT ASSESSMENT EXAMINATIONS

The Board of Regents of the New York State Department of Education requires that middle and high school students take skills and content assessment tests in different subject areas designed to measure whether they are achieving the state's academic standards. In order to earn a diploma, students must pass examinations in algebra, geometry, earth science, biology, english, foreign language, global history and geography, and U.S. history and government. The test questions are written by teams of teachers. Sample middle and high school level tests are available for examination on their Web site at: www.nysd.gov/ciai/assess.html.

Questions to Consider:

Select and evaluate a national, state, or district standardized test in your content area.

1. What types of questions are being asked?
2. In your opinion, are the content and level of difficulty appropriate to the grade level of students being assessed?
3. If you were on a committee of teachers invited to submit questions for the test, what kind of questions would you add? Why?

SECTION E: WHAT DOES A STUDENT PORTFOLIO LOOK LIKE?

Student portfolios have been offered as a way to more effectively evaluate the full range of a student's mastery of a subject or a skill. A portfolio can include different types of writing, projects, reports, presentations, and even tests, but it is not simply a collection of student work. For it to be a useful document, it should be integrated into the instructional and assessment fabric of a school's program and provide students with opportunities to reflect on their growth and learning and explain why they selected a particular piece for inclusion in their portfolio. Effective portfolio programs also need to provide students and teachers with specific guidelines for creating, assembling, and evaluating student work.

A multitude of questions have to be addressed when a teacher or school establishes a portfolio program:

- Who defines what goes into a portfolio—individual students and teachers, the academic department, school or district administrators, or a state's regulatory body?
- Can portfolios accurately measure the full range of skills, attitudes, content knowledge, and conceptual understanding developed during a course or multiyear program?
- Will students be involved in defining portfolio topics and projects, deciding on the products that will be evaluated, and the evaluation process itself?
- Are portfolios comprehensive documents showing the full span of a student's work, or do they contain a selection of typical, or perhaps exemplary, efforts?
- How much weight will be given to effort, the process of creation, and the final product in assessing student work?
- Does individual growth count or only a student's final achievement?
- How will growth, the process of creation, and effort be measured?
- Can portfolios include group as well as individual work? If they can, how will a student's participation in a group project be evaluated?
- What standards should be used to evaluate the quality of work at different points in a student's secondary school career?
- Can evaluation be objective or even systematic?
- How do programs avoid the mechanical application of portfolio design and assessment?
- Will schools and districts sacrifice student experimentation and creativity as they try to ensure that minimum guidelines are met?
- Can portfolio assignments and even entire portfolios receive meaningful number or letter grades?

The Center on Learning, Assessment, and School Structure (Wiggins, 1996–1997; Wiggins & McTighe, 1998) addresses some of these questions in proposals for integrating portfolio creation and assessment into classrooms. It recommends involving students in clearly defined and guided multistep projects that are evaluated at different points in the creative process. It also recommends detailed assessment rubrics that examine both content and presentation.

The Central Park East Secondary School (CPESS) in New York City, which is part of the Coalition for Essential Schools, offers an even more radical departure from traditional assessment. CPESS requires that seniors create and defend 14 portfolios to graduate (Meier & Schwartz, 1995). Each student selects seven major areas and seven minor areas for portfolio development. Four of the major areas are required of every student: science/technology, mathematics, history and social studies, and literature.

At CPESS, student portfolios reflect cumulative knowledge and skills acquired by students while at the school. They demonstrate students' command of information about the subject, their ability to explain their own and other people's points of view, their ability to draw connections between different topics, their ability to think creatively about the subject, and their ability to explain the broader relevance of their work. Students work with staff advisors to prepare their final portfolios and a presentation to the graduation committee for review and evaluation. The committee assesses a student's portfolio using an established scoring grid that weighs both the substance and style of the work. When portfolios need to be modified or expanded, students are given the opportunity to complete the necessary work and resubmit the portfolio for approval.

The majority of the material included by students in their portfolios is originally done as coursework. The inclusion of collaborative work is encouraged. Interdisciplinary projects can be submitted in more than one portfolio area. Because each student works at a different pace and in a different way, and because students bring a diversity of academic, social, and cultural experiences with them to their work, CPESS has no single prescribed formula for completing the portfolio-assessment process.

JOIN THE CONVERSATION—CHEATING AND PLAGIARISM

In a survey of 21,000 students by Josephson Institute of Ethics, 70% of high school and 54% of middle school students admitted cheating on an exam (Altschuler, 2001). Also, 97% of high school students let someone copy their work. The Internet and word processors have also made it easier for students to acquire and camouflage other people's work. Teachers have one of two options. The first is to crack down on students by monitoring their work and punishing malefactors more severely. The second is to integrate instruction and assessment so students are continually producing and updating work and the end product is the result of an ongoing process.

Questions to Consider:

1. Do you believe there has been an expansion of student cheating in school in recent years? Explain your views.

2. The Judeo-Christian Bible recommends that someone who is "without sin" should throw the first stone at a person accused of an infraction such as cheating. When you were in school, did you cheat on tests and reports? Why? What would have made you stop?

3. In your opinion, which of the strategies described previously would be more effective at reducing cheating by students? Explain.

SECTION F: HOW SHOULD TEACHERS ASSESS THEIR OWN PRACTICE?

One of the main reasons for teachers to assess student learning is to understand our own performance. Examining student work makes it possible to evaluate the effectiveness of teaching practices and curricula and to decide whether individual lessons and activities connect to and scaffold on prior student understanding and experience. The assessment of students helps teachers figure out how to better prepare, to more successfully present ideas in class, and to achieve goals. It makes possible what Dewey and other educators have called *reflective practice.*

Dewey (1933) believed that human beings have "an innate disposition to draw inferences, an inherent desire to experiment and test. The mind ... entertains suggestions, tests them by observation of objects and events, reaches conclusions, tries them in action, finds them confirmed or in need of correction or rejection" (p. 9). In my experience, what Dewey called an *innate disposition* is better understood as a *potential.* Human beings have the capacity to reevaluate, draw connections, and learn, but that does not mean we always engage in reflective practice.

Reflective practice, the idea that teachers, individually and collectively, need to constantly reevaluate their performance in order to assess whether they are achieving their goals, can be approached in a number of ways. It can be informal or take place in regularly scheduled support meetings. David Morris (whom you met in chap. 3) and I used to discuss our teaching on a daily basis over lunch. For many years, Rhonda Eisenberg (whom you met in chap. 2) and I met informally with other young teachers once a week at a local community center. The New Teachers Network enables teachers to share ideas and discuss issues at bimonthly meetings and via the Internet. Rachel Gaglione (whom you met in chap. 6) has lessons videotaped so she can observe, evaluate, and change her performance as a teacher.

Classroom observation forms can be especially useful for focusing attention on what is actually taking place in the classroom. Section G in this chapter includes forms for observing individual students, classroom interaction, and teacher decision making.

Michael Pezone and Lynda Costello-Herrara (chap. 1), Nichole Williams (chap. 5), and Adeola Tella (chap. 9) participated in field-testing the New York State Great Irish Famine curriculum in their classes (see chap. 7) as part of an action research project. The value of including action research in our teaching is that it encourages us to more systematically evaluate our ideas, knowledge of curriculum, and teaching methods. Using action research in class, teacher-researchers can identify particular issues or questions; develop strategies for addressing them; and, through recurring cycles of teaching, observation, conversation, and reflection, test and revise our teaching strategies.

Myles Horton (Horton & Freire, 1990) suggested an additional dimension for action research. He called on teacher-researchers to "Experiment *with* people not *on* people. ... They're in on the experiment. They're in on the process" (p. 148). This is a valuable idea for a number of reasons. Involving students in action research projects adds to their sense of ownership over what goes on in classes, and it helps them understand what it means to be a historian or scientist. Additionally, when students are part of the research team, assessment of student learning becomes less a battle of wills and more a part of the learning process.

At this point, I want to return to the *Army Air Corps Technical Schools Teachers' Manual* for one last visit. In an effort to encourage reflective practice and self-evaluation, the manual offers new teachers a 34 point checklist to consider as they assess their performance. I think it is a very useful list.

FIG. 8.7 Evaluating your performance as a teacher.

(With help from the World War II Army Air Corps Technical Schools Teachers' Manual)

1. Am I really interested in teaching this class, or is it just another chore for me?
2. Am I punctual in getting to class and do I start and close my class on schedule time?
3. Do I systematically check ventilation, light, heat, seating, and cleanliness of my classroom?
4. Do I make an effort to study the men and women in my classes as individuals so that knowing their peculiar weaknesses, difficulties, and needs, I can help them better?
5. Am I reasonably friendly and cordial with my students, or am I impersonal and distant?
6. Am I at ease before my students? Have I any annoying or distracting mannerisms?
7. Am I resourceful and adaptable? Do I feel the pulse of the class, know when to tell a good story, crack a joke, or let them rest for a minute or two?
8. Am I easily irritated? Am I ever sarcastic?
9. Is my voice clear, pleasing, and well modulated?
10. Am I guilty of patronization?
11. What do my students think of my class? Have I ever discovered their real opinions? Have I ever asked them at the completion of my course to let me have their unsigned, honest comments, criticisms, and suggestions?
12. Do I encourage students by finding something to praise in the work of every earnest and industrious worker?
13. Am I patient with the slower students, and do I provide enough suitable work for the quick learners to challenge their ability?
14. Do I merely hear recitations, or do I really teach my subject so that its real value in the lives of these learners and in the work of the world is made clear?
15. Do I prepare my lessons carefully before coming to class, making sure of a definite aim for each lesson, the steps to be taken, the materials to be used, the points to be made, the method to be used, and the means of measuring the results?
16. Before teaching a new lesson or taking up a new job, do I prepare my class for it by reviewing previous lessons and experiences and by explaining the new work clearly?
17. Do I make sufficient use of illustrations, concrete examples, maps, blackboard diagrams, and charts to make instruction clear?
18. Do I use models, pictures, cut-away parts, slides, and movies to demonstrate and illustrate the points I wish to make?
19. Do I make every effort to interest and to arouse these learners, to guide them in conference and discussion, and to influence them helpfully?
20. In my teaching, do I use language that is simple and clear to all? Do I talk too much?
21. Does my teaching develop sound thinking procedures?
22. Do I set definite standards for my students to attain, and do I insist that each student meets them?
23. Do I check on each job done in my shop or class, to see that it meets the standards for neatness, accuracy, and excellence?
24. Am I sure that each student understands fully and exactly the particular job she or he is to do?

FIG. 8.7 *(Continued)*

25. Am I sure that a student really understands what she or he says?

26. Do I help a student to correct his or her mistakes and misunderstandings or do I merely reveal them?

27. Have I learned to question effectively? Do my questions reach and stimulate all in the class? Are they clear, simple in phrasing, and always addressed to the entire class? Do I call on the slower and the normal students, or do I usually direct my questions to the bright students?

28. Do I insist on proper answers addressed to the class? Do I permit the class to answer in concert?

29. Do I check, through questioning, to see whether students really understand what I say? Do they really understand how to perform the required operations in any job?

30. Do I make definite and regular assignments and do I hold my classes strictly accountable for the preparation of such work?

31. Do I always make sure that my students are ready and prepared for the new assignment?

32. Am I in full control of my group at all times? Do I know what each student is doing? Do I see and hear all that goes on?

33. Do I stand while teaching? Do I move about the classroom occasionally?

34. Do I measure the success of my teaching by what my students know and do as the result of having worked with them—not by my prior record?

JOIN THE CONVERSATION—EVALUATING YOUR PERFORMANCE

Questions to Consider:

1. I have argued that teachers need to empathize with students and have a sense of "mission" to be successful. Would you add these qualities to this list? Why?

2. Which of these questions do you consider most important for evaluating the performance of a teacher? Select five and explain your choices.

3. Which of these areas are your greatest concerns as you prepare to become a teacher? Select three and explain your choices.

4. Which of these areas or questions would you drop as of limited importance for evaluating the performance of teachers? Explain your choices.

SECTION G: CLASSROOM OBSERVATION FORMS

The observation forms that follow are designed help preservice, student, and beginner teachers focus on what is taking place in a classroom and assess a teacher's performance based on the involvement of students in a lesson. Ask other teachers if you can use the form while observing their lessons and videotape and assess your own performance.

FIG. 8.8 Observing students. Observe an individual student for a class or day and complete the form at the end of session.

Student's Name _____ Class _____ Date/Period _____

KEY: A—Always   B—Usually   C—Sometimes   D—Rarely   E—Never

Student:

___ 1. Listens carefully during class time.

___ 2. Asks questions about what is not understood.

___ 3. Volunteers to answer questions posed to class.

___ 4. Follows directions.

___ 5. Respects classroom procedures.

___ 6. Respects teacher.

___ 7. Respects classmates.

___ 8. Is a leader in group activities.

___ 9. Is a good team member in group activities.

___ 10. Completes classroom assignments timely, accurately, and clearly.

___ 11. Completes homework assignments timely, accurately, and clearly.

___ 12. Participates in voluntary projects.

___ 13. Attends class regularly.

___ 14. Arrives in class punctually.

___ 14. Performs well on formal classroom assessments.

___ 15. Performs well on assigned projects.

FIG. 8.9 Teaching time. During each time segment, place a mark in the appropriate box every time a teacher engages in the activity. At the end of the class period tally the marks in each column.

Time	Explaining	Questioning	Demon-strating	Recording	Managing	Interacting (Groups)	Coaching Individuals	Other
0–5 min								
5–10 min								
10–15 min								
15–20 min								
20–25 min								
25–30 min								
30–35 min								
35–40 min								
40–45 min								
Total								

FIG. 8.10   Quantitative classroom mapping. Complete seating chart. Mark the box each time a student actively participates in the lesson.

Can you identify patterns in classroom participation? Explain.

FIG. 8.11   Qualitative classroom mapping. Complete seating chart. Place an appropriate code marking in the box each time a student participates in the lesson.

Codes:

AP—Answers or asks procedural question.   AC—Answers content question.
AO—Answers conceptual or opinion question. BC—Asks content question.
BO—Asks conceptual or opinion question.   DS—Dialogues with other students.
RA—Reads aloud.   P—Participates in full class activity.
                                             O—Other active participation.

Can you identify patterns in classroom participation? Explain.

REFERENCES AND SUGGESTIONS FOR FURTHER READING

Altschuler, G. (2001, January 7). College prep: Battling the cheats. *The New York Times Education Life,* pp. 4A, 15.

Dewey, J. (1933). *How we think: A restatement of the relation of reflective thinking to the educative process.* (Boston: Heath).

Gates, H. (1987). *The classic slave narratives.* (New York: New American Library).

Holmes, S. (2001, July 1). Leveling the playing field, but for whom? *The New York Times,* p. 6.

Horton, M., & Freire, P. (1990). *We make the road by walking.* (Philadelphia: Temple University Press).

Meier, D., & Schwartz, P. (1995). Central Park East Secondary School: The hard part is making it happen. In M. Apple & J. Beane (Eds.), *Democratic schools* (pp. 26–40). Alexandria, VA: Association for Supervision and Curriculum Development.

National Commission on Excellence in Education. (1983). *A nation at risk.* Washington, DC: U.S. Government Printing Office.

Ross, E. W. (Ed.). (1994). *Reflective practice in social studies.* Washington, DC: National Council for the Social Studies.

Steele, C. (1999, August). Thin ice: "Stereotype threat" and Black college students. *The Atlantic Monthly, 284*(2), 44–54.

Swope, K., & Miner, B. (Ed.). (2000). *Failing our kids: Why the testing craze won't fix our schools.* Milwaukee, WI: Rethinking Schools.

Wiggins, G. (1996–1997). Practicing what we preach in designing authentic assessment. *Educational Leadership, 54*(4), 18–25.

Wiggins, G. (1998). *Educative assessment: Designing assessments to inform and improve performance.* San Francisco: Jossey-Bass.

Wiggins, G., & McTighe, J. (1998). *Understanding by design.* Alexandria, VA: Association for Supervision and Curriculum Development.

9

SUPPORT: HOW CAN TEACHERS PROVIDE SUPPORT FOR STUDENTS HAVING DIFFICULTY IN SCHOOL AND LIFE?

In order to do well in school, most adolescents need places where they feel safe and "normal." Those of you who remember being teenagers, or who already have teenaged children, know that finding such a space in school, at home, in a community-based program, or in a social group is not always easy.

Teenagers need a place that is theirs, a place with which they can identify and for which they can take responsibility. A classroom, even when it is organized as a community, can be large and overwhelming. Teenagers need to be related to each other and to adults in smaller, often less structured spaces (e.g., teams and clubs). When I was in middle school my homeroom teacher, Miss Berkowitz, took me under her wing. She was also my algebra teacher and she encouraged me to be on the school's (her) math team. The team met during lunch period, a time when I normally played ball in the school yard. One thing Miss Berkowitz always did was to make sure we ate lunch. I lived in a single-parent family and sometimes my father would forget to leave lunch money when he rushed out early in the morning. On days when I did not have money for lunch, Miss Berkowitz always lent me what I needed. I stayed with the math team, and missed a number of ball games, largely because of my relationship with her.

Sometimes providing support means that a teacher needs to give a student a little space. Everybody has "bad hair days." Treat students the way you would want to be treated if you had just had a fight with your mother, were overtired, or just plain grumpy. Instead of backing a student into a corner and provoking an explosion, give them that space.

This chapter opens with an essay by Judith Kaufman, a professor of human development and educational psychology at Hofstra University, on the difficult world children and adolescents can face in our society. It is followed by statements from members of the Hofstra New Teachers Network on their own experiences as teenagers, the kind of support they needed, and the way their experiences shape them as teachers. Sections also discuss at-risk youth and the problem of violence in schools. The final essay is about the New Teachers Network and the fact that teachers, especially new teachers, need support too.

SECTION A: WHAT SHOULD TEACHERS KNOW ABOUT THE WORLD OF CHILDREN AND ADOLESCENTS?

Valuing What Our Students Know
By Judith Kaufman

Judith Kaufman teaches child and adolescent development to elementary and secondary education students in the Hofstra University School of Education and Allied Human Services. She believes that most of the problems associated with adolescence arise because "teenagers are trapped in a world where they are no longer allowed to act like children, but are not permitted to be adults." According to Judy, "Adolescence is not a natural phenomenon or developmental stage, but rather a modern social construction."–Alan Singer

Who we are as individuals is a product of the social context of our lives. We become who we become because of the experiences we have as members of families, communities, ethnic and religious groups, social classes and societies, and the way we are perceived and treated because of our race and gender. This perspective on human development is called social constructivism.

Of course, there are biological aspects of being human, but we cannot isolate those aspects from who we are as social and cultural beings. All human potential is expressed through a particular culture. I think that we are born with almost infinite potential, but once we become a part of a cultural environment, we are fundamentally altered and shaped by that environment. Our neural structure is shaped by each encounter in our worlds; connections are established and severed and potential ways of being are both nourished and starved. This process continues throughout our lives. As we experience new things, we continually grow and change.

As a social constructivist, I believe that to be effective, teachers need to understand that both they and their students shape and are shaped by the communities in which they live. I want to start off discussing who I am and how my social context has shaped my understanding of schools, children, and adolescents, and then discuss my views on what it means to be a teenager in this society and the implications this has for the way we organize schools.

I teach human development in a teacher education program and I am a former elementary school teacher. I was born in 1955 and raised in Worcester, Massachusetts. I have one brother, who is 4 years older than I am. The neighborhood I grew up in was a post-World War II suburban community built up with help from federally subsidized mortgages. It was ethnically mixed with Jewish and Irish Catholic two-parent families. The children in our neighborhood grew up together and went to the same public schools.

My parents were traditionally Jewish in the sense that education was highly valued and my brother and I received religious instruction in the afternoon after the regular school day. There was never a question that my brother and I would go to college. However, it was not as important for me to go to a "good college" because I was a girl.

The Jewish community in Worcester was, it seemed to me, a middle-class community and my parents seemed to be the only working-class Jews. Looking back as an adult, however, the community was quite diverse, wealthy and poor, secular and ultra religious, and everything in between. As a child, though, most of my classmates appeared to be from wealthier families and I felt marginalized. Their fathers were large business owners whereas my father was always struggling to earn a living. I think I accepted the anti-Semitic stereotype that Jews were supposed to be successful and I was always wondering why my family did not look like everybody else's.

My father did not graduate from college. When he was in high school he thought about becoming an engineer, but was discouraged by his guidance counselor who told him that Jews did not become engineers. He joined the Navy instead and served there during World War II. After the war, he married my mother and opened a gas station with my grandfather. He and my grandfather ran the gas station for a few years, but it never generated enough money. He opened another station and bought a truck and worked as a truck driver for about 10 years. Later, he went to work for another company and hated not being his own boss. He opened a bar, and finally a bar and a restaurant.

My mother grew up in a working-class town north of Boston. Her parents divorced and my grandmother married a man who later became a lawyer. This made it possible for my mother to attend art school for 2 years. She was fixed up with my father after the war. They dated for a short period of time and then were married. My mother never worked outside of the home as I was growing up.

When I was a child, there were different gender expectations for my brother and myself, and this made me angry. I was a tomboy and I always wanted the cultural advantages that men received, the greater freedom of choice and power. I did not fit into the traditional "girl" stereotype. I played sports. I played on the street with the boys. I loved tree houses and snow forts. I preferred Erector sets to dolls.

Acting like a tomboy gave me some male privilege, but never enough. For example, my brother could go with my father on truck-driving trips. When I asked to go, I was told it was "no place for a girl." My father and I were close, but I think he felt that he needed to contain me because the qualities he admired were just for boys. This was especially true when I started to enter adolescence.

I remember one incident when I was in either the third or fourth grade that taught me a lot about gender role expectations in school. In the wintertime my mother made me wear corduroy pants under my skirt so that I would be warm. The skirt looked ridiculous to me so I would take it off and stuff it in a milk box when I left the house. When I returned home, I would take it out and put it on again. My problem was in school, where the teachers and children made fun of me because girls were not supposed to wear pants. The teachers called me a boy and tried to pressure me into wearing a skirt. They wanted me to act like a little girl and I had to be punished for crossing gender boundaries.

One of the most painful school experiences for me was being held back in first grade. My birthday was in November, so at first I was one of the younger children. Half way through the school year my teacher called my parents and told them that I could not read yet and did not know my numbers. She complained that I played all the time, did not listen, and was always making trouble. Later she told my parents that I was not developmentally ready for the second grade and that I needed to be retained for a year.

Looking back, I am not sure whether I was held over because of my academic performance or because I was a tomboy and did not fit the image of appropriate behavior for a girl. A good deal of what school is about is learning to conform and I did not pay enough attention to the teacher's expectations for female first graders. Boys, however, were given extra space. My brother had the same problems as I did in school, but they did not keep him back.

As a result of being kept back in first grade, my sense of who I was in the world was changed. In my second go around in first grade, my classmates were younger and I felt old, big, and dumb. The other children did not make fun of me overtly, but the issue of age was always important. Children always ask each other, "How old are you?" I would have to "come out" about my age and they would think, "She's been left back, she must be dumb." Since then, I have always felt insecure about my intelligence. It has been a demon my entire life. I think that part of the reason I pursued a Ph.D. was to help beat that demon into the ground.

One of the ways I finally learned to survive and even succeed was to separate from the environment around me. I became another person, projecting the proper appearance in an effort to control the way other people saw me. I had a couple of close friends, but essentially I remained detached from the rest of the social scene. I strove to get into honor classes and then avoided taking academic risks. I felt I had tricked everyone into thinking that I was a good student. I could never let anyone know how insecure I felt; they might discover that I was really stupid.

I was marginalized in school, but I am White, I speak Standard English, and though my parents are working class, they have middle-class values. After experiencing the humiliation and pain of being held back, I learned to compromise with the system and started to obey its rules. I was given the benefit of the doubt and allowed to succeed. Children who do not have privilege based on their skin color or class membership or who have experiences that are at variance with the middle-class expectations of public schools often find school a devastating experience. They are labeled and tracked into the lowest rungs of the school and rarely given the benefit of a doubt or the opportunity to succeed.

When I started college, I originally planned to go into psychology; however, I had an "educational moment" that redirected me toward teaching. I took a class with a visiting professor from the University of Chicago. He told the class that he did not value our ability to repeat what was in textbooks. He wanted to hear our ideas about what we had read. Nobody had ever valued my thinking before. In that class, I went from being someone who received knowledge and information from others and reproduced what they thought to someone who could produce ideas that were significant. As a result of this experience and the professor's recommendation, I entered the school's elementary education program, received my teaching certification, and taught for 3 years. Then I decided to combine my love of psychology with my love of teaching. I earned a doctorate and became a teacher educator.

A perspective that I present in my education classes is that schools are designed to mold children to fit into very particular boxes. If teachers want to help children explore possibilities beyond the limits of these boxes, they must learn about the lives of the students they are going to be teaching. If we ignore their experiences, we deny children the possibility of exploring who they can be in the world; we put them in a box where they are constrained and defined.

Teachers need to find out as much as possible about their students and their families. They need to know about the neighborhoods they live in, their faith, language, and culture. More generally, teachers need to find out what their students already know about the world. If teachers begin with where students are they can provide an environment in which students use what they know to gain access to what they do not know. If students do not believe that teachers value what they know, they will resist and what they learn will have little to do with explicit classroom goals and objectives.

When I ask my own students what they learned in traditional classrooms, they rarely discuss subject matter content. Instead, they remember that they learned about what counted as good behavior or bad behavior, they learned about rules and schedules, and they learned about power and who had it. In short, they learned about the boxes they were expected to fit into and not about possibility and potential and how what they already knew about the world can provide the basis for learning so much more.

When I discuss adolescence with my students, I begin by dispelling the myth that adolescence is a time of raging hormones and uncontrolled emotions. Although it is certainly true that as children get older their lives get more complicated, most of the problems associated with adolescence stem from the way this period of life is framed by the popular culture. Teenagers are trapped in a world where they are no longer allowed to act like children but are not permitted to be adults. They are denied the rights and responsibilities of adulthood, but they are expected to act like adults. This irony creates many of the conflicts that we attribute to the turbulence of adolescence.

I argue that adolescence is not a natural phenomenon or developmental stage, but rather a modern social construction. The adolescent years are not problematic in cultures in which young people are legitimately integrated into their communities and are expected to increasingly contribute as workers and citizens. Adolescence is a phenomenon of the U.S. capitalist economy that began with the Industrial Revolution. It functions to keep teenagers out of the permanent labor force. In effect, the concept of adolescence lowers unemployment rates, provides teenagers with low-wage occupational training, and socializes them into a hierarchical and authoritarian work environment.

In this system, high schools function as containment facilities where teenagers are warehoused until society has a place for them. We justify this containment by arguing that the economy requires a skilled work force, but it is not clear that this training must take place in "schools as we know them" and with teenagers forced into suspended animation. The psychological cost of this system is young people disengaged from the adult community, concentrated into large age-segregated buildings, and living with increased surveillance and loss of privacy.

During the 1997–1998 school year, there was a series of highly publicized shootings in schools that contributed to growing national concern about teenage violence. However, while pundits were busy blaming movies and music lyrics for what seemed like an increase in violence, statistics showed there had actually been a slight decrease in school shooting deaths since 1992. (Donohue, Schiraldi, & Ziedenberg, 1998) Teenagers are used as political scapegoats and the corporate media perpetuate this by demonizing young people instead of confronting the problems of overall social violence and widespread gun ownership. It is far easier to blame youth culture than it is seek solutions through challenging powerful political lobbies protecting the interests of, for example, weapons manufacturers. The consequence is that teenagers are marginalized and further alienated from the adult community.

Sexuality is another area where teenagers are under attack. The problems facing adolescents are not their raging hormones, but the contradictory messages and the limited information they receive about appropriate sexual behavior. At the same time that teenagers are told to put off sex until marriage, they are immersed in advertising that exploits sexuality to sell all kinds of products and maintain consumer demand. Additionally, this culture drastically limits the information that youth need to be responsible sexual beings. It is difficult to get good information in schools about birth control and abortion, and we do not make condoms freely available in schools. Instead of encouraging teenagers to raise questions about their identities and sexualities, we silence them by establishing narrow, rigid categories of acceptable behavior and by defining many forms of normal human sexual activity as immoral or evil.

By politicizing and commercializing sex and by withholding information about healthy sexuality, our society victimizes young people. The United States has the highest rate of teen pregnancy in the northern hemisphere (American Academy of Pediatrics [AAP], 1999), twice the rate in England or Wales and nine times higher than The Netherlands or Canada (The Alan Guttmacher Institute, 1999). Within the United States, adolescents as a group make up a growing percentage of new HIV infections. Almost 25% of the estimated 40,000 new HIV infections in the United States occur among 13- to 21-year-olds, and at least one teenager is infected with HIV every hour (Szekeres, 1999).

Schools must provide children and adolescents with good information about human sexuality, reproduction, and sexually transmitted diseases. We know that prohibition and information control is ineffective. We also know that if you provide people with good information, they make better choices. For example, rates of sexual activity among western European teenagers are similar or higher than rates for teenagers in the United States; however, teens in western Europe have far lower rates of unintended pregnancy. They also have lower rates of sexually transmitted diseases and fewer abortions (Berne & Huberman, 1999). The reasons for these differences are not clear, but European adolescents have greater access to contraception and universal sexuality education in some European countries (AAP, 1999). The problem in the United States is not raging hormones, but a vocal and powerful conservative minority that denies that sexual expression is a part of healthy development.

There is a racist and classist fear in the United States that extending freedoms and responsibility to teenagers instead of intensifying control in schools might be effective in middle-class professional communities where it is thought that adolescents generally accept society's expectations, but would not work in poor communities of color where it is thought that teenage pregnancy, resistance to authority, and violence are epidemic. I would not classify resistance to authority as a problem, but it is clear that violence and unintended pregnancy cut straight across race and class lines. The widely publicized school shootings in the last few years have occurred in White suburban and rural communities, and White adolescents in the United States have higher birth rates than their counterparts in industrialized northern hemisphere countries (AAP, 1999).

A study by Ann Locke Davidson (1996) powerfully illustrates that teenagers will respond to a combination of respect, responsibility, and freedom. Among her findings, Davidson includes a case study of a teenager from East St. Louis, Illinois, who felt the community did not value him or his school. This young man gave up on any possibility of achieving success through the standard routes. He became a member of a youth gang and was involved with drugs and violence. He joined the gang because membership provided him with both a sense of power and of belonging.

The young man's mother, in an effort to help her son, sent him to live with a brother in Los Angeles, where he entered a high school program with other teenagers who had been involved in gang-related activities. In this program, he was given responsibilities that showed he was respected, he took courses that reflected his history and ethnic roots, and he learned about college opportunities. He went from a school where he was viewed as a delinquent and denied information and the right to participate as a full member of the community to an environment where those in power sent a clear message that they cared about him and his future. In this new setting, instead of being a dropout, he went to school every day and invested in his learning.

Understanding this young man's experience, and the experience of similar young men and women, can help educators develop models for secondary schools that respond to the needs of teenagers. For example, most community programs that are run for teenagers try to divert their attention away from their lives by providing them with recreational opportunities. Although these are valuable, they do not offer teens the chance to be constructive, responsible adults and citizens. I believe that successful schools and youth programs must help teenagers link up with their futures and allow them to participate as valued members of the community. Secondary education should expand freedom and responsibility together, extending teenagers both privilege and power. The adult community will need to cede some control if it is willing to share power and allow teenagers to make significant decisions.

What would schools look like if students had more power and responsibility? In many classes for academically elite students, ideas are respected and students are allowed to engage in independent and group projects in which they pursue information and construct their own knowledge and understanding. This approach to teaching is appropriate for all students in all schools and communicates to students that they have something significant to contribute to the educational enterprise. Secondary education can also be linked to paid internships where students can explore possible career paths and engage in work that is valued by their communities. Part of the high school experience can include community involvement in service that really matters. We need to integrate what happens in the classroom with what goes on in the community outside the classroom walls.

Kathleen Kesson and Celia Oyler (1999) describe the efforts of Rebecca Jim, a guidance counselor in northeastern Oklahoma who organized the Cherokee Volunteer Society for middle and high school students (both Native American and other teenagers), an extracurricular group that committed their efforts to environmental problems in the area. The students took on Tar Creek, named a Superfund site in 1983 but largely ignored by the federal and local authorities. Jim knew that she and her students could accomplish far more if they involved classroom teachers who would agree to integrate the environmental work in their curricula. Science teachers taught students how to collect water samples and monitor water quality. The senior classes of two English teachers put together an anthology of writing on Tar Creek intended to make information on the environmental problems accessible to the local community. The students involved also organize an annual Tar Creek Fish Tournament and Toxic Tour, which heightens public awareness and reminds the community that no fish can survive in the creek. The students in this area are involved in challenging work that brings the school and community together. They are honing valuable academic skills through work on issues that have immediate relevance for themselves and their community. Many of the students and their families are experiencing a wide range of serious health problems and they are optimistic that their work can make a difference, if not for them, then for future generations. These adolescents, through their work in school are making a legitimate and valuable contribution to their community and in turn they are perceived as valued community members.

This approach to secondary education means schools can stop focusing on what students do not know, a deficit model of education, and start focusing on what they can contribute to the world and their communities. Skill acquisition and knowledge construction are exciting and worth doing when young people have a reason for learning. The question for educators is, "How do we work with and develop the tremendous amount of knowledge, talent, and potential that students bring with them to class?" and "How do we help them channel their skills and knowledge in ways that have meaning and relevance to their lives and the communities they are living in?"

In my human development classes for preservice teachers, I introduce research and theory, but I try to focus discussion on three sources of knowledge. We talk about my students' own experiences as teenagers, their observations in schools, and the literature and theory about teenage life. An example of the literature we read is Michael Dorris's (1988) *A Yellow Raft in Blue Water*, which depicts the life of a Native and African American teenager and her search for identity and community. It is also about her discovery of the strong and complex bonds she shares with her mother and grandmother. Among other books we read is Paul Monette's (1992) *Becoming a Man: Half a Life Story*. It is about a gay male growing up in the 1960s and his struggle with homophobia and coming to terms with his identity. My students find these coming-of-age stories exceedingly useful for exploring the world of adolescents and figuring out what it means to be both a teenager and a teacher. The diversity of the literature helps them go beyond the media images of adolescence that are familiar and seemingly simple and to develop images of youth that have depth and complexity.

Schools should be organized to create experiences for children and adolescents that reflect who they are in the world. Schools should also be places where it is possible for students to both acquire and critique the values of the adult community. Forcing students to learn ideas they feel little connection with is successful for reproducing society exactly as it is, but unsuccessful in nourishing a generation in which individuals feel like legitimate stakeholders who can make a difference in the moral and democratic life of their communities. Immersing students in relevant and challenging work and learning and sharing decision-making power will significantly change the landscape of schools and how we think about adolescence. We will come to accept as commonplace the view that adolescents can act responsibly, learn, and make significant contributions to society.

* * *

JOIN THE CONVERSATION—HUMAN DEVELOPMENT

Judy Kaufman's beliefs about education are rooted in her ideas about child and adolescent development. They are summarized here.

1. Humans are born with almost infinite potentials.
2. Children who do not have privilege based on their skin color or class membership, or who have experiences that are at variance with the middle-class expectations of public schools, often find school a devastating experience.
3. If teachers want to help children explore possibilities for being and acting in the world that far exceed the limits of particular boxes, they must strive to learn about the lives of the students they are going to be teaching.
4. Most problems associated with adolescence arise because teenagers are trapped in a world where they are no longer allowed to act like children but are not permitted to be adults.
5. Adolescence is not a natural phenomenon or developmental stage, but rather a modern social construction. Adolescence is a phenomenon of the U.S. capitalist economy that began with the Industrial Revolution. It functions to keep teenagers out of the permanent labor force.
6. The problems facing adolescents are not their raging hormones, but the contradictory messages and limited information they receive about appropriate sexual behavior.
7. Schools should be organized to create experiences for children and adolescents that reflect who they are in the world and that make it possible for them to both acquire and critique the values of the adult community.

Questions to Consider:

Which of these statements by Judy Kaufman do you agree with? Which do you disagree with? Why?

SECTION B: BECOMING A TEACHER 6:
WHAT KIND OF SUPPORT DO TEENAGERS NEED?

In this section, members of the Hofstra New Teachers Network who had to overcome adversity as teenagers in order to receive an education, start a career, understand themselves, or even to survive discuss their personal experiences. As teenagers, these teachers struggled with difficult issues such as coming to terms with sexual identity, eating disorders, migration to a new country, juvenile delinquency, poverty, and gang violence. They explain what life was like for them as teenagers, the support they received from teachers and other adults, the kind of support that would have been helpful to them, and the way their personal experience influences the way they respond to their students.

Nobody Ever Told Me I Was Special
By Lauren Rosenberg

I worked with Lauren Rosenberg when she was a student teacher and observed her classroom while she was still a beginner. Lauren is a fabulous teacher who lights up her classroom with her smile. However, in teacher education classes, she tended to be very quiet. Lauren says she is the same way in most situations with adults. In this essay she tells about her experience as a teenager and young woman with low self-esteem who suffered from an eating disorder. She wishes to thank two teachers, her 11th-grade history teacher and a graduate school professor who taught a class on gender issues in education, for modeling ways that teachers can make a difference in the lives of their students.—Alan Singer

In middle school and high school I was a very conscientious, quiet, shy, and insecure young woman. I was the type of student who secretly begged for attention from teachers but never got it. I thought teachers overlooked me and could not even remember my name. Nobody in school ever told me I was special.

In most classes I would not raise my hand. I feared I would give a wrong answer and be called stupid. One experience I had that was different was in my 11th-grade history class. That teacher was the only one to encourage me to speak up and he helped me develop a sense of self-worth. He is one of the reasons I decided to become a social studies teacher.

As a teenager, I always had friends, but I was never confident in myself. I felt like an outsider. We lived in an ethnically homogeneous community, but this did not make me feel comfortable. Most of the students came from families that had more money than we had. Their parents were doctors, lawyers, and accountants; mine were teachers. We were a middle-class family living in an affluent community, and I felt we did not belong.

My eating problems began in junior high school. I was not really heavy, but I thought I was obese and I felt ugly. I also felt miserable about my hair because it was curly, black, and frizzy, whereas everyone else seemed to have blonde or brown straight hair. In high school, when I came home from school feeling down I would open the refrigerator and start eating. Food comforted me in a way that nothing else could.

I went to the state university and it was like being in high school all over again. I was with many of the same people I knew from before and I had the same feelings of inadequacy. In my sophomore year in college I started working out heavily to lose weight and I developed an obsession about food. Everything else in life—family, friends, school, my facial features—were beyond my control. But I could curb the amount I ate and reduce my weight and it gave me a sense of power that I never experienced before.

I started exercising more and eating less and less. I wanted no fat in my diet whatsoever. If I ate an extra carrot I would feel guilty and run longer on the treadmill the next day. I was obsessed to the point that food and exercise were all I thought about. Everyday, I wrote in my diary what I would eat the next day, how much I was going to run, and how much time I would spend on the treadmill.

At the same time, on the weekends when I would go out with my friends to bars, I was getting positive attention from men that I never received before. They commented on how great I looked and how thin I was. Getting this attention fed into my illness. I loved it and was encouraged to eat less and workout even more. I understood the correlation; lose weight and get the attention I craved. I thought, if only I had been thinner in high school, I would not have been ignored.

For more than a year, I did not menstruate. My hair was falling out, my skin was pale, I was always chilled, and I was not sleeping very much. But when you are anorexic nothing else matters. You become totally self-absorbed with being thin. In the morning, the first thing I did was check my rib cage and shoulders to make sure I could feel the bones.

During one spring break I went away with friends. We were staying together and they could see all of my eating and exercise "rituals." All I would eat for breakfast was an apple, and if I could not find one, I did not eat. One day I passed out. When we came home, they spoke with my parents. My mother started to cry when she saw me, but I refused to believe anything was wrong. I resisted for weeks. Finally, my parents got me admitted to a hospital with a program for people with eating disorders.

Recovery was a long, hard process. I was in the hospital program for 3 months during the summer and in out-patient therapy for years after that. While under treatment, there was so much pressure on me to eat that I became bulimic—binge eating and throwing up. I was ill for about 3 years.

I went to law school after graduating from college and was so miserable that my condition worsened. It was not until I dropped out of law school and decided to be a teacher that things came together for me. Now I am fine, but my condition is always on my mind. I still wake up each day and think what am I going to eat today. I am careful to avoid "emotional eating." I never skip a meal or starve myself. If I am having a bad day, I make sure I do not overeat in reaction. Sometimes my feelings of inadequacy come back. When I first started teaching, I felt like I was an impostor and was afraid that people would discover it.

Nobody ever told me I was special when I was younger and I needed to hear it. Now I know that everybody needs to hear it. As a teacher, I learned that a little bit of personal attention can mean a lot to a lonely teenager. The first day of class I have students write down their likes and dislikes, so that during the semester I can use stories that appeal to them and their interests. I do my best to get them to speak and to let everyone know that I think what they have to say is important. I tell students that being wrong is really not a big deal.

I put smiley faces on homework. I have 17-year-olds who come up to me and ask if they can get a smiley face. If a student has not shown up in class for a while and comes back or hands in homework after missing a few assignments, I write them a personal note saying its great to see you doing your work.

I now realize that many teachers ignore quiet girls, so I pay special attention to them. I notice them a lot, although I do not usually call on them unless they volunteer. I know if some of my teachers had called on me, I probably would have cried. Instead, I go over to the quiet ones after class and encourage them to join in. Sometimes it works and they become more willing to participate.

Last semester, a girl wanted to read me an essay she wrote for her English class about bulimia. She was signaling that she had an eating problem and was reaching out to me. I told her my story, was able to persuade her to speak with a counselor, and she is now getting help. In the future, I want to help young women deal with self-esteem issues so they can address their feelings before they turn into eating disorders.

As teachers, we often get caught up in lesson planning and the details of what we have to do the next day. We forget that teaching is really about the students. Helping young people feel special is the most important part of teaching for me.

A Couple Since They Were 14

Samuel Charles and Ruth Santos are pseudonyms. The authors of these essays were inner-city youth targeted for failure in our society. They decided to use pseudonyms to respect the privacy of family members. Samuel and Ruth grew up in the Baychester section of the Bronx in New York City. It is a neighborhood dominated by a large public housing project where poverty and drug-related crime were endemic during their teen years. In school, they both resisted placement in academically advanced classes because they did not want to be teased by the other children.

Samuel's father was a "numbers" runner for an illegal gambling operation, one of the few jobs available for an African American male in his community. He abandoned the family while Samuel was a young boy and Samuel's mother had to work two jobs to keep them together. Because of this, Samuel had major responsibilities supervising his younger brother. As they grew older, Samuel turned to sports, whereas his brother became involved with drugs and violence, eventually ending up in jail.

Ruth's grandparents migrated to New York from Puerto Rico but her family has not lived the "American dream." Her father, who was incarcerated on drug charges and died of HIV/AIDS, was never really part of her life. While Ruth was in fourth grade, her stepfather, a Viet Nam veteran who had been exposed to Agent Orange, died of a liver-related disease. For much of her childhood and adolescence the family depended on public assistance.

Ruth and Samuel have been a couple since they were 14-years-old and students in junior high school. They believe their relationship with each other was the most important element in their survival and success. After attending a suburban college they returned to live and work in the Bronx. They now have two children and are both teachers. Ruth teaches mathematics at a magnet secondary school (grades 7–12) for gifted youth in the African American community of Harlem. Samuel is a social studies teacher and the dean at the Bronx high school he attended as a teenager. In these essays they explain what made it possible for them to survive and succeed against the odds.—Alan Singer

* * *

I Am Tired of Seeing Black and Latino Students Not Succeeding
By Samuel Charles

I grew up in the Bronx three or four blocks from Edenwald projects. Edenwald had a really bad reputation. There were shootings there and drug dealers. I grew up in the late 1980s and early 1990s when crack was big time. Some of my friends had older brothers who were big-time dealers with reputations in the community before they went to jail. Two of my best friends got locked up after an accident in a stolen car. I never stole cars, but I rode in them because it was something fun to do, not something that we thought of as criminal.

My brother was involved in drugs and violence. He was younger than I am, but he was a tough guy. Everybody in the community knew him and knew not to mess with him. I was into sports, but he thought money was glamorous. He liked to have a wad of money. My brother went to a special education school and was suspended numerous times. He had to go because of his behavior. He could not read well and teachers did not help him out. I think he felt, "I can't do this work, why am I even bothering to try?" He became a street kid and there was no one home to stop him. He was an angry guy and when he turned 21 he got in heavy trouble with the law and was sent "upstate."

There were no organized gangs like the Bloods and Crips are today. We defined our identity by the block where we lived; every block had its own "posse." I was involved in fights with my posse, but we did not have guns. As a teenager, I was part of the Five-Percenters. The group was quasi-religious and philosophical. You joined this group because you were searching for knowledge of self as a young black male. A lot of us did not have fathers at home, so we turned to people who seemed to have knowledge of the world like the Five-Percenters and the Nation of Islam.

One of the things that made a difference for me was that I had confidence in myself that I was able to do the schoolwork. I had the ability, so when I was motivated I experienced success in school and wanted to do it more. School was like a game for me; when I was winning I wanted to play more. But if you keep losing you lose your zest to want to play and give up. When teachers realized I had the ability and wanted to succeed they invested in me. My fourth-grade teacher brought me to her house and taught me to use her computer.

When I went to junior high school I was placed in the smartest class but I forced them to kick me out. The first day at school we were all sitting in the auditorium as they called out each class. There were new kids that I had never seen in my life. When they called my name with 7SPE (special program enrichment) and the kids in the back yelled, "Nerds, nerds, nerds," I sunk down in my chair and tried to disappear. From that day on I did whatever I could to get transferred into a regular class. I had the ability to do the work but I did not want to be there. Until I was in ninth grade, I did the minimum amount of work necessary to pass my classes. My best friends never went to school. They still do not have their diplomas.

In ninth grade, I joined the school baseball team and started to go out with Ruth who was in the 9SPE. Being with Ruth made it cooler to be smart and being on the team grounded me. Ruth helped me in math and we would get together and do homework. I was still absent from school a lot and cut the day we filled out applications for high school. Because I was not there I did not get into the school where I wanted to play ball. When they did not accept me, it was the worst day in my life. I went to the neighborhood high school instead and planned to transfer as soon as possible, but after joining the football team, I decided to stay.

From my earliest youth, sports provided me with male role models, gave me something to do that kept me out of trouble, and shaped my goals. Because of team sports, I had something to look forward to each day, responsibilities to live up to, and a foundation for my life. In high school, I played football and baseball and ran track. I was a starter and a captain so people looked up to me.

In high school, I had teachers who saw that I had ability and wanted to learn. I was placed in college-bound classes. I did not care about Arista and the honor's society, but teachers introduced me to these things. My English teacher encouraged me to join the debate team and even called my house to recruit me.

Their idea of caring about students is what shapes me now as a teacher. When I walk into a classroom I tell the class, "I do not care if you are the best student or the worst student, it is my job to care about each and every one of you." I insist that every student have a notebook binder, paper, and a pen. I get mad if they do not do their homework. I give them a hard time when they are late. I call home and speak with parents over the smallest things. Because I care, some of them complain that I am too mean.

As a high school student, I did not want to disappoint people who felt I could do better. I remember I passed the standardized math final exam with a 68. My teacher expected me to score more than 90 and I felt bad that I let this teacher down. When teachers care about students they try harder because they do not want to let you down.

The teachers that students considered good when I was in high school were the teachers that made the class interesting. I believe when a teacher makes the class interesting, students will want to learn. Someone may not be a "rocket scientist" in every subject, but if a student enjoys class, he or she will grasp the main ideas and become a better student.

I try to use the introduction to a lesson to connect the subject matter with the lives of students in my class. We may start out talking about the way people are treated because of their race, gender, sexuality, or beliefs, and suddenly we are learning about conditions for slaves in ancient Rome.

I became a dean because it makes it possible for me to deal with a larger number of students, not just the ones in my classes. I want to turn the school around. I am tired of seeing Black and Latino students not succeeding in school and in life. No one seems to understand why these kids cannot read. No one seems to understand why they do not want to come to school. But I do know. I know we can read and will attend if teachers and schools care about us.

I Did Not Want to Be Another Hispanic Statistic
By Ruth Santos

My mother moved us around a lot when I was a little girl. We lived in the South Bronx until I was in second grade, moved to Baychester for a couple of years, and then to the Edenwald area near Samuel's family. My mother had me and my older sister by her first husband and two children by her second husband. My mother did not graduate from high school because she got pregnant with my sister. However, when she was older, she got her GED and an associate's degree. Most of the time we were on welfare or had social security and veterans benefits because of my stepfather.

As a young girl I was really embarrassed about being on welfare. The kids in school made fun of you if you were on welfare or had to use food stamps. From as early as kindergarten I wanted to do well and make something out of my life. I wanted to be important, a professional with a good job. When I first started school I was sent to the resource room with other kids for special help in reading. But I was faster than everyone else and eventually I was put in a regular class. I was always a good math student, but I am not sure why. I remember that when I was in kindergarten the teacher gave me a math game and I loved it. I must have been lucky to have elementary school teachers with solid math backgrounds.

When I did well in seventh grade, they put me in the 8SPE class (special program enrichment), but like Samuel, I was embarrassed and did not do that well. I did not fail, but I was never in the top group. In ninth grade, I started to do well. It was the love of math that got me through. I found high school easy. I was never concerned if teachers were boring. I figured they had a job to do and I had a job to do. I just went to class, took notes, and did my homework. I got exceptional grades; I was always a 90 student, because I did my work.

I was always a quiet person and kept mostly to myself. I cannot think of any teachers who reached out specially to help me before I got to college. My motivation to succeed came from inside me. I joined the debate team because I wanted to compete against Samuel and his school. The mock trial coach sought me out for the team but I quit because there were students on the team who made fun of me because I was so nervous. When one of the cool kids laughed at me, I quit. The coach never came after me to find out why.

My older sister had a baby when she was 14 years old. But she still graduated from high school and went to a 2-year college. My mother and the rest of our family helped her pull through. Luckily, I did not get pregnant, even though Samuel and I had unprotected sex. We had a lot of free time together and did not really know what we were doing. We tried condoms and other methods but we were not always careful. If I got pregnant in high school, my mother would have wanted me to have an abortion, but I think I would have kept it like my sister. I always believed if you were dealt it, you could deal with it. I finally did get pregnant with my son when I was eighteen and a freshman in college. I was frightened it would destroy my dreams, but I would not let it. I took off one semester but then continued with my plans. I did not want to be another Hispanic statistic.

I experimented with alcohol when I was 12 or 13 but I stopped. Samuel and I managed to avoid drugs. I saw what it did to people in my family. Samuel was an athlete so he looked down on drug use and alcohol. Samuel and I were together so we were able to resist peer pressure to use drugs. We supported each other and protected each other.

I probably am a pretty traditional teacher. The big difference in what I do is that many math teachers make things too complicated by using sophisticated mathematical language that interferes with student learning. I always try to teach in ways that students will understand. As a math teacher, I could have a higher paying job in the suburbs but I always promised myself that I would return to the city. I feel an obligation to give back to young people growing up like I did. Money was never the most important thing for me. I feel I could have done anything I wanted to do, but I decided to become a math teacher in the city to make a difference.

A lot of my students remind me of myself, especially the girls. I am not sure if I do the best job for them. I am a very private person. I do not like people to pry into my life and I try to respect their privacy. I always feel I could do better as a teacher. The students say I am good, but I do not feel I am good enough. There are still students I do not reach and I cannot make them love math. I want to do more; I just do not know how to yet.

* * *

I Was in Sixth Grade and Could Not Read
By Adeola Tella

*During her first 2 years as a teacher, Adeola Tella involved her classes in the reading buddies pro-
gram discussed in chapter 4 and in the development of differentiated texts for the Great Irish Famine curriculum (see chap. 7). She was a superior student in the teacher education program and is
now an outstanding teacher. I was surprised when I learned that Adeola had had difficulty in
school and could not read until she was in sixth grade. Her story illustrates the potential for excellence possessed by many students, a potential that is often ignored because of problems with language.—Alan Singer*

My mother was born in rural Jamaica in the Caribbean and my father is Yoruba from Nigeria
in West Africa. They met while my mother was a nursing student in Scotland and my father,
an engineer, was there on business. At first they went to live in the United States, where I
was born. However, when I was 2 years old, we moved to Illora, my father's ancestral village.
I finally returned to the United States permanently when I was 12 years old.

In Nigeria I learned to speak Yoruba, though I still spoke English with my mother. School
was taught in Yoruba, and because my mother left for the United States when I was 9, that
was my primary language. Possibly because of my mixed-language background, I never really learned to read and write while in Nigeria. No one ever took the time to help me or to
find out why I was having difficulty.

When I joined my mother, we lived in a primarily African American community. I was excited to be reunited with her and to return to this country. Although we were all Black, I was
teased by the other children in school because I was from Africa. They called me "charcoal"
and claimed that I smelled "funny." They also teased me because I was in sixth grade and
could not read.

I was placed in a regular class and the school assigned a special tutor to help me in reading. By the end of the year, I had pretty much caught up with the other students in my class
and was doing very well in math. My experience is important because many people believe
that immigrants who are not literate in their home language will never learn to read and
write English well.

The next year, in middle school, students were tracked by reading scores and I was assigned to a remedial class. I started high school in the more advanced math class, was transferred to an academic social studies class in 10th grade, and to an academic English class in
11th grade. My mother was still concerned with my academic progress and arranged for me
to get extra help in a reading clinic at a local college.

The teasing ended in high school, partly because I fit in better, but also because with an
influx of Jamaican immigrants, our school became more diverse. My sisters and I had our
own "African" style, which was becoming popular in the Black community.

Looking back, I always wanted to be a teacher. As a little girl, I used to play school with my
dolls. But I finally decided to take the step because of my own experience. I had too many
teachers who did not care about me and made no effort to recognize my problems and figure out the help I needed. Basically the rule in school was, "If you were not smart, forget it."

A lot of students, especially immigrants, have the same difficulties that I had. I know what
their problems are because I went through them and I know how to help them. Just because
a student is in middle school and has not yet learned how to read is no excuse to give up on
them. I know that everyone can learn.

I did have a few teachers who modeled what it means to be a good teacher. They were
passionate and interesting and would become engrossed in what they taught. I try to be like
them. I love to tell stories to capture student interest.

My students always complain that I am too strict, but I do it for them. I try to pay attention to everything that is going on in the room so I can help students when they need it and stop problems before they begin. I was always able to do better in school when I had a strict teacher. I needed a well-structured classroom, and I try to provide one for my students.

I also try to show students that I care about them. I have a special relationship with my homeroom class so that students know they always have a place to go. I make sure that my room really is their home.

I Needed to Be Accepted; I Needed to Feel Safe
By J. B. Barton

J. B. Barton is a pseudonym. The author of this essay is a young European American woman who "grew up in a suburban community where it was very important to fit in and not be different from everyone else." She discusses grappling with her sexual identity, her realization that she is gay, and the impact of her experience and understanding on her teaching. When she wrote this, she was 23 years old and had just completed her first year teaching English in a suburban middle school. She decided to use a pseudonym because of homophobia in our society and concern that it would prevent her from earning tenure.—Alan Singer

I grew up in a suburban community where it was very important to fit in and not be different from everyone else. My family moved there when I was a little girl, just before I started school. I had a tight-knit group of about 10 friends who stayed together until we finished high school. I am now 23 years old and just completed my first year of teaching English. I work in a community not far from where I lived and went to school.

In high school, I was a cheerleader and played on the girl's softball team. I began to feel different from other people when my friends became deeply involved in emotional and physical relationships with a group of boys from the football team. I did not want to be different and experimented with dating, but nothing seemed to happen.

I always felt close to women and emulated female teachers and friends. While in high school, I developed "idols" such as Ellen DeGeneres, Martina Navratilova, and Melissa Etheridge, who appealed to me and I looked up to them. I am not sure why this happened, because I did not consciously know they were gay. My friends would tease me and dismiss them as lesbians, but I refused to believe it. In my personal journal, I wrote about how I felt different from everyone in my crowd, and the debate over whether these women were gay, but I never addressed my own sexuality.

I often think about what it would have been like if I was aware of my "otherness" and came out about my sexuality in high school. I do not think my friends could have handled it and there would have been no place in our school for me to go and talk with anyone. The cheerleading team was very close and in our routines we had to have physical contact during the lifts. I am sure it would have made my teammates uncomfortable.

It is very hard and lonely to be different in a small, closed community where everybody knows everyone else. Students used "gay," "dyke," and "fag" to put people down. There were rumors that one of the coaches of the softball team was a lesbian and students gossiped about her. I needed to be accepted, I needed to feel safe. I did not want to be labeled or the subject of gossip.

Homosexuality was and is a taboo subject, rarely discussed in school. During my senior year, I remember that a gay man spoke to our government class about discrimination and intolerance. My mother found a response journal I wrote about the lesson where my comments were very homophobic. I think this is a common phenomenon. Many gay youth espouse homophobia because they are afraid of their difference, do not want other people to know, and cannot let themselves confront it.

I did not come out as a lesbian until I was in college, primarily because I did not really know until then. I joined the rugby team and met women who were open about their sexuality and accepting about the sexuality of others. Suddenly I was able to see homosexuality as "normal" and I could focus on my identity. Once I met people who were openly gay, I was finally free to be me. I was able to have an emotional and physical relationship with another woman and to come out to my family. I am not sure why gay women frequently go into sports. I think it is because sports provide a community of people where you can be comfortable being yourself, where it is okay to celebrate being physical, and where you are respected by others, including straight people. I know that I was attracted to the camaraderie and the freedom.

During my freshman year in college I began to speak with my mother about what was going on in my life. She asked me lots of questions and was very supportive. When I was involved in my first serious relationship, I decided I had to tell my father about my sexuality. He said that he already knew and assured me that he would love me no matter what. My younger brother has found it difficult to accept who I am, but he is coming around.

In college I was able to get support as I tried to sort out my feelings. A professor gave me material to read and urged me to write about what I read and about myself. I was able to discuss my ideas with her one on one and felt free to truly say how I felt. I also joined a woman's alliance in which it was acceptable to be gay, and I participated in a gay men's and women's group in which we discussed issues we faced and organized a conference. These were important relationships because I met a broad range of people who were openly gay and lesbian, not just rugby players. It made it more comfortable and I finally felt accepted and safe.

An important moment for me was the murder of a young gay man, living in Wyoming, named Matthew Shepard. When he was killed, he was about the same age as I was and I found it very frightening. My mother called me when she heard the news on television and was crying. A professor distributed a newspaper article on what happened and we discussed it in class. I hung up the article in my apartment and began to actively raise issues about gay rights with friends.

I graduated from college with a major in English, a minor in women's studies, and no idea what I wanted to do. At first I turned to teaching by default, but the more I thought about it, the more excited I became. I remembered teachers who had pushed and helped me, and I figured it would be a way to combine my love of reading and writing with my desire to affect the lives of young people. In my teacher education program, I became more outspoken on gay rights issues. I helped organize a workshop for student teachers where we discussed how to provide support for gay and lesbian youth in our classes.

I am open about my identity with my friends and family, but I have not discussed it at work. As a first-year teacher, I had too many other issues to deal with. However, I am proud of the way I integrated respect for gays and lesbians into the curriculum. The main themes we study in middle school English literature are prejudice and tolerance. This year my seventh-grade classes read *The Light in the Forest* (Richter, 1994), *The Witch of Blackbird Pond* (Speare, 1991), *Tom Sawyer* (Twain, 1983), *When the Legends Die* (Borland, 1972), *The Yearling* (Rawlings, 1961), and *The Giver* (Lowry, 1993). All types of issues are introduced through this adolescent literature, but attitudes toward sexual orientation and discrimination against gays are ignored. I decided to design a lesson about the murder of Matthew Shepard using a political cartoon, a popular song, and poetry. I also reorganized the material for use on one of the school's standardized assessment tests. Students had to respond to the cartoon and a passage from the song and compare themes from these sources with a piece of literature they read in class. This was an important activity because it helped prepare students to meet state English language and literature standards. One of the other teachers questioned whether this topic was acceptable for middle school. But when I said that I thought it was precisely what the curriculum is supposed to be about, she backed off.

In middle school, students are first thinking about their sexuality. I have not yet had to address the needs of a student who is grappling with being gay. However, I have actively challenged the use of homophobic language in class and encouraged students to respect difference. In discussions about Matthew Shepard, we compared accepting differences of sexual orientation with differences in race. After the Matthew Shepard lesson, some of my students watched a biography of his life on MTV and talked about it with their families. One girl made her brothers promise never to call someone "fag" again.

* * *

FIG. 9.1 Teaching about Matthew Shepard—a lesson for middle school students.

Aim: What can happen when prejudice goes unchallenged?

Objective: Students will:

- Listen to a newspaper article and understand and explain its content.
- Compare information garnered from one source with information presented in another format.
- Identify and discuss prejudice against people who are perceived as different from themselves.
- Express their own ideas on prejudice in the form of a poem.

Materials:

- "Far Side" cartoon on human diversity and prejudice.
- Lyrics to "Scarecrow" by Melissa Etheridge and the CD *Breakdown*.
- Newspaper editorial, "The Lesson of Matthew Shepard," *The New York Times*, October 17, 1998, 14.

Do Now: Students will examine a "Far Side" cartoon on human diversity and prejudice. Students will write their view of the main idea of the cartoon.

Motivation: Discuss the question: "How can stereotypes and prejudices lead to hate crimes?"

Activities:

- Review student responses to the "Far Side" cartoon.
- Teacher will put poem structure on board and review with class.

One Noun
Two Adjectives
Three Verbs
One Question
One Answer

- Teacher reads excerpts from the newspaper editorial to the class twice. First time, listen only. Second time, write down words and phrases that evoke emotions.
- Students write poems about the newspaper editorial using this format.
- Volunteers read their poems to the class.
- Students read aloud the words to the song "Scarecrow," which was inspired by the Matthew Shepard case.
- Class will listen to recorded version and class discuss its meaning.

Summary Question: Should people accept human differences? Why?

JOIN THE CONVERSATION—IS IT THE RESPONSIBILITY OF TEACHERS?

Questions to Consider:

1. In your view, is it the responsibility of schools and teachers to deal with problems such as the ones discussed in these autobiographies? Explain.
2. Lauren Rosenberg, Samuel Charles, Ruth Santos, Adeola Tella, and J. B. Barton tell stories that are moving and painful for them. If you had a story like these, would you be willing to share it would other teachers? Would you be willing to share it with students who are experiencing similar difficulties? Explain.

SECTION C: WHY ARE STUDENTS AT RISK?

Every Student Here Is At Risk
By Alan Singer

From 1982 until 1990, I taught at Franklin K. Lane High School in Brooklyn, New York, a school with more than 4,000 students and 300 teachers. Most of my students were from ethnic and racial minority groups, and many were from poor families. Individually and collectively they were considered at risk of failure in school and in life. David Santana and Eric Larson (not their actual names) were students in my 11th-grade social studies classes. An earlier version of this essay was published in the Spring 1991 issue of Democracy and Education.—Alan Singer

David Santana was older than the other students in my 11th-grade class, and standardized tests showed that he was reading at significantly below grade level. He had a long history of failure in school. During the spring semester he became involved in our class oral history project, working with a group of students who helped to draw up a questionnaire for the class. Later, he interviewed his grandfather about migration from Puerto Rico to New York City.

David's interview with his grandfather was impressive. With assistance from other students, he edited his work and it was published in a school magazine. The interview became part of the social studies curriculum and was used to help students have a better understanding of the experience of recent immigrants to the United States. Later, it was included in an article about the use of oral history in high school and published in a social studies education journal.

To the best of my knowledge, David never learned about his accomplishments. Toward the end of the term, he started to skip school. I called him at home and he told me that he was having problems but he would try to come to class. Eventually he stopped attending school altogether. The next year I spotted David in the neighborhood with a group of drug abusers and he did not look well. I never saw him after that. David Santana was at risk as a student and in life, and I do not believe he made it.

Eric Larson was a tall, athletic, West Indian immigrant to the United States. In 11th-grade, he became involved in the school's political action club. Eric believed it was important for Black males to give positive leadership. He became a spokesperson for the club, attended a rally in Washington, D.C., testified at board of education hearings, appeared on a cable television talk show, and organized students to participate in activities when Nelson Mandela of South Africa visited New York City in 1990.

Eric was intelligent and outspoken, though he was not always responsible about tasks and time (after all, he was a teenager). We met with his guidance counselor and he was transferred into an honors class in the second half of 11th-grade.

Eric was an only child living with his mother and grandmother in an apartment on a stable block in a predominately working-class and poor community. One morning on his way to school, Eric was arrested when the police ran a drug enforcement sweep on his block. He was quickly released and no legal charges were ever made against him. However, the affair left Eric extremely bitter.

As the school year progressed, it became apparent that Eric was failing a number of courses. His soccer team coach and I both met with him and tried to keep Eric focused on school. Eventually, he passed all of his subjects and the coach was able to get him a summer job at a sleep-away camp out of the city. The next year he graduated from high school, joined the Navy, and moved away from the community for good. Eric Larson was at risk, but with strong support he was able to make it through a difficult school year and summer, graduate from high school, and get his life organized.

In neighborhoods like the one where David and Eric lived and went to school, every student is at risk. Daily life places them at risk of poverty, disease, drug abuse, pregnancy, criminality, and victimization. Herbert Kohl (1994) believes that these conditions contribute to resistance to learning by students who experience life and school as a series of irrational conditions, arbitrary demands, and injustices. In her book, *Framing Dropouts* (1991), Michelle Fine argues that many high schools use boredom, humiliation, and bureaucracy to drive these students out, and that dropping out of school is often the only choice that allows them to retain any sense of dignity. Strategies that are supposed to make students learn often only insure that they do not learn.

Deciding to resist learning or to drop out of school are only part of a series of complex and difficult choices that face these teenagers. The problem of redirecting teenagers goes far beyond the confines of a school. It is a problem of our society as a whole, how it is structured, and what kind of future it is prepared to offer young people. But despite the broader dimensions of the problems, it is my experience that teachers can affect the lives of their students.

I try to make it possible for students to enjoy learning by connecting topics with their lives, such as the oral history project David Santana completed with his grandfather. I do not mean just entertaining students. A lot of the pleasure people experience in learning comes when they master something that is difficult, something they did not think they were going to understand. Suddenly the world is less of a mystery, and they have a sense that they can control it.

For schools to be successful, teachers must establish communities where students have a sense of ownership, of relationship with adults and each other, of creating shared expectancies, and of democratic decision making. Our students are part of an unjust world in which they feel they have no control. They need fairness and a sense that they are respected and can make a difference. Eric Larson's role as an activist and his ability to give leadership to other students were crucial in sustaining him during a difficult period of his life.

One of the things I like best about school, when I was a youngster and as a teacher, is that in September you have a blank slate and can start all over again. No matter how poorly you performed in the past, you get another chance. Within the at risk student population there are teenagers who have decided they want direction. They want to learn. Their situation has changed and they want to try again. A boy becomes a little more mature and is not so quick to lose his temper. A girl is scared by her sister's pregnancy or drug addiction. A teenager gets a part-time job and begins to have a sense of possibility. Parents get their lives together so home is stabilized. In whatever way, and for whatever reason, a student decides to shoot for something more in life. If teachers create structured, motivating learning communities, these young people have a chance.

As a teacher, I expect to be treated like a human being, and I try to treat my students as human beings also. But I realize that they are teenagers and that they frequently live under very difficult and disorganized circumstances. One of my primary battles is to provide some structure for their lives. Whatever reason that they come to school, I expect them to work and learn. When necessary, I provide pencil, pens, and paper. I show them how to organize their notebooks. I meet with guidance counselors and I call homes, both to speak with parents about potential problems and to report advances and achievements. I visit homes when necessary. When students run foul of the dean, I go down to the dean's office and speak up for them. I mediate disputes with other teachers, write references for court appearances, and refer students to social service agencies. I want to win a future for every one of my students, although I realize I cannot. But the only way I can support students who are ready for my help is to try to support everyone.

* * *

JOIN THE CONVERSATION—AT-RISK STUDENTS

Questions to Consider:

1. I believe that in neighborhoods like the one where David and Eric lived and went to school, every student is at risk. Do you agree with this statement? Would you extend it to every teenager? Explain.

2. I feel that the only way I can reach students who are ready to be helped is to try to reach everyone. This can be a tremendous emotional drain on a teacher. In your view, is it fair to ask teachers to make this commitment? Why?

SECTION D: WHY DID PEOPLE DIE AT COLUMBINE?

I attended an elite public high school during the 1960s where I felt pretty much like a misplaced piece of furniture. I had passed the stiff admissions test, but the school was set up for the privileged few, and the rest of us received little support or attention.

At school, I had a group of friends who could fairly be described as weird. Where possible, we sat in the back of rooms and tried to remain anonymous. During our free time we read and discussed science fiction and fantasy novels. Our particular favorite was Doc Savage and we imagined joining his band of superheroes.

For three alienating years, we listened to dark and heavy music such as the Doors, the Animals, and the Stones; experimented with alcohol and hallucinogenic drugs; and dreamed of having girlfriends. At one point we organized our own mythic religion, which we called Zo'olium, and we discussed building a rocket ship in shop class and blowing up the school.

We did not want to hurt anybody, but we did want to do away with a hated place that we experienced as a prison.

My friends and I were pretty serious about some of our fantasies. After graduation, two of us spent the summer searching for Bigfoot in the Pacific Northwest and the following year three of us traipsed through the Andes and along the Amazon River in South America. Our parents were deeply worried about our behavior, our sullen demeanor, and our use of drugs, but there was little they could do to change things. Mostly they just hung on to tenuous relationships, hoping we would grow up before we hurt ourselves or ruined our lives. I have lost track of most of the guys from Zo'olium, but from what I have heard, they have generally done all right with their lives. A couple of them are engineers, one is a restaurateur, one is an astronomer, one is a postal worker and part-time author, and I am a teacher.

I think about my friends and our high school experiences whenever I hear about another new case of school or teenage violence. I suspect that many other adults have also been rethinking their pasts as a result of the shooting deaths at places like Columbine High School in Littleton, Colorado. What I have tried to figure out is what was different then, and why we did not take the same destructive path.

Many commentators have called for increased vigilance by school authorities to target suspect youth before they have a chance to injure themselves or others. Sometimes this profiling would be coupled with psychological support services, but usually it just means keeping an eye on teenagers that people find "too different" because of their appearance, music, or ideas. Some have suggested that the solution to this type of violence is increased school security. They want teachers and principals to have the power to search and suspend students, metal detectors installed at entrances, and police officers assigned to buildings.

These proposals share three things in common: They are premised on the idea that alienated young people are somehow different from the rest of us and do not deserve our concern; they violate fundamental democratic rights that are cherished in our society such as freedom of speech, the right to due process, and the right to privacy; and they generally ignore why those two young men at Columbine High School were able to kill and injure so many other people and then to kill themselves.

As I think back on the past and my friends, what emerges most clearly is that our culture has changed. Today, we live in a culture that glorifies violence in sports and the movies and where the evening news celebrates the death of others through hygienic strategic bombings. It is a society that promotes the need for instant gratification and uses youthful alienation to sell products, where those who do not fit in are ignored, where schools still rank and sort out young people and brand them as failures. And we live in a country where unhappy people have easy access to plans to make bombs on the Internet and can purchase weapons of immense destructive capacity.

Although I do not absolve them of responsibility for their actions, there is more to blame for what happened in Columbine than those two young men. I can only think of two solutions that would help prevent future violent explosions like this one. As a former high school teacher, I am convinced that if these young men had had a place where they felt they belonged, where people cared about them, they might not have committed those violent acts against others.

But even more crucially, if our country had strict gun control laws, no one would have died in the incident at Columbine. When I was in high school, we were weird and we were alienated, but we did not have guns.

FIG. 9.2   Resolving a conflict between students before it escalates.

Building classroom community and supporting students requires mediating conflicts between students before they escalate. One approach is to help students view the conflict from the perspective of other people who are involved. Before students sit down to "talk it out," it may be helpful to have them complete the following report.

List the participants in this conflict: _____

_____

What was the immediate cause of the conflict?_____

_____

_____

Do you know the underlying causes of the conflict? If so, what were they? _____

_____

_____

Describe what happened from your perspective. _____

_____

_____

How do you think the other person or people view what happened? _____

_____

_____

What choices did you make that escalated the conflict? _____

_____

_____

What could you have done differently before the conflict?_____

_____

_____

What could you have done differently at the time of the conflict? _____

_____

In your view, how would these different courses of action have shaped the conflict? _____

_____

_____

In your view, what should be the result of the conflict? Explain. _____

_____

_____

JOIN THE CONVERSATION—DEALING WITH VIOLENCE IN SCHOOLS

Questions to Consider:

1. In your view, what is the relationship between adolescent acts of violence and violence in the broader society? Explain.

2. In your view, how are you similar to or different from the young people who have committed violent acts?

3. Do you think you and your friends could have been capable of violent behavior toward people or property while in high school? Explain.

4. In your opinion, would programs like the one described earlier help to prevent violent eruptions in schools? Explain.

SECTION E: HOW SHOULD SCHOOLS DEAL WITH TRAGIC EVENTS?

In the aftermath of the destruction of the World Trade Center in New York City in September 2001, there was widespread discussion of how to support children who lost family members or were upset by events. Many school districts had decided that the best policy was not to discuss the events, even after some students had witnessed the explosions from their classroom windows. Maureen Murphy, S. Maxwell Hines, and I encouraged teachers from the New Teachers Network to give students an opportunity to voice their concerns and fears in class in a supportive environment with peers and adults that they knew and trusted. Otherwise, the option for many students was to learn about what was happening from rumors circulating around the building or from friends after school. Most leading psychologists agreed with confronting events openly, that it is a mistake to try to protect children by avoiding discussion.

The National Education Association in conjunction with the American Federation of Teachers, the National PTA, and the National Association of School Psychologists circulated a list of recommendations for parents, teachers, and caring adults, which we support. Although it primarily addresses the needs of younger children, its approach is definitely appropriate for adolescents as well. The list included the following recommendations:

- Model calm and compassionate behavior and remind children how much we love and care about them.

- Establish routines that provide structure and comfort in daily life—have dinner together, read a bedtime story together, and help with homework.

- Jumpstart a conversation with a question, share your feelings, and be a good listener. Ask what they know and how they are feeling. Allowing children to voice their views provides a greater sense of control over their environment.

- Observe and be responsive to children's emotional state. Be prepared for some regressive behavior and "acting out." Children will express their emotions differently. Provide time for writing, drawing, and other ways to express feelings.

- Design a family or school activity that involves children in helping others.

- Tell children the truth. Grieving is natural and the process should be acknowledged and shared.

JOIN THE CONVERSATION—ADDRESSING TRAGEDY

Question to Consider:

Should teachers give students an opportunity to voice their concerns and fears about tragic events such as the destruction of the World Trade Center in New York City or the 1995 Oklahoma City bombing of a federal office building? Explain.

SECTION F: WHAT KIND OF SUPPORT DO TEACHERS NEED?

Teachers Need Support, Too: The New Teachers Networks' Response to the Amadou Diallo Case
By S. Maxwell Hines, Maureen Murphy, Alan Singer, and Sandra Stacki

Many of the essays in this book are biographical sketches by young teachers who are members of the Hofstra University New Teachers Network. The network is a School of Education alumni group that builds on trusting relationships developed between teachers and between teachers and university faculty during preservice teacher education programs. These relationships are maintained through faculty visits to secondary school classrooms; participation by new teachers in School of Education classes; and as hosts for participant-observers from the preservice teacher education program, peer mentoring by more experienced classroom teachers, regular support meetings, network-sponsored conferences, e-mail contact, and involvement in professional activities. The network offers new teachers the opportunity to be part of a supportive community where they are valued as resources and partners rather than employees, clients or students. S. Maxwell Hines, Maureen Murphy, Alan Singer, and Sandra Stacki are the Hofstra University New Teachers Network faculty advisors. A version of this section was published in the December 2002 issue of Phi Delta Kappan magazine.—Alan Singer

On Friday, February 25, 2000, four White New York City police officers charged with the wrongful death of an African immigrant to the city were acquitted of all charges at a widely followed trial. That evening, three participants in the Hofstra University New Teachers Network circulated, via the network's 100-member e-mail list, a proposal for responding to racial violence and the jury verdict in their classrooms.

By Monday night, 13 teachers had replied with ideas for proceeding. One teacher submitted a lesson plan downloaded from *The New York Times* Web page. Another copied, pasted, and sent out news releases and editorials to use to open class discussion. Many New Teachers Network members expressed their own hopes or frustrations as they collectively tried to grapple with the difficult issues of racism, injustices in the judicial system, and police brutality.

One White woman teaching at a suburban ethnic minority middle school wrote:

> I had my kids write journals today about their reaction to the verdict. My problem and/or question is: Many students were taking sides based on race and not the facts of the case and were VERY influenced by reactions at home. Some students did not want to discuss it at all because (and this is my own guess) they are getting opinions at home that may not be appropriate for school discussion. Whatever people say, RACE is a REAL issue for my students where the black vs. white line is VERY much there. How do I deal with this?

FIG. 9.3   Remembering Amadou Diallo.

How should teachers talk with students, particularly African American, Caribbean, and Latino students, but also White students, about the acquittal of four police officers in the murder of Amadou Diallo? Clearly, teachers must let students speak. But what else? What can come from the discussion that is constructive?

Should students simply vent or learn that they must be careful when approached by police officers? We believe one way to remember Amadou Diallo and to work for change is to use his death as a symbol to help organize against injustice.

According to *The New York Times,* 62.7% of all people stopped by the New York City Police Department's Street Crime Unit in "stop-and-frisk" operations are Black and 16 Black people are stopped for every Black person who is arrested.[1]

We suggest that for the next 3 months, students create a log and write up descriptions of all interactions they, their family members, and their friends have with members of the police department—both positive and negative. If possible, they should include in their logs the ethnicity, gender, and age of both the person stopped and the police officer.

At the end of 3 months we can correlate our results, write a report, and send it to the New York State Attorney General's office, the Attorney General of the United States, and the press. What do you think?

[1]Dan Barry, "One Legacy of a 41-Bullet Barrage Is a Hard Look at Aggressive Tactics on the Street," *The New York Times,* February 27, 2000, p. 42.

An African American woman working in an urban high school responded: "I have been crying since the verdict. I have experienced being stopped for no reason by a red-faced police officer who, when he realized I was a woman, told me to drive on. I knew he was going to kick some poor Black person's behind before the night was out. But who would believe me if I reported this?

"You asked what students could do in a situation like Diallo's. Students should speak to their government representatives. They should meet with the police captains in their neighborhoods and make alliances with good police officers. They should ask for neighborhood policing with regular patrol officers who would know their names and the people and the feel of the community. Students should be encouraged to help the officers when they can by letting them know of people who would turn our neighborhoods into cesspools. I am not minimizing the difficulty of doing any of the suggestions. But it can be done. It must be done."

The e-mail dialogue continued for 2 weeks and eventually revealed sharply different views about race in American society among New Teachers Network members. In one interchange, a white woman teaching in a suburban ethnic minority community wrote:

Let me state for the record that I am not in any way justifying the police officers in the Diallo shooting or in any recent case of wrongful shooting. But I need to vent. I am so tired of listening to the news and reading the paper and hearing the excuse of racism. Is it really that bad? Yes, those police officers made mistakes and should be punished in some way. Yes, Black men are profiled the most. But don't most violent crimes occur in Black and Hispanic communities?

We all have been abused and treated unjustly at some point in our history. Its time to stop making excuses and treat everyone equally. I don't remember people making excuses for me and my fellow classmates when I was in school. I survived. I carried all of my heavy textbooks to school, I did my homework every night, and I studied for my tests, and NO way in this world did I grow up in a "Brady Bunch" family. If we keep using racism as an excuse, we are only hindering other groups from moving forward. Can we ignore it? No, it does exist. But it is becoming the excuse for everything these days. It is time to move forward. We've beaten this thing to death. I'm sure I'll get some responses from this one ... but you know what ... I'm sure there's more than just me out there that's tired of all this.

An African American woman teaching in a suburban alternative high school, who was an undergraduate student in the program with this woman, wrote back:

As history teachers can you please tell me when a police state has been successful? I am a black mother of a black boy. You do not know the fear that I have to deal with. Just because my son may be "walking while Black" he is targeted. Having a loved one who is in the NYPD has given me insight into how the New York City Police Department is divided—even the locker rooms are segregated. Please explain to me how they are supposed to protect and serve? We are talking about individuals who grew up outside of the city and telling them to protect areas that they are not the least bit familiar with. Not just Black, but Jewish, Spanish, Muslims and Italian areas where the culture, language, and lifestyle is very different. My friend told me that some white cops are so scared that they carry two and three guns. When is this going to stop? Combating racism should not divide teachers, but unite us so we can avoid this happening in the future. I am sorry, I cannot act like nothing has happened.

To answer her question, yes, it really is that bad. When someone cannot walk down the street without worrying about being killed by the "good guys"—yes, it is that bad. When people believe that the end justifies the means—yes, it is that bad. When people question the victim—yes, it is that bad. Have you ever really feared for your life from the "good guys"? Ask any Black man walking down the street, and he will tell you—yes, it is that bad. It has nothing to do with socio-economic status, it has to do with race. Please, let's not run from the truth. I am tired of race being a factor in the death of my people. I will talk about it and fight against it so my son will not be next.

Although response to the Diallo verdict was more dramatic and personal than most e-mail interchanges and discussions at network meetings, we believe it is indicative of the way that the New Teachers Network provides support and professional development for new teachers as they address difficult issues in their classrooms.

Members of the New Teachers Network report that participation supports their ability to teach in troubled urban and suburban minority schools. It helps them overcome their inexperience and sense of isolation so they can affect the lives of young people. A statement prepared by one of the teachers for the network's annual conference indicates the influence programs like the New Teachers Network can have on the life and pedagogical practice of new teachers and their students.

I began attending New Teacher Network meetings during my first year of teaching. I was teaching 6th and 7th grade science in a New York City middle school even though my certification area was social studies. I am currently in my fourth year of teaching and I continue to attend Saturday morning network meetings on a regular basis. My fiancee, who is also a teacher, often wonders what happens at the meetings to keep me attending so religiously. The best way for me to answer this question is to describe how I feel when I leave a network meeting.

We all know how happy we feel on Friday afternoon when that last bell rings and it's time to go home. I'm no different. I often stay late at work, but rarely on Fridays after a long and tiring week dealing with 8th grade hormones and their endless stores of energy. I struggle to get myself out of bed on Saturday morning, but once I grab my coffee and I'm on my way my mind starts to roll. I imagine the conversations that will take place and I begin to think of questions or concerns I want to bring up. I know that whatever professional concerns are on my mind, I'll be able to talk about them there. The dynamic of the group is electric. I never feel so much like a professional as I do when I'm there. We're all there to help each other. Sometimes the topics are focused on classroom management, sometimes on how to deal with supervisors or colleagues who do not share a similar teaching philosophy and sometimes on new lesson or project ideas. No matter what, we always share our love for being with the kids. Throughout the meetings, I sit and write down all the new ideas I'm getting, either as suggestions from others or ideas that I thought up as a natural progression from our discussion. When I leave the meeting I am rejuvenated. I rush home and begin planning out all these new activities.

The network keeps the pleasure I feel when I teach fresh, and listening to the concerns and problems of the newer teachers keeps me grounded in reality. I hear that many teachers burn out in their first five years, but I am going just as strong as I was the day I started. I'm sure it's because I have a group of people to talk to, listen to, bounce ideas off of and to give me support.

Yes, teachers need support, too.

JOIN THE CONVERSATION—THE NEW TEACHERS NETWORK

Questions to Consider:

1. Is "race" such a sharp point of division in your community? Explain.
2. During the e-mail exchange, people responded to each other harshly. Under the circumstances, why do you think people remained involved in the dialogue and in the network?
3. As a new teacher, if you have the opportunity, will you become involved in a group like the New Teachers Network? Explain.

REFERENCES AND SUGGESTIONS FOR FURTHER READING

The Alan Guttmacher Institute. (1999). *Teen sex and pregnancy.* New York: Author.

American Academy of Pediatrics. (1999). Adolescent pregnancy: Current trends and issues: 1998 (RE9828). *Pediatrics, 103*(2), 516–520.

Berne, L., & Huberman, B. (1999). *European approaches to adolescent sexual behavior and responsibility.* Washington, DC: Advocates for Youth.

Borland, H. (1972). *When the legends die.* New York: Bantam Doubleday.

Davidson, A. L. (1996). *Making and molding identity in schools: Student narratives on race, gender, and academic achievement.* Albany: State University of New York Press.

Donohue, E., Schiraldi, V., & Ziedenberg, J. (1998). *School house hype: The school shootings, and the real risks kids face in America.* Washington, DC: The Justice Policy Institute.

Dorris, M. (1988). *A yellow raft in blue water.* New York: Warner Books.

Fine, M. (1991). *Framing dropouts: Notes on the politics of an urban public high school.* Albany, NY: State University of New York Press.

Kesson, K., & Oyler, C. (1999). Integrated curriculum and service learning: Linking school-based knowledge and social action. *English Education, 31*(2), 135–149.

Kohl, H. (1994). *I won't learn from you and other thoughts on creative maladjustment.* New York: New Press.

Lowry, L. (1993). *The giver.* Boston, MA: Houghton Mifflin.

Monette, P. (1992). *Becoming a man: Half a life story.* New York: Harcourt Brace Jovanovich.

Rawlings, M. (1961). *The yearling.* New York: Scribner.

Richter, C. (1994). *The light in the forest.* New York: Random House.

Speare, E. (1991). *The witch of Blackbird Pond.* Bantam Doubleday.

Szekeres, G. (1999). HIV/AIDS in adolescence [Year-end special edition]. *Bulletin of Experimental Treatment for AIDS.* (http://www.sfaf.org/treatment/beta/b42/b42adolescence.html).

Twain, M. (1983). *Adventures of Tom Sawyer.* New York: Penguin.

10

STRUGGLE: HOW CAN WE STRUGGLE TO BE MORE EFFECTIVE TEACHERS AND BUILD BETTER SCHOOLS?

Frederick Douglass, born a slave in Maryland in 1817, escaped to freedom as a young man and became an abolitionist, author, orator, U.S. government official, and an international spokesperson for human rights. In a letter written in 1849, Douglass argued, "The whole history of the progress of human liberty shows that all concessions yet made to her august claims have been born of earnest struggle. . . . If there is no struggle, there is no progress" (Seldes, 1966, p. 214).

Margaret Mead was a path-breaking anthropologist who argued that scientists had to understand traditional cultures on their own terms, rather than measure them against supposedly more advanced civilizations. Mead is credited with the statement: "Never doubt that a small group of thoughtful, committed citizens can change the world; indeed, it's the only thing that ever does."

The quotes from Douglass and Mead have become the unofficial maxims of the Hofstra New Teachers Network as we struggle to become more effective teachers, build better schools, and have an impact on and influence the lives of our students. As a teacher, you will be involved in multiple struggles throughout your career. Some of these struggles are personal ones as you grapple with adult and professional responsibilities and define your goals and practice as a teacher. You will need to learn how to struggle with and for your students and to function as an ally and occasional prod to colleagues. You will have to decide whether to support or question union leadership and school systems, communities, and a society that do not always value and invest in the education of young people.

In chapter 5, I introduced you to Thomas Gradgrind, an industrialist who is the headmaster of a school in Charles Dickens's *Hard Times* (1854/1973). The book opens with Gradgrind explaining his philosophy of education. "Now, what I want is, Facts. Teach these boys and girls nothing but Facts. Facts alone are wanted in life. Plant nothing else, and root out everything else. You can only form the minds of reasoning animals upon Facts: nothing else will ever be of any service to them. This is the principle on which I bring up my children, and this is the principle on which I bring up these children. Stick to Facts, sir!" (p. 47).

Dickens's purpose in the book is to satirize Gradgrind and expose the dreary schools and factories where children and workers were reduced to interchangeable numbers and virtually enslaved to machinery. Charlie Chaplin's movie *Modern Times* (1936) has a similar image of work in industrialized society.

The scariest thing about Gradgrind's school is how closely the caricature resembles the reality of that day. According to historian David Craig, "The first two chapters of the novel are an almost straight copy of the teaching system in schools run by the two societies for educating the poor. In the Manchester Lancasterian School a thousand children were taught in one huge room, controlled by a kind of military drill with monitors and a monitor-general. . . . Groups of facts, mechanically classified, were drummed in by methods that might have been meant to squash forever the children's urge to find out or understand anything for themselves" (Dickens, 1973, p. 22).

This "mechanical system of education" was developed by John Lancaster who also provided an "elaborate code of rewards and punishments" including " 'the log', a piece of wood weighing four to six pounds, which was fixed to the neck of the child guilty of his (or her) first talking offence. . . . More serious offences found their appropriate punishment in the Lancasterian code; handcuffs, the 'caravan,' the pillory and stocks, and 'the cage.' The latter was a sack or basket in which more serious offenders were suspended from the ceiling" (Dickens, 1973, p. 23). British public opinion solidly approved of this system, which was discussed and praised in the British House of Commons and in academic journals. However, Craig also cited a school inspector who complained that the "elaborate methods for destroying meaning" caused the children's "faculties" to be "stunted in their growth, and they sink into inert listlessness."

Despite these horrific images, the Lancaster–Gradgrind approach to pedagogy remains with us today. Although it continues to be satirized, for example, in the movie *Ferris Bueller's Day Off* (1986), it is also championed by prominent educators such as William Bennett (Bennett, Finn, & Cribb, 1996), Chester Finn and Diane Ravitch (1987), and E. D. Hirsch (1987, 1996). They have written widely promoting lists of facts to be memorized by children at different age levels and in different grades and have received government support for their proposals. In one of her books, Ravitch (2000) launched a savage assault on "progressive education" and the Deweyian movement to educate children for understanding and participation in democratic society.

One argument for the Lancaster–Gradgrind approach to teaching (especially in schools for youth from immigrant, non-English-speaking, working-class, and poor families) is that the supposed ends—cultural literacy, higher scores on standardized exams, and better behaved children—justify the means—oppressive classrooms and the rote learning of decontextualized information.

It is difficult to respond to their claims to a miracle cure for what ails education other than by saying that, based on my experience as a student and classroom teacher, I know it will not work. The French philosopher Albert Camus (1956/1991) offers a more intellectual way of looking at "reforms" that ignore means in the name of a higher good, a utopian ideal that will be achieved in the future. Camus argues that ends can never be known in advance, so suspension of judgment on means is never justified. In fact, the means that we experience are the only things we can evaluate.

I truly believe there is no magic pill that will make you a better teacher or simple solution that will improve education and our schools. Being an effective teacher means engaging in a long-term struggle to convince students that your goals for the class make sense and are worth examining and that your means (your approach to teaching or pedagogy) will treat them with dignity as thinking human beings and feeling members of a classroom community. As a concluding chapter, this chapter on struggle discusses the politics of education (e.g., standards debates), schools we want, and how teachers can be involved in building them. It concludes with an essay that discusses support groups, professional organizations, and site-based management teams. It includes an essay on student teaching and excerpts from a student teacher's reflective journal.

JOIN THE CONVERSATION—SCRIPTED LEARNING

David Craig presents a "model dialogue" between a monitor and student from an 1840s training manual. I find it eerily reminiscent of contemporary scripted learning programs that are supposed to "teacher-proof" classroom instruction and provide easier means for assessing student learning (Dickens, 1973, p. 22).

Monitor: What have you been reading about?

Boy: Ruminating animals.

Monitor: Another name for ruminating?

Boy: Cud-chewing.

Monitor: What is the root of the word?

Boy: Rumen, the cud.

Monitor: You read in the lesson the enamel is disposed in crescent-shaped ridges. What is the enamel?

Boy: The hard, shining part of the tooth.

Monitor: What part of the tooth is it?

Boy: The covering of that part that is out of the jawbone.

Monitor: What do you mean by disposed?

Boy: Placed.

Monitor: The root?

Boy: Pono, I place.

Questions to Consider:

1. How does the "boy" demonstrate what he has learned? What is missing from his education?
2. Scripted learning programs such as "Success for All" have been developed and promoted by major institutions and scholars such as Robert Slavin of John Hopkins University. They have been endorsed by school systems that see them as solutions to the problem of boosting scores on standardized exams in poor communities. Their proposals have been sharply debated in educational magazines such as *Phi Delta Kappan* (Pogrow, 2000; Slavin & Madden, 2000; Slavin, Madden, Dolan, Wasik, Ross, et al., 1994). Do you think these programs have value? Would you want to teach in a school that used this kind of model for teaching? If you had children, would you want them in schools using this type of program? Explain your views.

SECTION A: WHAT SHOULD YOU THINK ABOUT AS YOU PREPARE TO STUDENT TEACH OR START YOUR FIRST TEACHING POSITION?

Some of you will find these suggestions a little silly, especially if you are a second-career teacher or someone who has significant work experience. However, I know that when I was in my early 20s these were very real issues for me as I struggled to figure out what it meant to be a responsible adult, worker, and professional.

General Things to Think About

1. Why you want to be a teacher.
2. Your long-term career goals.
3. Things you liked as a student.
4. Things you did not like as a student.
5. What it means to be "in charge."
6. Why you are taking student teaching (or becoming a teacher).
7. How you can experiment with different ways to teach.
8. How you can experiment with being a different "you."
9. What it means to be a responsible worker.
10. What it means to be a responsible adult.
11. What it means to be a professional teacher.
12. How you want to be related to your colleagues, your students, your supervisors, the community.

Being Prepared for Work

1. How will I get up in the morning?
2. What will I wear?
3. How will I travel?
4. What materials will I need?
5. What will I need to learn?
6. When will I prepare?
7. How will I schedule my time at the school?
8. How will I get my own class work completed?
9. What is the layout of the school?
10. Who "carries clout" at the school—principal, assistant principal, superintendent, chairperson, school board, parents, colleagues, union, guidance counselor, dean?
11. When will I eat lunch? What will I eat?
12. What is available in the library? the AV? the computer center?

Preparing to Observe a Class and Teacher

1. Whom will I observe?
2. When will I observe?
3. Where do they want me to sit?
4. Do they want me to participate in any way?
5. What should I look for?
6. What is the teacher doing?
7. What are the students doing?
8. Are the teacher and the students having the "same" lesson?
9. What are the goals of the lesson?
10. Are the goals being achieved? How?
11. Do I want to teach this kind of lesson?

About the Students and Their Families

1. Who are the students—academically and by ethnicity and social class?
2. What is the community like?
3. Are students and staff from similar or different backgrounds? Is this a problem?
4. Are parents involved in the school? How?
5. Does the school have established procedures for contacting families?
6. Who are the resource people who can help you learn more about students?

Preparing to Teach

1. When will I begin to teach?
2. How many classes will I teach?
3. What will I teach?
4. What are my responsibilities for the class?
5. How much freedom to experiment do I have?
6. Do I know the "stuff"?
7. How can I best prepare lessons?
8. Where can I get help?
9. What should I do if I am unhappy in my "situation"?
10. What should I do if I disagree with my supervisor?

JOIN THE CONVERSATION—PREPARING TO TEACH

Question to Consider:

What are your concerns about yourself as you prepare to student teach or begin your first job as a teacher?

SECTION B: WHAT WILL STUDENT TEACHING BE LIKE?

Many of the best veteran teachers I know cannot sleep the night before the first day of school. Their minds race with ideas and they worry whether they will be able to engage a new group of students. Part of the problem is that teachers keep getting older while students remain the same age. Usually, but not always, their anxiety eases after the first day. One trick that helps me get some rest is to keep a note pad by my bedside so I can write myself "urgent" messages.

Student teachers and new teachers, who do not have the knowledge that they have done it all before, are often plagued with apprehension, even when they are very good. Some stop eating, whereas others cannot stop. No matter how much I or one of the other field supervisors reassures them of their ability, they remain tense. In my experience, two things have aided them as they work through their nervousness—discussions with peers in seminars or teaching networks and keeping a journal. Both are vital elements of reflective practice.

I was never a big journal writer, but some student teachers find it helps them focus on what actually happened in their classes. They can vent their frustrations with individual students, whole classes, cooperating teachers and supervisors, the "system," or the world.

They can also rethink their practice, decide on new strategies, engage in dialogues with authors, and enter debates over educational ideas.

The journal that follows was kept by Dawn Brigante for a reflective practice seminar while she was an English student teacher (supervised by Maureen Murphy). Dawn expressed many insecurities about her performance in the journal, but an inner strength allowed her to share them with other student teachers in the class and with this broader audience. In the journal entries reproduced here, Dawn compares her own experience and ideas with the ideas and experiences of authors she read in the teacher education program. The journal has been edited to remove some personal references; however, Dawn and I believe it remains true to the spirit of the original document.

A Student Teacher's Journey
By Dawn Brigante

Journal Entry 1: I am having a lot of doubts.

Rereading Linda Christensen's "Building Community from Chaos" now that I am a student teacher, I can relate a lot easier to what she has to say. My first placement is in a racially and ethnically diverse middle school, and I am becoming more aware that some of the students in my classes have different needs than others, like the ones I grew up with in my segregated, white, middle-class community. I hear teachers talk about the "baggage" kids carry to school with them, and I am definitely beginning to see it for myself. But I won't use this an excuse to give up on my students.

I am starting to understand how Linda feels when she goes into a classroom expecting to accomplish specific academic goals and is not being able to achieve any of them. Like Linda, I am learning that content must sometimes take a back seat to children's needs. This isn't a bad thing, especially when it creates a "teachable moment" in class. Reaching students is more important to me than insisting that the class strictly adhere to the day's agenda.

I strongly believe teachers must provide students with opportunities to talk about the anger and sadness in their lives. Often it is considered unacceptable to express feelings such as sadness, depression and anger in school. That is how students learn to bottle-up their emotions, but they can only bottle them up for so long before they explode. Teachers and students should work together to design curricula and choose literature to read based on the interests of students.

When I have my own classroom, I hope to use Linda's suggestions for breaking down walls and stereotypes among students and creating classroom communities. It is important that students talk to one another. Many think they know everything they need to know about their peers: whose parents are divorced, who has no parents, who hangs out with the "wrong" crowd. They think that their first judgment is the final word. But when they get to really know others, when they find out that everyone has his or her own story, that everyone feels pain, and experiences hardships and joys, they will think twice before doing anything hurtful or selfish.

I like Linda's idea of having older students teach lessons to elementary school children. The opportunity to act as role models provides positive experiences for the teenagers and for the younger students. Having high school students rewrite children's books is a good way for students to express their understanding of the world, a world in which happy endings are not handed out on a silver platter; they must be struggled for and sometimes they never occur.

I particularly responded to Linda's ideas because right now I feel as if I am a kid teaching kids. I know right from wrong well enough, but that does not mean that I do the right thing all of the time. On Friday, I cursed while talking to a student, and I don't know if I have lost or gained ground with him (maybe a little of both). I wonder if I have the right to say to kids, "Hey, listen to me because I am your teacher, and I will teach you right from wrong." Who am I to assume that position? I am probably more confused than most of my students.

I am having a lot of doubts about teaching lately. I am unsure as to whether this is for me. However, I have decided not to make any decisions about the future until after the semester is over.

Journal Entry 2: Where do teachers begin?

When I began reading Herbert Kohl's *I Won't Learn From You*, I did not understand what "willed not learning" meant. I had read Kohl in the past, but I was unable to relate to what he was saying about the way certain students felt about school. It was not until recently that I began to understand the implications of his ideas.

When Kohl talks about students who choose not to learn because of their life experience or experiences in school with stereotypical, racist, or chauvinist curriculum and materials, he is taking the blame for failure off of the students. He makes it the teacher's job to find solutions. I never really thought much about this before. As a high school and college student, I believed people didn't learn because they had a lower ability level or because they gave in to peer pressure; it never was and probably still is not cool to be too smart.

Recently I came face-to-face with an example of willed not learning. I met a young man in one of the classes I was observing who did nothing all period long, day in and day out. He was not motivated by anything related to school or school work. The only thing that interested him was dramatic performances. He was eager to play any character, eager to be someone he was not, even if only for a moment. It was very difficult for me to understand how he could be so unmotivated and lifeless one moment and eager to perform the next.

After observing him for a while, I noticed that this boy was extremely intelligent. When we could get him to take the tests, he easily got better test grades than those who had participated and studied. I asked some of his other teachers about him and found out that he did nothing in any of his classes, but they also thought he was very intelligent. One teacher told me that he had been through some kind of terrible tragedy more than a year before and that he had become unresponsive as a result. I could not understand why none of them had bothered to find out what the problem was and why no one was attempting to break through his wall. I tried to reach out to him the best way that I could. Although he was not my student, I remarked on how intelligent he was and told him he could do anything he tried, but that he had to try first. I did not accept blank test sheets when he handed them in. I gave them back to him and told him to make educated guesses. I could not change his life, but I tried to change his experiences for a few moments at a time.

The questions I am left with for Kohl are "How does a teacher find out why a student has chosen not to learn?" and "Where do we, as teachers, begin?" I don't know if this young man's case would be considered "willed not learning" in Kohl's eyes because his problem is not with the curriculum or the materials, but with himself and his reality. Maybe he feels as if he has been through enough and cannot deal with the trivialities of the day-to-day school routine. Maybe he feels alone, so he has turned off completely. I do not know where the root of the problem lies; I only know that I would never allow a student to choose to fail without doing everything in my ability to bring him or her back.

I have decided that I can only be a teacher if I have the opportunity to truly help my students. I want to work with the students that Kohl talks about because I believe that I am capable of getting through to them. I am sure that there is a lot of work involved with Kohl's ideas for restructuring a class, but it is the kind of work teachers must be willing to do if they are teaching students and not simply content.

Journal Entry 3: Say yes to students.

Of all the books I read during my short "career" as an education student, none had quite the impact that Judy Logan's *Teaching Stories* had on me. As a middle school English teacher, I can completely relate to Judy's classroom and her approach to teaching, and I appreciate the candor with which she deals with the critical issues that confront adolescents and their teachers. Since completing the book, I have begun to think long and hard about the individual needs of my students and the ways a teacher can reach each one of them.

One of the most important things I learned from Judy Logan is to say "yes" to students. Sometimes saying "yes" will be hard, but if I really want to make a difference and to make education relevant, I must take the risk. It will mean learning to loosen the reins and letting students pursue avenues that interest them.

As a student teacher, I do not really control what is happening in the classroom, though when my cooperating teacher said a class was mine, I tried to make decisions I thought were right. On several occasions, students came to me with alternative ideas for assignments. I knew the only way I could empower them was to say "Do it your way," but I was afraid my cooperating teacher would feel I used poor judgment. I decided to say "yes" anyway, but kept it a secret between us. When they handed in their work, I was very pleased with the results.

Recently I began a unit on how to write research papers, a subject that usually is a drag for students and teachers. After reading Judy Logan's piece about her Woman's History Quilt Project, I decided that papers should be about a famous woman in American history. I excluded contemporary pop culture personalities and some students were disappointed with this limitation. As I went around the classroom to help them decide on people, several students asked if I would allow them to do musicians such as Courtney Love, Mariah Carey, Selena, and Janis Joplin. I hesitated at first, but I heard Judy Logan's voice inside my head saying "Yes! Yes!" and I answered with a resounding, "Yes!!!" I detected a look of disappointment on my cooperating teacher's face, but I did not let it change my decision. I asked myself what the goal was for this unit. My goal was to teach students how to write a research paper, and if they could learn that while writing about someone they were interested in, then I had done my part. I'm not here to make education a drag for kids.

I also want my students to learn that there are strong women who are not written about in the history books and encyclopedias. In conjunction with the research paper assignment, I had them write about a positive female role model from their everyday lives. Many of them wrote about their mothers, family friends, and teachers, people who have had a profound influence in their lives. I think it was a good opportunity for students to see how much women do and are capable of doing.

Emily Styles' metaphor of curriculum as a window and mirror is a lot like Judy Logan's approach to teaching and an important idea for new teachers to consider. Styles believes that students should be able to see themselves mirrored in the content of the curriculum, and they should also be able to look through the windows of curriculum to see other people's stories. I think students who are given the opportunity to tell their own stories will be better listeners to the stories told by other people. Empowering students to talk with and to listen to one another is one of the first steps to creating a democratic, liberating dialogue in the classroom. When students believe that their voices are worth hearing, they will speak loudly and clearly and more often. This is one of the major goals I have for my classroom and my students. I want to provide students with a forum that frees them from the restrictions that bind them and so they can begin telling their own stories. I thank Judy Logan for showing me how it can be done.

Journal Entry 4: I wondered if everything I had learned was a waste.

When I began student teaching, I believed on faith that experiential learning was the best way for a student to experience education. I believed that every lesson had to be hands-on and if I could not find an engaging way to teach something, I was a failure. But as my student teaching experience progressed, I kept asking myself, "Are my students really learning?" I constantly wondered if students in an experiential classroom are short-changed. Maybe these students need a teacher to get up in front of the room and say, "You need to know this . . ." or "This means this . . ." I began to doubt myself more and more as I heard veteran teachers refer to experiential classrooms as "cut and paste" classrooms. I wondered if everything I had learned to that point was a waste. When I read John Dewey's *Experience and Education*, I was relieved to see he was addressing some of my questions. Dewey discusses the "problem of discovering the connection which actually exists within experience between the achievements of the past and the issues of the present."

While Dewey raises points worth considering, his writing was very difficult to get through and I was left unsatisfied. I was waiting anxiously for him to provide me with the answers. What I now realize is that experiential learning means that teachers have to come to their own conclusions based on experiences working with students in their classrooms.

I have begun to notice that different classes need to be taught differently. One of my classes is filled with an academic mix of "lower than grade-level" and "grade-level" students. This makes it difficult to aim lessons at everyone. Sometimes I feel as though I am either leaving some students behind or teaching "down" to the group. I must admit that my expectations are not as high as with my other classes. If I can get them to read, to understand, and to think critically from time to time, I feel that I am doing my best. But am I? Sometimes I find myself accepting "I don't know" and silence when I know that they are capable of much more.

Recently I did a timeline project with them, and I could tell that they were excited to be doing something other than reading and discussing the text. If I had realized this at the start, I would have done a lot of things differently. But I was told early on that it was not in this "class's make-up" to participate in open discussions or presentations. More than anyone else, these students need to have intellectually exciting experiences that provide them with incentives to attend class and learn. Reading and discussing the textbook does not motivate them to do anything but wait for the bell to ring.

Journal Entry 5: A pedagogy of hope.

I really cannot relate to Paulo Freire's *Pedagogy of Hope*. I cannot find the connection between the types of oppression he talks about and my duty as an educator. This may not be due to any fault of mine or of Freire's. It may be, as he suggests, a shortcoming of education in the United States.

I know this sounds confusing, but it took me a while to disentangle my thoughts so it might take you a while to make sense of them. Until now, I had absolutely no need to understand ideas like those presented by Freire. They are not part of education in the suburban schools where I was a student and now student teach. They are not tested on final exams or requirements for admission to top colleges. There is no time in the day set aside for a teacher to investigate the cultural backgrounds of students, to get to know their needs, and to develop strategies to help them overcome oppression. Maybe these are priorities in other countries or other parts of the United States, but not here. Here, as Herbert Kohl points out, "students are judged by their conformity and obedience rather than their intelligence in dealing with the problems that they and their communities face." Maybe that explains why Freire seems so alien to "mainstream" America.

I don't know what a new teacher in a traditional suburban school district can do to bring Freire's ideas and hopes into fruition; I don't know if a new teacher can really do anything. I hear more about not rocking the boat than I hear about helping to provide students with a "democratic, liberating education."

I definitely agree with Freire's claim that traditional schooling consists of "banking" information into students' minds and that this system assumes they bring nothing worth knowing with them. I have tried to open up the lines of communication with students and to let an uninhibited dialogue flow. There is an awful lot I do not know and I am willing to be taught by them. Unfortunately, many of my students are uncomfortable expressing themselves in class. I worry that Freire's approach is threatening to students, teachers and the parents whose hard earned dollars pay my salary.

I am not sure where to go from here or what to do about the things raised by Freire. To what degree can I really make a difference? The problem with reading literature such as this book is that once we are confronted with the issues, we can no longer claim ignorance; we can never turn back.

Journal Entry 6: The hardest thing I have ever had to do in my life.

I was asked what I learned during my student teaching experience. I find that question difficult to answer because I learned so many things about the type of person and educator I am, about people in general, and about the students in my classes. With all of the knowledge I gained, I still have many unanswered questions, and some feelings I have not even formulated into questions yet. I hope to find some answers as I write this, and I hope that other answers, and new questions, become clearer to me when I am teaching.

I feel as though I have changed drastically as a person over the past months. I faced a challenge and I am proud of what I have accomplished. I survived all of those days when I thought that I could not last another moment or that I could not possibly face another class filled with teenagers. I learned that stress can do strange things to your body and I found out it is okay to scream in your car and to vent your frustrations, as long as your windows are closed and the stereo is playing loudly. If I am ever a cooperating teacher, I will try my hardest to be supportive of my student teachers and to offer constructive criticism that actually is constructive. I have learned that I do know a lot about literature, but that I have a lot to learn about everything else. I realize now that teaching is not an easy job; there is so much involved beyond which can be taught in a methods class.

Student teaching was by far the hardest thing I have ever had to do in my life, but also the most rewarding. I gained valuable experience and I truly understand how difficult it is to teach a full day of classes. Having a support system in our seminar helped me gain insight into myself as a teacher and a person. The books and articles we read and wrote about provoked my thoughts about what I want to accomplish as a teacher and how to go about accomplishing them.

* * *

JOIN THE CONVERSATION—DAWN'S JOURNEY

Questions to Consider:

1. Which of Dawn's journal entries comes closest to addressing your concerns as you prepare to student teach or become a beginning teacher? Explain.

2. Dawn appears to arrive at a new level of understanding of material she read in her
   teacher education program as she teaches and reflects on her experiences in the classroom. Have you found the articles and books you have read about teaching useful? Explain. What do you think of Dawn's discoveries?

3. In your experience, is keeping a journal such as this one useful to you as an individual? Explain.

4. Write a letter to Dawn responding to her experiences and discussing your own.

SECTION C: RECOMMENDATIONS FOR NEW TEACHERS

As a teacher you will attend many graduations and hear a number of speeches offering advice or challenging the audience to go off and remake the world. Perhaps the most famous
speech of this kind is by a character named Polonius in William Shakespeare's *Hamlet*.
Polonius sends his son off to study at the university with the phrase, "To thy own self be
true." Few people realize when they quote the speech that Polonius was a bit of a buffoon
and Shakespeare was poking fun at his pomposity. Realizing the risks involved in final words
of advice, Stephanie Hunte (whom you met in chap. 2), Michael Pezone (chap. 1), and I want
to offer some parting thoughts to young teachers as they voyage out into the "real" world.

FIG. 10.1 Polonius's advice to Laertes.
By William Shakespeare, *Hamlet*, Act I, Scene 3

Be thou familiar, but by no means vulgar.
Those friends thou hast, and their adoption tried,
Grapple them to thy soul with hoops of steel;
But do not dull thy palm with entertainment
Of each new-hatch'd, unfledged comrade. Beware
Of entrance to a quarrel, but being in,
Bear't that the opposed may beware of thee.
Give every man thy ear, but few thy voice;
Take each man's censure, but reserve thy judgment.
Costly thy habit as thy purse can buy,
But not express'd in fancy; rich, not gaudy;
For the apparel oft proclaims the man,
And they in France of the best rank and station
Are of a most select and generous chief in that.
Neither a borrower nor a lender be;
For loan oft loses both itself and friend,
And borrowing dulls the edge of husbandry.
This above all: to thine ownself be true,
And it must follow, as the night the day,
Thou canst not then be false to any man.

FIG. 10.2   Twelve end-of-my-first-month resolutions by Stephanie Hunte.

Stephanie Hunte found this list of resolutions in the teaching journal she kept during her first months of teaching. She confesses that she "broke" Resolution 2 within 3 weeks after she made it. Stephanie feels her journal and resolutions helped to keep her focused on her goals as a teacher during some very trying moments. She recommends the practice to all new teachers.

1. I have to learn patience.
2. I will no longer say "shut up" to any human being regardless of age or position.
3. I will plan at least one interesting lesson for each day.
4. I will use projects with all my classes.
5. I will have a more democratic classroom where kids can express themselves openly.
6. I will follow up on what I say. There is nothing worse than a lack of consistency.
7. I will be better organized. Paperwork is piling up.
8. I will incorporate at least one hands-on activity per lesson.
9. I won't use the mundane factoid lessons I find in the textbook.
10. I will prepare lessons 2 days in advance especially those that require photocopying.
11. I will not threaten students into learning by using coercive tactics.
12. I have to learn patience.

FIG. 10.3   Sports metaphors by Alan Singer.

Teaching is a lot like basketball.
Some days you cannot make a basket, but then suddenly you are "in the zone" and it seems like you will never miss a shot. Often that is how I feel in front of the room.

Some teachers compare teaching to football.
Football coaches like to compare their game with war, especially the need to plan short- and long-term strategies, the continuous movement of men and supplies, and the importance of field position. Football fans continually use the language of war—blitzes, end-around plays, fighting in the trenches. But if we put aside some of the violence, designing a game plan for football is a lot like planning to teach.

But mostly teaching is like baseball.
In the spring of 2000, the defending champion New York Yankees were mired in a five-game losing streak. Their defense was sloppy, pitching was erratic, the team's hitters were cold, and a number of players were nursing minor injuries. Manager Joe Torre daily reminded anxious reporters and panicking fans that it was a "162-game season"; that in baseball "no one wins every game"; and that the team was sound, would play through its problems, and would get back on the right track. As some commentators have noted, if you make out two thirds of the time, you are a candidate for the Hall of Fame in Cooperstown.

In numerous popular movies, including *Field of Dreams* (1989), *The Natural* (1984), and *A League of Their Own* (1992), to name a few of my favorites, baseball is a metaphor for the ebb and flow of life. It is a long flowing season with a mixture of ups and downs.

I want to make a simpler analogy—baseball as a metaphor for teaching. Although you try to get a hit with every at bat, no one does. You will not win every lesson or everyday. You need to think in terms of the full 180-day season: building, planning, and training for the long haul.

Remember, if something doesn't go right, don't panic. There is time to figure it out and fix it.

FIG. 10.4   The Zen teacher by Michael Pezone.

The following are traditional Zen Buddhist stories that Michael Pezone, a mentor teacher in the New Teachers Network, likes to share with people starting the teacher education program. He gives each tale his own particular twist.

1. A huge, rough samurai once went to see a little monk, hoping to acquire the secrets of the universe. "Monk," he said, in a voice accustomed to instant obedience, "teach me about heaven and hell." The little monk looked up at the mighty warrior in silence. Then, after a moment, he said to the samurai with utter disdain, "Teach YOU about heaven and hell? I couldn't teach you about anything. You're dirty. You smell. Your blade is rusty. You're a disgrace, an embarrassment to the samurai class. Get out of my sight at once. I can't stand you!" The samurai was furious. He began to shake all over from the anger that raced through him. A red flush spread over his face; he was speechless with rage. Quickly, menacingly, he pulled out his sword and raised it above his head, preparing to slay the monk. "That's hell," said the little monk quietly. The samurai was overwhelmed. Stunned. The compassion and surrender of this little man who had offered his life to give this teaching about hell! He slowly lowered his sword, filled with gratitude, and for reasons he could not explain his heart became suddenly peaceful. "And that's heaven," said the monk softly. As a teacher, I ask myself: "Am I in heaven or am I in hell?"

2. There once was a monastery that was very strict. Following a vow of silence, no one was allowed to speak at all. But there was one exception to this rule. Every 10 years, the monks were permitted to speak just two words. After spending his first 10 years at the monastery, one monk went to the head monk. "It has been 10 years," said the head monk. "What are the two words you would like to speak?" "Bed . . . hard . . ." said the monk. "I see," replied the head monk. Ten years later, the monk returned to the head monk's office. "It has been 10 more years," said the head monk. "What are the two words you'd like to speak?" "Food . . . stinks . . ." said the monk. "I see," replied the head monk. Yet another 10 years passed and the monk once again met with the head monk who asked, "What are your two words now, after these 10 years?" "I . . . quit!" said the monk. "Well, I can see why," replied the head monk. "All you ever do is complain." As a teacher, I ask myself: "How will I spend my 30 years?"

3. Two monks were washing their bowls in the river when they noticed a scorpion that was drowning. One monk immediately scooped it up and set it upon the bank. In the process he was stung. He went back to washing his bowl and again the scorpion fell in. The monk saved the scorpion and was again stung. The other monk asked him, "Friend, why do you continue to save the scorpion when you know it's nature is to sting?" "Because," the monk replied, "to save it is my nature." As a teacher, I ask myself: "Is it my nature to save the scorpion?"

JOIN THE CONVERSATION—ADVICE TO TEACHERS

Questions to Consider:

1. Whose advice is more useful to you? Explain.
2. What questions would you like to ask Stephanie, Alan, Michael, and Polonius? Why?
3. Make a list, write a poem or speech, tell an allegory, or draw a picture with your advice to someone beginning a career as a secondary school teacher.

SECTION D: WHAT CAN TEACHERS DO?[1]

Following e-mail exchanges involving dozens of teachers and a New Teachers Network meeting, Maureen Murphy, S. Maxwell Hines, Sandra Stacki, and I wrote and circulated the following statement on the destruction of the World Trade Center towers in New York City and the role of teachers at a time of national or local emergency.—Alan Singer

As teacher educators at Hofstra University, we are part of a support network for approximately two hundred beginning secondary school teachers (first three years) in the New York metropolitan area. We maintain regular e-mail contact and meet bi-monthly on Saturday mornings at the university. In this essay, Alan Singer expresses our collective response to the role of teachers at a time of national or local emergency.

On the morning of September 11, 2001, Alan was visiting a student teacher and two members of the New Teachers Network at a junior high school in Queens. He first learned of events at the World Trade Center when one of the teachers received a cell phone call from his sister. She was sobbing because her husband worked on a top floor in one of the towers and she feared he was dead.

Within minutes, school administrative personnel circulated around the building briefing teachers and telling us the school was in "lock down"—no one was permitted to enter or leave. Administrators and teachers were calm and professional, but clearly there was no broader plan in place to address what was happening and how to respond to students who suspected something was going on, heard rumors about catastrophe and war, or simply wanted to know why they could not leave. Within an hour a crowd of concerned parents were outside the building and visible from classroom windows. Many were crying.

That afternoon teachers in the New Teachers Network began to exchange e-mail messages. They described their experiences and fears with each other in an effort to come to terms with what had happened and to figure out how to help their students understand events. Mentor teachers from a number of schools in the area and teachers educators also met with over thirty new teachers for three hours on Saturday morning, September 15.

What emerged from our conversations was a picture of what had taken place in the area's secondary schools on the day of the attack and the days that followed. In a number of schools in the city and the suburbs, students and teachers, alerted by cell phone calls or late arrivals to school, witnessed the second plane crash and the collapse of both towers from school windows. In some of these schools, teachers and students discussed what they saw and turned on news broadcasts to try to learn what was happening. But in others, teachers were ordered to remain silent and carry on with business in their classes as usual.

Unlike the coordinated emergency services response, each school and district seemed to go in a different direction. On the following days, some tried to return to normalcy and pretended that nothing had happened, while others provided counseling for upset students but little else. A number of schools held memorial assemblies and then told students and teachers to get back to work. Some schools designated specific subject classes where events would be discussed, while other schools left it up to the discretion of individual teachers. Many New York City districts provided teachers with lesson plans. Some of these encouraged teachers to involve students in open discussion and to challenge ethnic stereotyping. However other plans limited teachers to responding to student questions with scripted answers.

Not one teacher in our network reported that districts involved them either in discussion of the events or asked how they thought they should respond to students. All they received were directives.

---

[1]Other versions of this essay have appeared in Alan Singer, *Social Studies for Secondary Schools*, 2nd ed. and the newsletter of the New York State Council for the Social Studies.

In a time of national and local crisis, when they were in the best position to help adolescents make meaning of events, the professionals most directly connected with young people were disempowered by our school systems. A number of teachers involved in the network reported to the group that as adults who know and are trusted by their students, they felt they had to act. They decided to "shut their doors," ignore the directives and proceed on their own, whatever the later administrative consequences. Many stressed they believe their decisions helped to establish their classrooms as a communities where students felt able to speak out, could depend on each other and were safe.

The English educator working with the New Teachers Network put together a package of poetry to help students understand their feelings and suggested writing exercises that allow them to express their thoughts and emotions. Many classes are writing letters of condolence to victims of the attack.

As the social studies educator working with the network, I distributed a simple lesson that a number of the teachers used in their classes. We divided the front board into four columns. What we know. What we need to know. How we feel about what happened. What we think should happen next. Working individually, in groups or as a full class, students filled in the columns and then discussed what they had written. Our goals were to help students distinguish between fact and opinion, substantiated information and rumor, and emotion and reason. We challenged stereotypes and stressed the difference between Islam, a religion of over a billion believers, many of whom live in the United States, and the actions of one organized group or a few individuals. We also wanted to lay the basis for a long term investigation of why the attack took place so students can analyze underlying and immediate causes, understand why many people in other countries believe they have been injured by the United States and its allies, and participate in debate over United States policy decisions. Many of the teachers will have students use the internet to collect newspaper articles from around the world on the attack and the United States response. Comparing reports will help students see multiple perspectives that may be overlooked by local media.

At our Saturday meeting, Robyn Tornabene, a young biology teacher asked how she could be involved since events did not easily fit into her subject area. The group recommended that every teacher press schools and districts as part of professional development to involve teachers in discussion of these events and in designing a response strategy that includes lessons for different subjects. The teachers also felt that whatever their individual areas of expertise, in their classrooms, in extracurricular clubs, in the hallways, on teams and in individual meetings, they needed to be there for their students, as emotional supports, as role models, to promote tolerance and to champion reason at a time when all of us may get swept up in a wave of irrationality.

JOIN THE CONVERSATION—WHAT CAN TEACHERS DO?

Questions to Consider:

1. A number of teachers shut their doors, ignored directives, and proceeded on their own, whatever the later administrative consequences. What do you think of their decisions? Would you join them? Would you support them if they were reprimanded? Explain.
2. What do you think of the group's recommendations? Why?
3. In your opinion, should teachers be involved in planning how schools respond to emergencies? Why?

SECTION E: POSTSCRIPT—NOT "ANOTHER BRICK IN THE WALL"

In chapter 1, I introduced two songs, "Another Brick in the Wall (Part II)" by Pink Floyd and "Fight the Power" by Public Enemy. As I said at the time, this book is based on the premise that every teacher must make a decision: Will you "fight the power" or become "another brick in the wall" of an educational system that rewards some students, tracks many into limited options, and leaves others behind? Maureen Murphy, S. Maxwell Hines, members of the New Teachers Network, and I have tried to offer education students, student teachers, and beginning teachers a research- and theory-based approach to teaching that makes it possible to affect the lives of students and schools. We hope you decide not to become "Another Brick in the Wall."

A lot of fuss is made by politicians and some educators about poor test scores and the need to raise academic standards in the United States. But they rarely ask the key question: **Why aren't all students doing well?** More than a century ago, Emile Durkheim (1897/1951), a French sociologist, rejected the idea that education could be the force to solve society's problems. Durkheim believed that education could be "reformed only if society itself" was reformed. He argued that education was "only the image and reflection of society. It imitates and reproduces the latter; . . . it does not create it" (pp. 372–373).

I think Durkheim is saying that we have the schools we have—not because teachers are bad or there is something wrong with children or their parents, but because it serves the interests of powerful forces in our society not to educate some children and to have teachers, parents, and children blame each other for the problems. If Durkheim is correct, a society has the school system it deserves. Denouncing the poor quality of education is like blaming a mirror because you do not like your reflection.

Blaming schools, while exempting our social system from scrutiny, allows those who support the status quo to propose relatively inexpensive, but ultimately ineffective, solutions to the problems affecting education. Instead of spending money to lower class size; build new, safe, welcoming schools for all children; enhance the development of teachers throughout their careers; and support research on promoting learning, they vote to raise standards, reshuffle curriculum content, create new tests, and demand foolproof teacher certification criteria. Few people ask what will happen in communities in which 80% of the students who complete high school are unable to earn diplomas. Instead, to punish these students for their failure, because failure is by definition their own fault, there is a movement to bar 4-year public colleges from providing them with remedial classes.

The first step in improving education is to recognize that the problems plaguing schools are rooted in the way our society is organized. The United States does not have a uniform school system that educates all children. It provides elite private schools for the children of the privileged, while some kids sit in overcrowded classrooms in crumbling buildings. Teachers need to ask ourselves, what kind of country is it where children who already have computers at home are the ones most likely to have access to them in school? I want every child in the United States to have the same education they provide in the fanciest private schools or in the most affluent suburban districts.

This being the case, I believe there are still real possibilities for improving public education. American educational ideology is inconsistent, valuing individualism, competition, and materialism, but also citizenship, democracy, and equality. Teachers can take advantage of this inconsistency to create democratic classroom communities where students learn to think critically, provide leadership, and care about others. For me, the crucial players in the struggle to transform schools (and society) are our students. If they experience concern and democracy in schools and learn to think critically about the world, they can become powerful agents for change. It is our job as teachers, a very difficult job, to find ways to help them.

In addition, teachers can build on the strengths of students while acknowledging weaknesses. Strategies to promote the love of learning must take both into account. Poverty, alienation, and discrimination have had a devastating impact on many communities in the United States. What young person could emerge out of these communities, and certainly out of many of our public schools, without some educational deficits? This is why teachers cannot ignore the social context of learning. As a high school teacher, I tried to connect with every student in the room, even when I realized it was not always possible; there were too many complicating factors in the lives of my students. What kept me going may have been obstinacy, but it was also the realization that I could not predict which students would respond, so the only way I could reach some of the students was to try to reach every one of them.

I think that conservative politicians and educators made a strategic error in their campaign for higher educational standards, and that their mistake opens up space for legal challenges to unequal school funding and for organizing the public to fight for a more equitable school system and society. State legislatures and courts generally endorse school systems that permit social inequality. National and state standards, by raising the minimum for acceptable school performance and by providing a new definition of a "sound basic education," make every school system subject to legal review. Teachers, parents, and our students can be major contributors to campaigns that insist that our school systems obey the law.

Many new teachers are frightened of being perceived of as activists or even of being seen as having a point of view. Some argue that they will wait until they have tenure before they express their views. However, my experience is that if you are afraid to speak out before you have tenure, you will not speak out later. School districts always have treats to offer or withhold, better rooms and equipment, advanced placement classes, extracurricular pay, or administrative assignments, so there is always another reason to remain silent.

As a teacher, you will have to decide whether you are going to remain silent; join those who blame parents, children, and other teachers; or become involved in the struggle to educate all children. None of us is born immune from the fear of losing a job or the prejudices that infect our society. But if teachers face up to who we are and examine our society, attitudes, and behavior with open eyes, we can overcome our limitations and help to change the world.

Ladies and gentlemen, we have a difficult but wondrous task in front of us. Get ready. Get set. Go out and teach.

JOIN THE CONVERSATION—SHOULD TEACHERS BE NEUTRAL?

In their book, *We Make the Road by Walking* (1990, p. 102), Myles Horton and Paulo Freire discuss the question whether it is possible or desirable for teachers to be "neutral" in their classrooms. Freire asks, "A biology teacher must know biology, but is it possible just to teach biology? What I want to know is whether it is possible to teach biology without discussing social conditions."

Horton believes, "There's no right I could claim that anybody else in the world can't claim, and I have to fight for their exercising that right just like I have to fight for my own. That doesn't mean I have to impose my ideas on people, but it means I have a responsibility to provide whatever light I can on the subject and share my ideas with people."

Discussions of the desirability and possibility of "teacher neutrality" have always produced sharp disagreements in my teacher education classes. In one interchange, Jewella Lynch explained, "I want my students to understand that I am a human being who comes to class with my own perspective on events and that they shape everything that I teach. That does not mean I give my personal views on every issue. I try to model for them what it means to be a thinking person who uses information to support opinions and the importance of being an activist. My goal is to have them develop and clearly state and support their own positions."

In response, Nicole Theo expressed concern that teachers would be impinging on the prerogatives of parents by conveying their personal opinions on moral issues. She does not want students to be forced to choose between "the belief systems of a teacher whom they admire and parents whom they love and depend on." Nicole believes that teachers must maintain strict neutrality and refrain from presenting their "personal agenda in class."

Questions to Consider:

1. In your opinion, is it possible or desirable for teachers to be neutral on controversial issues?

2. Is it possible for teachers to express opinions without proselytizing and while respecting the opinions of their students?

REFERENCES AND SUGGESTIONS FOR FURTHER READING

Bennett, W., Finn, Jr., C., & Cribb, J. (1996). *The educated child: A parent's guide from preschool through eighth grade.* New York: The Free Press.

Camus, A. (1991). *The rebel, An essay on man in revolt.* New York: Vintage. [Original work published 1956]

Christensen, L. (2000). Building community from chaos. In L. Christensen (Ed.), *Reading, writing and rising up* (pp. 2–9). Milwaukee, WI: Rethinking Schools.

Dewey, J. (1954). *Experience and education.* New York: Collier/Macmillian. [Original work published 1927]

Dickens, C. (1973). *Hard times* (D. Craig, Ed.). New York: Penguin. [Original work published 1854]

Durkheim, E. (1951). *Suicide, A study in sociology.* New York: The Free Press. [Original work published 1897]

Finn, Jr., C., & Ravitch, D. (1987). *What do our 17-year-olds know: A report on the first national assessment of history and literature.* New York: Harper & Row.

Hirsch, E., Jr. (1987). *Cultural literacy, What every American needs to know.* Boston: Houghton Mifflin.

Hirsch, E., Jr. (1996). *The schools we need & why we don't have them.* New York: Doubleday.

Horton, M., & Freire, P. (1990). *We make the road by walking.* Philadelphia: Temple University Press.

Kohl, H. (1994). *I won't learn from you and other thoughts on creative maladjustment.* New York: The New Press.

Logan, J. (1997). *Teaching stories.* New York: Kodansha America.

Pogrow, S. (2000). The unsubstantiated "success" of success for all. *Phi Delta Kappan, 81*(8), 596–600.

Ravitch, D. (2000). *Left back: A century of battles over school reform.* New York: Simon & Schuster.

Seldes, G. (Ed.). (1966). *The great quotations.* New York: Lyle Stuart.

Slavin, R., Madden, M., Dolan, L., Wasik, B., Ross, S., & Smith, L. (1994). Whenever and wherever we choose: The replication of "success for all." *Phi Delta Kappan, 75*(8), 639–640, 642–647.

Slavin, R., & Madden, N. (2000). Research on achievement outcomes of success for all: A summary and response to critics. *Phi Delta Kappan, 82*(1), 38–40, 59–66.

APPENDIX I: IDEAS FOR YOUR PROFESSIONAL PORTFOLIO, RESUME, AND COVER LETTER

When you apply for a job, you need to convince an individual or a committee that they should invite you to an interview from a crowded field, give you a chance to teach a demonstration lesson, and offer you a position. I recommend student teachers consider the following five things as they prepare a strategy that will secure them a teaching position:

1. Do not pad your resume. If a school is not interested in a beginner, they will not interview you (e.g., do not list afterschool jobs or describe everything you did as a student teacher).

2. Schools often want people who can do more than one thing. Make sure they can tell who you are and what you can do from your resume and cover letter (e.g., coach baseball, direct play).

3. Individualize cover letters. Show that you know something about the school or district (e.g., discuss your desire to work in a multiethnic community).

4. When you get an interview, be who you are, not whom you think they want. It is unlikely you will trick anyone. You do not really want to work in a school that has a radically different approach to education from yours.

5. Create a portfolio that demonstrates the kind of teacher you are. Place it on a Web site and bring a hard copy with you to interviews. Even if no one looks at it, the process of

FIG. 10.5 Creating a professional portfolio.

1. Why have a professional portfolio?
    a. It is a way to assess your teaching and professional preparation.
    b. It helps you visualize your development over time and redefine future goals.
    c. It is a way to present your teaching and professional preparation to others.
    d. It is a way to prepare yourself for job interviews.
2. What should I include in my professional portfolio?
    a. Personal and professional information.
        1. Cover letter
        2. Resume
        3. Certification
        4. Diploma
        5. Scores on qualifying exams
        6. Letters of recommendation
        7. Philosophical statement—"Why I want to be a teacher"
    b. Examples of knowledge and competence.
        1. Photographs of students
        2. Unit plan with handouts
        3. Student work
        4. Certificates of achievement
        5. Field observations
        6. Relevant written work
    c. Special achievements—student magazine, published material, playbill, newspaper articles.
3. How should I organize my professional portfolio?
    a. Personal approach—develop a strategy for presenting yourself.
    b. Standards approach.
        1. Knowledge of subject matter
        2. Knowledge of human development
        3. Adapting instruction for individual needs
        4. Multiple instructional strategies
        5. Classroom motivation and management skills
        6. Communication skills
        7. Instructional planning skills
        8. Assessment of student learning
        9. Professional commitment and responsibility
        10. Partnerships
4. How do I present my professional portfolio?
    a. Working portfolio/your file cabinet—a system for storing and sorting material for inclusion in your presentation portfolio.
    b. Presentation portfolio.
        1. Bound copy—insert binder
        2. Electronic delivery—Web site or CD-ROM

creating a professional portfolio helps you to crystalize your thinking about teaching and prepare for interview.

Sample Resume (For a beginner, limit to one or two sides maximum, one or two fonts)

Name, Address, and Phone (top, center, bold)

E-Mail Address and Web Site (these establish computer literacy)

Certification Area (e.g., New York, 7–12 Social Studies, Pending)

Education (listed in reverse chronological order)

Professional Experience (anything that is school or education related)

Other Work Experience (only things that show responsibility or special skills)

Special Achievements, Awards, and Activities (CRUCIAL—these separate you from the crowd)

Professional Memberships (these demonstrate your seriousness)

References (two or three, preferably people they know, definitely people easy to contact)

FIG. 10.6   Sample resume.

Alan Singer
123 Santa Fe Avenue
Brooklyn, NY 11235
718/123-4567   Singer@aol.com
www.geocities.com/Athens/Academy/1234

Certification: New York State 7–12 Social Studies (pending)

Education:

Master of Science in Education with Honors,	
Hofstra University, Hempstead, NY 11549,	December 1999
Bachelor of Arts, Major: History, Minor: Political Science, GPA: 3.6	
Hofstra University, Hempstead, NY 11549	May 1996

Professional Experience:

Student Teacher—Harrisburg High School, Global History and United States History; Dakota Middle School, United States History	Fall 1999
Tutor, Global History and United States History	1997–1999
Substitute Teacher—Freeport School District	1997–1999
Participant/Observer—Herricks Middle School, East Meadow High School	1998–1999
Assistant Coach, Hempstead High School J-V Football,	1998–2000
Counselor (Summers)—Camp Whatchamacallit, Saratoga, New York	1994–1997

Other Work Experience: Manager, Megabuster Video   1992–1994

Special Achievements: President, History Society; School Play; Editor, Magazine; Scholarships

Professional Memberships: National Council for the Social Studies

References:

Field Supervisor for Student Teaching, Department of Curriculum and Teaching, address/phone

Department chair of school where you student taught, address/phone

One other, address/phone

Professional File available upon request from university.

FIG. 10.7 Sample cover letter.

Alan Singer
123 Santa Fe Avenue
Brooklyn, NY 11235
718/123-4567   Singer@aol.com
www.geocities.com/Athens/Academy/1234

June 1, 2002

Jane Doe, Social Studies Chair
George Washington High School
Washingtonville, Vermont

Dear Ms. Doe,

I recently completed student teaching at AAA Middle School and BBB High School in CCC-ville, New Hampshire. I am a May 2001 graduate of DDD University where I majored in history with a minor in secondary education. I am currently certified to teach social studies grades 7–12 in Vermont.

I grew up in New York City, but fell in love with Vermont and New Hampshire while attending college and I plan to make my home in this area. I am particularly interested in the global history position advertised for your school because of my strong background in African and Asian history. During the summer between my junior and senior years I spent three months living and studying in Kenya and in my social studies methods class I developed units on Africa and Asia that I successfully taught as a student teacher. I would be pleased if you examined the units and the rest of my teaching portfolio on my Web site.

As an undergraduate, I did volunteer work in a dramatics program at the Youth Center in EEE-town. I also performed in university productions of "FFF" and "GGG." These experiences convinced me of the importance of drama for engaging young people in an exploration of our world. I know your school has an award winning dramatics program. If I am offered the teaching position, I hope to contribute to this tradition.

As an undergraduate student I joined the National Council for the Social Studies and attended workshops sponsored by the New Hampshire state council. I am especially interested in document-based instruction that achieves state learning standards. I plan to pursue this interest in graduate school and hope it is consistent with the goals of your program.

I hope to hear from you soon.

Sincerely,

APPENDIX II: RECOMMENDED WEB SITES FOR TEACHERS

The World Wide Web is difficult to navigate, constantly changing and idiosyncratic. Most of the teachers who helped assemble this list of recommended sites prefer Google as their search engine, but some disagree. Any directory of recommended sites is going to include sites that have moved or have closed shop. In addition, one person's best site can be someone else's dud. We encourage you to explore these sites for yourself and bookmark your own favorites.

Our recommendations are divided into three general categories (professional organizations, resources and lesson plans, and publishers and corporate-for-profit sites) and are listed alphabetically within each group. As you visit these sites, you will discover that most could be listed in more than one category. Special thanks for helping research this section go to Dean Bacigalupo, Richard DeLucia, Ken Dwyer, Ken Kaufman, Michelle Maniscalco, Tammy Manor, Stephanie Morris, Jason Noone, Jennifer Palacio, Sandra Stacki, Ken Tapfar, and Nicole Theo.

PROFESSIONAL ORGANIZATIONS

American Council on the Teaching of Foreign Languages (www.actfl.org). ACTFL is dedicated to the improvement and expansion of the teaching and learning of all languages at all levels of instruction. ACTFL is an individual membership organization of more than 7,000 foreign language teachers and administrators from elementary through graduate education, as well as government and industry.

American Federation of Teachers (www.aft.org). The mission of the American Federation of Teachers, AFL-CIO, is to improve the lives of its members and their families; to give voice to their legitimate professional, economic, and social aspirations; to strengthen the institutions in which they work; to improve the quality of the services they provide; to bring together all members to assist and support one another; and to promote democracy, human rights, and freedom in the union, nation, and world.

American Educational Research Association (www.aera.net). AERA is concerned with improving the educational process by encouraging scholarly inquiry related to education and by promoting the dissemination and practical application of research results. AERA is the most prominent international professional organization with the primary goal of advancing educational research and its practical application. Its more than 22,000 members are teachers; administrators; directors of research, testing, or evaluation in federal, state and local agencies; counselors; evaluators; graduate students; and behavioral scientists. The broad range of disciplines represented by the membership includes education, psychology, statistics, sociology, history, economics, philosophy, anthropology, and political science.

American Library Association (www.ala.org). ALA provides leadership for the development, promotion, and improvement of library and information services and the profession of librarianship in order to enhance learning and ensure access to information for all.

Association for Supervision and Curriculum Development (www.ascd.org). The ASCD is an international, nonprofit, nonpartisan education association committed to the mission of forging covenants in teaching and learning for the success of all learners. Founded in 1943, ASCD provides professional development in curriculum and supervision, initiates and supports activities to provide educational equity for all students, and serves as a world-class leader in education information services. ASCD publishes *Educational Leadership.*

Bilingual Education Network (www.rmplc.uk/orgs/blen). Based in the United Kingdom, this site offers information and ideas for teachers of English as a second language.

Children's Defense Fund (www.childrensdefense.org). CDF is a strong, effective voice for all the children of America who cannot vote, lobby, or speak for themselves. It pays particular attention to the needs of poor and minority children and those with disabilities. CDF educates the nation about the needs of children and encourages preventive investment before they get sick or into trouble, drop out of school, or suffer family breakdown.

Coalition of Essential Schools (www.essentialschools.org). CES is a national network of more than 1,000 schools, 19 regional centers, and a national office seeking to promote higher student achievement and to develop more nurturing and humane school communities. CES National supports the work of this network by providing professional development, conducting research, maintaining this Web site, and advocating for the CES Network.

Educators for Social Responsibility (www.esrnational.org). ESR's mission is to make teaching social responsibility a core practice in education so that young people develop the convictions and skills needed to shape a safe, sustainable, democratic, and just world. ESR supports social and emotional learning, character education, conflict resolution, violence prevention, and intergroup relations. It offers comprehensive programs, resources, and training for adults who teach children at every developmental level, preschool through high school.

ERIC (www.askeric.org). ERIC offers more than 3000 resources on a variety of educational issues. ERIC includes lesson plans, Internet sites, educational organizations, and electronic discussion groups. Lessons are offered in the following subject areas: arts, character education, foreign language, general lesson plans, health, information literacy, integrated interdisciplinary approach, language arts, mathematics, physical education, science, social studies, vocational education.

Foxfire (www.foxfire.org). Teachers and students develop creative and innovative ways to learn the curriculum in learner-centered, community-focused learning environments.

Gay, Lesbian, and Straight Education Network (www.glsen.org). GLSEN is one of the nation's leading voices for equality and safety in the educational system.

Global Schoolhouse (www.gsn.org). This site provides excellent resources for the information consumer, especially teachers who want to use the Internet in their classrooms.

Institute for Democracy in Education (www.ohiou.edu/ide). IDE was founded by local teachers in Southeastern Ohio dismayed that public school reform overlooked the historic purpose of public education—the development of participatory citizens who have cultivated democratic habits of heart and mind. IDE includes more than 20 regional offices across the United States and Canada.

Institute for Elementary and Secondary Educators (www.brown.edu/Departments/IESE). IESE is located at Brown University. It offers links to resources, projects, and examples of schools that use educational technology.

International Education and Resource Network (www.iearn.org). iEARN is a nonprofit organization made up of almost 4,000 schools in more than 90 countries that empowers teachers and young people (K–12) to work together online through a global telecommunications network. Through participation in iEARN projects, students develop the habit of getting involved in community issues, thus better equipping them for future citizenship participation.

International Society for Technology in Education (www.iste.org). ISTE publishes *Journal for Research on Technology in Education* and develops technology standards for schools.

Internet Public Library (www.ipl.org). IPL is a public service organization and learning and teaching environment at the University of Michigan School of Information. Activities include finding, evaluating, selecting, and organizing library material. IPL advocates a learn-by-doing approach to train information professionals and students to work in an increasingly digital environment.

MiddleWeb (www.middleweb.com). This site is dedicated to reform and innovation in middle schools, with an emphasis on urban issues. It provides links to other online resources and a listserv that connects middle school teachers interested in improving middle grades, teaching, and learning.

National Association for Multicultural Education (www.nameorg.org). NAME advocates for educational equity and social justice. Membership encompasses the spectrum of professional educators and specialists, including early childhood, classroom and higher education faculty, administrators, psychologists, social workers, counselors, curriculum specialists, librarians, scholars, and researchers. NAME publishes newsletter and a quarterly journal, *Multicultural Perspectives.*

National Center for Fair & Open Testing (www.fairtest.org). NCFOT is an advocacy organization working to end the abuses, misuses, and flaws of standardized testing and to ensure that evaluation of students and workers is fair, open, and educationally sound. It places special emphasis on eliminating the racial, class, gender, and cultural barriers to equal opportunity posed by standardized tests, and preventing their damage to the quality of education.

National Clearinghouse for Bilingual Education (www.ncbe.gwu.edu). NCBE is funded by the U.S. Department of Education's Office of Bilingual Education and Minority Languages Affairs (OBEMLA) to collect, analyze, and disseminate information relating to the effective education of linguistically and culturally diverse learners in the United States.

National Clearinghouse for Comprehensive School Reform (www.goodschools.gwu.edu). Newsletter examines educational reform programs that successfully meet the needs of diverse learners.

National Coalition of Education Activists (members.aol.com/nceaweb). NCEA is a multiracial network and membership organization of parents, school staff, union and community activists, and children's advocates working for equitable and excellent public schools. NCEA's quarterly newsletter, *Action for Better Schools*, provides an annotated list of practical resources.

National Commission on Teaching & America's Future (www.nctaf.org). NCTAF is a nonpartisan, nonprofit group dedicated to improving the quality of teaching nationwide as a means of meeting America's educational challenges. NCTAF's work is based on a solid body of research demonstrating that access to competent, qualified teachers is a crucial factor in determining student achievement.

National Committee for Languages and the **National Council for Languages and International Studies** (www.languagepolicy.org). JNCL and NCLIS are membership organizations united in their belief that all Americans must have the opportunity to learn and use English and at least one other language. The site provides links to individual language associations.

National Council for Accreditation of Teacher Education (www.ncate.org). NCATE is a coalition of professional associations of teachers, teacher educators, content specialists, and local and state policymakers committed to quality teaching. Through the process of professional accreditation of schools, colleges, and departments of education, NCATE works to make a difference in the quality of teaching and teacher preparation today, tomorrow, and for the next century.

National Council for the Social Studies (www.socialstudies.org). NCSS provides leadership, service, and support for all social studies teachers. It serves as an umbrella organization for elementary, secondary, and college teachers of history, geography, economics, political science, sociology, psychology, anthropology, and law-related education. NCSS publishes curriculum journals for teachers working in elementary, middle, and secondary schools, and a social studies research journal.

National Council of Teachers of English (www.ncte.org). NCTE is devoted to improving the teaching and learning of English and the language arts at all levels of education. It provides a forum for the profession, opportunities for teachers to continue professional growth throughout their careers, and a framework for cooperation to deal with issues that affect the teaching of English.

National Council of Teachers of Mathematics (www.nctm.org). NCTM provides the vision and leadership necessary to ensure a mathematics education of the highest quality for all students. NCTM publishes four professional journals: *Teaching Children Mathematics, Mathematics Teaching in the Middle School, the Mathematics Teacher,* and the *Journal for Research in Mathematics Education.*

National Education Association (www.nea.org). NEA is America's oldest and largest organization committed to advancing the cause of public education. NEA conducts professional workshops, supports members involved in contractual negotiations, lobbies state and federal legislative bodies, and promotes dialogue on major educational issues.

National Endowment for the Humanities (www.neh.fed.us). NEH is an independent grant-making agency of the U.S. government dedicated to supporting research, education, and public programs in the humanities.

National Endowment for the Sciences (www.nes.fed.us). NES is an independent grant-making agency of the U.S. government dedicated to supporting research, education, and public programs in the sciences.

National Middle School Association (www.nmsa.org). NMSA is a resource center for middle school teachers.

National Science Teachers Association (www.nsta.org). NSTA promotes excellence and innovation in science teaching and learning. Membership includes science teachers, supervisors, administrators, scientists, business and industry representatives, and others involved in science education. NSTA publishes a professional journal for each level of science teaching.

National Writing Project (www.writingproject.org). NWP promotes exemplary instruction of writing in every classroom in America. It recognizes that our lives and practices are enriched when those with whom we interact represent diversities of race, gender, class, ethnicity, and language.

Network of Educators on Central America (www.teachingforchange.org). Teaching for Change provides curriculum guides and other resources to help teachers engage students in innovative classroom activities that deal with issues of equity and social justice.

Phi Delta Kappan (www.pdkintl.org). Kappan is an advocate for research-based school reform. *Kappan* provides a forum for debate on controversial subjects. It is disseminated to all members of Phi Delta Kappa International and is available by subscription to nonmembers.

Rethinking Schools (www.rethinkingschools.org). This organization began as a local effort by Milwaukee-area teachers to address problems such as basal readers, standardized testing, and textbook-dominated curriculum. It has grown into a nationally prominent publisher of educational materials. It remains committed to equity and to the vision that public education is central to the creation of a humane, caring, multiracial democracy.

Secondary School Educators (7-12educators.about.com/mbody.htm). This site offers ideas for handling hot topics in the classroom and provides links to subject-area links and lesson plans.

Secondary Teachers (www.tenet.edu/jumpstart/secondary.html). This University of Texas–Austin site provides links to curriculum resources, calls for grants, and professional organizations.

Science Learning Network (www.sln.org). SLN is a project sponsored by the National Science Foundation. It provides an online science learning community for teachers, students, and teaching institutions such as museums.

Success in School Equals Success in Life (www.schoolsuccessinfo.org). This is a partnership of People for the American Way and NAACP. It urges parents, particularly those with the least available resources, to get involved in their children's education.

Teachers Network (www.teachersnetwork.org). This is a national, educational, nonprofit organization that identifies and connects innovative teachers exemplifying professionalism and creativity within public school systems. Site includes: Daily Classroom Specials, Videos for Teachers, For New Teachers, Grants for Teachers, Talk with Teachers, and Teacher Bookstore.

Teacher Talk (education.indiana.edu/cas/tt/tthmpg.html). Center for Adolescent Studies at Indiana University offers forum for teachers.

Teach for America (www.tfanetwork.org). This is a national corps of outstanding and diverse recent college graduates of all academic majors who commit 2 years to teach in urban and rural public schools. After their 2 years, Teach for America alumni bring their unique perspective and experience to every sector of professional life, where they remain lifelong advocates for making an excellent education available to all children.

United Nations (www.un.org/cyberschoolbus). This site provides information and activities linking teachers and students with UN-sponsored projects around the world.

United States Department of Education (www.ed.gov/free). DOE offers hundreds of education resources supported by agencies across the U.S. federal government. Subjects include: arts, educational technology, foreign languages, health and safety, language arts, mathematics, physical education, science, social studies, and vocational education. DOE also provides a survival guide for new teachers at www.ed.gov/pubs/survivalguide.

What Kids Can Do (www.whatkidscando.org). This site highlights innovative programs that show the power of young people to shape our world.

RESOURCES AND LESSON PLANS

Armadillo's K–12 WWW Resources (chico.rice.edu/armadillo). Rice University maintains this site with subject area links to resources for K–12 teachers.

Awesome Library (www.awesomelibrary.org). This site organizes the Web with 17,000 carefully reviewed resources, including the top 5% in education.

Beginning Teachers Tool Box (www.education-world.com). This is a "survival kit" for new teachers that includes a newsletter and professional and classroom resources.

Busy Teacher (www.ceismc.gatech.edu/busyt). Georgia Tech maintains this site with subject area links to resources for K–12 teachers.

Cagle/Slate (cagle.slate.msn.com/teacher). This site is a source for cartoons by world-renowned cartoonists. It is maintained by a member of the Professional Cartoonists Society and a classroom teacher.

Creative Teaching (www.creativeteachingsite.com). This is a nonprofit site financed by the author to help teachers develop more creative teaching ideas and to help teachers more thoroughly enjoy their profession. The creator of this site has been teaching and teaching teachers for 30 years.

Edutrail (www.edutrail.com). Edutrail is designed to allow teachers to easily post and exchange lesson ideas.

IBIBLIO (www.ibiblio.org). This site is one of the largest "collection of collections." Collaboration between the Center for the Public Domain and the University of North Carolina–Chapel Hill offers free software and information on music, literature, art, history, science, politics, and cultural studies.

Instructional Materials Center (www.amkc.edu). The University of Missouri–Kansas City School of Education maintains a useful site with teaching tips, links, recommended books and advice for new teachers.

Lesson Planz (www.lessonplanz.com). This site is a clearinghouse with more than 4,000 lesson plans organized by content and theme. It includes a chat room where teachers share ideas.

Library of Congress American Memory (memory.loc.gov/ammem). This is a gateway to rich primary source materials relating to the history and culture of the United States. The site offers more than 7 million digital items from more than 100 historical collections.

Merrow Report (www.pbs.org/merrow). This site is an engaging documentary series about learning, about stretching your mind, and about television that educates. The Merrow Report looks at issues that shape the ways all of us live and work and learn.

PBS Teacher Source (www.pbs.org/teachersource). This site provides teacher-developed materials, television programming, and professional development information.

Smithsonian Institute (educate.si.edu). The Smithsonian Institute in Washington, D.C., designed this site to introduce teachers to programs offered at the museum. It provides lesson ideas in a range of subject areas.

Tag Teacher (www.tagteacher.net). A comprehensive site based in the United Kingdom, Tag Teacher is designed to support teachers. It offers an online newsletter, a chat room, and lesson-planning resources. It provides a global perspective on classroom issues.

Teacher's Corner (www.theteacherscorner.com). This site provides lesson plans, thematic units, lesson calendars, and pen pals.

Teachers First (www.teachersfirst.com). On this site, lessons and resources are organized by subject area.

Teachers Helping Teachers (www.pacificnet.net/~mandel). This site is designed to help teachers share lessons and teaching ideas.

Teachers.Net (www.teachers.net). This site is a large teacher resource site.

PUBLISHERS AND CORPORATE-FOR-PROFIT SITES

Copernicus (www.edgate.com). Gateway's corporate site for teachers, students, and parents has a range of educational links and resources. It offers extra help for students and allows teachers to post assignments online.

Discover (www.discover.com). This is the home of the Schrock guide to integrating the Internet into the curriculum. It offers numerous resource links and lesson ideas.

Education Week (www.edweek.org). This is an online newspaper that discusses current news, special events, and professional and social issues of significance to teachers.

Encarta (encarta.msn.com). This is an online encyclopedia maintained by Microsoft.

Encyclopedia Britannica (www.britannica.com). This is one of America's leading encyclopedias with everything from the origins of the universe to current events.

Grolier's Encyclopedia (www.gi.grolier.com). This is an excellent reference library.

Houghton Mifflin (www.eduplace.com). The Web site provides supplemental material that parallels and expands on the parent company's texts.

K–12 Teaching & Learning Center (www.k12tlc.org). This is a privately owned and operated Web site for K–12 educators, students, and families. It charges a nominal membership fee.

Learning Network's Teacher Channel (www.TeacherVision.com). This corporate-sponsored Web site offers lesson plans, free e-mail newsletters and literature tie-ins, quizzes, and printables to help teachers enhance learning and incorporate technology into their classrooms.

McDougal Littel (www.mcdougallittell.com). This site provides resources in all subject areas.

Merriam-Webster Online (www.merriam-webster.com). This is an online English language dictionary and thesaurus.

My School on Line (MySchoolOnline.com). This site provides a range of Internet and Web site solutions, from teaching teachers how to use the Web to providing easy-to-use Web-site-building tools and education-focused content.

The New York Times (www.nytimes.com/learning). This is a New York City-based newspaper with broad national coverage of events. It includes lesson ideas and sample assessments.

Prentice Hall (www.phschool.com). This site provides resources in all subject areas. It offers teachers the ability to interact with textbooks and create their own Web sites, and it provides state-specific curriculum information.

TeachWave (www.teachwave.com). Created to link job seeking teachers and administrators with K–12 schools in need of qualified professionals, TeachWave offers free job posting.

World Book (www.worldbook.com). This site provides access to the *World Book Encyclopedia.*

Yahoo's Education Directory (dir.yahoo.com/Education/K_12/Teaching). This is a directory of reference materials, online learning communities, and links to resources on classroom management, lesson planning, and library resources.

Laurence_Klein.Edu

Middle school teacher Larry Klein and his students maintain four Web sites for use by his social studies classes. All the sites are free to teachers and easily accessible by parents. Larry uses a site on TeacherWeb.com (TeacherWeb.com/NY/168/Klein/index.html) to post announcements, homework assignments, a class calendar, and answers to frequently asked questions. It also contains a number of study links. This Web site is updated daily by students from Larry's ninth-grade classes who have the class password.

Larry has a WWW.Geocities.Com (WWW.Geocities.com/jhs168q) site that includes class rules, a joke page, information for parents, fun and educational links, and a list of "useless" social studies facts.

WWW.Think.Com is a secure Web space that allows students to develop and post Web-based multimedia projects. Each student has her or his own password that permits her or him to enter, view, and change material on her or his site. As the teacher, Larry is listed as site manager and has access to every student's page. The site also allows students to dialogue on controversial or interesting questions.

Larry is also responsible for maintaining the school's Web page at WWW.Parsons168.com. This is a much more formal site that has letters addressed to students and parents, explanations of state learning standards and assessments, and copies of trip permission slips.

Larry's Recommendations for Building Your Own Web Sites

TeacherWeb (teacherweb.com/). This site provides easy-to-create, easy-to-update personal Web sites for teachers.

Developing School Web Pages (www.siec.k12.in.us/~west/online/index.html). This site offers tips for creating a content rich, visually appealing Web page for your school site.

Webmaster Resource Page (www.pekin.net/pekin108/webmasters/resources.html). This is a Pekin, Illinois School District site. Features include: Yahoo's List of K–12 Schools, Beginner–Intermediate–Advanced Level Web Design, A Guide to Creating a Successful Web Page, Great Web Site Design Tips, Art and the Zen of Web Sites, The Tao of Web Sites, Top Ten Mistakes in Web Design, Web Pages That Suck, and Detailed Descriptions for gif vs. jpeg.

Internet 101 (www.internet101.org/). Created for those who want to know just the basics, this site provides enough knowledge to have fun on the Internet, yet it will not bore you with too many details. Think of this as a set of instructions for people who don't like to read instructions.

Lisa Explains (www.lissaexplains.com/). This is Web page design for kids. Topics include HTML, how to create home pages, make a Web page, hex codes, rgb color chart, free guestbooks, projects, counters, guestbooks, JavaScript, scripts, downloads, e-mail, tutorial, guide, java script, tables, lake and snow applet, applets, search engines, graphics, copy, paste.

Homeroom.Net (www.homeroom.net/). This is an Internet community of school Web sites, links, and education related information.

Web66 (web66.coled.umn.edu/schools.html). This site is designed to facilitate the introduction of this technology into K–12 schools. The goals of this project are to help teachers learn how to set up their own Internet servers; to link teachers, students, and schools; and to help teachers find and use appropriate resources on the Web.

Backgrounds for Educators and Others (arthur.k12.il.us/arthurgs/aesbggr.htm). This site provides borders and tiled backgrounds that might be useful to teachers or students developing home pages.

Presenting Java (www.december.com/works/java.html). Java is a computer programming language that brings animation and a level of interactivity to the Web. With Java, you can create animations, simulations, and applications for Web pages that are truly interactive.

Simple JavaScript (www.uen.org/utahlink/public_html/handouts/js/simpljs.htm). This site provides information on using Simple JavaScripts, JavaScript Basics, and Online Resources.

Website Abstraction—Free JavaScripts (wsabstract.com/cutpastejava.shtml). This site offers comprehensive JavaScript tutorials and more than 400 free scripts.

The Free Site (www.thefreesite.com/). This provides listings and reviews of the best freebies available on the Net: e-mail freebies, free fonts, fun freebies, free games, free graphics, free Java & Javascript, free postcards, free software, free sounds, free technical support, free Web space for hosting your site, Web master freebies (free tools, Web site resources).

Free Web Graphics Tools and Resources (www.gifcruncher.com/resources/links.html). This lists free sites useful for designers and Web masters.

Fontsnthings.com (www.fontsnthings.com/collected/whoami.html). This site provides a collection of unusual freeware and shareware fonts.

Web Page Formatting (www.uen.org/utahlink/public_html/handouts/handouts.html). A training resource provided by UtahLink, this site provides handouts that may be used for classroom and personal education. Features include: 15 ways that computers can save an educator's time, building instructional materials with the Internet, Internet integration ideas across the curriculum, working with graphics on the Web, HTML tags for formatting text, using simple JavaScripts.

School Icons (www.schoolicons.com/eng/index.html). This site provides free Web graphics—educational icons, clipart, backgrounds, buttons, counter digits, and more.

IconBAZAAR (www.iconbazaar.com). This is a gallery of free clipart, graphics, images, webdings, and webart for use in HTML development.

ClipArt Review (www.webplaces.com/html/clipart.htm). This site is a guide to free graphics on the Web: icons, backgrounds, textures, animated gifs, buttons, bars, lines, rules, bullets, clip art.

Cool Archive (www.coolarchive.com). This site offers a huge free vault of clipart images, fonts, icons, hundreds of animations, buttons, bullets, arrows, bars, html and photoshop tips, sounds. Plus it offers an online logo generator and button maker to create your own graphics.

Earl's ClipArt Page (library.hilton.kzn.school.za/Mainpgs/clipart&.htm). This site offers clipart, sounds, and fonts galore.

Author Index

Note: Page number followed by *f* indicates figure.
Page number followed by *n* indicates note.

A

Agosti-Dircks, Christina, 17–18, 56, 209*f*
Albers, D., 24
Altschuler, G., 218, *224*
Apple, M., xiv, xv, 12, 13, 104, *122*
Atwell, N., 51–52, *148*

B

Bacigalupo, D., 102*f*
Baker, M., 12
Baldwin, J., 120–121, *122*
Bambino, Jennifer, 44–45, 48
Barry, D., 249*n*.1
Beagle, P. S., 35, *57*
Bellamy, E., 182, *199*
Bennett, L., 15
Bennett, W., 254, *270*
Benenson, G., 196–197
Berkowitz, B., 105
Berne, L., 230, *251*
Bigelow, W., *62, 148*, 153
Bloom, B., 193
Bologna, S., 41
Bonds, R., 202
Borland, H., 240, *251*
Bowe, F., 87
Bowler, C., 24
Bowles, S., *148*
Brigante, D., 258–263
Brown, C., 13
Brown, M. W., 99*f*

C

Callahan, R., 124, *148*
Camus, A., 254, *270*
Caponi, C., 40–41
Carini, P., 108, *122*
Casey, ?., 13
Chaucer, G., 14, *16*
Christenson, L., *62, 148*, 152–154, *166*, 183, *199*, 258–259, *270*
Clark, S., 10–11
Cobb, C., Jr., 183–184, *199*
Costello, L., 187, *199*
Costello-Herrera, L., 45–46, 48, 210*f*, 219
Cotten, S., 42–43, 48
Counts, G., xiv, xv, 12, 13
Covello, L., 125, *148*
Cribb, J., 254, *270*
Crick, F. H. C., 189*f*
Cronin, C., 91

D

D'Agostino, G., 125, *148*
Daniels, H., *149*
Darling-Hammond, L., 35, *57*
Darwin, C., 92–94
Davidson, A. L., 230, *251*
Deen, R., 51, *57*
Delpit, L., xiv, xv, 12, 13, *62*, 103, *122*
Dewey, J., xiv, xv, 8–9, 12, 219, *224*, 261, *270*
Dickens, C., 130–131, *148*, 253–254, 255, *270*
Dircks, H., 134
Dmuchowski, S., 24

Subject Index

Note: Page number followed by *f* indicates figure.
Page number followed by *n* indicates note.